D0062661

CAMBODIA

TOM VATER

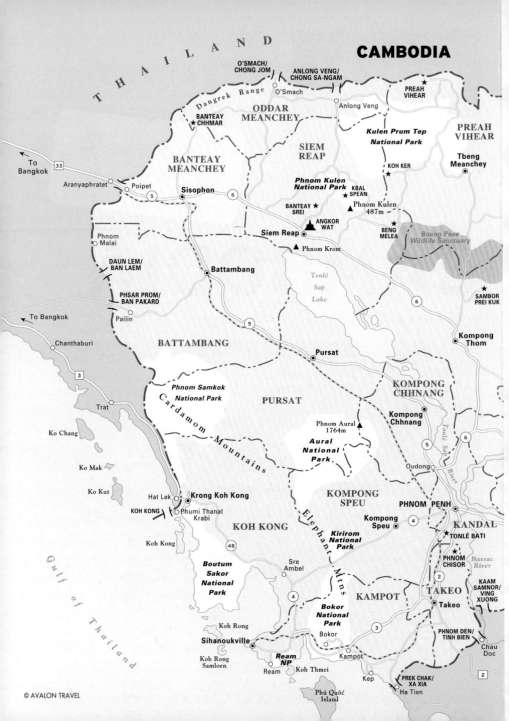

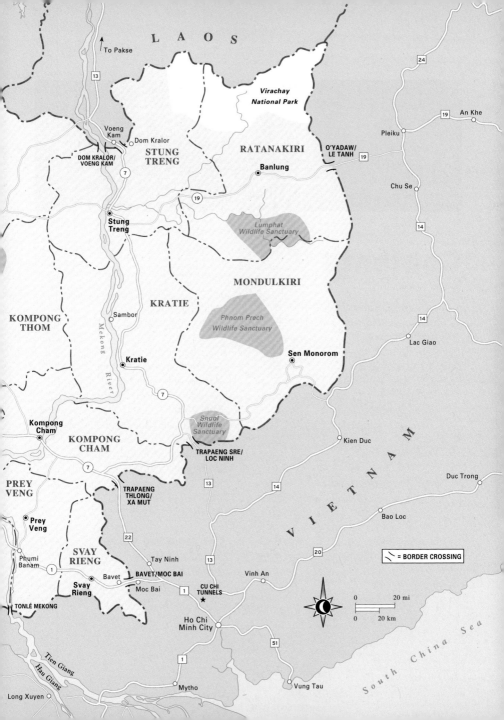

Contents

Discover Cambodia

The first rays of the sun touch the central towers of Angkor Wat. The rice paddies and golden temple roofs shimmer in the morning sun. Old women, their heads hidden under red headscarves, rest in the shade of giant banyan trees, chewing betel. Monks collect alms and policemen collect bribes. The smell of fried food wafts across the street. Children pass on bare feet, laughing. Old men silently sit at roadside cafés, nudging glasses of thick sweet coffee. After sunset, young lovers race their bikes through darkened, potholed city streets, thousands of insects hover around flickering streetlamps, and sidewalk restaurants are crowded with celebrating families.

These could be a visitor's first impressions of Cambodia, recorded 40 years ago, but it's also the way I first encountered the country, barely 15 years ago, as well as just last month. Kampuchea, as the Khmer call their homeland, has a timeless, mysterious, and somewhat anarchic quality. It's a quality barely discovered by the outside world.

The temple ruins of Angkor — the Khmer Empire that ruled much of Southeast Asia almost a thousand years ago — have put the country on the map, and attract more than a million foreign visitors a year. No one leaves disappointed. Yet, for the independent traveler, Cambodia has much more in store. From bustling markets in the capital Phnom Penh to quiet tropical

beaches around Sihanoukville, from lush jungles in Mondulkiri to the remains of French colonial heritage and traditional country life rarely seen in the 21st century, a journey through Cambodia is an adventure.

Above and beyond the magnificent sights, visitors are rewarded by the warm welcome of Cambodia's people. Despite the country's tragic and disturbing recent history, despite poverty and years of isolation, the *sourir khmer,* the smile of the Khmer, remains intact. Amid traces of three decades of war and genocide, the Khmer have begun to pick up the pieces and are looking toward a peaceful future with cautious optimism, which makes a visit a real experience you are likely to cherish forever.

And things are getting better, slowly. As the infrastructure and economy improve steadily, partly thanks to tourism, Cambodia invites us to partake in its rebirth, in a celebration of its ancient culture, conveyed in every moment of travel in this quiet kingdom by the Mekong.

Planning Your Trip

► WHERE TO GO

Cambodia is Southeast Asia's most adventurous country, bar none. It also offers the most grandiose architecture. The magnificent ruins of the Angkor Empire, located predominantly in the northwestern part of the country, are reason enough to visit, but there is much more to do and to see for visitors who bring curiosity and, most importantly, energy. Even after 10 years of peace, the country's infrastructure is limited, and, once away from the temples and the bustling capital of Phnom Penh, your initiative often determines how much you are likely to get out of the experience.

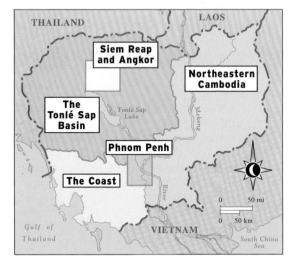

Apart from the sometimes hair-raising traffic, Cambodia has become a very safe country to travel in. The main roads have now been largely rebuilt, except in the northeast. Armed robbery of foreigners is virtually unheard of nowadays, and unless you are looking for trouble, you are unlikely to find any.

What makes Cambodia so different from

Kep Beach, on Cambodia's coast

IF YOU HAVE...

- **ONE WEEK:** Visit the Angkor temples and Phnom Penh. Get a three-day pass to see the magnificent ruins near Siem Reap, then travel to Phnom Penh by air, boat, bus, or taxi and indulge in a long weekend of markets, bars, and some of the best riverfront views Southeast Asia has to offer.

- **TWO WEEKS:** Take your time visiting the Angkor temples and hanging loose in Phnom Penh. Then, depending on whether you want a holiday or an adventure, head for a beach resort in Sihanoukville or into one of the remote northeastern provinces, Ratanakiri and Mondulkiri, for some elephant trekking or a walk though a national park.

- **THREE WEEKS:** Visit the Angkor temples, Phnom Penh, and one of the remote northeastern provinces before rounding off your trip on a beach in Sihanoukville.

- **FOUR WEEKS:** This is enough time to get a great overall impression of Cambodia. Take your time at the temples and try to visit one of the remote temple sites, stop over in Phnom Penh, head for one of the remote northeastern provinces for a few days of trekking, explore the coastal communities of Kep and Kampot, and finish off on the beach in Sihanoukville.

a farm hut in Mondulkiri, in northeastern Cambodia

its larger neighbors is its unique, grandiose, and disturbing past, which the Cambodians are now only too glad to leave behind. Most of all, travel in Cambodia promises a certain freshness, call it an edge or a vibe, that invites exploration, because it has not been explored by hundreds of thousands of others.

Siem Reap and Angkor

Temples, temples, and more temples. Several huge imperial capitals of the Khmer Empire flourished around the town of Siem Reap in the northwestern part of Cambodia between the 10th and the 15th century and ruled Cambodia, as well as large parts of today's Thailand, Laos, and Vietnam. Today, only temple ruins, magnificent dreams in stone, remain, and the Angkor Archaeological Park, a UNESCO World Heritage Site, is not only a tourist magnet attracting two million visitors a year, but also the spiritual and cultural heart of

colonial and Khmer-style architecture in the Royal Palace compound in Phnom Penh

Cambodia. Due to its proximity to Angkor, Siem Reap has grown enormously in recent years and is the country's cleanest, safest, and best organized town.

Phnom Penh

Cambodia's capital has come a long way in the last decade, from dangerous backwater to boomtown, and has rediscovered some of its old world charm in the process. Yes, the streets are (pretty) safe and hundreds of restaurants, bars, and clubs await visitors who can party around the clock against a background of colonial architecture and Cambodia's newfound, if grossly uneven, economic regeneration. Add to that street markets, art galleries, and a few museums that do a good job presenting both Cambodia's Angkor era as well as its more recent catastrophic turmoil.

The Coast

Almost 500 kilometers of coastline await beach bums, divers, and adventure seekers. While development in Sihanoukville, the country's prime beach resort, appears to be accelerating, plenty of offshore islands receive barely any visitors, while others are turning into exclusive casino resorts. Decent coral reefs are beginning to attract scuba divers and the coastal towns of Kampot and Kep offer great accommodations and history lessons from Cambodia's recent past, all at a pace slow enough to seduce even the most jaded traveler.

The Tonlé Sap Basin

The Tonlé Sap Lake is a huge and shallow expanse of water in the center of Cambodia.

selling souvenirs on Serendipity Beach in Sihanoukville

On the lake, floating village communities welcome visitors, while several towns along its shores offer colonial architecture, several remarkable Angkor-era temples. and fantastic insights into daily life. Battambang is the most attractive town in the region, offering temple ruins, several grim war sites, colonial architecture, and one of the strangest train rides in the world: the Norry or Bamboo Train.

Northeastern Cambodia

Southeast Asia's mightiest river, the Mekong, runs through Cambodia, its shores lined with small, picturesque towns. Endangered dolphins and river trips attract visitors, many of them on their way to the country's most remote provinces, Ratanakiri and Mondulkiri. Home to most of Cambodia's indigenous people, the Khmer Loeu, as well as much of the country's rapidly dwindling forest and wildlife, these two regions do not have any paved roads and beyond the provincial capitals, the free-wheeling business practices of the kingdom are turning one of the world's last great wilderness areas into plantations and desert. Enjoy this otherworldly region while some of its spectacular resources remain.

▶ WHEN TO GO

Cambodia's climate is tropical year-round, except for the highlands in the northeastern part of the country, where it can get cool. The best time to visit is in the cool season between October and early March. But that's also the busiest time of year around the Angkor temples. During the hot season, from late March into June, much of the country turns into a furnace, so that's definitely the time to head for the cooler provinces of Ratanakiri and Mondulkiri, though Khmer New Year in April is a special experience anywhere, especially around Angkor. The rainy season, from June to September, is a great time to explore the temple ruins, as there are fewer visitors, but much of the rest of the country is inaccessible due to the terrible road conditions. In October, head to Phnom Penh for Bonn Om Tuk, the annual water festival with three-day boat races and a city bursting at its seams with visitors from the provinces.

The cool season is a great time to visit Cambodia's temples.

► BEFORE YOU GO

Passports and Visas

All visitors to Cambodia must have a passport valid for at least six months. It's possible to apply for a one-month tourist visa online or in person at any Cambodian embassy or consulate in your own country or another country. Alternatively, visitors are issued a visa upon arrival at the international airports in Phnom Penh and Siem Reap and at a number of border crossings from Thailand, Laos, and Vietnam.

Vaccinations

It's essential that your tetanus and diphtheria shots are up to date. It is generally recommended that travelers be immunized against typhoid and tuberculosis, and sometimes for Hepatitis B as well. For visitors who intend to spend prolonged periods in remote areas, rabies shots and a vaccination against Japanese encephalitis might be appropriate. Those who are likely to have blood contact with locals or other travelers should consider taking a course of Hepatitis A vaccinations. During the rainy season, malaria is prevalent in border areas and remote jungle locations. It's best to visit your doctor eight weeks before departure, as some vaccinations require several shots over a period of time. All inoculations should be recorded on an International Vaccination Card. The Cambodian authorities require visitors to have yellow fever vaccinations if they arrive from a potentially affected area, such as parts of Africa and South America.

Finally, it's highly recommended that travelers purchase good travel insurance covering their entire length of stay in Cambodia. Health facilities are at best rudimentary.

Transportation

Distances in Cambodia are short, but the roads, though improving, are bad. The main

traveling by motorbike in Siem Reap

population centers are connected by tarmac highways, but out in the provinces, it's graded or ungraded laterite, which creates dust storms that turn clothes red and destroy cameras. The journey from Siem Reap to Phnom Penh can be undertaken by plane, boat, bus, or taxi. The rest of the country is mostly reachable by bus or taxi, though some of the remoter corners of Cambodia can only be reached by pickup or four-wheel-drive—or just by motorbike.

Driving yourself is possible if risky, given local driving culture, the state of the roads, and the lack of medical facilities. But it's also a great adventure driving through Cambodia in or on your own vehicle and in the country-side, locals welcome anyone passing by with open arms.

Explore Cambodia

► BEST OF CAMBODIA

A 14-day tour of Cambodia gives you enough time to take in the temples around Angkor, move on to the delights of the capital Phnom Penh for a few days, and finally head for the beaches—or, if you are longing for something a little more adventurous, on a trip to the wild northeast.

Day 1

Arrive at the international airport in Siem Reap and transfer to a hotel in town. In the late afternoon, rent a tuk-tuk, motorbike, taxi, or bicycle and head out to the Angkor Archaeological Park. Purchase a three-day pass, starting officially on the following day—but entitling you to enter the temple area for the rest of the afternoon, which gives you the opportunity to catch the sunset at Phnom Bakheng. In the evening, take a stroll around Pub Street and the Old Market area.

Day 2

Start early in the morning and visit Angkor Wat before the crowds arrive. At midday, head to one of the modest eateries around the main temples, enjoy a quick lunch, and take a break from the sun. In the afternoon, visit the imperial city of Angkor Thom and marvel at the Bayon, its most spectacular structure, before heading back into town. If you have any energy after a day among the ruins, consider catching a traditional dance performance.

Day 3

With another early start, you'll have plenty of time to explore the more far-flung temples of Preah Khan, cross the Eastern Baray, and take in Ta Prohm (the jungle temple) and Ta

a wall of the Bayon, in the imperial city of Angkor Thom

Keo (a simple sandstone pyramid with great views) on the way back to Angkor Thom.

Day 4

On the last day your pass is valid, head out to the exquisite temple Banteay Srei, and explore Kbal Spean, a nearby riverbed full of stone carvings. A visit to the Cambodian Land Mine Museum could be an interesting diversion from the temples. In the evening, check out the night market or the craft boutiques around town for some souvenir hunting.

Day 5

Visit one of the temples outside the Angkor Archaeological Park, such as Beng Melea,

a bungalow at the Tree Top Eco-Lodge in Banlung

or do something entirely different: You could play a round of golf, take a boat trip to a floating village or protected biosphere, join a horse safari, do a Khmer cooking course, or even jump aboard a helicopter flight across the temple ruins.

Day 6

Grab a bus, boat, or taxi from Siem Reap to Phnom Penh, check into a hotel, and take a late-afternoon stroll down Sisowath Quay to soak up the atmosphere of Cambodia's capital.

Day 7

Explore Phnom Penh's main historical sights: the Royal Palace and Silver Pagoda. In the afternoon, visit the National Museum, which has the best collection of Angkorian artifacts in the country.

Day 8

Take a look at Cambodia's recent tragic past by visiting the Choeung Ek Killing Fields, 15 kilometers outside of town, where thousands of people were exterminated. Most of the people killed here came from Tuol Sleng S-21, a former school turned into torture center back in town, now a museum. Finish the day by visiting the Russian Market, a great place to hunt for souvenirs or just have a cup of coffee.

Day 9

Take a bus or taxi south to Sihanoukville and head for Serendipity or Occheuteal Beach to find the best accommodations.

Days 10-12

Soak up the beach, or if you don't succumb to the laid-back vibe, rent one of a variety of seagoing vessels—kayaks, sailboats, Jet-Skis, or windsurfing boards. To help you recover from any strenuous activity, plenty of beach shacks offer sumptuous seafood barbecues, cold beers, and even cocktails in the evenings.

Day 13

Take a bus or taxi back to Phnom Penh. Enjoy an afternoon river cruise and an early-evening drink at Maxine's before heading back into town for dinner and your last night in Cambodia.

Day 14

Grab a taxi, tuk-tuk, or minivan to Phnom Penh International Airport.

ALTERNATE ROUTE

If you're not beach-inclined—and providing it's the dry season—head for the northeast instead.

Day 9

Get an early morning bus or taxi from Phnom Penh to Banlung, the provincial capital of Ratanakiri. Check into one of the excellent eco-lodges around town.

Day 10

Visit the town's market in them morning, then head for serene Yeak Lom Lake for an afternoon dip.

Day 11

Rent a motorbike and head for An Dong Meas, from where it's possible to catch a boat up the Tonlé Se San River to visit intriguing Charay cemeteries near the Vietnam border.

Day 12

Rent a motorbike and head for Lumphat, the old provincial capital that fell victim to the Vietnam War.

Day 13

Check out of your lodge in Banlung and take a bus or taxi back to Phnom Penh. Enjoy an afternoon river cruise and an early-evening drink at Maxine's before heading back into town for dinner and your last night in Cambodia.

Day 14

Grab a taxi, tuk-tuk, or minivan to Phnom Penh International Airport.

▶ TOTAL CAMBODIA

One month is enough time to see the country's highlights, get a feel for Cambodia's people and atmosphere, and find a few days to relax on a beach.

Days 1-5

Start in Phnom Penh, the country's fascinating capital. Allow three days for the tourist sites and the best shopping Cambodia has to offer, and, depending on your predisposition, another few days to recover from the city's unhinged nightlife. If you have the time, several trips out of town, such as a visit to the Choeung Ek Killing Fields or to the site of the old capital at Oudong, are worth considering. From Oudong it's not far to Kompong Chhnang, one of the most attractive towns around the Tonlé Sap Lake.

a fishing village near Kompong Chhnang

fish *amok,* one of Cambodia's most popular dishes

Days 6-10

Follow Route 5, along the southern shore of the Tonlé Sap Lake, past the floating village of Kompong Luong, near Pursat, all the way to the attractive riverside town of Battambang, which exudes colonial flair and is surrounded by a number of attractive temple mountains bearing the scars of Cambodia's civil war. A number of attractive hotels, suiting all budgets, make Battambang a great place to linger for a few days.

Days 11-18

A boat from Battambang along the Sangker River and across the Tonlé Sap Lake, or a bus, will take you north to Siem Reap, your base for exploring Angkor Wat and the other temples of Angkor. For any but the most jaded travelers, three days among the temples makes most sense, and Siem Reap—with its markets, cultural shows, nightlife, and museums—tempts many visitors to stay longer. Some of Cambodia's most remote and spectacular temple sites lurk in the jungle north and west of town. Siem Reap also serves as a base to reach Anlong Veng, a former Khmer Rouge

stronghold that's now the site of several macabre reminders of the country's darkest period.

Days 19-24

Return to Phnom Penh, by boat, plane, taxi, or bus, and head to one of the country's remote provinces in the northeast. Ratanakiri, on the border of Laos and Vietnam, offers minority villages, jungle treks and river trips, and some of the country's best accommodations. In Mondulkiri, the Bunong minority, former elephant hunters, offer treks on the backs of pachyderms and there are a number of spectacular waterfalls to visit. Visitors to Ratanakiri stay in Banlung, while visitors to Mondulkiri generally stay in Sen Monorom.

Days 25-31

From northeastern Cambodia, return to the capital, before heading south to Cambodia's 500-kilometer coastline. Kampot and Kep are sleepy seaside communities with great accommodations and interesting sites, while Sihanoukville offers the best beaches and is the place to laze around and lose yourself in the azure waters of the Gulf of Thailand.

▶ THE TEMPLES OF ANGKOR

A week is sufficient time to get well acquainted with Cambodia's cultural heritage. The main temples of Angkor can be seen in a day, but that hardly does justice to this UNESCO World Heritage Site. In three days, it's possible to see all the major temples around Angkor Thom. In a week, you can visit pretty much all the sites in the Angkor Archaeological Park at your leisure. If you're not templed out after that, day trips and overnights to some of the more remote temple compounds can be a real adventure.

One Day in Angkor

If you only have a single day to visit the temples of Angkor, consider buying a ticket in the late afternoon before the day you intend to visit the temples, which will enable you to catch the sunset from Phnom Bakheng. Start early the next morning and plow through Angkor Wat, Angkor Thom, and The Bayon. Stop for lunch in a shady spot for an hour before heading to Preah Khan and Neak Pean to the north, then round out the day with visits to the jungle temple of Ta Prohm and a climb up the sandstone pyramid of Ta Keo.

Three Days in Angkor

Three days in Angkor gives you enough time to soak up the main structures at leisure and get a good impression of the former might of the Khmer culture.

DAY 1

Start early in the morning. Visit Angkor Wat and take your time exploring the bas-relief galleries and inner courtyards. Numerous lunch places around Angkor Wat will keep you from returning to town at midday. Head on to Angkor Thom, the imperial city. The Bayon is the most

the west gate of Angkor Thom

CAMBODIA'S TOP 10 TEMPLES

The god kings of the Khmer Empire built a huge number of temples across Cambodia, as well as in what is now southern Laos and parts of Thailand. The most famous, Angkor Wat, now attracts up to 6,000 visitors a day. Others, almost as spectacular but more remote, attract but a handful of tourists. Any list of favorites is subjective, of course, but these 10 buildings (in order of preference and relative importance) will not disappoint.

· **Angkor Wat** – The largest religious building in the world is awesome and stupendous. Don't miss it.

· **The Bayon** – The enigmatic smiles of the *bodhisattva* follow visitors around this mysterious temple complex in the heart of Angkor Thom.

· **Beng Melea** – Subsumed and enveloped by forest, this off-the-beaten-track complex has a unique, disquieting atmosphere, especially just after the rains.

· **Ta Prohm** – This sprawling temple

THAILAND LAOS

0   50 mi
0   50 km

Mekong

Anlong Veng   ★ Preah Vihear

★ Banteay Chhmar

Banteay Srei   Koh Ker ★   Tbeng Meanchey ○   Banlung ○

SEE DETAIL   ▲ Angkor Wat   ★ Beng Melea   Stung Treng ○

Siem Reap ○

Battambang ○

★ Sambor Prei Kuk

Tonlé Sap Lake

River

Sen Monorom ○

Pursat ○   Kompong Thom ○   Kratie ○

Kompong Chhnang ○   Kompong Cham ○

Tonlé Sap River

VIETNAM

Krong Koh Kong ○   PHNOM PENH ⊛   Prey Veng ○

Ko Kut ○

Kompong Speu ○

Koh Kong ○   Svay Rieng ○

Takeo ○

Koh Rong ○   Sihanoukville ○   Kampot ○

Kep ○

Gulf of Thailand   Phú Quốc Island   Phnom Penh

ANGKOR TEMPLES

Neak Pean ★

WALL   WALL   Eastern Baray

Bayon ★

Western Baray   Ta Prohm ★

Angkor Wat ▲   Siem Reap River

© AVALON TRAVEL

compound is preserved as the French explorers of 19th-century Angkor saw it.

- **Banteay Srei** – Marvel at the Khmer Empire's finest carvings at this small temple just off the Angkor Circuit but within easy distance of Siem Reap.

- **Koh Ker** – This remote, jungle-bound former Khmer capital and temple complex has a fascinating pyramid as its main monument. More than a hundred structures deep in the forest make the journey worthwhile.

- **Preah Vihear** – Politically controversial, this cliff-top temple on the Cambodian-Thai border has incredible views over the Cambodian plains.

- **Banteay Chhmar** – Adventurous types will get a kick out of this rarely visited temple complex between Siem Reap and the Thai border – looted, overgrown, and remote enough to invoke delusions of being on an Indiana Jones-type mission.

- **Sambor Prei Kuk** – A Pre-Angkorian temple city near Kompong Thom shows the way of things to come.

tree root at Angkor Wat

- **Neak Pean** – A minor ruin on the Grand Circuit, this small temple constructed in a pond comes into its own during and after the rainy season. A small romantic gem of a building, it's a personal favorite.

spectacular structure, but the Terrace of the Elephants and the Baphuon are also worth visiting, as are some of the smaller structures within the city walls.

DAY 2

Start early once more and head through Angkor Thom to the forest temples of Preah Khan and Neak Pean. Explore the temple mountain of Pre Rup before heading to the fantastic jungle temple of Ta Prohm, and finally to Ta Keo on the way back to Angkor Thom.

DAY 3

No visit to the Angkor Archaeological Park would be complete without a walk around Banteay Srei, an exquisitely carved sandstone temple nearly 40 kilometers from Siem Reap. There's time to explore Kbal Spean, a nearby riverbed full of stone carvings.

One Week in Angkor

One week in Angkor allows visitors wowed by Khmer temple architecture to look at all the main sites in detail and explore a couple of the more remote and outlying temple sites near Siem Reap.

DAY 1

Visit Angkor Wat and The Bayon in the imperial city of Angkor Thom.

a temple wall at Beng Melea, overgrown by the roots of a ficus tree

DAY 2

Explore Angkor Thom in the morning before moving north of the Eastern Baray to see Preah Khan and Neak Pean, a couple of overgrown temple compounds.

DAY 3

Explore the structures south of the Eastern Baray: the temple mountain of Preah Rup, the spectacular and gigantic Ta Prohm, subsumed by jungle, and Ta Keo, a simple but imposing sandstone pyramid.

DAY 4

Drive out in the morning to the Roluos Group of temples, the remnants of the first major Khmer capital, 10 kilometers west of Siem Reap, and then visit Wat Athvea, a tiny and very quiet temple to the south of Siem Reap, in the afternoon.

DAY 5

Visit one of Angkor's architectural highlights, Banteay Srei, which features some of the Khmer empire's most exquisite carvings. This 10th-century temple is almost 40 kilometers from Siem Reap; the carved riverbed of Kbal Spean and the Cambodia Land Mine Museum make ideal afternoon destinations in the same area.

DAY 6

Enjoy a boat trip on the Western Baray, with a visit to the Western Mebon. Have a picnic on the banks of the reservoir.

DAY 7

Rent a car and visit Beng Melea, a spectacular jungle temple northeast of Angkor. Enjoy your last sunset at Angkor Wat or Phnom Bakheng.

▶ FROM COAST TO COAST

For those who don't want to see any temples, a 14-day tour from the Thai to the Vietnamese border right along the Gulf of Thailand may be just the thing. This tour follows the shoreline, starting at the border town of Koh Kong, a good base for treks and trips to offshore islands. Farther east, Cambodia's most popular beach destination, Sihanoukville, has ambitions, as yet unrealized, to become Southeast Asia's Acapulco. Towards Vietnam, Kampot and Kep make for plenty of soft adventure.

Day 1
Enter Cambodia overland from Thailand at Koh Kong and find a hotel. Visit the local market and riverfront.

Day 2
Take an island cruise or go scuba diving off the coast of Koh Kong, or join a jungle trek to a waterfall in the Cardamom Mountains.

Day 3
Take a ferry, bus, or taxi to Sihanoukville and find accommodations on Serendipity or Occheuteal Beach.

Days 4-5
Enjoy Sihanoukville's beaches, fresh seafood, and nightlife, and visit the famous Independence Hotel.

Day 6
Join an all-day fishing trip with evening barbecue.

Day 7
Take a boat trip (in a rented kayak or sailboat) around the outlying islands or embark on a scuba diving day trip.

Day 8
Take a bus or taxi to sleepy and romantic Kampot and choose from colonial-style and riverside accommodations.

Otres Beach, Sihanoukville's most remote beach

a street scene in Kampot with well-restored colonial buildings

Day 9

If the road to the spectacular mountaintop Bokor National Park, with its eerie colonial casino ruin, is open, join a day trip from Kampot or drive your own dirt bike to the top. If the road is closed due to construction work, you could always trek to the top in a long day hike with a guide and spend the night at the ranger station before descending the following day.

Day 10

Explore the intriguing caves of Phnom Chhnork and Phnom Sorsia near Kampot, featuring strange rock formations and Buddhist shrines dating back to the 4th century.

Day 11

Join a boat trip to the Kampot estuary or visit local pepper plantations and salt fields.

Day 12

Move on east to Kep, formerly the "Cambodian Riviera," now a ghost town of hundreds of ruined villas, with some excellent newly opened resorts. Explore the ruins and grab a meal at the crab market, which is famous all over the country.

Day 13

Rent a boat to head out to Koh Tonsay, also called Rabbit Island, which has a fine beach and some basic restaurants offering excellent seafood.

Day 14

Hire a taxi to take you to the Vietnamese border at Prek Chak/Ha Tien.

▶ THE WILD NORTHEAST

Take an 11-day trip through some of the country's remaining wilderness, including two days on Cambodia's hardest road. This adventurous motorbike trip should only be attempted by experienced riders or on the back of a Cambodian driver's bike.

Day 1

Rent a dirt bike, start early, and drive from Phnom Penh to Sen Monorom, Mondulkiri's capital. The first part of the journey leads across the Mekong on good roads to the small town of Snuol on Route 7, where riders can stop for lunch. Then follow the old logging road through meandering hills to Sen Monorom.

Day 2

Drive out to a Bunong village and join a day-long elephant trek across rolling hills and through dense jungle, before returning to Sen Monorom in the evening.

Day 3

After a late breakfast in Sen Monorom, take the good dirt road to Khon Nhek, the last settlement on the road between Sen Monorom and Banlung, Ratanakiri's capital. Arrive in the afternoon and find a place to sleep.

Day 4

Leave early in the morning from Khon Nhek and drive to Banlung, Ratanakiri's provincial capital, via Lumphat. There's no road as such, just a series of sandy trails, punctuated by occasional villages. Several rivers need to be crossed and it's best to hire some locals to help carry the bikes. After a grueling 8–10 hours, you'll reach Lumphat on the Srepok River in the

fishing boats on a tributary of the Mekong River near Kratie

HAPPY NEW YEAR, CAMBODIA STYLE

For three days in mid-April, Choul Chnam, the Khmer New Year, celebrates the beginning of the Buddhist religion. The year 2010 corresponds to 2553 in the Buddhist calendar. Traditionally, people gather in their local temples to make offerings. The Khmer, like the Thais, enjoy throwing copious amounts of water and talcum powder at each other and at tourists during the celebrations. Thousands of Cambodians head for the Angkor temples to celebrate, picnic, and sightsee. For many Cambodians, it's their first time seeing the temples. Bear in mind that this is the most crowded time of the year around the ruins.

During the first day of the celebrations, **Moha Songkran,** the Khmer light incense at shrines and pray. In the morning they wash their faces, at lunch their chests and in the evenings their feet with blessed water in order to attract good luck for the coming year. On the second day of the celebrations, **Wanabat,** people give to charitable causes and pray for the ancestors at the local temple. On the third and final day of the celebrations, **Tngai Laeung,** people bathe the Buddha statues in the temples, which is thought to bring good luck and longevity. They also wash the hands of their parents or grandparents, a sign of respect for the authority of elders, in the hope to be blessed by their best wishes and to receive their advice.

Angkor can be fun during the New Year and foreign visitors have a chance to observe locals in the new pagodas around Angkor, such as at Wat Athvea, as they honor monks, bathe their Buddha statues, and even engage in water fights inside some of the prayer halls. If you happen to be in Cambodia during the New Year holidays, **Siem Reap** and **Phnom Penh** are the best places to see the festivities. In the countryside, visitors are likely to be invited to local celebrations. Prepare to get wet – and drunk.

later afternoon. From here it's only an hour or two on a logging road to Banlung.

Day 5

Relax in Banlung and visit Yeak Lom Lake for a swim.

Days 6-9

Take a well-earned break from your bike saddle and embark on a three-night trek into Virachay National Park. Return from the trek to Banlung.

Day 10

Drive, in one long but comfortable day, from Banlung to Kratie, on the banks of the Mekong. The first stretch along Route 19 is unsurfaced and passes through forest and agricultural land, but beyond Stung Treng, Route 7 south to Kratie is one of the best roads in the country.

Day 11

After a hearty breakfast at Red Sun Falling in Kratie, follow the Mekong back to Phnom Penh. In the dry season, you could pass through the old French planter's town of Chhlong. In the rainy season, it's best to stick to the surfaced road via Snuol (Route 7).

SIEM REAP AND ANGKOR

The magnificent temple ruins of Angkor are amongst the great, ancient wonders of the world. The gigantic temple complex in Siem Reap Province in northwestern Cambodia, once the heart of an empire that stretched from South Vietnam to Laos and central Siam, is now a UNESCO World Heritage Site and the country's biggest tourist draw. Almost two million visitors descended onto the monuments in 2008. The Angkor Empire flourished between the 7th and 14th century, before it was subsumed by the aggressive policies of its stronger neighbors, and perhaps by its own delusions of grandeur.

Only in the mid-19th century did the French expedition of Henri Mouhot "rediscover" the temples for the rest of the world. Since then, the jungle that had grown over the sacred stones for centuries has slowly been stripped away, a process that continues to this day at the more remote temple locations in the province. While work on the temples halted between 1973 and 1992, mine-clearing programs and restoration projects are slowly restoring these true wonders of the world to glory; even outlying temples such as Beng Melea, which could only be reached by four-wheel-drive or helicopter a few years ago, are now easily accessible. At the same time, the Angkor ruins are beginning to show the strain of the millions of visitors and, if tourism in the area is to be sustainable, the industry will have to diversify to other more remote locations. Some of the temples may have to cap visitor numbers. For the moment though, any thought of sustainability goes against the grain of the development Siem Reap has seen in recent years.

© AROON THAEWCHATTURAT

HIGHLIGHTS

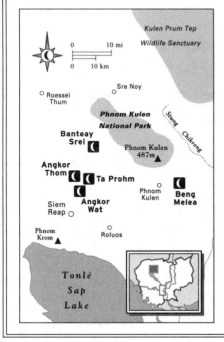

(Angkor Wat: The greatest of great temples, Angkor Wat is a monumental dream in stone (page 58).

(Angkor Thom: Cambodia's last imperial city is surrounded by a three-kilometer wall and moat. Right in its center is the Bayon, a spectacular temple dominated by towers adorned with the enigmatic smiling faces of the *bodhisattva* (page 63).

(Ta Prohm: The jungle-covered temple of *Tomb Raider* fame is the most romantic ruin in the Angkor Archaeological Park (page 71).

(Banteay Srei: This small 10th-century temple features some of the most exquisite carvings of the Khmer empire (page 79).

(Beng Melea: Away from the crowds and subsumed by jungle, this remote temple offers visitors one of the most atmospheric experiences of any Khmer temple (page 82).

LOOK FOR (TO FIND RECOMMENDED SIGHTS, ACTIVITIES, DINING, AND LODGING.

To ordinary Cambodians, Angkor symbolizes much more than the projected power of a forgotten time. Angkor is Cambodia's spiritual and economic heart. Monks and pilgrims from all over the country continue to visit the temples, especially around Khmer New Year in April. Siem Reap may appear strange to them—the formerly small market town with a couple of blocks of crumbling French colonial architecture has grown into the country's second capital—a city with more than 8,000 hotel beds, countless restaurants, souvenir shops, casinos, and bars. For those visitors who have any energy left after the temples, a number of interesting exhibitions, a couple of war museums, a pagoda with a killing field, as well as distractions such as golf courses and horse rides, could be of interest.

PLANNING YOUR TIME

If you are incredibly pressed for time, a quick one-day turn through Angkor Wat, Angkor Thom, including the Bayon, Ta Prohm, and Banteay Srei will at least give you a superficial impression of the Khmer Empire. Three days are a must for all those who want to soak up the architectural majesty of the former Angkor Empire. A week allows you to visit outlying and remote temples. Farther afield sights such as the temples Beng Melea or Koh Ker or the biosphere and floating village on the Tonlé Sap can be reached in day trips.

Siem Reap is by far the most affluent place in Cambodia and the shopping's not bad (though the markets in Phnom Penh offer a greater selection of goods at slightly better prices), which may tempt some visitors to hang around a few days longer than they'd planned.

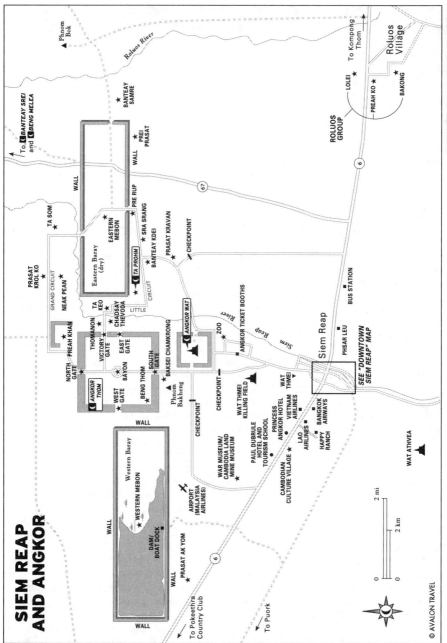

SIEM REAP AND ANGKOR

To Kompong Thom

Roluos Village

LOLEI ★

PREAH KO ★ BAKONG ★

ROLUOS GROUP

▲ Phnom Bok

Roluos River

To BANTEAY SREI and BENG MELEA →

BANTEAY SAMRE ★

WALL

PREI PRASAT ★

WALL

PRE RUP ★

TA SOM ★

EASTERN MEBON ★

Eastern Baray (dry)

SRA SRANG ★

BANTEAY KDEI ★

PRASAT KRAVAN ★

CHECKPOINT

BUS STATION

PRASAT KROL KO ★

NEAK PEAN ★

GRAND CIRCUIT

TA KEO ★

TA PROHM

LITTLE CIRCUIT

PREAH KHAN ★

THOMANON ★
CHAODSAY THEVODA ★

NORTH GATE

VICTORY GATE

EAST GATE

BAYON

SOUTH GATE

ANGKOR THOM

WEST GATE

BENG THOM

BAKSEI CHAMKRONG ★

Phnom Bakheng ★

ANGKOR WAT

ZOO

ANGKOR TICKET BOOTHS

Siem Reap River

Siem Reap

PHSAR LEU

SEE "DOWNTOWN SIEM REAP" MAP

CHECKPOINT

CHECKPOINT

WAT THMEI KILLING FIELD

WAT THMEI ▼

PRINCESS ANGKOR HOTEL

VIETNAM AIRLINES ▼

BANGKOK AIRWAYS

WALL

Western Baray

WESTERN MEBON ★

CHECKPOINT

WAR MUSEUM/ CAMBODIA LAND MINE MUSEUM

PAUL DUBRULE HOTEL AND TOURISM SCHOOL

CAMBODIAN CULTURE VILLAGE ★

LAO AIRLINES

HAPPY RANCH

AIRPORT (MALAYSIA AIRLINES)

WAT ATHVEA ▲

WALL

DAM/ BOAT DOCK

PRASAT AK YOM ★

WALL

To Pokeethra Country Club

To Puork

67

67

6

6

2 mi

2 km

0

0

© AVALON TRAVEL

Siem Reap

The town nearest to the Angkor temples has grown from a tiny village a hundred years ago into Cambodia's second-largest city. Some locals call it the unofficial capital, thanks to the millions of tourist dollars that have been rolling in since the late 1990s. Siem Reap translates as "Defeated Thailand," a reference to the Khmer Empire at a time it controlled large swathes of Siam (today's Thailand) for several centuries. Following the sacking of Angkor by the Siamese in 1431, the tables turned and the Angkor ruins, as well as Siem Reap, were administered by Siam.

The town of Siem Reap really came into its own at the beginning of the 20th century, when the first wave of international tourists arrived. Le Grand Hotel D'Angkor opened in 1932 and tourism grew steadily until World War II. Following the war, Angkor became trendy once more and remained on the global tourist circuit until the late 1960s, when increasing turmoil in Cambodia and the neighboring war in Vietnam put an end to tourism. French archaeologists remained at the temple and tried to continue working, even as the war reached Siem Reap, but in 1975, the Khmer Rouge emptied the town and drove all its inhabitants into the countryside, where many perished. When the Vietnamese pushed the Khmer Rouge out of the government in 1979, the new occupiers put their own troops into Siem Reap. The Khmer Rouge escaped into the forests around the town and embarked on a 15-year terror campaign on Siem Reap's citizens, the Vietnamese, and, later, the United Nations Transitional Authority in Cambodia (UNTAC), which culminated in a final large-scale attack in 1993.

Today, Siem Reap is the safest city in the country and Cambodia's boomtown. In just 10 years, this sleepy backwater has turned into a thriving, chaotic metropolis. I remember the installation of Siem Reap's first traffic lights in 2001. Three policemen manned the chosen crossing, each armed with a megaphone, and spent all day explaining the traffic lights' function to passing traffic participants. At 6 P.M., the officers went home and the lights immediately became mere decoration. The traffic on the main roads is the biggest hazard around town. In 2007, the Angkor International Hospital, Cambodia's first international-standard clinic, opened—and now provides competent treatment to accident victims. Thankfully, the French town center has been tastefully restored and it's still possible to go for a quiet walk under the trees by the Siem Reap River. Many of the villages around town have lost little of their simple charm and seem barely affected by the tourist circus. Hustle, prostitution, and drugs are kept to a minimum, and if you are not looking for any trouble you are very unlikely to find any.

Siem Reap will continue to evolve and expand, and there's talk of a second airport. As long as Angkor remains one of the world's most popular archaeological sites, Siem Reap is unlikely to stop growing.

SIGHTS
The Old Market Area

Just eight years ago, the area around Old Market (Phsar Chas), right in the heart of Siem Reap and close to the river, was a run-down, dilapidated affair, a little unsavory at night. Since then, investment and restoration have taken place and the colonial buildings around the covered market have recaptured their former grace. All this makes for a francophone ambience, a nostalgic vibe with more than a whiff of l'Indochine, and a very nice space to move around in. Several downtown areas of Cambodian cities retain substantial colonial architecture, but only here has it been completely rehabilitated. The market itself has largely been given over to things tourists might buy—from DVD documentaries on the Khmer Rouge to silk scarves, rice paper prints of *apsaras,* opium pipes, and the ubiquitous *krama*, Cambodia's all-purpose head scarf. About half of the market still sells products for

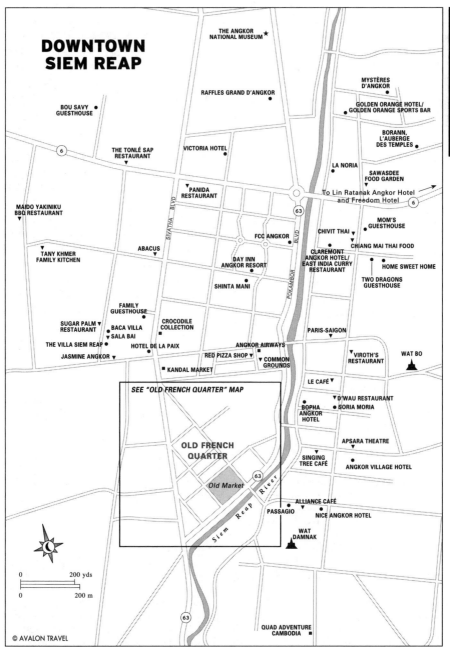

DOWNTOWN SIEM REAP

THE ANGKOR NATIONAL MUSEUM ★

MYSTÈRES D'ANGKOR ●

RAFFLES GRAND D'ANGKOR ●

GOLDEN ORANGE HOTEL/ GOLDEN ORANGE SPORTS BAR ●

BOU SAVY GUESTHOUSE ●

BORANN, L'AUBERGE DES TEMPLES ●

6

THE TONLÉ SAP RESTAURANT ▼

VICTORIA HOTEL ●

LA NORIA ●

SAWASDEE FOOD GARDEN ▼

To Lin Ratanak Angkor Hotel and Freedom Hotel   6

PANIDA RESTAURANT ▼

SIVATHA BLVD

63

MAIDO YAKINIKU BBQ RESTAURANT ▼

MOM'S GUESTHOUSE ●

CHIVIT THAI ▼

FCC ANGKOR ●

CHIANG MAI THAI FOOD

ABACUS ●

POKAMBOR BLVD

CLAREMONT ANGKOR HOTEL/ EAST INDIA CURRY RESTAURANT ●

TANY KHMER FAMILY KITCHEN ▼

DAY INN ANGKOR RESORT ●

HOME SWEET HOME ●

SHINTA MANI ●

TWO DRAGONS GUESTHOUSE ●

FAMILY GUESTHOUSE ●

SUGAR PALM RESTAURANT ▼

CROCODILE COLLECTION ■

BACA VILLA ● SALA BAI ●

PARIS-SAIGON ●

THE VILLA SIEM REAP ●

HOTEL DE LA PAIX ●

ANGKOR AIRWAYS ●

VIROTH'S RESTAURANT ▼

WAT BO ▲

JASMINE ANGKOR ▼

RED PIZZA SHOP ▼

COMMON GROUNDS ▼

KANDAL MARKET ■

LE CAFÉ ▼

SEE "OLD FRENCH QUARTER" MAP

D'WAU RESTAURANT ▼

BOPHA ANGKOR HOTEL ●

SORIA MORIA ●

APSARA THEATRE ●

OLD FRENCH QUARTER

SINGING TREE CAFÉ ▼

ANGKOR VILLAGE HOTEL ●

63

Old Market

ALLIANCE CAFÉ ●

Siem Reap River

PASSAGIO ●

NICE ANGKOR HOTEL ●

WAT DAMNAK ▲

0   200 yds

0   200 m

63

QUAD ADVENTURE CAMBODIA ■

© AVALON TRAVEL

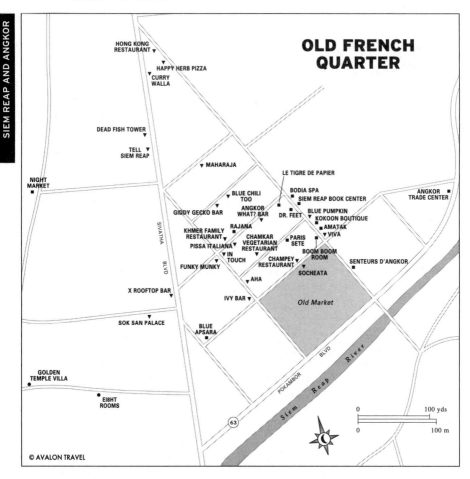

OLD FRENCH QUARTER

HONG KONG RESTAURANT ▼

HAPPY HERB PIZZA ▼

CURRY WALLA ▼

DEAD FISH TOWER ▼

TELL ▼ SIEM REAP

MAHARAJA ▼

NIGHT MARKET ■

LE TIGRE DE PAPIER

BLUE CHILI ▼ TOO

BODIA SPA ■

SIEM REAP BOOK CENTER ■

ANGKOR TRADE CENTER ■

GIDDY GECKO BAR ▼

ANGKOR WHAT? BAR ▼   DR. FEET ■

BLUE PUMPKIN ■ KOKOON BOUTIQUE ▼

SIVATHA

KHMER FAMILY RESTAURANT ▼

RAJANA ■

AMATAK ■ VIVA ▼

PISSA ITALIANA ▼

CHAMKAR VEGETARIAN RESTAURANT ▼

PARIS ■ SETE ▼

IN ▼ TOUCH

BOOM BOOM ▼ ROOM

FUNKY MUNKY ▼

CHAMPEY ▼ RESTAURANT

SENTEURS D'ANGKOR ■

BLVD

SOCHEATA ▼

AHA ▼

X ROOFTOP BAR ▼

IVY BAR ▼

Old Market

SOK SAN PALACE ▼

BLUE APSARA ■

POKAMBOR   BLVD

Siem Reap River

GOLDEN TEMPLE VILLA ●

EIGHT ROOMS ●

63

0   100 yds

0   100 m

© AVALON TRAVEL

the local community, including fruit, machine parts, and clothes. The streets around the market are lined with eateries (some budget, others upscale), shops, Internet cafés, and bars—making for a great stroll in the early evening. The stalls selling local products open from the crack of dawn until early evening, while the shops selling curios open around 10 A.M. and close around 7 P.M.

Wat Bo

One of the oldest temples in Siem Reap, the 18th-century Wat Bo (entrance free), on the eastern side of the river, has some interesting frescoes on the walls of the prayer hall, including the depiction of an opium-smoking Chinese trader.

Wat Damnak

Located on the eastern side of the river, this large temple compound (entrance free) was once a royal palace and has been beautifully restored. In the afternoons, locals come to sit by a large stone basin filled with lotus flowers and catfish. The Center of Khmer Studies is located in a handsome building dating back

© AROON THAEWCHATTURAT

Wat Athvea, a small Angkor-era temple, is in a village between Siem Reap and Phnom Krom.

to the early 20th century, located within the temple compound.

Wat Athvea

Wat Athvea (entrance free) is a very special place. The active monastery lies in the shade of a bamboo grove, right next door to a small, but very handsome and well-preserved Angkor-era temple. The pagoda is never empty—monks, village elders, and musicians can usually be found in the prayer hall. An open reception hall and a prayer hall, as well as wooden huts that serve as accommodation for the monks, make up the compound. In the prayer hall, hundreds of Buddha statues are gathered around a central shrine and the walls are covered in frescoes depicting the life of the Buddha. Once a year, during Khmer New Year, all the statues are washed by the local community, a ceremony that entails a wild water battle.

The 12th-century temple next door, surrounded by a high laterite wall, is often deserted, although local people conduct merit-making ceremonies in its single main tower.

Wat Athvea is a great place to gain an impression of what the atmosphere around the temples was like before tourists rediscovered Angkor. Just a few minutes away from Cambodia's busiest shopping streets, an incredibly peaceful and relaxed ambience pervades the temple buildings. The two buildings are off the main road between Siem Reap and Phnom Krom. The turn-off to the temple is marked by a large gate on the right-hand side, about four kilometers south of Phsar Chas (Old Market). It's not necessary to have a pass for Angkor to visit this ruin.

Beyond the temples, a small village—with traditional family homes on stilts—is full of friendly teenagers keen to take visitors around the area. Some of the kids speak English fairly well and have a few facts about temple and country life ready, but don't expect a real "tour." It's the experience rather than the facts that counts here. A donation of a few dollars for the young guides is expected.

Wat Thmei Killing Field

Although the Khmer Rouge never dared to attack the temple ruins of Angkor, many people died in the area during and after the communist reign. Siem Reap Province contains numerous killing fields. Wat Thmei (entrance free), an active temple on a side road from Siem Reap to Angkor, has a glass-paneled stupa in its courtyard, which is filled with the bones of victims of the Khmer Rouge.

The Angkor National Museum

The Angkor National Museum (tel. 063/966601, www.angkornationalmuseum.com, daily 9 A.M.–7 P.M.), on the road to the temples, just beyond the Le Grand Hotel d'Angkor, opened in late 2007 and serves as a light introduction to the magic of the Angkorian Empire. Visitors to this massive complex, a project run by a private company in conjunction with the Cambodian Ministry of Culture and Fine Arts, will be left wondering whether they are in a shopping mall or a museum, but that's not to say that a visit is a waste of time. Several exhibition galleries on Khmer civilization, Angkor Wat, and Angkor Thom contain some fine examples of Angkorian artifacts and statues. A number of rooms equipped with comfortable seating show short, informative movies in nine different languages. Audio tours of the entire facility are also available. The pieces on show come from the storage of the National Museum in Phnom Penh and from Conservation d'Angkor. A highlight is the Hall of a Thousand Buddhas, which is very nicely lit and does indeed contain 1,000 Buddha statues. A dome with a giant screen split into three parts almost delivers an IMAX experience. Contemporary artists also find a space here, with regular exhibitions related to Angkor held in a smaller domed hall inside the museum. The museum's exit leads straight into a souvenir shop.

All in all, the number of artifacts is a bit light, but the museum is still finding its feet and, anyway, this is edutainment. It doesn't compare to the National Museum in Phnom Penh, but it isn't trying to. The only real criticism is the ticket price: US$12 for foreigners, US$3 for Khmer.

The Cambodian Cultural Village

This rather unsophisticated theme park (tel. 063/963836, www.cambodianculturalvillage.com, daily 9 A.M.–9 P.M.), located on the airport road, whisks visitors through Cambodia's turbulent history. Exhibits include replicas of temples, miniature versions of entire villages (including a so-called millionaire house, "a place where ancient rich men stayed") as well as life-size re-creations of scenes from Cambodia's past. Traditional dance performances from around the country take place at several locations in the village. Check the website for times. The place made headlines in 2003 when a display illustrating the presence of UNTAC in the country was limited to a foreign soldier embracing a Khmer sex worker. That particular item has been removed, but the US$11 entrance fee for foreigners is still not entirely justified.

The War Museum and the Cambodia Land Mine Museum

Two museums remind visitors of the 30 years of war in the latter half of the 20th century and the legacy of conflict that Cambodia has endured. The War Museum (no phone, daily 9 A.M.–5 P.M., US$1), built and managed by the Department of Defense, is close to town, just north of Route 6 towards the airport. The official ad reads, original spelling intact, "The War Museum is very unique, all kinds of old weapons used during almost 3 decades of wars in Cambodia. Tanks, Armored Personal Carrier, Artilleries, Mortars, Land mines and small arms...etc. So you spend just thirty minutes or 1 hour. You'll see all these weapons."

The museum is not dedicated to any specific conflict, nor, it seems, are its planners aware of any chronological relevance of recent warfare on Cambodian soil supposedly illustrated here. Tanks, mortars, and anti-aircraft guns rust in the sun, while a dilapidated collection of firearms is kept in an open shed. Some of the weaponry on show was manufactured as early as the 1930s and hails from places as diverse as Vietnam, China, the Soviet Union, and East Germany. There are mock mine fields and a large collection of landmines remind visitors of the continuing scourge of these weapons in Cambodia.

The Aki Ra Mine Action Museum (tel. 012/598951, www.cambodialandminemuseum.org, daily 7:30 A.M.–5:30 P.M., US$1), also called the Cambodia Land Mine Museum Relief Facility, is managed by a Canadian NGO. It's located out near Banteay Srei, and is best visited during a trip to this outlying temple. There's information on land mines and a large collection of war scrap dug up from the surrounding countryside, and visitors can challenge themselves by walking through a mock mine field and booby traps.

ENTERTAINMENT AND EVENTS

There are plenty of nighttime hangouts competing for those who still have some energy left at the end of the day. Bars-cum-restaurants are in the majority, and a couple of venues offer live music. The suspect ambience so typical of many of Phnom Penh's bars and clubs is virtually nonexistent in Siem Reap. For those in search of some traditional entertainment, *apsara* dance performances are put on by several upscale hotels and numerous restaurants. And there's always the Night Market, with its bar and food court.

Bars and Clubs
BARS

Right in the heart of old Siem Reap, Pub Street offers some appealing venues. Restaurants, bars, and clubs line this narrow road; street vendors sell anything they can think of; and the atmosphere is safe and relaxed. Best of all, the police cordon the area off at night, so there's no motorized traffic to worry about, should you stumble onto the street at 2 A.M.

Not as old as the temples, but open for business since 1998, the **Angkor What? Bar** (daily 5 P.M.–very late) has grown from a hole-in-the-wall late-night filling station with a beer-spattered pool table into a much larger, spacey affair—every inch of wall space is covered in guests' signatures. Join the club. Tables out front are a perfect vantage point to survey the action on the street.

Reassuringly pop-tastic, both in name and character, is the Western-style **Funky Munky** (www.funkymunkycambodia.com, noon–very late except on Mon.) on Pub Street, which spins contemporary dance tunes and serves a wide range of cocktails late into the night. The **Blue Chili Too** (daily 6 P.M.–2 A.M.), located in a narrow alley behind Pub Street, is Siem Reap's gay-friendly nighttime hangout. It follows the same concept as its brother operation in Phnom Penh: soft lighting, nice decor, and company.

The **Ivy Bar** (daily 7 A.M.–very late), on the southwestern corner of the Old Market area, has been around for years and remains a good meeting spot. Its claim to fame is Pol Pot's toilet seat, spirited away from Brother Number 1's last home in Anlong Veng in 2000, and now proudly displayed in a frame on the wall, offset by some of Gordon Sharpless' enigmatic Cambodia images and a pool table. The pub food and breakfasts, both Western and Asian, are not bad either. The **Giddy Gecko Bar** (daily 5 P.M.–very late) is located on the first floor of a corner building in the Old Market area, hence offering great views over the nighttime action in the heart of Siem Reap. It's a laid-back place where you can sip a cocktail, surf your laptop with Wi-Fi access, or smoke a hookah.

In the forecourt of the Golden Orange Hotel in the Wat Bo area, across the river from the Old Market, the friendly **Golden Orange Sports Bar** (daily 6 P.M.–midnight) is a small island of Americana. Hotel guests and visitors can relax to music familiar to American ears (anything from The Rolling Stones to the Carpenters), enjoy a free game of pool, drink a cold beer, surf the Internet, and watch Hollywood movies, all at the same time if necessary.

NIGHTCLUBS

Siem Reap's premier nightclub suitable for tourists (there are quite a few very rowdy Khmer clubs around as well) is the **Sok San Palace,** which plays house, R&B, hip hop, and funk. It serves drinks that aren't overpriced and features laser lighting, dancing girls, and karaoke rooms. The club is located in central Siem Reap, on a side street off Sivatha Boulevard, a little south of X Bar.

LIVE MUSIC

A cross between an American roadhouse bar and a Thai beer hall (the owner is Thai), the eclectic and huge **Dead Fish Tower,** located in the heart of town on Sivatha Boulevard, provides seating on three levels with a small stage on the first level. Traditional dance performances and live bands are featured regularly and the steaks are pretty good (US$6–12). Their advertising reads "We don't serve Dog, Cat, Rat or Worm," though there's a page on the menu entitled "Scary Dishes" (with pig's heart, eel, and frogs, for example). Most diners are impressed by the crocodile pit on the way to the restrooms. A plate of fish to feed the large and very much alive reptiles is just US$0.50, and the jaded creatures start snapping their jaws as soon as you raise your arm above them. This is the perfect place to get rid of those pesky travel companions you have been trying to shake for a week.

In Touch (daily 11 A.M.–2 A.M.), a bar-cum-restaurant serving Thai food, located amongst the bustle of Pub Street, hosts live cover bands (mostly light jazz) upstairs from 9 P.M.

Performing Arts

Many of the upscale hotels in town put on traditional Khmer dance performances during their dinners. These usually include both classical and folk dances and tend to last about an hour. One of the most professional troupes works the *apsara* dance on the Apsara Terrace at the **Raffles Grand Hotel d'Angkor** (tel. 063/963888). Dinner performances run Mondays, Wednesdays, and Fridays at 7:45 P.M. from October to May and it's US$32 a head. Other similarly sumptuous dinner events can be attended at the **Sofitel Royal Angkor** (tel. 063/964600), on the road to the temples and the **Victoria Angkor** (tel. 063/760428).

Outside the high-end hotels, the **Apsara**

Theatre (tel. 063/963561), a massive wooden Khmer-style auditorium, is probably your best bet to see cultural dances in Siem Reap; it's located in the Wat Bo area, opposite the Angkor Village Hotel. Traditional *apsara* dance performances take place on Tuesdays, Thursdays, and Saturdays 7–9 P.M. with a set menu Khmer dinner. Dinner and performance are US$22. The **Tonlé Sap Restaurant** on the airport road is really a package tour affair, with buffet dinners including a traditional dance performance for US$12. Shows start at 7:30 P.M. From 7–9 P.M., performances by a Khmer dancer are also held at the **Dead Fish Tower** on Sivatha Boulevard, but they tend to be subsumed within the venue's youthful, cosmopolitan atmosphere.

Traditional Cambodian shadow puppet theater (Speik Thom and Speik Toot), featuring stories from the *Reamker,* the Khmer version of the Indian epic the *Ramayana,* as well as popular folk stories can be seen at the hotel **La Noria** (tel. 063/964242) on the eastern side of the river on Wednesdays (7–9 P.M.) and at the **Butterflies Garden Restaurant** (tel. 063/761211, www.butterfliesofangkor.com), on the road to the airport. For the latter venue's schedules, check the website.

With his weekly solo cello performances and talks, **Beatocello** (www.beatocello.com), or Dr. Beat Richner, raises much-needed funds for the Jayavarman VII Hospital in Siem Reap and the Kantha Bopha 1 and 2 Children's Hospitals in Phnom Penh. Shows take place every Saturday at 7:15 P.M. at the Jayavarman VII Hospital on the road to the Angkor ruins. Entrance is free, but a donation is appropriate. In the day time, the Jayavarman VII Hospital also welcomes blood donations. On Tuesdays and Thursdays, a film about Dr. Beat Richner, entitled *Doctor Beat and the Passive Genocide of Children* is shown at 7:15 P.M. at the Jayavarman VII Hospital. Entrance is free.

Art Galleries

One of the smartest galleries–cum–drinking dens in Siem Reap is the spacious retro-futuristic **Arts Lounge** in the Hotel de la Paix. Regular exhibition of traditional and

HEAVENLY *APSARAS:*
THE KHMER NATIONAL BALLET

Khmer ballet, or classical dance, is one of three categories of Cambodian dance (the others being folk and vernacular dance). Originally the ballet was performed exclusively for the royal court. With independence from France, classical dance was introduced to the Cambodian public to celebrate Khmer culture. During the Khmer Rouge years, the art form was almost lost, but since the early 1990s, the School of Fine Arts in Phnom Penh has been training new batches of dancers. The dancers, all female, have to learn more than 3,500 movements, each of which has its own specific meaning, often symbolizing aspects of nature, such as the opening of a flower. Students are trained for 9 or 12 years to learn the intricate positions and movements the

dances entail. Other dances tell the story of Cambodia's origins, a union between a hermit named Kampu and a woman called Apsara Mera. The dancing *apsaras,* who grace many temple walls, suggest that the royal ballet was most popular in the 10th to 12th centuries. The School of Fine Arts shows off the results of their endurance training on special occasions such as during Khmer New Year in front of Angkor Wat.

Since mass tourism has arrived in Cambodia in recent years, many hotels and restaurants in Siem Reap and Phnom Penh offer Khmer classical dance performances as a dinner accompaniment. One of the best places to catch a high-quality performance is the Grand Hotel d'Angkor in Siem Reap.

contemporary Cambodian artists are presented here at monthly intervals. The **Red Gallery** (www.redgalleryasia.com), on the premises of the FCC Angkor, promotes and exhibits paintings and sculptures by some of Cambodia's most established international and local artists in a relaxed and intimate environment. Exhibits change every now and then, and the quality of the work is consistently high. Drop by for insight into a slowly emerging contemporary Cambodian art aesthetic.

The **McDermott Gallery** (www.mcdermottgallery.com), located next to AHA in The Passage by the Old Market is one of the most attractive exhibition spaces in Cambodia and features fine art photography from a number of well-established as well as emerging artists. It's well worth a visit. A second McDermott Gallery can be found on the property of FCC Angkor. Here, photographer John McDermott exhibits his otherworldly and idiosyncratic infrared black-and-white photographs of the Angkor ruins. Large prints retail US$450–3,000.

Another enigmatic photographer, the Italian Pierre Poretti, exhibits his work at the **Klick Gallery** (www.iklektik.com/photography)

located in The Passage by the Old Market. Poretti shoots in black and white and then hand-tints his images. His series of photographs of the Angkor ruins have a nostalgic look. Other series include pictures from Bali, Myanmar, Vietnam, and Laos, as well as portraits of Grace Jones.

Stephane Delapree, a French-Canadian cartoonist, paints extremely colorful naive canvasses of Cambodian scenes. The artist calls his work Happy Paintings (www.happypainting.net) and he has a gallery called **Happy Cambodia** in the Old Market area, as well as another branch in Phnom Penh.

Cultural Events and Festivals
KHMER NEW YEAR
During Khmer New Year, which falls in April, be prepared to share Angkor with thousands of celebrating Cambodians, who travel from all over the country to picnic and celebrate amongst the ruins.

THE ANGKOR PHOTO FESTIVAL
The Angkor Photo Festival (www.photographyforchange.net) was created in 2005 and

now draws both famous and passionate photographers from around the world to Siem Reap in November each year. Outdoor projections showcase regional and international photographers in different locations in Siem Reap.

The festival also has social goals. During their stay, well-established photographers from all over the world will tutor free workshops for emerging Asian shooters and the festival will also present its outreach programs for vulnerable people.

SHOPPING
Markets

Old Market, known to the locals as Phsar Chas, has become more commercial since visitor numbers really picked up in 2003, but this most traditional of Siem Reap markets is still divided down the middle into stalls selling curios and souvenirs and, across a central courtyard alive with vegetable vendors, stalls that sell household goods and cheap electronics to local people. Along its western side, a number of well-priced Khmer restaurants cater both to foreign visitors and Cambodians. The area around the market is lined with boutiques selling handicrafts, often produced by underprivileged and marginalized people.

Kandal Market, in English Center Market, is Siem Reap's largest market hall, squarely aimed at foreign souvenir hunters. Besides fine silks and clothing, it sells every type of tack imaginable, much of it brought in from neighboring countries. Haggle for everything and don't be surprised when the only other customers in here are tour groups.

The **Night Market** (www.angkornightmarket.com), opened in 2007 in its own little compound a few minutes' walk to the west of the Old Market area. A huge collection of stalls selling silks, handicrafts, and curios—many of them imported from neighboring countries—is on display. Orphans and people with disabilities get stalls at a discount and NGOs also exhibit and sell their products here, but most of what you'll see are generic souvenirs. Several movies about aspects of Cambodian history are shown nightly. A food court (not always open)

and a bar will keep you fuelled up in between browsing silks, bootleg DVDs, or jewelry. The market opens daily at 4 P.M., and stalls remain open till midnight.

Shopping Mall

Siem Reap's first shopping mall, the **Angkor Trade Center,** located just by the river a little north of the Old Market area, is a rather modest creation, with branches of Swensen's and the Pizza Company (as well as a small supermarket) on the ground floor and a cheap food court on the second floor. In between, stalls sell bootleg DVDs and clothes.

Craft and Book Shops

A number of fashionable boutiques are located in the Old Market area. These outlets have fixed prices and are not cheap, but you will find items here not available in the markets. **Senteurs d'Angkor** sells spices, tea, coffee, soaps, oils, and Khmer wine, as well as silks. Very similar yet different is **Kokoon Boutique,** which sells some pottery as well as silks and home decoration items. **Amatak** sells handprinted T-shirts, hats, and silks. The NGO-based **Rajana,** on Sivatha Boulevard, sells articles made from wood, as well as silks and other handmade souvenirs. More on the noisy and youthful side is the **Boom Boom Room,** also near the Old Market, where you can upload a vast range of music to your iPod or any MP3 player at a fraction of its original retail price. Similar outlets exist in Phnom Penh and Sihanoukville. Besides music, trendy club wear and drinks are for sale.

The **Crocodile Collection** on Sivatha Boulevard sells reptilian belts, shoes, and wallets, not just made of crocodile leather, but also of stingray, cobra, and ostrich leather. A little army of stuffed crocs welcomes visitors at the door. A croc wallet is around US$100. One would assume that the crocodile and ostrich leather is derived from animals bred specifically for this purpose. Cobras and stingrays are much more likely to be caught in the wild.

Numerous mobile book vendors, many

of them maimed by land mines, move through the Old Market area and usually carry a selection of nonfiction titles about Cambodia. Inside the Old Market, several book stalls carry the same limited choice. For a wide selection of books, some genuine, some pirated, including a whole shelf full of American underground writers, as well as bestsellers, classics, travel guides, and nonfiction on Cambodia, Vietnam, and Laos, head to **Blue Apsara.** This shop just south of the Old Market area is probably Siem Reap's best-stocked secondhand bookstore. **Monument Books** at the FCC Shopping Plaza sells new books, but they come at a high price. There's a second branch at the airport. The **Siem Reap Book Center** near the Old Market looks like an old trader's shop in India and sells a decent selection of history and photo books, as well as stationary, office supplies, countless souvenirs of doubtful taste, and chocolate bars.

A curious and incongruous outlet to hang around in is **Paris Sete** on Pub Street. This French shop specializes in beautiful if expensive lacquer images of Tintin cartoons and Expressionist art, imported from Saigon. The collection of photos and postcards on sale—including recruitment posters for the French colonial efforts of the 20th century—is worth perusing, and browsers may even find a couple of original rare books, posters, and artifacts.

SPORTS AND RECREATION
Swimming
While bathing in the river that runs through Siem Reap is not recommended, a few hotel pools open to outsiders and can offer some respite from the heat. The largest pools in town can be found at the **Princess Angkor Hotel** (tel. 063/760056, www.princessangkor.com) on the road to the airport; the **Lin Ratanak Angkor Hotel** (tel. 063/969888, www.lin-ratanakangkor.com), behind Phsar Samaki off Route 6; and the **Raffles Grand Hotel d'Angkor** (tel. 063/963888, www.raffles.com/en_ra/property/rga) in the heart of town.

Cycling
As foreigners are no longer allowed to drive their own motorized vehicles around Siem Reap or Angkor, the only alternative for visitors determined to see the area on their own terms is pedal power. Please note that while the roads around the temples are pretty flat, it does get very hot on the long stretches where the tree cover has been cut. Bring sun protection and drink plenty of water. Bicycles can be rented from guesthouses at US$2–3 a day.

Golf
The closest 18-hole golf course to Siem Reap is the Nick Faldo–designed **Angkor Golf Resort** (tel. 063/392288, www.angkor-golf.com), just six kilometers from the city along the road to the airport. A second professional-standard course, the **Pokeethra Country Club** (tel. 063/964600, www.pokeethra.com) lies some 16 kilometers from Siem Reap on Route 6. This 18-hole course, complete with driving range, restaurant, and pro-shop, is managed by Sofitel.

Cooking School
Le Tigre de Papier (tel. 063/760930, www.letigredepapier.com), a restaurant on Pub Street, offers half-day introductions to the Cambodian kitchen. The course (US$12) includes a trip to Old Market (Phsar Chas) to purchase ingredients and two hours of supervised preparations, including both cooking and food presentation. Participants get to check out each other's creations at lunch.

Horseback Riding
For avid riders, countryside horse trails can be explored from **Happy Ranch** (tel. 012/920002, www.thehappyranch.com), located a couple of kilometers from downtown Siem Reap. Rides are US$18 an hour, or US$31 for two hours. Group lessons are US$18 per student, one-on-one lessons are US$22. Riders must weigh less than 90 kilograms (200 pounds).

Quad Bike Tours
If you fancy racing a quad car through the Cambodian countryside, then look no

further than **Quad Adventure Cambodia** (tel. 017/784-727, www.quad-adventure-cambodia. com), located on the eastern side of the river, not far from Wat Damnak. Different tour packages on American-made Polaris Trail Boss quads are available, from two-hour romps to longer full-day trips to remote corners of the province.

Massage and Spas

Many of the upscale hotels and resorts in Siem Reap have their own spas or massage services. Outside of the hotel scene, head for **Bodia Spa** (www.bodia-spa.com), which includes a fashionable boutique and café. Bodia is located right next to U-Care Pharmacy in the Old Market area. **Islands Massage** (body massage US$8/hr) and **BE VIP Massage** (body massage US$6/hr), a few doors down, and **Dr. Feet** (foot reflexology US$6/hr), across the road, are all respectable.

ACCOMMODATIONS
Under US$15

One of the most reliable cheapies in town, though a bit off the beaten track, is the friendly **(Bou Savy Guesthouse** (tel. 063/964967, www.bousavyguesthouse.com, US$9 without a/c, US$15 with a/c), located on a garden property in a small lane just past Wat Kesararam on Route 6. The Khmer family who owns this place has a hands-on management policy, which translates into simple but clean rooms, personable, caring service, and all the usual travel and tour programs. All rooms have en-suite bathrooms and TV.

The **Baca Villa** (tel. 063/965328, www.baca-villa.com, US$8 without a/c, US$15 with a/c) is a good budget option on Taphul Road. The en-suite rooms are nothing to write home about, but they are clean, large enough, and have a TV. The guesthouse has a good garden restaurant that serves a large selection of Cambodian dishes, as well as backpacker fare, and organizes its own bike and four-wheel-drive tours.

Another rock-bottom place is the **Family Guesthouse** (tel. 092/968960, familyguest-house@gmail.com, US$6 without a/c, US$13

with a/c), located on a small side street off Sivatha Boulevard, a hundred meters north of Kandal Market. The small, clean rooms are a steal, though they have few amenities. There's Wi-Fi and a decent rooftop restaurant.

Located on a quiet side street in the Wat Bo area, **Home Sweet Home** (tel. 012/824626, www.homesweethomeangkor.com, US$6 without a/c, US$12 with a/c) might not have any great thrills, but it's a good value. The decent-size rooms are clean, and have en-suite baths and TV and either fans or air-conditioning. Should you be bored or burnt out on CNN, BBC, and HBO, or simply require more high-brow entertainment, it's possible to rent DVD players and movies for US$2. The Internet service downstairs in the restaurant is free for guests. This guesthouse, like most operations of its size, also offers a travel and visa service and laundry.

The **Nice Angkor Hotel** (tel. 063/966247, www.niceangkor.com, US$15) is really quite nice, just as the name suggests. This bargain basement guesthouse, located on the eastern side of the river, not too far from the Old Market, offers clean and simple air-conditioned rooms, most with their own small balconies (though not the rooms on the ground floor, of course). Guests can access the Internet free of charge and the restaurant serves Khmer and international standards.

US$15-25

If you are looking for a good mid-range guest-house with great service, check out the **(Two Dragons Guesthouse** (tel. 063/965107, http:// talesofasia.com/cambodia-twodragons.htm, US$17–27), near Wat Po. The Two Dragons offers 13 spotless if small rooms and is fronted by a restaurant that turns out good Thai dishes. The main reason to stay here, however, is the establishment's owner, American writer/ photographer and tireless pundit Gordon Sharpless, whose website, http://talesofasia. com, has been informing Cambodia travelers about the state of the roads, the temples, and the country for many years. Needless to say, the Two Dragons is a mine of information and

Gordon's photo-portraits of life in Cambodia are not bad either. There's free Wi-Fi access and a no-smoking policy in the rooms.

Not far away, but on the noisier Wat Bo Road is **Mom's Guesthouse** (tel. 012/630170, www.momguesthouse.com), which was once located in a traditional wooden building, but moved into a more swanky, newly built townhouse in 2007. Mom has decent sized but slightly dark air-conditioned rooms for US$20 including breakfast, or brighter deluxe rooms for the same price, but excluding the breakfast. The guesthouse offers all the usual travel services and has an ATM on the premises.

A stylish and low-cost accommodation option is the youthful and trendy **Ei8ht Rooms** (tel. 063/969788, www.ei8htrooms. com, US$16–22), located in two buildings on opposite sides of a side street off Sivatha Boulevard to the south of the Old Market area. Both common areas and the spacious air-conditioned rooms are carefully decorated with silks and black and white furniture. All rooms come with DVD players and a large selection of movies free of charge. Internet access in the lobby is free for guests. Several grass-roof pavilions on the roof make for a nice spot to watch the sun go down.

Golden Temple Villa (tel. 012/943459, www.goldentemplevilla.com, US$8–30), on the same lane as Ei8ht Rooms, is an orange-themed building, and both the outside and inside sport a uniform color tone. It's located in a luscious garden, overgrown with fully grown bamboo clusters. The 40 smallish rooms (all en-suite with tubs) are clean and smartly kept with silk curtains around the beds. Some rooms have air-conditioning, some have balconies. Downstairs, there's free Internet service for guests and the restaurant serves typical Khmer and Western dishes.

US$25-50

On the east side of the river, not far from Wat Bo, the **Bopha Angkor Hotel** (tel. 063/964928, www.bopha-angkor.com, US$38–58) offers smart and stylish rooms with traditional decor; some rooms have private balconies. The

attractive restaurant, serving mostly Khmer dishes, is popular, even with people who don't stay here. Try the excellent dim sum breakfast (US$3.50). A decent-sized pool will help weary temple visitors relax.

Anonymous but clean and spacious air-conditioned rooms welcome guests at the friendly and helpful **Freedom Hotel** (tel. 063/963473, www.freedomhotel.info, US$15–50), which has a very nice pool and a gym. Located on Route 6, west of Phsar Leu, this large budget place also has its own silk outlet.

French-owned **La Noria** (tel. 063/964242, www.lanoriaangkor.com, US$29–39), near Wat Bo Lanka, offers small but smart air-conditioned rooms decorated with traditional Khmer handicrafts in two-story bungalows, located around a small pool in a luscious garden. The poolside bar might just be the thing after a day at the temples. Alternatively you could avail yourself to a massage treatment on the premises. Following the same concept as La Noria, the smart two-story boutique bungalows set in a lush open garden promise a pleasant stay at the friendly **Borann, l'Auberge des Temples** (tel. 063/964740, www.borann. com, US$33, or US$44 with balcony), which is located off Wat Bo Road. Each good-size, en-suite, air-conditioned room (four per bungalow) is carefully designed with (partly antique) redwood furniture and cow-hide shadow puppets from the *Reamker,* and opens onto a private terrace. The in-house restaurant serves light Khmer and Western dishes, with main courses around US$6. And there's a pool.

The **Paul Dubrule Hotel and Tourism School** (tel. 063/963672, www.ecolepauldu-brule.org, US$25–50), way out on the road to the airport, is not really a hotel at all, but Siem Reap's first school training young and underprivileged Cambodians in the arts of the hotel business. The school turns out about 100 students a year, most of whom find work in the industry. Best of all, the school has four beautifully and individually designed rooms, each one donated by a different five-star hotel. These rooms are used for training purposes, hence the low rates. If you don't mind staying a little farther from the action, you can enjoy first-class international facilities at a budget price and get the chance to observe this commendable school close-up. During term time, from October to July, **Le Jardin des Delices,** an adjacent restaurant, serves the creations of the trainee cooks. The school also offers half-day upscale cooking classes.

(The Villa Siem Reap (tel. 063/761036, www.thevillasiemreap.com, US$15–40), located on Thapul Road a few minutes' walk from the Old Market area, is something of a concept guesthouse; itt makes the most of its budget facilities and offers simple air-conditioned rooms with brilliant purple color schemes. All rooms have Wi-Fi, the restaurant downstairs has an agreeable atmosphere and dishes from around US$5, and guests have free use of the large swimming pool at the Princess Angkor Hotel on Route 6. The staff is young and friendly and the whole place exudes positive energy. Highly recommended and a bargain to boot are the eco-tours that the guesthouse offers, especially the trips to Beng Melea, tours through Cambodian villages that take several NGOs and their activities on board, as well as trips on the Tonlé Sap that protect visitors from the money-making operations that control access to the lake villages. Groups are small (maximum eight people) and always accompanied by an experienced English-speaking guide. Participants can teach English at a local school, partake in the rice harvest, or try the local rice wine.

A modest but smart choice is the very neat and Swiss-German managed **Passagio** (tel. 063/964732, www.passagio-hotel.com, US$30 including breakfast), just north of Wat Damnak on the eastern side of the river. Spacious and spotless air-conditioned rooms with tasteful decor and furnishings, TV, and en-suite hot water are located in a modern townhouse surrounded by a small garden. A small pool gives you a chance to cool off after a long day amongst the ruins. The restaurant serves Khmer cuisine and international favorites with a Swiss leaning—Cordon Bleu is US$8.50.

The recommended **(Golden Orange Hotel** (tel. 063/965389, www.goldenorange-hotel.com, US$25 including breakfast), located in the Wat Po Lanka area, is run by Doug, a somewhat abrasive but friendly American, and offers nicely turned-out, spotless, international-standard air-conditioned rooms. Some rooms have Jacuzzi-style bath tubs, just the thing after a long day visiting the temples. Broadband LAN and Wi-Fi Internet access, a restaurant serving Asian and Western food, a roof-top terrace with a great view across parts of Siem Reap, and all the usual services—such as tours, ticket service, and even a sports bar with a pool table—round out the picture. You bet!

US$50-100

Located behind Wat Po Lanka, the quiet, very private and francophone **Mystères d'Angkor** (tel. 063/963639, www.mysteres-angkor.com, US$49–74) has handsome wood and stone air-conditioned pavilions (four rooms to a building) around a small swimming pool set in a wonderful tropical garden, complete with mango trees and coconut palms. The rooms are bright and beautifully furnished with traditional rosewood furniture. The main building houses the reception area, a pool table, and an excellent restaurant that serves mostly Khmer dishes. A set-menu dinner is US$8.50.

The four-story boutique hotel **Soria Moria** (tel. 063/964768, www.thesoriamoria.com, US$45–90) is located in the Wat Bo area and offers large and bright, air-conditioned European-style rooms with carefully selected furnishings, TV, Wi-Fi, and minibar. The in-house fusion restaurant serves Scandinavian and Japanese cuisine. On Wednesdays, from 5 P.M.–10 P.M., all dishes and drinks cost just US$1. The rooftop bar, with a whirlpool tub, is a good place to relax in the evenings. Spa treatment is also available. An *apsara* dance show, organized by the Sankheum Center for Children (www.sangkheum.org), takes place every night and is free for guests, though donations to the NGO are appreciated.

The **Lin Ratanak Angkor Hotel** (tel. 063/969888, www.linratanakangkor.com,

US$60–120), behind Phsar Samaki off Route 6, is a typical upscale Cambodian hotel offering medium-size, spotless, carpeted rooms with en-suite bathrooms, TV, minibar, air-conditioning, and Wi-Fi. One of the main advantages of this hotel is the larger-than-average swimming pool. The restaurant serves Western and Khmer standards. Breakfast is included in the room price and children under 12 are free.

The **Day Inn Angkor Resort** (tel. 063/760503, www.dayinnangkor.com, US$90) is a smart mid-range colonial-style hotel right in the heart of Siem Reap behind the post office. Large, attractive, air-conditioned rooms with tropical rattan furnishings are located around a large pool. Rates include breakfast.

A good mid-range option in the Wat Bo area is the **Claremont Angkor Hotel** (tel. 063/966898, www.claremontangkor.com), an Australian-owned place that offers smart, good-sized rooms with a cool ambience and real bathtubs. Doubles cost around US$70 for walk-ins, or US$55 if you book over the Internet. Guests also have the use of a fully functional gym, a small swimming pool, and Internet, and there's an in-house Indian restaurant on the sixth floor.

US$100-200

Located next to Siem Reap's Royal Residence, the **Foreign Correspondents Club Angkor (FCC Angkor)** (tel. 063/760280, www.fcccambodia.com, US$170 garden view, US$150 pool view) is not a media hangout as one might suspect, but this smart boutique hotel and restaurant does follow the same philosophical and aesthetic concept as the original FCC in Phnom Penh. The rooms are of modest size but feature a real sense of planning and carefully arranged decor and have a cosmopolitan international boutique feel. Expect attractive bathrooms. The small saltwater pool is a welcome break from the heat and there's an in-house spa.

There are countless mid-range and upscale hotels on the road to the airport catering to tour groups—many of them run-down after less than a decade in service. One of the best

of these massive complexes is the **Princess Angkor Hotel** (tel. 063/760056, www.princessangkor.com, US$100–120 rooms, US$180 suites), which offers international-standard but fairly anonymous, spacious rooms and suites with thick carpets—all with air-conditioning, TV, minibar, and complimentary tea, coffee, and water. Guests can also avail themselves of massage services and a gym. The real advantage of this hotel over many of its neighbors is its large swimming pool. Oh, and there's a casino attached.

A unique hotel experience is the **Angkor Village Hotel** (tel. 063/963561, www.angkorvillage.com, US$109–199) in the Wat Bo area. This collection of traditional Khmer wooden stilt houses is set in a beautiful, spacious, jungle-like garden compound with fully grown rain-trees, coconut palms, banana plants, and bamboo clusters. The wooden houses all feature en-suite bathrooms, air-conditioning, TV, and Internet access, and there's a swimming pool.

The **Shinta Mani** (tel. 063/761998, www.shintamani.com, US$100–140), which looks a bit like a Cambodian government building, is just around the corner from the post office. It's a small and pleasant upscale hotel, with just 18 spacious, tastefully furnished, air-conditioned rooms, located in cool whitewashed galleries around a medium-size swimming pool (US$5 for nonguests). Internet service is available in the lobby area. This hotel is connected to the Institute of Hospitality, a school teaching Western culinary skills to local youngsters. The students get a small stipend and virtually all participants find work in the industry after completing their nine-month course. The attached spa offers massages, body scrubs, therapeutic facials, and hand and foot care.

If you can do without total authenticity, but will enjoy the best possible copy of something that never really existed—namely the colonial paradise—then the **Victoria Hotel** (tel. 063/760428, www.victoriahotels-asia.com), just to the west of the Royal Independence Gardens, will fulfill your expectations. Located in a massive colonial-style compound designed with a great eye for detail, this French-owned property might only be five years old, but conveys all the nostalgia you will need. The airy reception area is invitingly intimate and yet formal, and the rooms (all with air-conditioning, TV, minibar, LAN and Wi-Fi, and private balcony, US$115–125) are furnished with perfect copies of sumptuous period furniture. The spacious suites (US$330) have all been designed to individual concepts—such as the Maharajah Suite and Governor Suite, each with their personal color schemes and decor. The steel cage elevators add a nice touch and there's a good-size swimming pool in a central courtyard. Best of all, guests may choose to be driven around the temples in vintage Citroëns—now that's hard to beat for a classy way to see the wonders of Angkor.

Over US$200

For the ultimate colonial-era experience in Siem Reap, look no further than the historic **Raffles Grand Hotel d'Angkor** (tel. 063/963888, www.raffles.com/en_ra/property/rga, US$300–2,000), situated just north of the beautifully kept Royal Independence Gardens. From the moment you approach the perfectly restored building, the old world ambience is unbeatable. The Grand d'Angkor first opened in 1932, then catering to the upscale French travelers visiting the ruins of Angkor. Later, illustrious celebrities such as Charlie Chaplin and Jackie Kennedy stayed here. Today the hotel still caters to Cambodia's most affluent guests and the large rooms and suites offer all international-standard amenities, always in a tasteful, francophone, colonial context. The swimming pool is one of the largest in town and the Elephant Bar in the basement exudes quiet retro charm. The Grand d'Angkor is a bit formal, but that's part of the ambience. *Apsara* dance show dinners, performed on the hotel stage behind the pool, take place between October and July and cost US$32. Guests may also avail themselves to the hotel's tennis courts. The Café d'Angkor offers international cuisine and breakfast and

the Restaurant Le Grand serves an exclusive selection of the best of Khmer cuisine. The Grand D'Angkor organizes exclusive tours into the surrounding countryside (including a Khmer-style ranch barbecue combined with a horseback ride) and can even provide food and beverage catering for your private jet. Finally, to get rid of your aches and pains, visit the in-house Amrita Spa, which offers massage therapies, body wraps, packs, and masks, as well as specialized skin care treatments, salt rubs, and manicures. You will be pampered.

Bombastic style, dramatic history, overwhelming architecture, cool retro ambience, and an extremely high standard of services make the **Hotel de la Paix** (tel. 063/966000, www.hoteldelapaixangkor.com, US$330–715) one of the most exclusive, smart, and impressive hotel experiences in the region. The original Hotel de la Paix was built in the 1950s and saw much of Cambodia's tragic history unfold within its walls. Built by a Khmer warlord and anti-French guerilla, who was thought to have magical powers, the hotel has served as the private residence of a Lon Nol commander, as a rice depot for the Khmer Rouge, as government guesthouse during the Vietnamese presence, and finally as the Directorate of UNTAC. In 1993, the old building was knocked down and construction started on the massive art deco edifice the hotel has now become. Arranged around a courtyard with an old banyan tree in its center, more than a hundred luxurious, spacious, and carefully designed rooms cater to every whim. The suites have bathtubs right in the center of the master bedroom, a perfect honeymoon indulgence. All rooms feature pre-programmed iPods, a safe, fridge, and complimentary Wi-Fi. The in-house restaurant, Meric, offers first-class Cambodian cuisine as well as international dishes (main courses around US$25). Guests can choose to dine sitting on swinging platforms, or more conventionally, at a table. Last but not least, the spacious and idiosyncratic pool, complete with an ornate bridge crossing it, is fit for a Roman orgy.

FOOD
Street Cafés and Bakeries

Common Grounds (tel. 063/965687, daily 7 A.M.–10 P.M.) is an agreeable, modern American-style coffeehouse behind Phsar Kandal, with a great collection of teas, cakes, and tarts, free Wi-Fi, and fast Internet terminals. All profits go to NGO projects in Cambodia.

Right next to the French Cultural Center just off Wat Bo Road, **Le Café** (tel. 092/271392, daily 7:30 A.M.–10 P.M.) is located in a quiet garden and offers sandwiches, salads, cakes, and fruit juices, all prepared by the Paul Dubrule Hotel and Tourism School, an NGO training young Cambodians in the hotel and catering business.

The laid-back **Singing Tree Café** (tel. 092/635500, www.singingtreecafe.com) is located in a wooden house in a pretty garden on the eastern side of the river, not more than a few minutes' walk from the Old Market. The food is mostly vegetarian, but also includes sushi. The café is part of the NGO scene in Siem Reap and several worthy causes are promoted here. Movies, often interesting documentaries, are shown in the upstairs lounge area every Thursday at 7 P.M. There are Pilates lessons on Tuesdays, Wednesdays, and Fridays; meditation on Wednesdays; and a monk chat— a chance to interact with and ask questions of Buddhist monks—every Saturday. Check the website for exact times. A small shop sells locally made souvenirs and T-shirts, and the coffee's not bad, either.

Khmer

Several cheap Khmer restaurants can be found tucked to the northeastern side of the Old Market. They all serve good-quality local dishes, most around US$2. Lots of Khmer eat here, which is as good a recommendation as any. All these eateries have English menus with photos. The best of the lot might be **Socheata,** which does an excellent fish *amok* for US$3. Don't be intimidated by the no-thrills decor, since this might be your best chance to taste genuine Khmer cuisine if you are only visiting Seam Reap. Young Cambodians are trained to work in the restaurant business at the nonprofit "School of Rice" **Sala Bai** (tel. 063/963329, www.salabai.com), a small eatery on Taphul Road, which only opens during term time, from October to July. The restaurant is open on weekdays for lunch only between noon–2 P.M. The students serve quality Asian and Western three-course set menus.

Located on the first-floor terrace of a traditional wooden house on Oum Khun Street to the west of Taphul Road, the **Tany Khmer Family Kitchen** (tel. 063/964118, daily lunch and dinner) offers moderately priced (most courses around US$4) Cambodian dishes, as well as a Khmer Set Menu (US$11). Great home cooking and informal atmosphere make this a very unpretentious, relaxing choice.

The attractive **Sugar Palm Restaurant** (tel. 063/964838, daily 11 A.M.–10 P.M.) on Taphul Road is located on the first floor of a wooden house, a nicely furnished open balcony space, and serves superior Khmer cuisine. Grilled eggplant with minced pork (US$5) and, for the more courageous, frog legs in ginger (US$6) are typical dishes and the wine list is extensive. Diners can also enjoy Cambodia's national dish here: *prahoc* (fermented fish-paste).

The **Khmer Family Restaurant** (tel. 015/999909, daily 11 A.M.–10 P.M.) is part of a colonial block reaching all the way from The Passage, a narrow alley of galleries and restaurants, to the road west of the Old Market. It serves cheap Khmer dishes in a relaxed atmosphere. Try fried morning glory with chicken, pork, beef, fish, or tofu for US$2.50, or fried pumpkin with a choice of the same add-ons for US$3.

Also located in The Passage, the tiny and comfortable **Chamkar Vegetarian Restaurant** (Mon.–Sat. 11 A.M.–10 P.M.) offers a small but very attractive menu of vegetarian Khmer dishes, along with some great cakes.

An altogether different dining experience in the Old Market area is the ultra-trendy **AHA** (tel. 063/965501), founded by the owner of the Hotel de la Paix. Enjoy fine wines and Cambodian and Western snack food and marvel at the contemporary interior design, more than a million miles from the rice fields of Cambodia, and yet somehow sitting (metaphorically speaking) right amongst them. Start with tapas and move on to chicken spring rolls. The restaurant is linked to the McDermott Photo Gallery, creating an artistic, up-market ambience unrivalled in Siem Reap.

On the southern half of Wat Bo Road, the upscale **Viroth's Restaurant** (tel. 012/826346, daily 11 A.M.–2 P.M. for lunch and 6–10:30 P.M. for dinner) has great ambience, with soft lighting and Cambodian tapestries providing a romantic backdrop to the excellent Khmer cuisine. Fish and beef *amok* are favorites. Main dishes cost around US$7.

Facing the west side of the Old Market, the **Champey Restaurant** and the **Amok Restaurant** almost flow into each other across a narrow alley. The former has yellow decor, the latter is kept all in blue; both eateries share the same owner and menus of great Khmer cuisine, and are open daily 9 A.M.–11 P.M. Main courses are around US$5.

Asian

For those who'd like to try health-conscious Asian cuisine, the **Panida Restaurant** (tel. 011/741628, daily 7 A.M.–10 P.M.) offers a decent variety of vegetarian Thai food, guaranteed free of MSG, along with fruit shakes and coffees. Most dishes are around US$4. It's located on the way to the airport, but still close enough to the downtown area to walk there.

The excellent **Chivit Thai** (tel. 012/830761, daily 7 A.M.–10 P.M.) is located in a wooden pavilion fronting a small garden on Wat Bo Road and serves a wide variety of authentic Thai cuisine. Try the *nam prik pla pon,* a fiery fish paste dip served with raw and cooked vegetables, or for a more conventional taste, the excellent chicken cashew. Most dishes are a very reasonable US$4, the food is nicely presented, and the service is prompt. If only they did not play airport lounge music all day...

Right next door, the **Chiang Mai Thai Food** (tel. 012/980833, daily 7 A.M.–midnight) is equally authentic and reliable, but is located in an air-conditioned building. The food here is slightly cheaper than at the Chivit Thai, but it tastes just as good and there's a large variety of dishes to choose from.

The **Sawasdee Food Garden** (tel. 063/964456, www.yaklom.com, daily 6:30 A.M.–10 P.M.) on Wat Bo Road, just north of Route 6, serves decent Thai food in a laid-back atmosphere. *Tom yum kung,* shrimp soup, as spicy as you order it, is US$5.

The **Paris-Saigon** (tel. 063/965408, daily 11 A.M.–10 P.M.) is a cozy restaurant in the Wat Bo area, with attractive red-brick decor. The menu is predominantly French, but there are a few Vietnamese courses as well, and a good selection of wines. Try the beef fillet (US$9.50) and *phoe bho beef* (Vietnamese beef soup, US$6). It's a great place for a quiet dinner for two.

Located in a family house and decorated with Japanese paintings, the **Maido Yakiniku BBQ Restaurant** (tel. 063/761947, daily lunch and dinner), on a road parallel and west of Taphul Road, is as low-key a Japanese restaurant as you could hope for, with common and private VIP rooms (for groups of up to six). Dishes include sushi as well as some Khmer dishes, such as grill-it-yourself barbecues of beef imported from Australia.

The **Hong Kong Restaurant** (tel. 063/966226, daily 9 A.M.–10 P.M.), to the north of the Old Market and just south of Center Market, is a small, bright, fast-food-style Chinese eatery, offering dim sum and a wide range of standard Chinese rice dishes.

The **d'Wau Restaurant** (tel. 012/356030, daily 7 A.M.–10 P.M.), on Wat Bo Road, is a smart and trendy-looking Malaysian restaurant with an extensive menu of curries. Guests can dine in tiny wooden pavilions in a small garden out front or in the large air-conditioned restaurant. Try the chicken satay (US$3). The d'Wau is 100 percent halal and does not sell alcohol. It's possible to have food delivered to your hotel.

Little India (tel. 012/652398, daily 9 A.M.–late), located right in the heart of the Old

Market area, is actually a Sri Lankan place, but serves reliable Indian cooking. *Thalis* are US$3–4, depending on whether you prefer vegetables or meat, and you can sit right on the curbside to watch the nightlife action.

The cheap and cheerful **Maharaja** (tel. 063/966221) manages to conjure magic at a small price in the heart of the Old Market area. Vegetarian *thalis* cost just US$2.50 and they are not bad. Guests may choose from five different levels of spiciness. All the usual Indian and Pakistani standards are available, from trusty chicken tikka to creamy *korma* dishes, with most main courses around US$4. Service is prompt and friendly.

The **East India Curry Restaurant** (tel. 063/966898) on the sixth floor of the Claremont Angkor Hotel serves a huge choice of Indian and South Asian dishes. Meat standards such as chicken tikka are around US$6, while vegetarian courses will set you back around US$4. The East India has two terraces, both offering good views over Siem Reap.

Possibly the tastiest Indian restaurant is **Curry Walla** (tel. 063/965451), a Punjabi place on Sibvatha Boulevard that does very good *dal makhni*. Most dishes, both vegetarian and non-vegetarian, are around US$3.

International

North of the Old Market and almost next door to the Hong Kong Restaurant, the **Happy Herb Pizza** (daily 7 A.M.–11 P.M.) serves budget Khmer dishes and pizzas, as "happy"—meaning topped with marijuana—as you like 'em. It's part of a franchise with outlets in Phnom Penh.

Tell Siem Reap (tel. 063/963289, daily 11 A.M.–10 P.M.) on Sivatha Boulevard, like its namesake in Phnom Penh, offers a large variety of German and Asian dishes from around US$7 in an air-conditioned, family-friendly environment; there's a good choice of German beers and liquors.

The **X Rooftop Bar** (daily 4 P.M.–sunrise) on Sivatha Boulevard is one of the most popular after-dark hangouts in Siem Reap. Movies, free Wi-Fi, Western comfort food, cigars, wine, and a great view make this a great stopover on any tour through the town's nightlife area.

One of the best-restored, spectacular-looking, colonial-style restaurants is **Le Malraux** (tel. 063/966041, www.le-malraux-siem-reap.com), located on Sivatha Boulevard opposite the road that leads to the Angkor Night Market. A modern art-deco dream, with a menu and wine list to suit the ambience, Le Malraux is the kind of place you might head (scrubbed and showered, of course) after a dusty day amongst the Angkor ruins, to enjoy a cigar and a cognac and debate the legacy of the French Republic in the Kingdom of Cambodia. Main dishes are around US$12.

The **Abacus** (tel. 012/644286, daily 10 A.M.–11 P.M.), just off Taphul Street, is an agreeable French and Khmer restaurant in a traditional Cambodian house located in a small garden. It sports a short but interesting menu. The eatery feels almost like the living room of an absent-minded academic, with books and magazines piled on shelves everywhere and small tables separated by low walls inviting guests to linger over food and wines. Dishes include fish fillet tamarind (US$7.50), mashed pumpkin, and grilled eggplant; the crocodile tail curry (US$13) is highly recommended for more adventurous diners.

Le Jardin des Délices, an excellent restaurant that is part of the Paul Dubrule Hotel and Tourism School (tel. 063/963672, www.ecolepauldubrule.org), way out on the road to the airport, opens only from October to July, during the school's term time. Set lunches prepared by the students are US$11. Call ahead.

On the corner of Corner Oum Khun Street and Street 14, in the Wat Bo area, **L'Escale des Arts & des Sens** (tel. 063/761442) serves upscale French cuisine in a large comfortable pavilion. Grilled duck foie gras with lemongrass, ginger juice, and talamma seed is US$24. Set menus are between US$18–24. Occasional dance and music performances are put on in high season.

Viva (tel. 092/209154, daily 11:30 A.M.–late) is Siem Reap's only Mexican restaurant. Located on a corner to the northern side of the Old

Market, this is obviously the place to go if you have a craving for burritos and enchiladas and want to watch the world go by from street level. Expect to pay about US$5 a main course.

Located in a whitewashed colonial building near Wat Damnak, the stylish **Alliance Café** (tel. 063/964940, daily 10 A.M.–midnight) is a smart French restaurant run by a French chef, made especially attractive by the works of Cambodian and French artists. Usually two or three artists exhibit their work at any given time. There's also outdoor seating. Red tuna coated with sesame (US$16) is recommended. Several Khmer dishes are also on offer.

The **Red Pizza Shop** (daily 10 A.M.– 10 P.M.), near Kandal Market, smacks of a well-known American franchise, but offers pizzas unheard of in the United States. Try Pizza Tom Yum and other combinations catering to Asian tastes, as well as more conventional cheese and meat toppings.

Pissa Italiana (daily 11 A.M.–11 P.M., except closed Sun. lunch) on Pub Street is a reliable Italian eatery, serving pastas, pizzas, salads, and delicious homemade lemon tarts.

The **Jasmine Angkor** (tel. 012/808881, 24 hours a day) on Samdech Tep Vong Street near the corner of Taphul Road, is not particularly cozy, but it does offer air-conditioning and a huge menu of Khmer and European dishes (main courses around US$4). Traditional dance performances take place occasionally in the evenings.

One of the trendiest and most cosmopolitan places in town is the futuristic **Blue Pumpkin** (tel. 063/963574), on the road north of the Old Market. It offers not just a comfortable, air-conditioned, first-floor lounge with Wi-Fi access, but also has some of Siem Reap's best sandwiches, salads, cakes, and tarts on its menu. It's no wonder this place is enormously popular with the backpacker set.

INFORMATION AND SERVICES
Tourist Information

The Tourist Office, next to Le Grand d'Angkor Hotel, is not terribly informed and most visitors cull their information from local guides, hotels and guesthouses, and the ever-present free Canby guides, which list hotels and restaurants. Cambodia Pocket Guides publish a couple of booklets featuring shopping, dining, and drinking. These publications promote only businesses that advertise.

Libraries and Permanent Exhibitions
THE CENTRE OF KHMER STUDIES AT WAT DAMNAK

This excellent non-lending library (tel. 063/96438, www.khmerstudies.org/library/library.htm), located on the eastern side of the river within the Wat Damnak temple compound, is open to the public Monday–Saturday 8 A.M.–noon and 2–5 P.M. The Centre of Khmer Studies promotes research, teaching, and public service in the social sciences, arts, and humanities. The library holds a large collection of books and academic texts in English, French, Khmer, and several other languages. It's possible to have texts photocopied.

THE TONLÉ SAP EXHIBITION

Out on the road to the temples, the NGO Krousar Thmey, a foundation helping deprived children, has set up a small exhibition on Khmer heritage and the ecology of the Tonlé Sap Lake. The exhibits (daily 8 A.M.– noon and 1:30–5:30 P.M.) look a bit dated, but a relaxing massage by blind masseurs trained by physiotherapists (US$5/hour) is also available here. You can just drop by or call ahead for an appointment (tel. 063/964694).

Money

Siem Reap is dotted with banks and ATMs and there are unofficial money changers at Phsar Kandal (Center Market) that offer a marginally better rate than the banks. Banks are usually open Monday–Friday 8 A.M.–3 or 4 P.M., and sometimes until 11:30 A.M. on Saturdays.

All ATMs, including those at the airport, dispense U.S. dollars. Large ripped dollar notes will not be accepted by local businesses.

Credit cards (especially Visa, MasterCard, and JCB) are widely accepted, but businesses usually charge a commission (of a few percent) for transactions. Travelers checks are accepted at most banks, at some hotels, and by some money changers.

Health and Emergencies

In case of a serious accident or illness, head for the 24-hour **Royal Angkor International Hospital** (tel. 063/761888, 012/235888, 063/399111, www.royalangkorhospital.com) on the road to the airport, which provides high-quality medical services (including an ICU and blood bank), as well as an all-Cambodia ambulance service. The hospital can also organize medical evacuations in very serious situations.

The most recommended pharmacies are U-Care in the Old Market area (tel. 063/965396) and at the airport. Make sure you have medical insurance (highly recommended in Cambodia), as hospital bills can be astronomical.

Internet Access

Siem Reap is extremely well-connected to the digital global village. In fact, virtually every guesthouse and hotel provides Internet access to its guests, either on communal terminals or with Wi-Fi access in the rooms. Sometimes, especially in mid-range places, this service is free of charge; at other establishments, you might have to buy a card or charge the time spent online to your bill. Some bars and restaurants, including the Blue Pumpkin, Common Grounds, and the X Bar, have free Wi-Fi access, and there are plenty of Internet cafés around town from where Skype calls are usually possible. Rates average US$1 per hour.

Post Office

The post office, located on the western side of the river, a little south of the FCC, is open daily 7:30 A.M.–5:30 P.M. and there's no vouching as to how reliable it is. If you're shipping something valuable, then DHL (Phsar Kandal, tel. 063/964949) might be the ticket.

Laundry

Virtually all hotels, from budget flophouses to first-class boutique hotels, offer a laundry service.

GETTING THERE
Air

Most of the two million international travelers who visit the Angkor ruins each year arrive at Siem Reap's modern airport. As Bangkok Airways/Siem Reap Airways have a monopoly on flights from Thailand, prices on this route, the busiest, are unreasonably high; it's actually cheaper to fly into Phnom Penh with Air Asia and then on to Siem Reap on a domestic flight with Siem Reap Airways, though this of course is a lot of hassle. Still, while the road between the Thai border and Siem Reap is still unfinished, Bangkok Airways is the most convenient choice, with five direct Bangkok–Siem Reap flights a day. This monopoly may end upon completion of the highway.

It's also possible to fly into Siem Reap from Singapore on Silk Air, from Kuala Lumpur on Malaysia Airlines and Air Asia, from Ho Chi Minh City and Hanoi on Vietnam Airlines, from Kunming in China on China Eastern Airlines, from Cheng Du on Angkor Airways, from Inchon in South Korea on Korean Air and Asiana Airlines, and from Hong Kong with Dragon Air and Siem Reap Airways.

The airport is six kilometers from town; a taxi costs US$5, and a *motodup* will take you for US$1. Note that the domestic departure tax is US$6, while the international departure tax is US$25. Many hotels provide free pick-ups and drop-offs, if you make arrangements in advance.

AIRLINE OFFICES

Siem Reap has the following airline offices:

- **Angkor Airways:** 564, Mondul Village, tel. 063/964878, www.angkorairways.com
- **Bangkok Airways/Siem Reap Airways:** National Route No. 6, tel. 063/965442, www.bangkokair.com

- **China Eastern Airlines:** 304, Steung Thmey Village, Svay Dangkum Commune, tel. 063/965229, www.ce-air.com
- **Korean Air:** Room 120, Airlines Office Building, Siem Reap International Airport, tel. 063/964881, www.koreanair.com
- **Lao Airlines:** 114, Sala Khanseng Village, National Route No. 6, tel. 063/963283, www.laoairlines.com
- **Malaysia Airlines:** Rooms 117–119, Siem Reap International Airport, tel. 063/964761, www.malaysiaairlines.com.my
- **Silk Air:** Room 122–123, Airline Office Building, Siem Reap International Airport, tel. 063/964993
- **Vietnam Airlines:** 342, National Route No. 6, tel. 063/964488, www.vietnamairlines.com

Boat

The boat rides from Phnom Penh and Battambang are enjoyable in the wet and cool season, but several accidents have happened in the past, with vessels breaking down mid-lake (or running out of gas) and luggage being lost. What with road conditions getting better all the time and passenger numbers on the ferry dropping off, the boat operators have raised the prices. Still, if you are itching for a bit of adventure, try the run to Phnom Penh for US$30, or to Battambang for US$20. The four- to six-hour ferry ride to Phnom Penh is only moderately scenic, but the trip to Battambang (6–8 hours) definitely has its moments, as the boat passes several traditional fishing villages on stilts before entering the Sangker River, which snakes through numerous small settlements before reaching Cambodia's second city.

These ferries are not altogether safe by Western standards, and the buses are considerably cheaper and faster.

Regional Road Transport

Numerous bus companies do the Phnom Penh to Siem Reap run, which costs US$8–11,

depending on the on-board facilities (all buses on this route are air-conditioned). Buses by Sorya Transport (tel. 023/210359), Mekong Express (tel. 063/963662), which has deluxe, air-conditioned buses, Paramount Angkor (tel. 063/761912), and Capitol Guesthouse (tel. 023/217627) all leave from the Chong Kov Sou Bus Station, off Route 6, a couple of kilometers to the west of Siem Reap. *Motodups* will take you there for US$2, tuk-tuks for US$3. Journey times are typically 5–6 hours and buses leave very frequently 7 A.M.–14:30 P.M. Most guesthouses and hotels are happy to get the tickets for you, but may charge an extra dollar for the service.

With rising gas prices and affluent tourists, taxi fares from Siem Reap have risen to almost extortionate heights. A private taxi to Phnom Penh is pricy at US$75, while a ride to Battambang is US$50. A ride to the border town of Poipet will set you back about US$60. Coming from Phnom Penh or Battambang might be cheaper. Coming from the border, you will have to deal with the Poipet taxi mafia who might demand anything from US$40 to US$70. The price will partly depend on your bargaining skills.

The Siem Reap-Bangkok Run

It's possible to travel from Siem Reap to Bangkok overland in one long day. Numerous operators offer the trip, which takes around 9–12 hours. Ask your guesthouse or hotel for details. From Bangkok, a number of operators on Khao San Road offer the trip for US$10–20, but this is fraught with scams and rip-offs. Sometimes passengers are taken through the Pailin border, at other times, the buses on the Cambodian side are so slow that travelers arrive late and tired in Siem Reap, more likely than not to accept the choice of accommodation offered by the bus touts, who collect commission. Going it alone from Siem Reap need not be more expensive, as there is now a bus for US$10 to the border in Poipet. Alternatively, you can take a taxi (US$50–70, 3–4 hours). On the Thai side, you can choose between bus (150–200 baht), minibus (300–400 baht), or train (50 baht) all the way to the Thai capital—or, if you arrive late, to a decent hotel or guesthouse in Aranyaprathet, the town closest to the border on the Thai side. Avoid staying overnight in Poipet at all costs.

GETTING AROUND

Downtown Siem Reap is small enough to walk around, but if you are staying a bit farther out, there's a range of local transport you can use to get around town. Besides hiring a bicycle from a guesthouse for a couple of dollars a day, the cheapest options are the trusty *motodups*,

motorcycle taxis that will charge about 1,000 riel for a short ride, up to US$1 for a longer distance. Prices increase as soon as the sun's gone down. A tuk-tuk is a safer, more comfortable, and slightly more expensive option—with rides in town for around 2,000 riel to US$1. Unless you are going to the airport (US$5), a taxi around town seems hardly worth it.

Foreigners are not allowed to drive themselves in the Siem Reap area, unless they are residents. This guarantees income to the *motodups* and tuk-tuk drivers who depend on tourist dollars.

Angkor

Most visitors to Cambodia come to see the temples of Angkor. Located in forests to the northwest of the Tonlé Sap Lake, the sprawling ruins of the Angkor Empire are simply without equal in Southeast Asia. It is the interplay between forest and ruins that gives the former Khmer capital its otherworldly, fantastical atmosphere. Even widely traveled and jaded culture-hounds cannot help but be moved by the scale and sensuousness of these buildings.

More than two million visitors entered the Angkor Archaeological Park in 2008. For Cambodians, Angkor lies at the heart of the national identity: as much an ancient success story and an object of immense pride as a psychological burden for a country with such a tragic recent history.

For more than 500 years, Angkor dominated the political and cultural affairs of much of Southeast Asia and the Khmer Empire spread into large parts of Thailand, as well as Laos and Vietnam—restored temples in Thailand and Laos attest to this—before being subsumed by its own grandeur and the jungle in the 15th century.

Angkor Wat is the largest religious building in the world, and its surroundings play host to the highest concentration of temples in the world. The temples were declared a UNESCO World Heritage site in 1992. Around the

© AROON THAEWCHATTURAT

the central pyramid of Angkor Wat

temples, life goes on as it has done for hundreds of years. Siem Reap Province is one of the poorest in Cambodia and rice-fields continue to be tilled by oxen and plow, just as they were during the Khmer Empire's hey-day. In fact, many aspects of Cambodian life have not changed much in the past thousand years. Since the fall of Angkor in 1431 at the hands of the Siamese, the country has been sliding from one tragedy into another, and many Cambodians dream of recapturing some of the country's former glory one day.

What is considered Angkor today (part of the Angkor Archaeological Park) spreads over an area of some 230 square kilometers, and besides Angkor Wat and the imperial city of Angkor Thom, this includes all other temples in the region. Most temples lie a few kilometers to the north of Siem Reap, while the structures known as the Roluos Group, which predates Angkor slightly, can be found 15 kilometers east of Siem Reap.

THE HISTORY OF THE ANGKOR EMPIRE

The wall of the city is some five miles in circumference. It has five gates, each with double portals. Two gates pierce the eastern side; the other sides have one gate only. Outside the wall stretches a great moat, across which access to the city is given by massive causeways. Flanking the causeways on each side are fifty-four divinities resembling warlords in stone, huge and terrifying. All five gates are similar. The parapets of the causeways are of solid stone, carved to represent nine-headed serpents. The fifty-four divinities grasp the serpents with their hands, seemingly to prevent their escape. Above each gate are grouped five gigantic heads of Buddha, four of them facing the four cardinal points of the compass, the fifth, brilliant with gold, holds a central position.

This is how Chou Ta-Kuan, a Chinese diplomat described the Khmer capital of Angkor Thom during his visit in the late 13th century in his account *The Customs of Cambodia* (The Siam Society, Bangkok, 1992). The visitor from the North was clearly impressed by the power and affluence projected by the city's monuments, which, at the time, were the culmination of 500

years of the rise and fall of one of the greatest empires of the Middle Ages. To put the glory of Angkor in perspective: When Chou Ta-Kuan visited, the imperial city of Angkor Thom had around one million inhabitants, and the temple of Ta Prohm alone had more than 80,000 servants and staff, while in Europe, Paris had a population of just 25,000.

The history of Angkor begins some 500 years prior to Chou Ta-Kuan's visit, at the dawn of the 9th century. In the preceding centuries, smaller empires and fiefdoms had fallen and risen in the region, which we now recognize as Cambodia. Most of them had fallen under the control of the court of Java in Indonesia, although some recent studies suggest that Java could in fact be Chenla, an earlier Khmer kingdom. Whatever the case, the first great Khmer king Jayavarman II (A.D. 802–850) declared himself *devaraja* (divine ruler) of the kingdom of Kambujadesa; he established several capitals, including one at Phnom Kulen, to the northeast of Siem Reap, and later another at Hariharalaya, near Roluos.

Towards the end of the 9th century, Indravarman I (A.D. 877–889) built the first of the great Angkor temples, Preah Ko, as well as the Bakong and began work on a huge *baray* (water reservoir), at Hariharalaya. His son, Yasovarman I (A.D. 889–900) expanded on his father's achievements, finished the *baray,* and created yet another royal city, Yashodarapura, located around Phnom Bakheng, today's most popular sunset spot within the Angkor Archaeological Park. Yasovarman I might also have been the Khmer king to begin constructions of the mountain temple of Preah Vihear. Other kings came and went, powers struggles between different royal families and with the neighboring Cham continued, and the capital briefly moved out to Koh Ker, before returning to the Angkor area.

Suryavarman II, who ascended to the throne in A.D. 1113, extended the Khmer Empire to its largest territory. He also built Angkor Wat, yet following his death in A.D. 1150, the empire fell apart once more. Only his cousin, Jayavarman VII, managed to reunite the kingdom under

CHOU TA-KUAN: ANGKOR'S CHRONICLER

Chou Ta-Kuan, a Chinese diplomat in the service of Emperor Chengzong of Yaun, grandson of Kublai Khan, traveled from Wenzhou, on the East China Sea coast, past Guangzhou and Hainan, along Vietnam's coast and up the Mekong River as far as Kompong Cham, from where he took a smaller vessel across the Tonlé Sap Lake to arrive at the imperial city of Angkor Thom in August 1296.

Chou Ta-Kuan was neither the first nor the last Chinese diplomat to visit the seat of the Angkor Empire, but he stayed for 11 months and took notes. *The Customs of*

Cambodia, the only surviving first-person account of life in the Khmer Empire, is one of the most important sources available to scholars and laymen to understand Angkor. Not only did the diplomat describe the city of Angkor Thom, he also shed some light on the daily lives of ordinary Cambodians. With his report, Chou Ta-Kuan gives today's visitors an opportunity to imagine how the ruined splendor of the temples must once have been a busy metropolis and how, at its height, a million people could have lived and worked here.

his crown in A.D. 1181, fight off the Cham, and commence the Khmer Empire's last great renaissance. Jayavarman VII converted from Hinduism to Mahayana Buddhism, founded the last great Khmer city, Angkor Thom, and oversaw Angkor's most prolific period of monument building. In less than 40 years, hundreds of temples—as well as libraries, *dharamshalas* (rest houses), and hospitals—were hastily constructed along new roads that now connected large parts of the kingdom. Many of the monuments built under Jayavarman VII are artistically inferior and stylistically impure because the speed of construction was so frenetic. It seemed like the last god-king knew that time was running out. It was Jayavarman VII who had some of Angkor's most enduring iconic buildings constructed, including Ta Prohm and the Bayon. In A.D. 1203, the king annexed Champa and effectively extended his empire to southern Vietnam. But, with the death of Jayavarman VII in A.D. 1218, the moment had passed and Angkor slowly went into decline.

Hinduism was briefly reintroduced by Jayavarman VIII in the late 13th century, resulting in a concerted and presumably costly act of vandalism that saw the defacing of many Buddhist monuments, including Ta Prohm and Preah Khan. Buddhism soon returned, but in a different form, as Theravada Buddhism, which has survived in Cambodia

to this day and which puts less emphasis on the divinity of the king. Perhaps this loss of spiritual authority affected later kings. Perhaps, as new research suggests, the Angkor Empire had overreached itself, ruined the environment around Siem Reap, and was ready to give way to something else.

Repeated incursions by the Siamese culminated in a seven-month siege of Angkor Thom in A.D. 1431, after which King Ponhea Yat moved the capital southwest to Phnom Penh. Other reasons for the demise of this great empire are also plausible. The Khmer Empire had been built on the back of an agrarian society and trade was becoming more important in Southeast Asia. Angkor Thom was too isolated, too far from the coast, and too far from the Mekong to be able to keep up with new challenges. Following the move to Phnom Penh, the temples remained active, yet were slowly subsumed by jungle.

THE "REDISCOVERY" OF ANGKOR

Angkor is unlikely to have ever been completely abandoned, though exact information on the activities around the ruins between the 15th and 18th century A.D. is sketchy. Following the last onslaught by the Thais in 1431 and the gradual shift of the capital towards Phnom Penh, monks continued to live around Angkor

Wat until the 16th century. The Cambodian court apparently returned to Angkor for brief periods during the 16th and 17th centuries.

Around the same time, an early report by the Portuguese writer Diego De Couto apparently referred to a Capuchin friar visiting the region in 1585 and finding the temples in ruins, overgrown by vegetation. So impressed were early visitors from Europe, the Middle East, and other parts of Asia that some wildly speculated that the Romans or Alexander the Great had built the temples.

A trickle of these adventurers and traders, many of whom had settled at the court in Phnom Penh in the 16th century, began to take note of the ruins, either by hearing other people's accounts or traveling there themselves, a 10-day journey at the time. A group of Spanish missionaries even hoped to rehabilitate the ruins and turn them into a center of Christian teaching. A Japanese interpreter, Kenryo Shimano, drew the first accurate ground plan of Angkor Wat in the early 17th century. Japanese writing on a pillar inside Angkor Wat is said to have been carved by his son, who later visited the site in honor of his adventurous father. Other foreigners—including an American, a Brit, and several French explorers—published their accounts of visiting the temples, but no one really took note.

In 1858, Henri Mouhot, a French naturalist who lived on the island of Jersey, set off on an expedition sponsored by the British Royal Geographical Society and reached Angkor in early 1860. Mouhot spent three weeks at Angkor, surveyed the temples, and continued up the Mekong into Laos, where he eventually died of a fever (possibly malaria). His notes were published in 1864, a year after Cambodia had become a French protectorate.

THE RESTORATION OF ANGKOR

In 1863, a year before Mouhot's report was published, Vice-Admiral Bonard, the governor of the French colony of Cochin China (South Vietnam), visited Angkor and decided that it had not been the Romans or any other foreign power who had built the magnificent temples, but the now-impoverished Cambodians.

The idea of restoring Cambodia and its people to its former grandeur encouraged the population back home in France to support the republic's quickly expanding and unpopular colonial efforts in Southeast Asia. Angkor became a symbol of this drive, and as a consequence, was soon very much a focus of attention at the highest political levels of the French administration. Thailand was already under the influence of the British (a British photographer, John Thomson, published the first images of Angkor Wat in the 1860s), and the race was on to find a trade route into China, which was just beginning to open up to foreign commerce. Cambodia and the Mekong were to play a key role in this race.

In 1866, the Mekong Exploration Commission, led by Doudart de Lagrée, France's representative in Cambodia, and accompanied by Francis Garnier, Louis Delaporte, a photographer named Gsell, and several others, set off to find out whether the Mekong was navigable. On the way, they made a planned detour to Angkor and took detailed, scientific notes. Louis Delaporte's watercolors and drawings, fanciful though they were, and Gsell's photographs of the temples, along with route maps and extensive descriptions of temples and the lives of Cambodians, were published in two volumes in 1873 as *Voyage d'exploration en Indo-Chine*. As the French public was not aware of Henri Mouhot's British-funded efforts, Garnier and Delaporte (de Lagré had died by this time) got all the credit for the "discovery" of Angkor. Their findings were well presented and included, for the first time, outlying temples such as Beng Melea, Preah Khan, and Wat Nokor, to the east of Angkor, as well as Khmer temples in southern Laos. Of course, in the eyes of superior-minded Europeans, the temples could not compete in grandeur with efforts back home and the early explorers claimed that "Cambodian art ought to perhaps rank its productions behind the greatest masterpieces in the West."

Yet, slowly, in the minds of these early

archaeologists and consequently the French public, the true dimensions of the Khmer Empire began to emerge. In 1867, at the Universal Exposition in Paris, visitors were presented with giant plaster cast reproductions of the temples. In the following years, Delaporte returned to Cambodia and began to systematically remove statues, sculptures, and stonework to Europe. Soon after, he became the director of the Indochinese Museum in Paris, which began to amass a collection of Angkorian artifacts. Around the same time, the first tourists began to arrive. They too took souvenirs with them, many of which disappeared into private homes in France. In 1887, the French architect Lucien Fournereau made extensive and detailed drawings of Angkor Wat and other temples, which for the first time, presented Europeans with accurate, scientific plans of Khmer architecture. Hendrick Kern, a Dutchman, managed to decipher the Sanskrit inscriptions on temple walls in 1879, and the French epigrapher Etienne Aymonier undertook a first inventory of the temples around Angkor, listing 910 monuments in all.

In 1898, the Ecole Francaise d'Extreme Orient (EFEO), founded by the colonial masters to study various aspects of their Far-Eastern possessions, began to work in Cambodia, and soon efforts were made to start clearing the jungle from some of the ruins. The EFEO created a road network around the ruins, the Petit Circuit and the Grand Circuit, which are still used by many visitors. To this day, the EFEO has been the most consistent body involved in the study and restoration of Angkor.

The Cambodians were never consulted about any of France's activities around Angkor. The French writer Pierre Loti remarked in 1912 that France "was idiotically desperate to rule over Asia, which has existed since time immemorial, and to disrupt the course of things there." Loti felt that the French presence was disrupting the continuity of Cambodia, where the royal dancers appeared to step out of the past into the present, unchanged by time. The writer stated: "Times we thought were forever past are revived here before our eyes; nothing

has changed here, either in the spirit of the people or in the heart of their palaces." The French artist Auguste Rodin was so taken with the dancers that he followed them around France on their visit in 1906.

At the time, Angkor, which lay in Siem Reap Province, still belonged to Siam. It was only in 1907 that France forced Siam to hand over three provinces under Siamese control, including Siem Reap. From then on, France, the colonial masters of Indochine, were in control of the temples—until the beginning of World War II, when the area briefly returned to Siamese territory, because Siam had aligned herself with the Japanese, who had wrested control of the colonies from the French (although it was officers from the collaborating Vichy France government that continued to administer the rest of Cambodia).

Following World War II, France regained control of Cambodia and the Angkor temples until independence in 1953. This long-term continuity meant that the EFEO had a total monopoly on the research conducted on Angkor, which enabled the scientists involved to develop a coherent body of work over the years. In 1908, Conservation d'Angkor, the archaeological directorate of the Cambodian government, was established in Siem Reap and became responsible for the maintenance of the ruins. The office's first curator, Jean Commaille, originally a painter who'd arrived with the Foreign Legion, lived in a straw hut by the causeway to Angkor Wat, and wrote the very first guidebook to Angkor before being killed by bandits in 1916.

Commaille's successors further cleared the jungle, and, in 1925, Angkor was officially opened as a park, designed to attract tourists. Soon the first batches of foreign visitors arrived, by car or boat, from Phnom Penh or Bangkok and guided tours on elephant back were conducted around the temples. Many of these early tourists, rich globetrotters for the most part, stole priceless items from amongst the ruins or carved their names into the ancient stones. Little could be done about the thefts, but to search a few posh hotel rooms. Tourism continued to increase, and, in 1936, even Charlie Chaplin did a round of the temples.

In the meantime, research techniques used by the EFEO continued to evolve and became more integrated. Initially, different specialists had worked on different aspects of reconstruction and research; it was only in the late 1920s that several disciplines were combined—with spectacular results. Only now could the Bayon and Banteay Srei be dated properly and Angkor's chronology finally took shape. Influenced by the Archaeological Service of the Dutch East Indies, the EFEO, under curator Henri Marchal, began to undertake complete reconstructions of temples in the 1930s, most notably of Banteay Srei. Following World War II, as Cambodia moved towards independence, the EFEO moved its headquarters to France, and Conservation d'Angkor now ran the largest archaeological dig in the world, the French staff slowly being complemented by (French-educated) students from Phnom Penh. Excavations further afield could now be undertaken, at locations like Sambor Prei Kuk, the pre-Angkorian ruins near Kompong Thom.

In the 1960s, Angkor began to be used as a backdrop for movies, most notably *Lord Jim* and some of King Sihanouk's feature films. The ever-growing popularity of the temples meant that looting increased and many statues had to be removed and replaced with new plaster models.

Soon there were new challenges to the continuing restoration efforts—war was coming. Following Sihanouk's fall from power in 1970, the French staff of the EFEO carried on working on the temples for another two years, when they were forced to leave as the Khmer Rouge were closing in. Local workers continued with their efforts until 1975, when the revolutionary communists forced them into the fields to work or executed them. Angkor was once again abandoned. Through the long years of communist revolution and the subsequent civil war, the temples remained off limits, both to researchers and casual visitors, and the jungle grew back over the monuments. The Khmer Rouge was too superstitious to destroy the temples (though they destroyed virtually every modern temple in the country), but many research documents went up in flames. Luckily, much of the work the EFEO had done since its inception, some 70 years of solid, systematic research, had been copied and taken to Paris.

Following the invasion of Vietnam, work slowly resumed in the 1980s. First, the Archaeological Survey of India sent a team to restore Angkor Wat. The efforts of this enterprise have been widely criticized, but it should be kept in mind how very dangerous a country Cambodia was at the time and that the Indian scientists had little materials and few local experts to work with. At the same time, a Polish scientific delegation engaged in excavations around the Bayon. In 1989, the Royal University of Fine Arts was re-opened in Phnom Penh in order to train a new generation of archaeologists.

In 1991, after 20 years of neglect and devastation, not just of the ruins of Angkor, but of Cambodia as a whole, UNESCO (United Nations Educational, Scientific and Cultural Organization) established an office in Cambodia. Soon after, the World Monuments Fund was the first NGO to establish a branch at Angkor, followed shortly after by the return of EFEO. France and Japan soon pledged large funds for safeguarding the ruins, which by now were once more being looted at a frightening rate. Throughout the 1990s, new information garnered from technologies not available prior to 1972, including aerial photographs, and even space radar imagery obtained from NASA's space shuttle Endeavour, began to be systematically assimilated into the larger research body.

In 1992, Angkor Wat, along with 400 other monuments in the area, was included in the UNESCO World Heritage List. This officially made Angkor one of the world's most important cultural sites, a move designed to protect the remnants of the Khmer Empire from further looting or indiscriminate development.

Cambodia now has an article in its constitution that calls on the state to preserve the country's ancient monuments. UNESCO is the international coordinator for international contributions towards the up-keep of the temples. While restoration efforts have continued, and while UNESCO has been pushing for sustainable development, the Cambodian government created APSARA (Authority for the Protection and Management of Angkor and the Region of Siem Reap), a nongovernmental organization in charge of research, protection and conservation of cultural heritage, as well as urban and tourist development, in 1995.

THE FUTURE OF ANGKOR

In the Angkor Archaeological Park, it's the sheer numbers of visitors that now pose the gravest threat to the ruins. Wooden walkways, such as at Ta Prohm and Beng Melea, reduce some of the damage caused by large number of visitors, but with current visitor figures at two million a year, questions of sustainability continue to arise. For this reason, APSARA has been a mixed blessing. Placed under the double supervision of the Presidency of the Council of Ministers (technical supervision) and the Ministry of Economy and Finance (financial supervision), the organization's responsibilities are split into two distinct and sometimes contradictory areas—protection and exploitation. In 1999, the Cambodian government awarded a 10-year lease to manage the income generated by the temples to a private company called Sokimex. Attempts by UNESCO to stem the worst commercial exploits, such as elevator and footwear projects that followed, have had some success.

But Siem Reap's urban infrastructure has not been able to keep pace with tourist development, leading to a breakdown in water distribution and a lack of drainage. This is turn is affecting the temples, which are slowly subsiding, along with the falling water table. The Bayon is sinking into the sandy ground and cracks widen between its carefully assembled stones. In high season, some 6,000 visitors a day clamber across the temples, traffic jams within the park have become commonplace, and the once-romantic sunset spot at Phnom Bakheng is now crowded by a few thousand tourists every evening.

Recent debates about sustainability have centered on diversifying tourism in Cambodia. But even if some of the almost two million or so tourists could be persuaded to look at temples further afield, most first-time visitors to the country will most likely still want to see Angkor. The Cambodian government would like to increase visitor numbers to Angkor to 10 million people a year, five times the current volume.

Incidentally, a French-Australian-Cambodian research project called the Greater Angkor Project indicates that, at its height, Angkor Thom was surrounded by an urban sprawl the size of modern-day Los Angeles and therefore was probably the world's largest pre-industrial urban settlement. According to scientists from Sydney University, the Khmer capital lay in an urbanized wasteland, stripped bare of its forests, its rivers diverted, dependent on a sophisticated irrigation system that proved unsustainable. This, the scientists suggest, was the reason for the collapse of one of the world's great empires. And, according to the Greater Angkor Project, the same mistakes are being made again.

INFORMATION
Entry Tickets and Hours of Operation

All visitors to the Angkor Archaeological Park must have valid tickets. Visitors are checked at virtually all the temples. If you lose your ticket, there's no replacement and you will have to buy another one.

Tickets are available at the main entrance on the road from Siem Reap to Angkor Wat. One-day (US$20), three-day (US$40), and seven-day (US$60) tickets are available and must be used on consecutive days. One-day tickets are also available at a second entrance off the airport road. Three-day and seven-day tickets need to have a photograph of the ticket holder attached. If you are planning to purchase either of these, it's best to bring your own picture, as queues at the free photography service counter can be long on busy days. The ticket booths on the main road open at 5 A.M. and entry to the temples is possible from 5:30 A.M.–sunset. Banteay Srei closes at 5 P.M., while Kbal Spean closes at 3 P.M. Don't buy tickets anywhere else, as they are likely to be fakes. Note that if you purchase a ticket for the Angkor temples around 5 P.M., it is valid that same evening as well as the next one, three, or seven days. Some visitors use the afternoon prior to their passes becoming valid to visit Phnom Bakheng for the sunset views.

Several of the more remote temples are not covered by the tickets. Entrance to Phnom Kulen costs an uncalled-for US$20, while visitors to Beng Melea have to shell out a reasonable US$5. The even more remote Koh Ker costs US$10.

Security

The Angkor Archaeological Park has been de-mined and robberies are virtually unheard of, making the area around the temples one of the safest places in Southeast Asia.

GETTING THERE AND AROUND

There are numerous ways to explore the temples of Angkor. The distance between the temples is too far to walk, not least because it's hot almost year-round, so it's best to have wheels of one sort or another.

For years, sitting on the back of a motorbike and having a local *motodup* take visitors around was the most common way to get around the Angkor Archaeological Park, and this is still possible. Daily rates are around US$8 and a tip is expected.

Tuk-tuks are becoming ever more popular, comfortably sit two (four people if necessary), and cost around US$15 a day. Note that for temples farther away from Siem Reap, such as Banteay Srei, higher rates apply. A taxi will set visitors back around US$30 per day; a mini-bus around US$50, more to the outlying temples. For more remote temples such as Preah Vihear, consider renting a Jeep or other four-wheel-drive, for around US$80. To reach Beng Melea and Koh Ker, from Siem Reap, a normal taxi is sufficient. Your hotel or guesthouse will be able to arrange all of these options.

An altogether different possibility is renting an electric bicycle, an option introduced in 2006. For US$4 a day, electric bikes can be rented on a small side road on the right-hand side of the road to Angkor, a few hundred meters before reaching the ticket booths. The bikes do a maximum of 30 kilometers with one charge; there are 14 charge points around the temples, so there's little danger of running out of juice. No doubt, these electric bikes leave the smallest carbon footprint—barring cycling, of course—but they take money out of the local economy. For every tourist who chooses to get around on an electric bike, a young *motodup* driver in Siem Reap loses a day's wages, some of the few tourist dollars that really trickle down to ordinary people, so crucial in one of Cambodia's poorest provinces.

VISITING THE TEMPLES

Most tourists follow the most logical routes, created by French archaeologists a hundred years ago: the **Petit Circuit,** the 17-kilometer short route, which leads past all the main temples. Alternatively, the **Grand Circuit,** the 26-kilometer long route, offers countryside vistas, but does not include some of the temple highlights, such as Ta Prohm. The temples of the Roluos Group are not part of either route and can be visited in a separate half-day excursion.

As one day is enough to time to complete the Petit Circuit, you might think that this is sufficient time to marvel at the temples. Indeed, it could be argued that visitors who spend just a single day amongst the ruins will have far less of an impact than three-day visitors. But perhaps too brief a glance at the Angkor temples, seen in passing as a series of monuments stuck in the dry soil of a poor country, does not do justice to Khmer culture and your own sense of discovery. To be sure, the majority of tourists who visit Angkor nowadays arrive as part of a package tour. They move about in air-conditioned buses, isolated from their environment, and when inside the temples, they are firmly tied to their guides and camcorders. In this sense, Angkor—like the pyramids of Giza,

CYCLE ANGKOR

Since many visitors have had motorcycle accidents on the roads around the temples, the local authorities have banned tourists from driving their own vehicles in Siem Reap. Bicycles are the exception to the rule.

The temple-park is ideal for cyclists, though on some of the roads between the main temples, tour-buses, taxis, and tuk-tuks cause traffic jams in the mornings and late afternoons. Generally, though, bicycles are the perfect alternative to motorized transportation, and are much more in tune with the magnificence of the temples and forest. All the roads between the temples are paved and there are no notable hills. While many of the roads lie in the shade of the forest, it does get infernally hot in the summertime, so make sure you drink plenty of water (available from stalls near every major temple) and use sunscreen. Also be sure you lock your bike anywhere you plan to leave it.

The ideal route is the 17-kilometer Petit Circuit, which starts at Angkor Wat, leads past Phnom Bakheng into Angkor Thom and past the Bayon, and leaves Angkor Thom towards Takeo and Ta Prohm before returning to Angkor Wat.

If you like the idea of a bike, but aren't too keen on cycling, the Angkor Archaeological Park might have just the thing for you – an electric bike. For US$4 a day, electric bikes can be rented a few hundred meters before reaching the ticket booths on the road to Angkor.

the time of day, the light, and the numbers of visitors and local people present.

Exploring the temples with a guide can definitely enhance the experience and deepen your understanding of the magnificent civilization that once ruled over these buildings. The **Khmer Angkor Tour Guides Association (KATGA)** (tel. 063/964347, www.khmerangkortourguide.com) is the organization for official tour guides based in Siem Reap Angkor. The guides are trained by the Ministry of Tourism and the APSARA Authority. English- and French-speaking guides cost US$20–30 per day. Guides fluent in other languages, such as Spanish, German, or Japanese, are likely to cost more.

Your hotel or guesthouse will be able to arrange for an English-speaking guide for around US$30 a day. Note that tuk-tuk drivers and *motodups* are not allowed to guide tourists through the temples.

Numerous travel agents offer guided day tours for around US$60. This includes the US$20 entrance fee to the temples, as well as a guide, transport, and lunch. Sometimes a visit to the Angkor National Museum is also included. Three-day/two-night hotel and temple packages with pick-up from the airport, transport, accommodations, temple pass, and English-speaking guide cost around US$170–250, or more, depending on the cost of accommodations and the number of people in the group, and can also be booked through a local agent. If you book a tour as a group with a local travel agent, significant discounts are likely. Four-, five-, and six-day packages to the temples are also offered. Some tour operators make sure they benefit the local communities through their involvement with various aid projects.

Tour Operators

The following travel agents in Siem Reap offer standard tour packages for Angkor from one day to a week, as well as longer itineraries for locations further afield.

AboutAsia (tel. 092/121059, U.S. tel. 914/595-6949, www.asiatravel-cambodia.com)

the Coliseum in Rome, and the Acropolis in Athens—has become part of the global archaeological tourist trench, traversed in the same manner by millions every year. Individual travelers can be more flexible and can take their time, giving the temples space to breathe and to fit into the country as a whole. Rather than tick off temple after temple, it might be worth lingering here and there. The atmosphere of each ruin changes significantly depending on

runs tour packages around the temples and the country that involve the local community.

Angkor T.K. Travel & Tours (tel. 063/963320, www.angkortk.com) also runs tour packages around the temples as well as cycling tours.

The Villa Siem Reap (tel. 063/761036, www.thevillasiemreap.com) offers very competitive tours aimed at a young clientele; their popular five-night Siem Reap package for US$260 is a good value and good fun.

The World of Cambodia (tel. 063/963637, www.angkor-cambodia.org) has a wide selection of temple tours to suit all timetables and budgets, as well as hotel offers and tours further afield in Cambodia.

Souvenirs

In the unlikely event that you are offered anything that looks like antiques or genuine artifacts from the Angkor era, refuse to purchase these items; otherwise, you will become part of the international illegal trade of cultural artifacts. If you get caught at the airport with ancient carvings or even Buddha statues from the 19th century, you will certainly be arrested and charged.

Replicas of virtually every major structure or sculpture seen around the Angkor temples can be bought in Siem Reap and around some of the temples, made from virtually every material imaginable (including wood, bone, marble, and metal) and to suit all budgets. Groups of children sell drinks, wooden cowbells, T-shirts, and other small items in front of some of the ruins. They can be persistent, but bear in mind that the money they earn goes to the villages, rather than in the pockets of businessmen and the government. A number of musical instruments, including drums, and an ingenious mouth-harp made from bamboo and a fiddle, its sound body usually covered in snakeskin, are also offered in front of some of the temples.

APSARA, the nongovernmental organization in charge of the temples, has been making efforts to get rid of unregistered vendors and has even banned some older local monks

from entering Angkor Wat, arguing that they might scare tourists.

❿ ANGKOR WAT

Angkor Wat, a Hindu temple or mausoleum, is the largest religious building in the world, and one of the most beautifully impressive structures built by humankind. It's up there with the pyramids and the Taj Mahal. Thousands labored for three decades to create this magnificent dream in stone. But this 12th-century temple is much more than its sublime architecture can convey: It is the heart and soul of Cambodia.

Most Cambodians have never had an opportunity to visit Angkor Wat, yet the temple represents the country's heritage and culture for every Khmer. Angkor Wat has been on every national flag in one shape or another since 1863. Since the mid-1990s, it has also become one of the world's best-known and most visited tourist sites. Angkor Wat means "royal monastery city," which is probably a variation on the Sanskrit word *nagara,* which means "capital." The word *wat* is Thai for "temple," and the term was probably added when the building became Buddhist.

I still vividly remember my first glimpse of the temple. I was riding a motorcycle along the wide tree-lined road from the ticket booths towards the temples, with a real air of excitement and anticipation. Monkeys swung from the trees and a couple of elephants stood in the shade, waiting for tourist passengers. Upon approaching the moat, I turned left, and followed the road that ran parallel to the dark green water towards the causeway. Suddenly, to my right and across the moat, I glimpsed, just for an instant, the massive central towers rising out of dense foliage. I remember it like a pleasant shock. A disbelief at form and dimension kicked in; the jungle ambience around me induced a real personal sense of discovery.

It's the sheer size, more than anything else, that throws the first-time visitor: The moat is 1.5 kilometers by 1.3 kilometers long and 200 meters wide, and it carries water to this day. Simply walking around the complex takes a couple of hours. The vastness of Angkor Wat makes it difficult to guess its exact shape, even as one stands on the causeway in front of the entry towers (take a few steps to your left, off the terrace that marks the start of the cause-way, and you will be able to see all five towers). The causeway is 250 meters long and 12 meters wide. Without the benefit of elevation though, it's hard to fathom just how far—and in which directions—the building spreads out. The view from Phnom Bakheng gives visitors a pretty good idea as to its size. The rectangular shape of the temple spreads across 210 hectares.

Angkor Wat was built during and perhaps beyond the reign of Suryavarman II (1113–1150), and is thought to have served as a temple and a mausoleum. The latter is more likely, as Khmer temple gates usually face east. At Angkor, the main gate faces west.

Angkor Wat is a classic temple-mountain, a replica of the Hindu universe. The five towers represent the different peaks of Mount Meru, home to the Hindu pantheon, which sits in the center of the universe. The walls surrounding the sanctuary stand for the mountain ranges at the

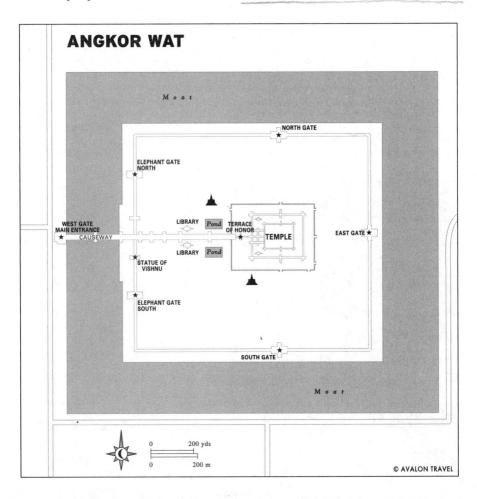

ANGKOR WAT

Moat

NORTH GATE

ELEPHANT GATE
NORTH

LIBRARY   Pond   TERRACE
OF HONOR

WEST GATE
MAIN ENTRANCE   TEMPLE   EAST GATE
CAUSEWAY

LIBRARY   Pond

STATUE OF
VISHNU

ELEPHANT GATE
SOUTH

SOUTH GATE

Moat

0   200 yds

0   200 m

© AVALON TRAVEL

edge of the world. The moat symbolizes the cosmic ocean. Angor Wat was dedicated to Shiva, and many of the temple's proportions and architectural elements correspond to aspects of Hindu cosmology. Like many other classic-era Khmer temples, Angkor Wat was built from sandstone blocks and laterite.

After crossing the causeway, visitors reach the outer enclosure running along the western side of the compound in the shape of a gallery, pierced by five entrances. Three towers, partially collapsed, sit on top of the enclosure. Underneath the central tower, a *gopura* (entrance hall) serves as an antechamber to the inner courtyard of the enclosure. Immediately to the right, inside the enclosure, rests a large statue of the Buddha, usually with a couple of old ladies in attendance lighting incense. As you step through the *gopura,* Angkor Wat rises straight ahead, at the end of another raised promenade, 350 meters long and 9 meters wide, that leads across open ground past two small libraries and a couple of lotus ponds. The magnitude of the building really becomes obvious as you approach

the sanctuary along this promenade. The pond on the right usually contains more water than the one on the left and is a great place to get atmospheric shots of Angkor in the late afternoon. Locals offer tourists the chance to sit on a horse and have their picture taken. Surprisingly, they get quite a few customers.

Angkor Wat is built on three levels, each one smaller and higher than the last, culminating in the 65-meter-high central tower.

The First Level

The **Terrace of Honor** connects the promenade to the first level, which is framed by galleries on all sides facing outwards. The galleries contain incredible bas-reliefs that cover almost all of the inner wall space. Ignoring those for the moment, and approaching from the promenade and walking straight on towards the central tower, visitors pass by two inner galleries, both in the shape of a cross.

To the left, the **Hall of Echoes** has great acoustics, if you manage to get a moment alone inside. To the right, the **Gallery of a**

apsara dancers carved on the wall of the outer enclosure around Angkor Wat

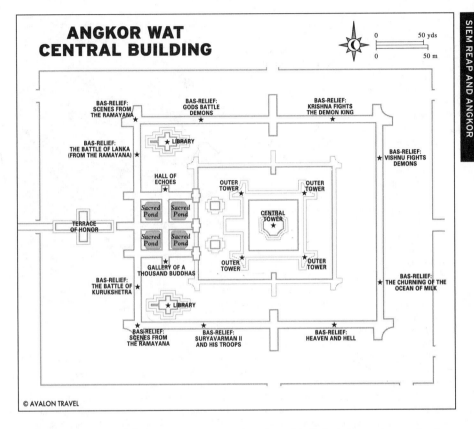

ANGKOR WAT CENTRAL BUILDING

0 50 yds
0 50 m

BAS-RELIEF: SCENES FROM THE RAMAYANA

BAS-RELIEF: GODS BATTLE DEMONS

BAS-RELIEF: KRISHNA FIGHTS THE DEMON KING

BAS-RELIEF: THE BATTLE OF LANKA (FROM THE RAMAYANA)

LIBRARY

BAS-RELIEF: VISHNU FIGHTS DEMONS

HALL OF ECHOES

OUTER TOWER

OUTER TOWER

Sacred Pond Sacred Pond

CENTRAL TOWER

TERRACE OF HONOR

Sacred Pond Sacred Pond

GALLERY OF A THOUSAND BUDDHAS

OUTER TOWER

OUTER TOWER

BAS-RELIEF: THE CHURNING OF THE OCEAN OF MILK

BAS-RELIEF: THE BATTLE OF KURUKSHETRA

LIBRARY

BAS-RELIEF: SCENES FROM THE RAMAYANA

BAS-RELIEF: SURYAVARMAN II AND HIS TROOPS

BAS-RELIEF: HEAVEN AND HELL

© AVALON TRAVEL

Thousand Buddhas did once contain many Buddha statues from the 14th century, a time when the Khmer Empire had permanently converted to Buddhism.

Beyond these two galleries, four courtyards with basins for ritual bathing feature windows with stone balusters made to look as if they'd been carved from wood, as well as a frieze of *apsaras*. The pillars around the pools feature Khmer and Sanskrit inscriptions.

THE BAS-RELIEFS

One of the highlights of visiting Angkor Wat, if not Cambodia, are the bas-reliefs that spread all around the galleries. Two meters high, this narrative in stone covers 1,200 square meters with kings and battles, gods and demons, heaven and hell, and the greatest stories from Hindu mythology.

Like a graphic novel for giants, drawn with incredible grace, an amazing eye for detail and atmosphere, the bas-reliefs are like a window into another world. The pillars that support the gallery roofs at regular intervals throw shadow patterns across the images that only enhance their energy. The bas-reliefs of Angkor Wat are truly a repository of sublime art, a testament to human creativity. Some of the bas-reliefs look like they have been polished. This could be due to them having been painted or because many people ran their hands over them.

Moving counter-clockwise from the Terrace of Honor:

The Battle of Kurukshetra: The southern

part of the western gallery depicts the battle of Kurukshetra, part of the *Mahabharata,* a Hindu epic, in which the clans of Kaurava and Pandava annihilate each other. The two armies march towards one another from opposite ends of the relief and clash in its center amongst elephants and chariots ridden by officers. Arrows fly in all directions and troops are engaged in bloody, close-quarters combat.

Scenes from the *Ramayana* (southwest): The pavilion on the southwestern corner contains a bas-relief depicting scenes from the *Ramayana,* another famous Hindu epic (the Khmer version is the *Reamker*), including Krishna lifting Mount Govardhana in order to defeat Indra. Some of the reliefs in this pavilion were damaged by leaks.

Suryavarman II and His Troops: The western part of the southern gallery features a historical scene, with Suryavarman II, the Khmer king who built Angkor Wat, sitting under royal parasols, inspecting his army and getting ready for battle.

Heaven and Hell: The eastern part of the southern gallery is nothing short of brutal. Yama, the god of hell, judges divides mankind into those who move upwards to heaven or downwards, through a trap door, into hell, where they are tortured, maimed, and killed over and over. The scenes of men with whips pushing endless chains of the condemned ahead of them seem like macabre visions of Cambodia's more recent past.

The Churning of the Ocean of Milk: On the southern side of the eastern gallery, the greatest of all the reliefs depicts one of the most important Hindu myths: the churning of the ocean of milk. Ninety-two *asuras* (demons) on the left and eighty-eight *devas* (gods) on the right grab the serpent Vasuki at opposite ends and pull back and forth for a thousand years, as they try to produce *amrita,* the nectar of immortality. The serpent coils around Mount Meru, which serves as the implement to churn the ocean. Gods and demons stretch across the entire panel. Above them, *apsaras* dance in the heavens. A four-armed Vishnu dances in the center of the panel. A demon king holds the

detail of the Suryavarman II and His Troops bas-relief on the western side of Angkor Wat's southern gallery

© AROON THAEWCHATTURAT

head of the serpent while the god of monkeys, Hanuman, holds its tail high over the *devas'* heads. Below the temple mount and the dancing Vishnu, Kurma, a reincarnation of Vishnu in the shape of a tortoise, provides a solid base in the churning ocean for Mount Meru to rest on. Mythical sea creatures swim around the bottom of the panel.

Vishnu Fights Demons: The northern part of the eastern gallery depicts Vishnu doing battle with innumerable demons. This relief is most likely of a later date, probably produced in the 16th century, somewhat less sublime than the main panels in this gallery, but still captivating.

Krishna Fights the Demon King: The eastern part of the northern gallery shows Krishna riding a *garuda*. Bana, the demon king, arrives from the opposite side. Krishna is stopped short by a burning city, Bana's home, but finally overcomes the demon with the help of the *garuda,* who manages to extinguish the flame.

Gods Battle Demons: On the western side of the northern gallery, a battle between gods and demons rages. The 21 Brahman gods all ride their traditional mounts—such as Brahma riding a goose and Vishnu mounted on a *garuda.*

Scenes from the *Ramayana* (northwest): In the northwestern pavilion, as in the southwestern pavilion, scenes from the *Ramayana* are played out, including a depiction of Vishnu with his wife Lakshmi by his feet, and numerous *apsaras* floating above his head.

The Battle of Lanka: The northern part of the western gallery displays a key scene from the *Ramayana,* the battle of Lanka, in which Rama fights with the demon king Ravana in order to claim his wife, who has been abducted to Lanka. In order to win the fierce battle, Rama calls upon the services of Hanuman, god of the monkeys, who attacks Ravana as the demon god rides a huge chariot and commands an army of brutal warriors. Once past this amazing tableau, the Terrace of Honor is just ahead.

The Second Level

Moving east from the galleries on the first level, steps lead to the second level. Its outside wall is undecorated, but on the inside, more than 1,500 *apsaras* vie for the attention of everyone passing. Alone or in small groups, each of the celestial dancers is slightly different from the next and it is hard to imagine a space more intent on celebrating the sensuousness of female beauty.

The Third Level

The third level was off-limits to all but the king and his high priest. It forms the base that the five towers, which represent the peaks of Mount Meru, stand on (with four of the towers on the corners and the fifth right in the center).

The views from the very top reveal the symmetrical nature of the temple complex and drive home what a wonder this building is. The third level is framed by an open gallery, which affords great views across the surrounding forest. Libraries, courtyards, and stairways surround the central tower, which rises 42 meters above the third level and 65 meters above the

ground. Originally, the small sanctuary underneath the tower housed a statue of Vishnu. Today, locals light incense in front of a contemporary Buddha statue here.

The stairs up the central tower, which ascend at an awe-inspiring 40 percent angle, can no longer be climbed, for fear of accidents. Plans to build a wooden stairway have yet to materialize.

◀ ANGKOR THOM

The crowning achievement of Jayavarman VII, the greatest of all the Khmer kings, was the construction of Angkor Thom, his "Great City," in the late 12th and early 13th centuries. Spread over an area of 10 square kilometers, this massive settlement is likely to have once supported a population of some one million people. It is surrounded by an eight-meter-high laterite wall, three kilometers long on each side, as well as 100-meter-wide moat.

Visitors enter via wide causeways that lead through five giant gates, crowned by *gopuras,* facing the cardinal directions (the eastern wall has two gates, the East Gate and the Gate of Victory, which connects the temple of Ta Prohm to the Terraces of the Leper King and Elephants), with four impassive faces of the *bodhisattva,* the enlightened one, staring at everyone arriving and departing.

The causeways are lined by two balustrades formed by 54 gods on the left and 54 demons to the right, with each group holding a *naga* snake, a reference to the Churning of the Ocean of Milk, the Hindu myth at the heart of Khmer culture. The roads running through the main gates all lead towards the Bayon, at the very center of Angkor Thom. The entire city is a representation of the Hindu universe, with the walls and moat symbolizing the mountain ranges and cosmic ocean surrounding Mount Meru.

The royal entourage, from the king down to the priests and generals, lived within the city walls, while the commoners lived in wooden houses, probably much like traditional Khmer houses today, beyond the outer enclosure.

In the heart of Angkor Thom, the Terrace of the Elephants and the Terrace of the Leper

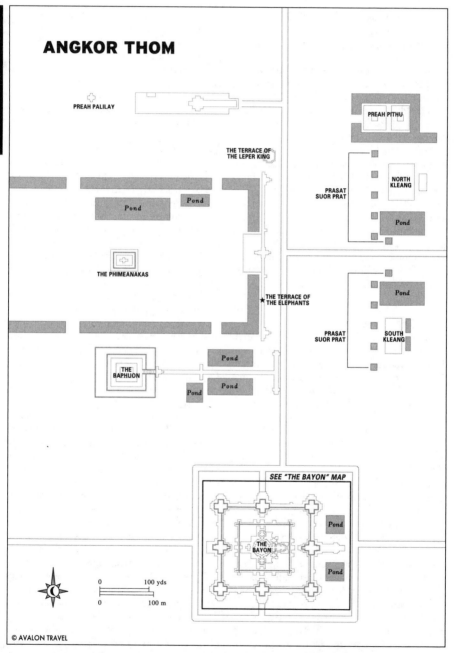

ANGKOR THOM

PREAH PALILAY

PREAH PITHU

THE TERRACE OF
THE LEPER KING

Pond

Pond

NORTH
KLEANG

PRASAT
SUOR PRAT

Pond

THE PHIMEANAKAS

★ THE TERRACE OF
THE ELEPHANTS

Pond

PRASAT
SUOR PRAT

SOUTH
KLEANG

Pond

THE
BAPHUON

Pond

Pond

Pond

SEE "THE BAYON" MAP

THE
BAYON

Pond

Pond

| 0 | 100 yds |
| 0 | 100 m |

© AVALON TRAVEL

© AROON THAEWCHATTURAT

The causeway to the south gate of Angkor Thom is lined with 54 heads of gods and demons.

King are most likely the foundations of a palace complex. The royal buildings were built from wood and no one is sure what they looked like. Nevertheless, the structures that are left give an impression as to the grandeur of Angkor Thom, the last great capital of the Khmer Empire.

The Bayon

More than 200 faces on 54 towers stare down at the world with what the French termed the *sourir Khmer* (the smile of the Khmer). Ambivalent, compassionate, and cruel at the same time, enigmatic for its mystery, the smile follows every visitor around the temple building, which is second in popularity only to Angkor Wat.

Some researchers believe the faces belong to the *bodhisattva* Avalokitshvara. Others think they represent the king himself: powerful, terrible, and compassionate, his eyes set on even the most remote parts of a vast kingdom at any given time. Perhaps both interpretations are true. What's sure is that visitors can feel the stares of the impassive faces wherever they are

inside the Bayon. Jayavarman VII was truly a Big Brother of antiquity.

The history of the Bayon is shrouded in as much mystery as the famous smiles on its towers. The temple was built on top of an older structure and was initially dated to the 9th century. It was discovered to be a Buddhist structure only in 1925, and the fact that the Bayon is at the exact center of the great city also eluded visitors for a long time. After the death of Jayavarman VII, who followed Mahayana Buddhism, the temple served as a Hindu and later Theravada Buddhist institution.

The Bayon is built on three levels. Incredible bas-reliefs cover some of the walls of the first and second levels, while the third level is dominated by the 54 towers and the central sanctuary. On the first level, an outer gallery is marked by eight *gopuras,* four of them at each corner and another four constructed at the middle point of each gallery. Inside the gallery of the first level, a couple of libraries can be found in the eastern courtyards.

The second level is bordered by another gallery, marked by four towers on the corners

THE BAYON

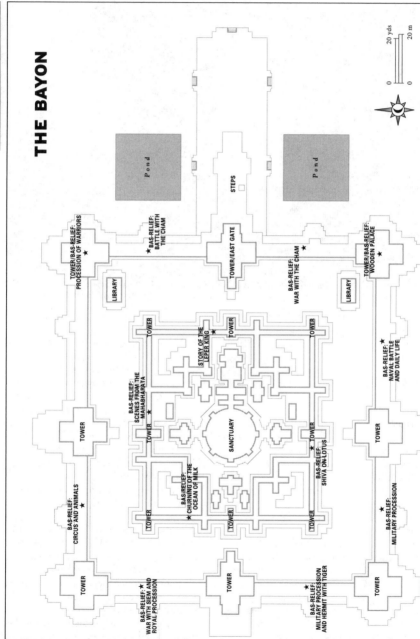

© AVALON TRAVEL

TOWER/BAS-RELIEF: PROCESSION OF WARRIORS ★

LIBRARY

BAS-RELIEF: BATTLE WITH THE CHAM ★

TOWER/EAST GATE

BAS-RELIEF: WAR WITH THE CHAM ★

LIBRARY

TOWER/BAS-RELIEF: WOODEN PALACE ★

TOWER

TOWER

TOWER

Pond

Pond

STEPS

BAS-RELIEF: SCENES FROM THE MAHABHARATA ★

STORY OF THE LEPER KING

TOWER

TOWER

TOWER

BAS-RELIEF: NAVAL BATTLE AND DAILY LIFE ★

SANCTUARY

TOWER

TOWER

TOWER

BAS-RELIEF: CHURNING OF THE OCEAN OF MILK ★

BAS-RELIEF: SHIVA ON LOTUS ★

BAS-RELIEF: CIRCUS AND ANIMALS ★

TOWER

TOWER

TOWER

TOWER

BAS-RELIEF: MILITARY PROCESSION

BAS-RELIEF: WAR WITH SIEM AND ROYAL PROCESSION ★

BAS-RELIEF: MILITARY PROCESSION AND HERMIT WITH TIGER ★

0   20 yds
0   20 m

one of the more than 200 carved faces that dominate the Bayon, the state temple in the center of Angkor Thom

© AROON THAEWCHATTURAT

and four *gopuras,* again at the middle point of each gallery. Quite a bit of the second level has collapsed and as you scramble across boulders and take small detours, it's easy to lose your orientation. Restoration work may also make access to some areas of the second level a little difficult.

The third level is circular in shape, unusual in Khmer temple architecture, and contains the faces of the *bodhisattva* Avalokitshvara arranged around the temple's central sanctuary.

THE BAS-RELIEFS

The incredible bas-reliefs of the Bayon cover an area of some 1.2 kilometers. The Bayon's main entrance faces east and the main bas-reliefs are briefly described starting from here, moving clockwise, with the reliefs on the right.

First Level

The reliefs on the first level were accessible to ordinary people and offer visitors a rare glimpse of what daily life for Cambodians must have been like during the Angkor era. Perhaps they served educational purposes: to inform the people of the merits of Buddhism. Some reliefs were never finished.

War with the Cham: The southern part of the eastern gallery is divided into three tiers and shows the Cambodian army on its way home, victorious after fighting the Cham. On the lowest tier, the army, moving on elephants and ox-carts, and accompanied by musicians, returns to Angkor. On the far right, Chinese traders can be seen. In the middle tier, fallen soldiers are returned home, and on the top tier, Jayavarman VII, protected by a parasol, heads a procession along with his commanders, on the back of an elephant.

Wooden Palace: The southeast corner pavilion contains unfinished reliefs of a wooden palace and a boat.

Naval Battle and Daily Life: The eastern part of the southern gallery is dedicated to the naval battle between the Khmer and the Cham that took place on the Tonlé Sap Lake in 1177. On the right, most easterly panel, hunters, men playing chess, women searching for head lice, and musicians are depicted on a lower tier. On the left panel, the battle is fierce and some soldiers are eaten by crocodiles after they have fallen into the water. On a lower tier, a woman gives birth, food is prepared, and another game of chess is in progress.

Military Procession: The western part of the southern gallery was never completed, though it does show a military procession, complete with crossbow-wielding soldiers mounted on elephants, as well as a sophisticated catapult on wheels.

Military Procession and Hermit with Tiger: The southern part of the western gallery is unfinished and shows a military procession passing through mountainous countryside, as well as a hermit climbing a tree to escape an attacking tiger. Farther on, a stand-off between two crowds is about to spill over into violence.

War with Siem and Royal Procession: The northern part of the western gallery contains scenes of close-up fighting between the Khmer

detail of the Naval Battle and Daily Life bas-relief on the Bayon's first level

and the Siamese, as well as a procession of the king on his way to meditate in the forest.

Circus and Animals: The northern gallery features a circus in its far-right corner, including jugglers and acrobats, while the royal court looks on. A procession of animals includes the now-extinct rhinoceros, as well as a pig, rabbit, deer, fish, and lobster. There's also a scene of meditating holy men in the forest and a group of women by a river receiving gifts.

Procession of Warriors: The northeast corner pavilion features yet another processions of warriors and their pachyderm rides.

Khmer Battle with the Cham: In the northern section of the eastern gallery, the Khmer appear to be gaining on the Cham in battle and even the elephants rip into each other.

Second Level

The bas-reliefs on the second inner level were accessible only to the king and his priests and feature scenes from Hindu mythology, as well as a few depictions of battle and everyday scenes. Given that Jayavarman VII introduced Mahayan Buddhism to the Khmer Empire,

this seems somewhat incongruous. But many things about the Bayon are not fully understood yet. The reliefs on the second level appear to either pre-date the rest of the temple by several hundred years—and were from the time of Yasovarman I, a Hindu king who ruled at the end of the 9th century—or they post-date Jayavarman VII's reign and were placed in the Bayon by Jayavarman VIII, a Hindu king, during the late 13th century. The panels of the inner galleries, separated by doors and towers, are smaller, not in as good condition, and are more fragmented than those on the outside.

Starting from the eastern entrance again, some of the highlights include several depictions of **Shiva** in the southern gallery; the **Churning of the Ocean of Milk** in the northern part of the western gallery; Shiva in several **scenes from the *Mahabharata*** on the eastern side of the north gallery; and the **story of the leper king,** which depicts a king being bitten while fighting a snake, then being observed and treated by a holy man and surrounded by women who examine his hands—just to the right of the main entrance in the eastern gallery.

The Baphuon

The Baphuon, a classic temple-mountain representing Mount Meru, was built in the 11th century, and therefore precedes Angkor Thom. Originally a Hindu temple, dedicated to Shiva, the Baphuon adjoins the royal palace enclosure. Its base measures 120 meters by 100 meters, and it's about 35 meters tall, minus its tower, which has collapsed. On its western side's second level, a reclining Buddha, nine meters tall and 70 meters long, was constructed in the 15th century.

In the 1960s, the EFEO began the huge reconstruction process, using the method of anastylosis, a technique that calls for the total dismantling and subsequent rebuilding of a structure. Unfortunately, by the time the Khmer Rouge made work on the temple impossible in 1972, this immense undertaking was unfinished and the plans were lost in the chaos that ensued. What was left was a sea of stones lying around in a loosely organized fashion.

The challenge of rebuilding the temple was taken up in 1995 and was still ongoing in 2009, though some parts of the temple, which contain interesting bas-reliefs, have become accessible once more.

The Phimeanakas

The Phimeanakas is a 10th-century temple-mountain close to the royal palace area of Angkor Thom. The central tower has collapsed and the three original levels have long been looted of its architectural subtleties. The royal enclosure too is largely in ruins. The royal palace would have been built from wood and there's no consensus on what it might have looked like.

The Terrace of the Elephants

This 350-meter-long terrace was once covered in wooden pavilions. From here, Jayavarman VII could inspect his troops as they marched into Angkor Thom from the Victory Gate. The terrace takes its name from the carved elephants on its eastern side and faces a central square where the troops would have marched in procession.

Carvings of lions and *garudas* can be found on the middle section of the terrace's retaining wall.

The Terrace of the Leper King

The jury is still out as to whether the 15th-century statue found on top of this platform to the north of the Terrace of the Elephants is a Khmer king with leprosy, or Yama, the Hindu god of death. The outer walls of the terrace are covered in reliefs of mythical beings and *apsaras*. The structure might have served as the royal crematorium. Most interestingly, there is a hidden inner wall on the terrace's south side. Visitors can walk along a narrow corridor crammed with several tiers of carved scenes in pristine condition, including *apsaras, nagas,* elephants, and a river with fish.

Other Structures

Many other ruins are dotted around the enormous enclosure of Angkor Thom. **Preah Palilay** is a small atmospheric Buddhist temple located to the north of the royal enclosure, erected during the reign of Jayavarman VII, with a chimney-like tower. Facing the Terrace of the Elephants across the central square, two so-called *kleangs* (the somewhat misleading Khmer word for storeroom) may have once served as royal guesthouses. The *kleangs* are older than Angkor Thom and were probably built in the 10th century. They are fronted by **Prasat Suor Prat**, a series of 12 laterite towers. Also built by Jayavarman VII, the towers once housed sacred statues or linga.

To the north of the *kleangs,* **Preah Pithu** is a group of five small temples, most of them Buddhist. Not too many visitors bother to come here and the atmosphere is very peaceful and relaxed.

THE TEMPLES OF ANGKOR
Phnom Wat Bakheng

Wat Bakheng was the very first temple-mountain constructed in the Angkor area. Dating back to the late 9th century, this Hindu temple marked the move from the smaller capitals around Roluos and sat at the

ANGKOR FROM THE AIR

Fancy a totally different view of the temples? Try Angkor from above. In all, there are three different possibilities to see Angkor from the air, each with their own merits.

The most straightforward way is to search for the **yellow balloon** (tel. 012/520810) that is tethered near Angkor Wat, on the road to the airport, and jump on board. The balloon (US$11 per person) rises to a height of 200 meters and the views of Angkor Wat, Phnom Bakheng, and the surrounding countryside are impressive.

Far more exclusive and expensive, but even more breathtaking, is a ride in a helicopter. Two outfits currently offer scenic flights starting at US$50 a head. **Sokha Helicopters** (tel. 016/731468, www. sokhahelicopters) is stationed right next to the big yellow balloon, while **Helicopters Cambodia** (tel. 012/814500, www. helicoterscambodia.com), a New Zealand outfit with an excellent safety track record, is based at the airport.

Finally, for those with high-altitude vertigo, a ride on an **elephant** may suffice. You still get better views than on foot, but there's no need to rise to extreme heights. During the day, elephants can be hired around the Bayon. In the afternoon, they tend to move to Phnom Bakheng in order to take visitors to this hilltop temple for the sunset. A 30-minute ride costs US$10-15.

heart of the royal capital of Yasodharapura. The temple's base is carved from the mountain itself and the climb up the front stairway is steep. Nevertheless, Wat Bakheng is the most popular sunset spot in the Angkor Archaeological Park and attracts thousands of visitors every night because it has fine views of Tonlé Sap Lake and Angkor Wat peeking out of the surrounding forest.

Elephant rides to the top are available (US$15). Rumors of an escalator to be constructed have persisted for years. Let's hope it will never happen.

Baksei Chamkrong

Located north of Phnom Bakheng, Baksei Chamkrong is a small but attractive pyramid-shaped temple built in the mid-10th century, just after the Khmer capital returned from Koh Ker to the Angkor area. The structure was originally dedicated to Shiva. Built from bricks and laterite, it has some sandstone decorations and is 12 meters tall.

Baksei Chamkrong means "the bird that shelters under its wings," a reference to a story about a Khmer king trying to flee Angkor as his city was besieged by a foreign army. A giant bird suddenly swooped from the sky and took the king under its wings, protecting him from the onslaught.

Thomanon

A contemporary of Angkor Wat, the small but graciously designed Thomanon was built in the early 12th century under the reign of Suryavarman II, and similarities are especially apparent in the design of the towers. Extensive restoration work in the 1960s did wonders for this Hindu temple, located on the left side of the road, just outside the Victory Gate on the way to Ta Keo.

Chaosay Tevoda

Just across the road from the Thomanon, this small temple has a similar floor plan and looks like it was built in conjunction. In fact, Chaosay Tevoda was built some years later. It features additional *gopuras* and a library, and is slowly being restored.

Ta Keo

A few hundred meters east of the Victory Gate, Ta Keo is a towering, unadorned temple pyramid that rises above the canopy of the surrounding forest. Built in the early 11th century during the reign of Jayavarman V from massive sandstone blocks, Ta Keo, facing east and dedicated to Shiva, was never completed, for reasons unknown. The total lack of decorations,

© AROON THAEWCHATTURAT

Ta Keo, an unadorned temple pyramid that was never completed

reliefs or otherwise, gives this temple a unique singularly powerful appearance—it seems built like a fortress. Nevertheless, the steep climb to the top, via any of the four stairways at the cardinal points, is worth the effort. The views across the trees are great and the ambience between the five towers up top is somehow quietly dignified, perhaps because not very many people come up here.

(Ta Prohm

More than any other major monument in the Angkor Archaeological Park, Ta Prohm is a trip back in time. When the French began to push the jungle back from the ruins at the beginning of the 20th century, the EFEO decided, for aesthetic reasons, that one temple should be left in its forest context, just the way French explorers had stumbled upon the ruins some 50 years prior to that. And that's the reason why some scenes of the movie *Tomb Raider* were shot inside the temple.

Of course, much work has been done on this huge sprawling temple complex and the jungle around the site has long been well managed—though several large silk cotton-wood and strangler fig trees have enormous roots sprouting across boulders and galleries, giving the site its unique Lost World feel.

Ta Prohm is a very handsome temple, built in the late 12th and early 13th centuries by the greatest of the Khmer kings, Jayavarman VII, to serve as a Mahayana Buddhism monastery and university. The rectangular temple complex is not a temple-mountain like Angkor Wat and is therefore not built in ascending levels. The temple sanctuary is surrounded by five walls and a series of long and low buildings. The outermost laterite wall is 1,000 by 700 meters long and the entire complex is 650,000 square meters in size.

In the 13th century, it was home to more than 12,000 people, including 18 high priests, 2,700 officials, and more than 600 dancers—with another 80,000 people living in 3,000 villages outside its walls to provide services. But the temple's possessions extended well beyond serfdom: Ta Prohm's vaults were said to hold more than 500 kilograms of golden dishes, 35 diamonds, 40,000 pearls, and 500 silk beds.

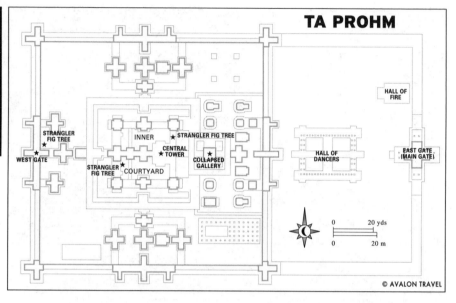

The monastic study center was a powerful concern indeed. Four *gopuras,* with heads similar to those on top the towers at the Bayon, provided access through the outermost wall into the complex, though today only the east and west entrance are open. Access is generally from the west, so most visitors get in via the back door. Have your driver drop you off at the eastern *gopura* and enter the temple the way it was designed to be entered.

Much of the ground between the fifth and fourth wall is overgrown by brush and large trees, but in its time, it must have been a small city, with wooden homes for the many staff. Two moats, on both sides of the fourth wall, have long dried up.

There are few bas-reliefs on the walls of Ta Prohm. Scholars speculate that these might have been destroyed, following Jayavarman VII's death and Angkor's reconversion to Hinduism, though there are some carvings of Buddhist iconography. Some of the *apsaras* had their heads cut off by looters many years ago. Several independent buildings stand freely within the complex. In the outermost enclosure, a **Hall of Fire,** a rest house or the home of a sacred flame,

stands alone to the east of the sanctuary. In the eastern part of the fourth enclosure, a **Hall of Dancers,** a structure Jayavarman VII had built in several of his temple complexes, features carvings of dancing *apsaras.* The central sanctuary is entirely unadorned. Its walls may have once been covered in silver.

But it's not so much the temple itself, though vast and gracious, as the interplay between stone and forest, that impresses visitors so much. And as many walls, corridors, and galleries have collapsed because of the jungle's intrusion, the temple's layout does not become apparent, because of the circuitous route visitors take. Several stretches of ground within the three central enclosures are so strewn with boulders that wooden walkways have been erected to make progress easier, and visitors are strongly discouraged to climb across collapsed walls. As Ta Prohm is afforded more shade by the forest than the other major monuments, the temple is not a bad place to visit when the sun is high up.

The scholar Claude Jacques remarked that Ta Prohm, more than any other Khmer temple, tempted writers into descriptive excess. Enough said.

© AROON THAEWCHATTURAT

the partially overgrown temple of Ta Prohm

Banteay Kdei

Just to the southeast of Ta Prohm, Banteay Kdei, built during the reign of Jayavarman VII, is yet another temple complex that served as a monastery. Due to inferior building materials, large parts of this temple have collapsed and much of the Buddhist imagery was vandalized in the 13th century, following the death of Jayavarman VII and the brief return of Angkor to Hinduism.

Banteay Kdei lies opposite Sra Srang, a reservoir that holds water year-round. In the dry season, a small island temple can be seen poking through the water's surface.

Prasat Kravan

This 10th-century Hindu temple was reconstructed by the French in the 19th century and sports its five original towers. Located to the south of Ta Prohm on the road back to Angkor Wat, Prasat Kravan was built from brick. Its interiors feature the only brick bas-reliefs in the Angkor area—notably depictions of Vishnu riding a *garuda* in the central tower,

and Lakshmi holding the trident of Shiva and the discus of Vishnu in the northernmost tower. Few visitors stop here and while it's not the most atmospheric location, the reliefs are worth checking out.

Pre Rup

Situated to the south of the Eastern Baray, Pre Rup, along with the Eastern Mebon, was one of the first temples built by King Rajendravarman II, after the capital moved back to Angkor from Koh Ker in the late 10th century. Pre Rup, Rajendravarman II's state temple, is a classic temple-mountain with five towers on a raised platform, dedicated to Shiva.

Built from red brick, laterite, and sandstone, the temple sits amidst two enclosure walls. Within the walls, the temple rests on a main platform built on three levels. Right in front of the temple within the outer wall and facing east, six towers flank the entrance. One tower, on the immediate right as you enter the complex, might never have been built or has been demolished. The second enclosure is entered

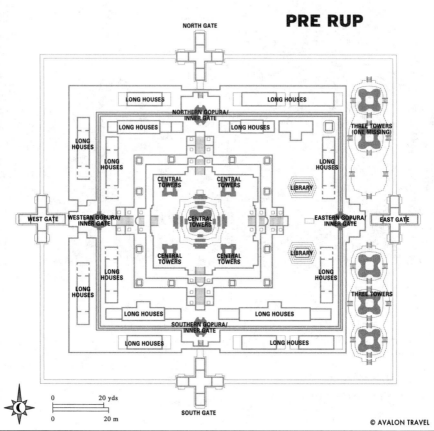

via four small *gopuras* at the cardinal points and contains several long houses, perhaps resting places for pilgrims. Two libraries with large towers are located just inside the courtyard entered through the eastern *gopura*.

The central platform of Pre Rup, split into three levels, is accessed via four stairways leading up from the *gopuras*. Next to the stairways, stone lions stand guard. The first two levels are built from laterite, while the third, top-most level is constructed from sandstone. On the first level, numerous small shrines containing linga, stand facing east. The five central towers on the third level, one in each corner and one

in the center of the top platform, contain some interesting bas-reliefs, notably Vishnu and his avatar, as well as flying *apsaras*.

Eastern Mebon

The construction of the Eastern Mebon precedes that of Pre Rup by a decade and the similarity in building style is obvious. The Eastern Mebon was the very first temple constructed by Rajendravarman II after the Khmer capital moved back from Koh Ker to Angkor, and was dedicated to his parents. It follows the same design as Pre Rup: It's a temple-mountain dedicated to Shiva, surrounded

PRESERVATION, BUSINESS, AND THE THEFT OF ANCIENT ARTIFACTS AT ANGKOR

When the Siamese sacked Angkor in 1431, they took whatever they could chisel off the walls with them. Ever since, the temples of the Angkor Empire have been looted – and Cambodia's cultural heritage continues to be plundered to this day.

After the Siamese, the Burmese looted Angkor in the 16th century and took more statues with them. In the 1870s, some years after Cambodia had become a French protectorate and Henri Mouhot had rediscovered the ruins, another Frenchman, Louis Delaporte, on an exploratory mission to the temples, took a wealth of statues and lintels back to France, where they can be seen at the Musée Guimet in Paris to this day. While this was sanctioned by the French government, the plan by the French writer André Malraux, who later became Minister of Culture in France, to steal several important pieces from Banteay Srei backfired when he was arrested for the trafficking of antiquities and thrown in jail. Malraux's connections soon got him out of this predicament though. In 1925, the area around the temples was declared a national park and looting subsided for a few years – until the chaos of World War II brought new opportunities for thieves; priceless objects disappeared in large numbers until Cambodia's independence in 1953. As the country slid into the Vietnam conflict in the late 1960s, a trickle of artifacts continued to move across its borders; following the Vietnamese liberation in 1979, the Khmer Rouge, who had retreated to the Cambodian Thai border, not far from the temples, engaged in the smuggling of statues.

But the worst was yet to come. As UNTAC moved into Cambodia in the early 1990s and the country's borders opened once more, the temples became accessible to an unprecedented wave of professional looters, some of them Cambodian police or military, who stole specific items for wealthy overseas collectors, destroying many significant structures that had weathered 800 years since being abandoned. The audacious removal of an entire temple wall from Banteay Chhmar near Sisophon in 1998 is one of the best-known examples of these widespread activities. Cambodian military spent four weeks carving the desired stones out of the temple with circular saws – luckily, in this case, the priceless carvings were intercepted at the Thai border and returned to Cambodia. Several American and European museums have also returned statues, and the United States and other countries have banned the import of Cambodian antiquities.

Looting also takes place on a smaller, less professional scale. Villagers or road builders sometimes come across temple structures and burial sites. In 2001, I passed through the village of Phum Snay, near Poipet. Within days of the discovery of a number pre-Angkorian graves, the local people had dug up their entire village, under the guidance of a foreigner who photographed and bagged each item found. The smuggler disappeared with the best pieces, and for weeks afterwards, locals stood by the roadside selling beads, precious stones, and pottery, until the site was entirely depleted.

As long as poverty is widespread in Cambodia, no amount of public campaigning or education will stop people from digging up and selling their national heritage for a few dollars.

by two walls, constructed on three levels, and crowned by five towers. The temple is built from a combination of brick, laterite, and sandstone, much like other early Angkorian structures. Impressive two-meter-high stone elephants guard the corners of the first and second levels. The towers were once covered in stucco. Today it's the red brick originally underneath, best photographed in the late afternoon, that's visible. Several lintels are covered in impressive carvings with themes from the Hindu pantheon.

It was built on an artificial island in the middle of the Eastern Baray, which is now dry. The Eastern Mebon stands just 1,200 meters to the north of Pre Rup on a direct north–south axis, and 6,800 meters to the east of the royal temple-mountain of Phimeanakas, on a direct east–west axis.

Neak Pean

Part of the Grand Circuit, Neak Pean is small, a bit out of the way, and otherworldly beautiful. Located to the east of Preah Khan on a direct east–west axis, this modest island temple was designed as an oasis of peace and reflection—part of a hospital constructed during the reign of Jayavarman VII, and hence dedicated to Buddha.

Neak Pean stands in the center of the Jayatataka Baray, which measured 3.5 kilometers by 900 meters and could only be reached by boat in its day. Today the reservoir is dry. In fact, Neak Pean stands on an island within a pond. The pond is surrounded by four more, smaller ponds. Four pavilions stand between the central pond and these smaller ponds, once used by pilgrims to absolve themselves of their sins. In each pavilion, a waterspout in the shape of a head conveyed water from the main pool into the smaller pools. There's an elephant head in the northern pavilion, a human head in the eastern one, a lion's head in the southern one, and a horse's head in the western one. These smaller ponds represent the elements of water, earth, wind, and fire, and it is thought that people with illnesses came to bathe here to reattain their natural balance with nature. Neak Pean was a Khmer spa. The entire complex sits in a walled enclosure, which in turn is located on an island in the *baray*. Access is from the north via a pier the French built.

Neak Pean, which means "entwined serpents," got its name from the two *naga* snakes that coil around the central island, which is round. The heads of the two snakes are separated, facing each other, and form an entrance to the sanctuary. The sculpture of a horse appears to be swimming away from the temple on its eastern side. The horse is a manifestation of the *bodhisattva* Avalokitshvara and was rebuilt from fragments by the EFEO during the temple's restoration in the 1920s.

Sometimes a group of blind musicians sits

under the bushes by the side of the pond and plays, lending this little location even more atmosphere. Neak Pean is best visited just after the rainy season in October or November, when some of the ponds may contain some water.

Ta Som

Also worth a visit is the northeastern-most temple on the Grand Circuit, the small and peaceful Ta Som. Built like a miniature version of Ta Prohm, and dedicated to the father of Jayavarman VII, this late-12th century Buddhist shrine has several *gopuras* with four smiling faces on top. The eastern *gopura* is being split and crushed simultaneously by a ficus tree and makes for a great photo. Surrounded by three laterite walls, the temple is built on a single level and contains some fine carvings.

Preah Khan

Located on the Grand Circuit and left, much like Ta Prohm, largely unrestored, Preah Khan is a huge sprawling temple complex of rectangular enclosures around a typically small Buddhist sanctuary. Also like Ta Prohm, the temple was built during the reign of Jayavarman VII in the late 12th and early 13th centuries, and served as a center of learning and meditation. It also had an equally impressive retinue. More than 100,000 people were connected to Preah Khan, a royal city in its hey-day, supporting more than 1,000 teachers as well as 1,000 dancers.

Preah Khan means "sacred sword," a reference to a sacred sword that Jayavarman II, the first Angkorian king, handed to his successor—and which was subsequently handed down from generation to generation. The words "Preah Khan" are Siamese. though, so the story of the sword could have originated there.

Consecrated in 1191, Preah Khan stands on two older palace complexes. The process of anastylosis, the dismantling and rebuilding of a structure, has been utilized here. In the 1930s, the jungle (except for the large trees) was removed, making the site much more accessible. Nevertheless, the trees around the site remain impressive, and with fewer visitors than Ta Prohm, Preah Khan is a good place to witness the interplay between stone and nature in peace.

Preah Khan was a temple of the Mahayana Buddhist sect, and many of its carvings were disfigured and destroyed following the death of Jayavarman VII and Angkor's brief return to Hinduism. Within its enclosure, Preah Khan contains many smaller independent Hindu shrines and temples. The temple complex was built right to the shore of the Jayataka Baray, to the east. It's best to enter from this side.

Preah Khan has four enclosure walls, the longest of which runs 700 by 800 meters. The complex was once surrounded by a moat and spreads across an area of some 140 hectares. This outer wall, constructed of laterite, contains sandstone sculptures of *garudas,* formerly topped by Buddhist images, long destroyed, at 50-meter intervals all the way around the complex. Four gates, at the cardinal points, offer access. Each entrance features a causeway crossing the moat, lined by gods and demons carrying *naga* snakes, similar to the causeways at the gates of Angkor Thom.

Visitors first come upon the Hall of Dancers. The lintels above the eight doorways all feature exquisite carvings of dancing *apsaras.* Just to the north of this building, a structure of unknown purpose has baffled scientists for decades: a two-story building with no discernable stairway and round columns, similar to Greek designs and unique to Angkor. The inner enclosures around the sanctuary can appear labyrinthine, due to the many galleries, low corridors, and walls with false windows. The walls used to be covered with huge bronze plates. The inner sanctuary today is a stone stupa, which was added many years after the temple's inception.

The Western Baray and Western Mebon

The Western Baray, located a few kilometers north of Siem Reap International Airport, is an incredible 8 kilometers by 2.3 kilometers wide, and continues to carry water year-round. On weekends, it's a favorite picnic spot. Snacks and drinks are sold at stalls along the dam on the southern side of the reservoir. In the center of the *baray,* the Western Mebon, a small temple in ruinous condition built in the 11th century during the reign of Udayadityavarman, can be visited by boat and features remarkable carvings of animals. The Western Baray is off the usual temple circuits, but it's worth a visit for its local life and the lack of crowds.

The Roluos Group

The Roluos Group of temples, named for its proximity to the modern village of Roluos, was part of the city of Hariharalaya, the first great Khmer capital. Located some 13 kilometers southeast of Siem Reap and founded by Jayavarman II in the early 9th century, Hariharalaya was the template for the later building frenzies of the Khmer kings. It was the first royal city established in the Angkor area and remained the capital of the Khmer for 70 years. Its last ruler, Yasovarman I, was the first king to build a temple at Angkor, at Phnom Bakheng, where he moved the capital in 905. The temples of this era were built of brick, and feature high and square towers on low bases. Structures such as *gopura* and libraries were first introduced during this time.

The detour to the Roluos temples is well worth the effort and entrance fees are covered by the pass to the Angkor Archaeological Park. There are three major temples at Roluos: Preah Ko, Bakong, and Lolei, all of them dedicated to Hindu deities.

Preah Ko was one of the very first temples built at Hariharalaya, and hence one of the first temples built in the Angkor area. Its outer walls have almost gone, so the temple complex seems quite small today, but it's well worth a visit, not least for its exquisite carvings. Preah Ko means "temple of the bull," named after stone *nandis* (sacred bulls), remnants of which stand on the eastern side of the temple. Originally, the building was surrounded by a moat and traversed by causeways. Beyond the *nandis,* a brick

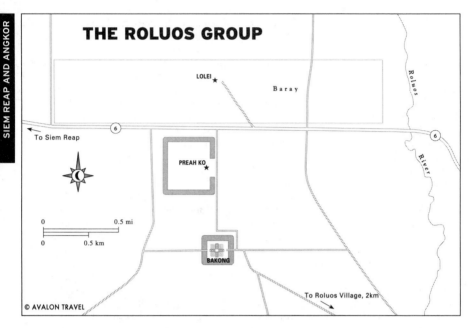

wall, pierced by two *gopuras* to the east and west, contains the sanctuary: a low platform with six brick towers. Unlike other temples, Preah Ko does not seem to be too concerned with symmetry. The six towers are not evenly spaced and those to the east are larger than the ones to the west. Preah Ko was dedicated to the king's ancestors and each tower contained a Hindu deity. The carved decorations on the towers' false doors, columns, and lintels are worth checking out. The three towers to the east feature male guardians and are thought to have been dedicated to paternal ancestors, while the towers to the west have female goddesses flanking the doorways and were most likely dedicated to maternal ancestors.

The **Bakong** was built after the death of Jayavarman II, and it became state temple of the Khmer Empire during the reign of Indravarman I. It stood at the heart of the city of Hariharalaya. The Bakong was the first temple-mountain built by a Khmer king and, dedicated to Shiva, its sanctuary probably contained a lingam. The site is surrounded by a rectangular wall 900 meters by 700 meters long, which in turn was surrounded by a moat. Causeways lead through the outer wall, lined with *naga* balustrades. An inner wall can be passed through four *gopuras* located at the cardinal points. The temple faces east, so it's best to enter from that side. As at Preah Khan, there's a processional space, lined with stone serpents to pass before reaching the inner compound. Numerous well-preserved buildings stand to the left and right: libraries, *dharam-shalas* (rest houses), and what are assumed to be crematoriums. Set around the platform that the sanctuary stands on are eight brick towers, open to the east only, their stairways guarded by stone lions. The towers have false doors in the other directions, featuring fine carvings. The platform the sanctuary sits on is built in five levels. On the first three levels, stone elephants—they get smaller as one ascends—stand on the corners. The fourth level is dominated by 12 sandstone towers, each of which contains a lingam. The sanctuary itself, a square tower with a lotus spire, was built later than the rest of the temple, probably in the 12th century.

The temple of **Lolei,** built a little later than the other two monuments at Roluos, was erected during the reign of Yasovarman I and was dedicated to Shiva. Originally Lolei stood on an island in the middle of a huge *baray,* which helped to irrigate the area around Hariharalaya and was the first reservoir built by a Khmer king. Lolei features just four brick towers, all of them in poor and overgrown condition, but some incredible carvings and inscriptions remain. An active modern pagoda operates within the temple compound.

Banteay Samre

Banteay Samre is a little bit out of the way and is best visited while on the way to or from Banteay Srei. It's worth the effort though, as the road to the temple leads through local villages and open countryside. The mid-12th century Hindu temple, built during the reign of Suryavarman II, is located on the eastern side of the Eastern Baray and resembles Angkor Wat in style, though not in dimensions. The temple's name refers to a group or tribe of people, possibly an indigenous minority related to the Khmer, who used to live around Phnom Kulen and is mentioned in an interesting folk story.

Banteay Samre has been reconstructed utilizing the anastylosis technique (the complete disassembling and rebuilding of a structure), and by all accounts was just a pile of rubble prior to the restoration works. The Banteay Samre complex is square in shape and features a moat, now dry, within its outermost enclosure wall, which in turn is pierced by four *gopuras* at the cardinal points. The wall around the inner temple complex is raised above floor level and features pavilions on its four corners. It's best to enter through the eastern *gopura* into the inner part of the temple. This route leads to a platform and a long hall that in turn leads to the central sanctuary. Two libraries can be seen to the north and south of the hall. Banteay Samre sees relatively few visitors. Curiously, the upper reliefs of the sanctuary feature Buddhist scenes.

THE STORY OF BANTEAY SAMRE

Once upon a time, a farmer named Pou, a member of the Samre community, an indigenous minority living near the Kulen mountain, got hold of seeds with supernatural powers. He planted the seeds and soon harvested the most delicious sweet cucumbers anyone had ever tasted. As a sign of respect, he took his harvest before the king, who found them so tasty that he ordered Pou to kill anyone who might enter his field. During the rainy season, the royal household ran out of cucumbers and the king himself decided to visit Pou for more. But the king arrived at Pou's field after dark and the farmer, thinking the monarch an intruder, killed him with a spear. Pou buried the king in the center of his field. As the king had no descendents, his advisors sought the wisdom of a Victory Elephant, as to who should be the successor. The elephant promptly marched to Pou's field and identified the farmer as the rightful ruler. Pou had himself crowned but the court dignitaries refused to show him respect; after all, he was just a Samre. Frustrated, Pou left the capital and moved to Banteay Samre. He called all the court's dignitaries, and all those who showed respect to the royal regalia of his predecessor were decapitated. Overcome by Pou's compassion, the remaining dignitaries accepted his authority and the kingdom has been ruled in harmony ever after.

☪ Banteay Srei

Banteay Srei, the "Citadel of Women," lies 38 kilometers (around 30–40 minutes in a tuk-tuk) from Siem Reap and is a little off the usual temple circuit. But this late-10th century temple complex, though modest in size, is one of the highlights of the Angkor Archaeological Park and should not be missed. It features some of the finest carvings in the world and has been extremely well restored.

Small by the usual bombastic dimensions of

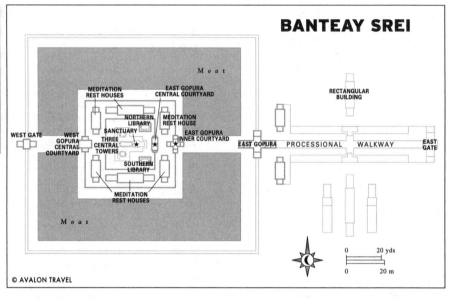

Khmer monuments, Banteay Srei was built during the reign of Rajendravarman. It's the only temple known to have been built not under the authority of a king, but by Yajnyavaraha, a Brahmin advisor to the king, who dedicated the complex to Shiva. Originally the site was called Tribhuvanamahesvara, or Isvarapura. Banteay Srei was once enclosed by three walls and a moat, though only two walls remain today. Entrance is best through a *gopura* on the temple's east side. Before reaching the central temple compound, visitors pass along a processional walkway flanked by galleries, walls, and more *gopuras*. To the north of the walkway, a single building features a brilliant carving of Vishnu as man-lion. Step into the inner compound through another *gopura* and you are facing the central part with the best carvings. All around the compound, six annex buildings may have served as meditation rest houses. Inside the temple compound, virtually every bit of wall space is covered in exquisite carvings. The soft, red sandstone can be carved almost like wood and therefore allows for incredible detail and texture. The central shrines, three in all, were dedicated to Shiva

and Vishnu and are guarded by mythical figures with human bodies and animal heads. These are replicas: The originals have been stolen or removed for safekeeping. The walls are covered with carved foliage, as well as geometric patterns. The central towers are covered with male and female divinities. The females wear such heavy earrings that their ear lobes are elongated. The lintels above the doorways to the central sanctuary are embellished with scenes from the *Ramayana,* including the abduction of Sita.

Two libraries to the east of the central sanctuary, made of brick, laterite, and sandstone, also feature outstanding carvings. The eastern side of the northern library (on the right as you approach from the east) is decorated by depictions of Indra, god of the sky, as he scatters celestial rain across the building's eastern side, while a *naga* snake rises from the deluge. The western side depicts Krishna killing his cruel uncle, King Kamsa, as shocked women look on.

The southern library's western side is covered in carvings telling the story of Parvati trying to attract Shiva, who is in deep meditation.

Parvati gets Kama, god of love, to shoot an arrow into Shiva's heart. Shiva promptly gets angry and burns Kama to ashes. He does notice Parvati, however, marries her, and brings Kama back to life. If only things were as simple in real life…

On the eastern side of the southern library, a scene from the *Ramayana* unfolds. Ravana, king of the demons of Lanka, tries to gain access to Mount Kailash, home of Shiva and Parvati. As he is barred from entering, he lifts the entire mountain and shakes it. Shiva in turn brings down the mountain on top of Ravana, who acknowledges Shiva's might and sings his name in praise for a thousand years.

Banteay Srei was further expanded in the 11th century and was probably in use until the 14th century. Yet the temple complex was not "discovered" by the French until 1914 and became famous only when celebrated French writer André Malraux tried to steal four *devatas* (goddesses) in 1923. During the 1930s, Banteay Srei was the first Angkor monument to benefit from the process of anastylosis, and it was only in 1936 that the true age of the temple was established. Sadly, the temple has been looted several times since Malraux's early efforts to deplete Cambodia's heritage and even concrete replicas of sculptures that have been moved to Angkor Conservation have been attacked.

Banteay Srei is best seen in the early morning or late afternoon, when the red sandstone really comes to life. Because of its modest size, the site tends to be overcrowded, but by late afternoon (the temple closes at 5 P.M.), the big groups have left.

Kbal Spean

Some 12 kilometers beyond Banteay Srei, the riverbed of Kbal Spean makes for an interesting detour during and after the rainy season. This "River of a Thousand Lingas" lies at the foot of Phnom Kulen and features impressive carvings of lingas and several figures in its rocky riverbed. To get to the river section with the carvings, it's a 40-minute walk. Note that this site closes at 3 P.M., so it's probably

PHALLIC OR NOT? – THE CULT OF THE LINGA

The linga, or lingam, according to Merriam-Webster's dictionary is "a stylized phallic symbol that is worshipped in Hinduism as a sign of generative power that represents the god Shiva." In fact, there is no agreement amongst scholars, mystics, and academics what the linga actually represents. It's thought that perhaps the linga was initially understood simply as a cylindrical shape which represented the formlessness of creation, and later became associated with Shiva. Later still, the linga came to be seen as the divine phallus of Shiva and was worshipped as a representation of the creator and destroyer of the universe.

Usually the linga rests on a square pedestal, called *uma*, or yoni, which is widely believed to represent the vagina. Some scholars and mystics such as Swami Vivekananda and Christopher Isherwood disagree with this latter interpretation.

Everyone agrees, though, that the linga has been worshipped for a very long time. It precedes Hinduism and has its origins either in early Buddhism or animism. It goes back at least to the Indus Valley civilization. In Cambodia, linga are found everywhere around Angkor and pre-Angkorian temple sites, perhaps first introduced by Jayavarman II. Linga are usually in temple sanctuaries, where worshippers have been pouring water over them for centuries. As a result, the water is said to become sacred. One of the most spectacular linga sites around Angkor is Kbal Spean, where hundreds of linga have been carved into the rocky riverbed. The water rushes across the carved stones and then feeds the rice fields below, perhaps symbolizing fertility. It's best to visit in the rainy season, or just after, when the river carries enough water to give the site some ambience.

best visited in the morning or around noon (as you'll be walking through forest, it shouldn't be too hot). The area around the carvings can be quite polluted by plastic, left by picnickers. Even here, some carvings have been hacked out of the river by looters in recent years. There's also a waterfall, with some carvings on top. Do not stroll off the well-trodden paths into the forest as the area may still be mined.

VICINITY OF ANGKOR
◖ Beng Melea

No doubt one of the most stunning temples in Cambodia, Beng Melea is still somewhat off the beaten track, but this atmospheric jungle ruin is bound to see a lot more visitors in the near future as roads improve. Built in the early 11th century during the reign of Suryavarman II, this temple compound is about one square kilometer in size, roughly precedes the design of Angkor Wat (though there are no bas-reliefs here), and stands on an ancient Khmer crossroad between Angkor, Koh Ker, and Preah Vihear.

More than any temple in the Angkor Archaeological Park, Beng Melea is an experience. Overgrown by jungle and collapsed on itself, the compound is a huge jumble of broken towers, underground galleries, and unidentifiable piles of rubble, massive walls, and corridors, adorned with false doors and windows and split open by roots that have been pushing apart the brickwork for centuries. Temples don't come any more Lost World than this.

Have a local guide show you incredible corners and pathways where the first rays of the sun break in long thin strips of bright light through the tall trees that grow out of the temple walls and play over the smiling faces of *apsaras,* the temple's celestial dancers. To make access a little easier, a wooden walkway was constructed during the shooting of the French movie *Two Brothers* by Jean-Jacques Annaud in 2002, a tale of two tiger cubs in colonial Cambodia.

The main temple itself is surrounded by a moat and several outbuildings, possibly libraries and *dharamshalas* (royal guesthouses), and is reached via a broad causeway lined with *naga* snakes. Until recently, Beng Melea was heavily

the central courtyard of Beng Melea at sunrise

© TOM VATER

BEYOND THE TOURIST TRAIL: CAMBODIA'S BEST REMOTE TEMPLE SITES

While the temples around Siem Reap now see literally millions of visitors, it requires only a little extra effort to escape the crowds and check out some more remote locations where you might find yourself almost alone amongst splendid Khmer ruins. And if you're interested in a trip deep into the Cambodian jungles, more gigantic temple complexes await you. Don't stray off the beaten tracks, though, as some remote temples could still be mined.

Here is a list of the country's best remote temple sites, in order of preference:

- **Beng Melea** – Spectacular 12th-century jungle temple, 70 kilometers northeast of Siem Reap, far enough away to avoid the crowds. Large parts of this huge compound have collapsed, and high walls, underground passages, and huge creeper trees make for an eerie atmosphere.

- **Koh Ker** – Almost an archaeological park in its own right, the 10th-century Koh Ker complex, a former Khmer capital 70 kilometers northeast of Siem Reap, contains almost a hundred monuments, including the impressive Prasat Thom, a seven-tiered pyramid in a jungle clearing. The area is still being de-mined, and despite good road connections, relatively few visitors make it out here.

- **Banteay Chhmar** – An overgrown, remote, 12th-century temple site featuring towers with the faces carrying the *sourir Khmer*, the famous Khmer smile. Despite heavy looting in recent times, this temple site, 61 kilometers north of Sisophon, is worth visiting for its ruined grandeur and sheer remoteness.

- **Preah Vihear** – Breathtaking views reward arduous travelers who brave dust and potholes to reach this cliff-top border temple, in recent times the center of political and military tensions between Cambodia and Thailand.

- **Preah Khan** – Truly a lost site in Preah Vihear Province, the roads to this remote temple complex north of Kompong Thom are so bad that the site is only accessible by motorbike – or, if you have the funds, by helicopter from Siem Reap. A road will no doubt be built soon, but for the moment, Preah Khan remains the most remote temple complex in Cambodia.

- **Wat Athvea** – A small Angkor-era temple in good condition, located just six kilometers south of Siem Reap on the road to the Tonlé Sap Lake, is flanked by an active pagoda and a friendly village. It's not truly remote, but it's rarely visited.

mined. On my first visit in 2001, warning signs still surrounded the entire compound and de-mining continued into 2007. Stick to the well-trodden paths.

In front of the temple, several small restaurants, which serve cheap Cambodian standards and cold drinks, are lined up by the roadside. Entrance to the temple is US$5 and tickets must be purchased from the guards on the causeway approaching the main (thoroughly collapsed) gate. The ticket for the Angkor Archaeological Park is not valid to visit this temple.

Beng Melea lies some 70 kilometers to the northeast of Siem Reap and can easily be reached on a one-day round-trip in a car or on a motorbike. Follow Route 6 from Siem Reap towards Phnom Penh and turn left at the small town of Dam Dek. From here it's another 35 kilometers. Alternatively, head for Banteay Srei and then Phnom Kulen and follow the base of the mountain for 25 kilometers until you reach a crossing where you turn left onto a mostly tarmac road, which takes you to the temple after another 10 kilometers. Note that this road is private; bikes have to pay US$1 while taxis are charged US$2.50, each way. Unfortunately, there are no accommodations around the temple yet. A taxi from Siem Reap should cost around US$60, and a *motodup* at least US$25.

Phnom Krom

For great views over the Tonlé Sap Lake, head for Phnom Krom mountain, some 10 kilometers to the south of Siem Reap on the shores of the lake. On top of the hill, an active pagoda is popular with locals and there are also a number of towers from the 11th century. Since 2006, Phnom Krom has been considered part of the Angkor Archaeological Park and can only be visited with a valid ticket. Though there's no ticket booth here, guards sometimes demand to see a pass, and as this minor ruin is far removed from other temples, very few people make it up here nowadays.

A tuk-tuk to Phnom Krom and back will cost you around US$5.

Chong Khneas Floating Village

Chong Khneas, populated largely by Vietnamese, is the floating village on the Tonlé Sap Lake closest to Siem Reap, and has seen a great deal of tourist traffic in recent years. As with other floating villages, expect to see schools, clinics, gas stations, and family homes, as well as souvenir shops. You will also see lots of boats filled with tour groups here. An interesting stopover in the village is the **Gecko Environment Center** (http://jinja.apsara.org/gecko/gecko.htm), which informs visitors about the unique biodiversity of the area. If you have time and want to see more of traditional life on the Tonlé Sap, skip Chong Khneas and visit Kompong Luong near Pursat or the floating community near Kompong Chhnang.

There are several possibilities to get out to see this waterborne community. The cheapest way might be to go directly to the boat dock and get on one of the many tour boats waiting. Two-hour trips should be about US$10, though you'll share the ride with a big group. More laid-back and intimate experiences are offered by **H2O** (tel. 012/809010), which operates a smart little aluminum boat that seats just eight passengers and offers cruises with drinks. Alternatively, the most stylish way to get on the water is with the **Tara River Boat** (tel. 092/957765, www.taraboat.com), a larger wooden vessel that offers a number of different trips on the lake. A half-day outing (four hours) is US$20 a person, and includes transportation from and to your hotel, a light meal, and drinks. Tours run at 7 A.M., 9 A.M., and 11 A.M. This trip also runs by a crocodile farm. A sunset trip, with dinner and unlimited drinks, costs US$30 and departs at 3:30 P.M.

To get there by yourself, take the road from Siem Reap to Phnom Krom, towards the lake. As you approach the lake, you'll reach the departure point for the ferries to Phnom Penh and Battambang. A tuk-tuk should be US$6 for the round-trip. Many tuk-tuk drivers get commission from agents offering boat tours. If you refuse to go with the outfit suggested by your driver, you may cause offense.

Prek Toal Bird Sanctuary

The biosphere and bird sanctuary Prek Toal is almost as over-run by commerce as Chong Khneas. It takes about two hours to get there in a boat, and you should expect to slide through tall grasses and brackish water. If you come in the dry season, you might be able to spot storks, ibis, pelicans, and eagles.

If you organize everything yourself, a boat to the Prek Toal Research Station will cost around US$50, where visitors have to pay an entrance fee of US$5—as well as another US$25 for a guided boat tour of the sanctuary itself. Many guesthouses and tour operators arrange packages at similar or just slightly higher prices. Try Peace of Angkor Tours (www.peaceofangkor. com). **Tara River Boat** (tel. 092/957765, www. taraboat.com) offers a day trip with transfers, all fees, drinks, and an English-speaking guide for US$60 per person.

Serious bird-watchers might want to check the website of the **Sam Veasna Center** (tel. 063/761597, www.samveasna.org), which specializes in bird-watching expeditions to remote sights.

To reach Prek Toal, use the same route as to Chong Khneas.

Kompong Phluk

This group of three traditional Khmer villages rises out of the Tonlé Sap floodplain on high stilts. About 3,000 people live here during the wet season among mangrove forests. In the dry season, when the lake's waters recede and leave the houses like stranded storks on their six-meter-high poles, many inhabitants move into smaller huts on stilts farther into the lake. The people of Kompong Phluk live off fishing and shrimp harvesting.

There are two ways to get to Kompong Phluk. In the rainy season, take a boat from Chong Khneas (US$50 for two passengers for a half-day excursion). In the dry season, when water levels are low, it's possible to drive all the way to the community, some 16 kilometers south of Siem Reap. Alternatively, depending on water levels, you might be able to get a boat from the village near the Roluos Group of temples.

Kompong Kleang

With more than 10,000 inhabitants, Kompong Kleang is the largest community on the lake. Most of the community, about 35 kilometers north of Siem Reap, is built on wooden poles anchored in the lakebed. The people here are Khmer and live off fishing. So far, visitor numbers are far fewer than at Chong Khneas, but more and more tour operators are putting this unique community on their itineraries. Around the village, flooded forest provides important spawning grounds for the Tonlé Sap's fish population. In the wet season, the houses are a couple of meters above the waterline, but once the waters have receded, the stilts can reach 10 meters above the muddy soil—quite a sight.

To get to Kompong Kleang, depending on the season and prevailing water levels, you might be able to head for Chong Khneas and catch a boat from there, or head east on Route 6 to Domdek Village, from where it's a short boat ride (US$10) in the wet season, or a longer bike ride all the way to Kompong Kleang in the dry season.

Phnom Kulen

Phnom Kulen is a mountain and something of a private national park. Inside the park, a waterfall is quite impressive in the rainy season. A River of a Thousand Lingas, on the other hand, is best seen in the dry season, when stone carvings (similar to those at Kbal Spean, a site that is included in the Angkor Pass) in the riverbed are clearly visible. Cambodians consider Phnom Kulen the cradle of the Khmer Empire—it was here that Jayavarman II declared a unified nation under a single ruler in A.D. 802. Hence the spot gets very crowded with picnickers on weekends and there can be quite a lot of garbage lying around.

What's more, entry to the site is US$20. (Entry to national parks in Cambodia is usually US$5, but Phnom Kulen is under the authority of a Cambodian businessman with good political connections.) The fee is as much as a day around Angkor Wat, even before your transportation costs are factored in; considering that there are no remarkable ruins to see here, for many it's not worth it—unless you're a waterfall fanatic.

It's possible to hire a *motodup* for the hundred-kilometer round-trip for around US$15, or a taxi for around US$30. From the ticket booth of the park entrance, it's 10 kilometers to the waterfall. If you are prepared to walk from here, the entrance fee is reduced to US$10.

PHNOM PENH

Just 10 years ago, Phnom Penh, located in the south-central region of Cambodia, at the confluence of the Tonlé Sap, Mekong, and Bassac Rivers, was one of the most dangerous and dilapidated capitals in the world. Gun crime was common, people slept on broken pavements, and hardly a road was surfaced. But recent relative political stability has had a miraculous effect: For the time being at least, Phnom Penh is once more becoming the "Pearl of Asia," a charming backwater capital on the banks of the Tonlé Sap River.

With the war truly over, some of the French colonial architecture intact, fascinating and sometimes grim traces of Cambodia's recent past lingering amongst accelerating renewed urban development, and more than 200 bars and restaurants catering to tourists, Phnom Penh is one of the most enigmatic of Southeast Asia's capitals—there's a great deal to be discovered. What's more, with a population of only two million and few high-rises, plenty of old world charm, and a real 20th-century urban feel, the city has so far resisted the kind of futuristic development seen in Bangkok and Kuala Lumpur.

Today, old men still slowly pedal their cyclos along the long Sisowath Quay, looking for a fare, just as they did in the 1960s. Around them, thousands of motorbikes swirl in mad abandon. Young lovers cavort on the manicured lawns around the riverfront and in the shadow of the Independence Monument, while the newly rich show off their imported cars on Sisowath Quay. Fishermen ride their long-tails on the choppy waters of the Tonlé

HIGHLIGHTS

((**The Silver Pagoda:** Located inside the Royal Palace complex, the Silver Pagoda contains priceless historical objects that survived the Khmer Rouge reign (page 100).

((**The National Museum:** Set in a luscious garden, this impressive 1920s building houses the country's largest collection of antiquities and hosts traveling exhibitions (page 101).

((**S-21 Tuol Sleng Museum:** No visit to Cambodia would be complete without taking a look at the country's recent tragic past. The Tuol Sleng Museum, a former Khmer Rouge interrogation center, is a memorial to the genocide that swept the kingdom between 1975 and 1979 (page 105).

((**Bophana:** At Cambodia's Audiovisual Resource Center, visitors can watch hundreds of hours of digitized film footage from Cambodia, from 100-year-old French reels to the movies of King Sihanouk (page 108).

((**Central Market:** Actually called New Market (Phsar Thmey in Khmer), this imposing art deco building, constructed in 1935, is one of the city's best-known landmarks and most visited and lively markets, offering anything from food produce to pirated clothes and books (page 113).

((**Choeung Ek Killing Fields:** Some 15 kilometers from Phnom Penh, Choeung Ek was the final destination for most of the prisoners held at S-21 and is just one of thousands such sites in Cambodia, a grim reminder of the reign of terror of the Khmer Rouge (page 131).

((**Oudong:** Several stupas cover three low hills to the west of Phnom Penh, all that's left of a former royal city that served as Cambodia's capital from the 17th century until 1866. The views from the top are spectacular (page 132).

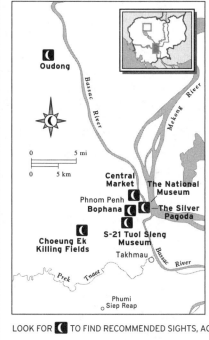

LOOK FOR ((TO FIND RECOMMENDED SIGHTS, ACTIVITIES, DINING, AND LODGING.

Sap River, making catches right in front of the Royal Palace, while half-naked kids use a makeshift platform to jump into the brown waters. There's even a resident elephant on the riverfront.

Modern-day Phnom Penh's population is 90 percent Khmer and 90 percent Buddhist. The largest minorities are the Vietnamese and the Chinese, but there's also a sizable community of Westerners living here. Cambodia's capital is a dynamic blend between old and new, the traditionally cultured and brash modernity. In years to come, traffic and encroachment of modern high-rise buildings are likely to replace some of the city's charm—enjoy it while it lasts.

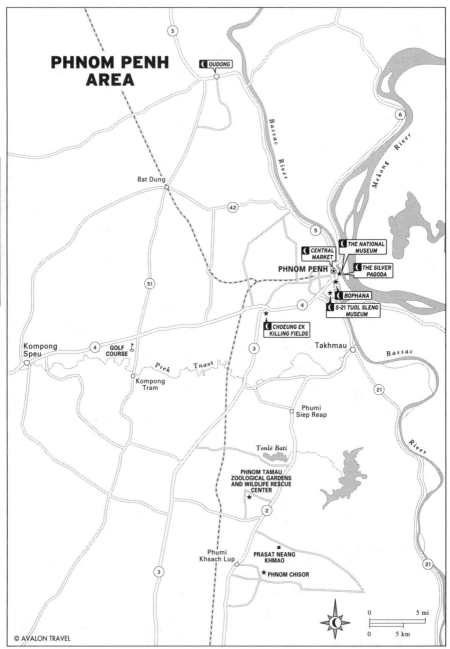

HISTORY

After Angkor was attacked by the Siamese in 1422, the Cambodian king Ponhea Yat moved the capital to Phnom Penh. Today, some historians argue that the Khmer king's main reason to shift his capital was not just Siamese aggression, but a regional economic shift from agriculture to trade. In a changing world, Angkor, far from the Mekong, was no longer a location central and accessible enough to sustain a nation. Phnom Penh, on the other hand, made an ideal trade location from where it was possible to could control river traffic from Laos, the flow of fish products and pottery from the Tonlé Sap basin, and the Chinese goods coming up from the Mekong Delta to the south.

Initially though, Phnom Penh remained capital for only a few decades and by 1494, the city had moved to Basan, later Lovek, and finally Oudong. By the 17th century, both the Vietnamese to the east and the Siamese to the West had begun to reassert themselves, and, caught between two stronger neighbors, Phnom Penh was sacked by the Siamese in 1772.

Due to shifting political alliances, Phnom Penh did not become the permanent capital until the French arrived in 1862 during the reign of King Norodom I. The new colonial masters occupied a city of some 25,000 people, introduced town planning, and quickly constructed canals and a port.

By the 1920s, Phnom Penh was known as the "Pearl of Asia," and the city continued to grow for the next 40 years. While the French left many important landmarks, the city really came into its own in the 1960s under the reign of King Sihanouk, until the Vietnam War spilled over into the kingdom in the early 1970s and Phnom Penh became a refugee center for millions of Cambodians.

When the victorious communists, the Khmer Rouge, eventually entered Phnom Penh on April 17, 1975, they immediately drove the city's entire population into the countryside. The Cambodian capital became a virtual ghost town, serving only as administrative center. People began to drift back into Phnom Penh after the Vietnamese invasion and liberation in

© TOM VATER

view of Phnom Penh, from the roof of the Sorya Mall

PHNOM PENH

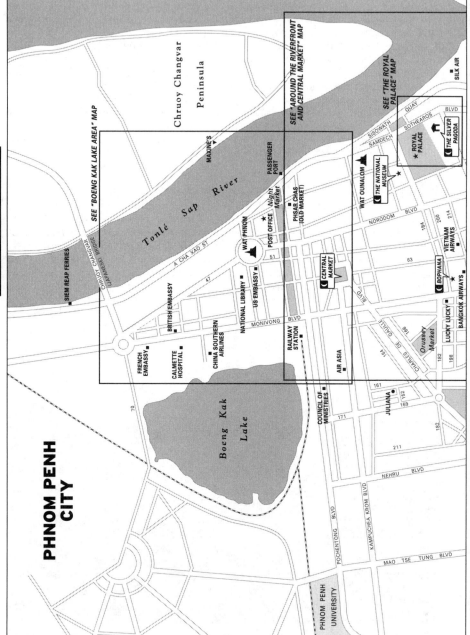

PHNOM PENH CITY

Chruoy Changvar Peninsula

Tonlé Sap River

SEE "BOENG KAK LAKE AREA" MAP

SEE "AROUND THE RIVERFRONT AND CENTRAL MARKET" MAP

SEE "THE ROYAL PALACE" MAP

SILK AIR ■

QUAY
SISOWATH
SAMDECH
SOTHEAROS BLVD

★ ROYAL PALACE
◀ THE SILVER PAGODA

Wat Ounalom ▲
◀ THE NATIONAL MUSEUM ★

MAXINE'S ▼

PASSENGER PORT ■

NORODOM BLVD

18A
200
214

VIETNAM AIRWAYS ■

Night Market
POST OFFICE ■
PHSAR CHAS (OLD MARKET)

WAT PHNOM ▲

A CHA XAO ST

51

63

◀ BOPHANA ★

BANGKOK AIRWAYS ■

CHRUOY CHANGVAR (JAPANESE BRIDGE)

SIEM REAP FERRIES ■

BRITISH EMBASSY ■

47

NATIONAL LIBRARY ■

US EMBASSY ■

◀ CENTRAL MARKET ▼

BLVD

LUCKY LUCKY ■

198

Orussey Market

CHARLES DE GAULLE

184

182

FRENCH EMBASSY ■

CALMETTE HOSPITAL ■

CHINA SOUTHERN AIRLINES ■

MONIVONG BLVD

RAILWAY STATION ■

AIR ASIA ■

COUNCIL OF MINISTRIES ■

161
152
169

JULIANA ■

171

211

192

70

Boeng Kak Lake

NEHRU BLVD

POCHENTONG BLVD

KAMPUCHEA KROM BLVD

MAO TSE TUNG BLVD

PHNOM PENH UNIVERSITY

PHNOM PENH

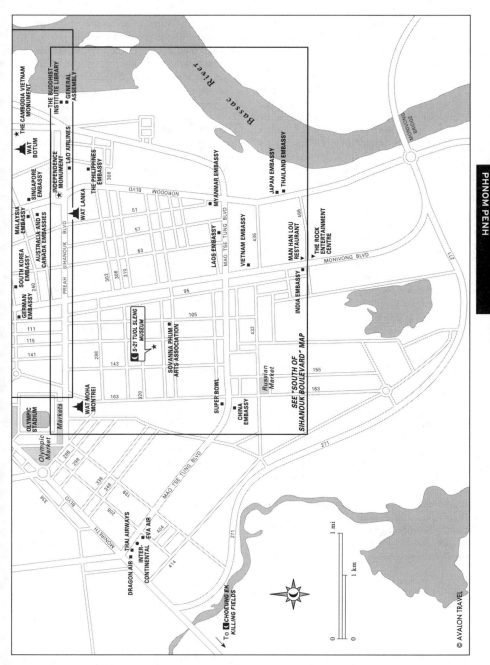

© AVALON TRAVEL

1979. But, as many of the city's original inhabitants had been killed, Phnom Penh was now largely populated by displaced refugees from the countryside.

When UNTAC showed up in 1992 with 22,000 soldiers and millions of dollars in their luggage, the capital immediately turned into a two-tier economy—one for foreigners, the other for locals; one powered with U.S. dollars, the other with Cambodian riel. This has not changed since the end of the United Nations mission a year later; U.S. dollars are still the currency dispensed by all ATMs around town.

Since 2003, most roads have been paved, public areas have been rehabilitated from rubbish dumps to green spaces, and the guns have disappeared from the streets—even if the disenfranchised poor remain just that. Some of the historical French buildings have been restored, but a fair number have also been knocked down and replaced by chrome and glass monstrosities, which point to a blander future. In 2009, the city's first skyscraper began to be constructed along the riverfront, not far from the Royal Palace—despite a law stipulating that buildings not be higher than Wat Phnom.

PLANNING YOUR TIME

While virtually all visitors to Cambodia head for the magnificent temples of Angkor, the country's capital is definitely worth a visit as well. It's possible to see the most important sights around town in a single long day. In three days, you can take it all in at a more leisurely pace.

Above all, it's the atmosphere of Phnom Penh that makes visitors stay longer than planned. Unlike neighboring metropolises Bangkok or Saigon, Phnom Penh remains, despite urban squalor, very much a manageable and often beautiful city. Wander the markets or the narrow streets off the riverfront or lose yourself after sundown in some of the hundreds of bars and restaurants around town; you may easily get stuck for a week, especially if you get sucked into the edgy nightlife the city offers after midnight.

ORIENTATION

Phnom Penh is an easy city to navigate. The French created their colonial capital on the drawing board and hence all roads in central Phnom Penh run roughly parallel. Even more convenient is the fact that all streets except for a few main thoroughfares were numbered in 1979, after street names had been changed countless times by different regimes in previous decades. Odd street numbers run parallel to the Tonlé Sap River, roughly from east to west, and increase the farther you travel west. Even street numbers run at a right angle to the river and increase towards the south.

The city's busiest road is Monivong Boulevard, which runs parallel to the river from north to south and is home to the largest number of businesses, as well as many mid-range hotels. Norodom Boulevard runs parallel to Monivong, but farther to the east and towards the river. This major thoroughfare, which starts at Wat Phnom and crosses Independence Monument, is lined by colonial villas and several embassies.

Sisowath Quay, also called "Riverside," runs directly along the Tonlé Sap River and is lined with hotels, restaurants, and small shops. Locals and tourists congregate along the landscaped river promenade in the afternoons, though the main stretch has been closed off and is being dug up to accommodate a new sewage system; it is not likely to be accessible again to the public until late 2010.

Sights

AROUND BOENG KAK AND WAT PHNOM AREA

In a city emerging from decades of conflict, development can be swift. Until a few years ago, the area around the Boeng Kak Lake was one of Phnom Penh's most notorious red light districts. Now, the alleys that stretch to the eastern shore of the lake serve as the city's backpacker quarter, which is on track to make way for new, luxury property developments in 2010.

The area around Wat Phnom symbolizes the city's history and continuity; it's the founding spot of Phnom Penh and, during the French occupation, the streets around this small hillock were the heart of the capital. Today, with many foreign embassies (including the new

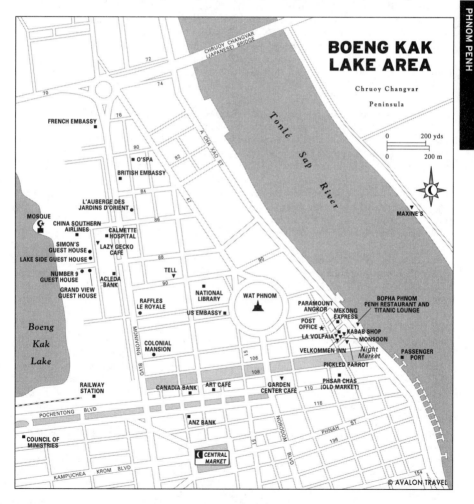

BOENG KAK LAKE AREA

U.S. mission) located in the neighborhood, it's once more a prosperous part of town.

Wat Phnom

Every great city starts with a legend and Phnom Penh is no exception. It's said that in the 14th century, a wealthy widow called Daun Penh discovered five Buddha statues that had been washed up on the shore of the Mekong in several tree trunks. To commemorate this miraculous event, Daun Penh had a small hill built, crowned by a temple to house the Buddha statues, which she named after herself and which is said to be today's Wat Phnom, the city's highest hill. The name of Cambodia's capital is a combination of the Khmer word for hill, *phnom,* and the name of the wealthy widow, Penh.

Today it costs US$1 to climb the wide staircase flanked by *naga* snakes to the temple at the top, which is usually busy with local visitors making offerings. The original structure has long disappeared, and the current building dates from 1926. Behind the temple, a small shrine dedicated to Daun Penh, who is today considered to be a powerful spirit, also draws a lot of visitors. A large white *chedi* contains the ashes of Ponhea Yat, the Khmer king who moved the capital from Angkor to Phnom Penh in 1422.

In 2008, the **Wat Phnom Fine Arts and Culture Museum** (no phone, daily 9 A.M.–5 P.M., US$2) opened in a building just below the temple. There's nothing much in the museum yet, but for several glass tanks (upstairs) filled with miniature figures and cardboard cut-outs re-enacting moments of Cambodian history. By far the most remarkable are the scenes of the Khmer Rouge's entry into Phnom Penh and the city's subsequent evacuation. Apart from that, it's barely worth the entrance fee.

There's plenty of activity around the base of the hill. Especially on weekends, Wat Phnom is a popular hangout, and there are fortune-tellers, gamblers, vendors, and even an elephant on hand to entertain people. Those who want to assure good luck for the future can get vendors to release birds from

tiny wooden cages (for a fee, of course). The vendors claim that the birds return after being set free. At times, a small stage is set up and noisy Khmer pop groups do their best not to scare people away.

Nearby is the National Library and Archives, also housed in a restored French building and situated in a small, well-maintained garden. Between Wat Phnom and the enormous and heavily fortified U.S. Embassy, a bronze statue of Daun Penh was erected in 2008. Be aware that if you attempt to photograph the embassy building, even from a passing tuk-tuk, you are likely to be stopped by security personnel who will insist you hand over your film or delete your images. Phnom Penh's only McDonald's is housed within the embassy walls.

The Post Office Square

Phnom Penh's central post office is housed in a beautiful ochre colonial building, which was restored in 2001. A few hundred meters east of Wat Phnom, the building faces a square, lined with French colonial buildings. It's easy to imagine the idyllic pre–Khmer Rouge atmosphere while strolling around the area.

The French Embassy

Located on Monivong Boulevard, the French Embassy is surrounded by a high wall and is not a tourist site as such. Nonetheless, some of the most dramatic scenes during the fall of Phnom Penh took place here in 1975. As the communists entered the city, most of the foreigners still in Phnom Penh, along with their Cambodian friends and families, sought refuge here. The Khmer Rouge ordered the French Embassy staff to hand over all Cambodians, except women married to foreigners. Refusal, the communists threatened, would lead to the death of everyone inside the embassy. The French had no choice but to hand over almost 600 Cambodians, most of whom were never seen again. Some 10 days later, the embassy was closed and the remaining foreigners were taken to the Thai border. Scenes in Roland Joffe's movie *The Killing Fields* recount this tragedy.

PHNOM PENH IN A DAY

Phnom Penh, despite its ever-growing volume of traffic, is still a great city to explore on foot, at least in parts. The main sites, including the two biggest markets, can be seen in a day.

A great place to start in the morning is **Sisowath Quay,** where numerous cafés, restaurants, and delis offer an astounding variety of breakfasts. Explore the **Royal Palace,** including the **Silver Pagoda,** and then head across to the **National Museum,** less than five minutes away on foot, to take a look at its huge collection of Angkor relics.

Street 178, which runs past the National Museum, is a good place to grab lunch and wander around the local art galleries. After lunch, visit the nearby art deco **Central Mar-**ket (Phsar Thmey), a few minutes' walk from the riverfront.

In the afternoon, hitch a ride south of the city, past the Independence Monument to **S-21 Tuol Sleng Museum,** as terrible and tragic as a sight can be. From this former Khmer Rouge prison, take another short ride to the **Russian Market** (Phsar Toul Tom Poung), which offers an enormous variety of souvenirs, silks, and bootleg DVDs and CDs. It's often very hot in this crowded, roofed market, so late afternoon is the best time to visit.

Round off the day where you started, on Sisowath Quay, to watch the sunset over the river from the **Foreign Correspondents' Club,** or relax in one of the many sidewalk restaurants.

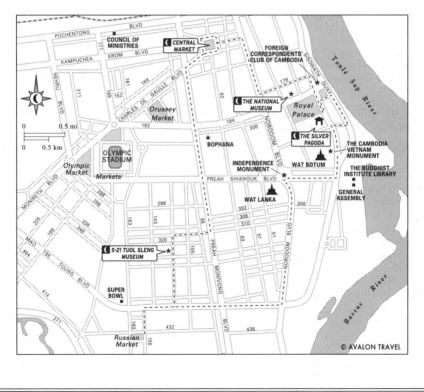

PHNOM PENH

© AVALON TRAVEL

GHOST TOWN 1975-1979

In the months prior to the collapse of the military government of General Lon Nol, thousands of refugees tried to flee the fighting between their own government troops, the NVA/NLF, the South Vietnamese, and the Khmer Rouge; they entered the city, which quickly grew from a population of half a million to more than two million people.

On April 17, 1975, the Khmer Rouge entered Phnom Penh. Initially there was some rejoicing as Pol Pot's revolutionary communists conquered the capital. This soon turned to terror, as the Khmer Rouge, many of them battle-hardened teenagers, immediately drove virtually all of Phnom Penh's inhabitants into the countryside, telling people that the United States was about to bomb the city, which was not the case.

The Khmer Rouge believed cities to be representations of capitalism and the root of all evil. Cambodia's urban centers were simply abandoned. Homes, schools, and hospitals were emptied in a matter of days and those who could not walk were killed or left to die. Wealthy and educated urbanites were branded as "New People" or "April 17 People" and treated especially harshly. Anyone connected to the old regime or the United States was killed. Forced into rural communes, many "New People" perished in the years that followed.

Phnom Penh turned into a ghost town, with money abolished, and banks, post offices, and schools closed. A few ministries and factories stayed open and the Tuol Svay Prey High School was turned into the infamous Tuol Sleng Prison, where alleged enemies of the state were interrogated and tortured, before being executed at the Choeung Ek Killing Fields 15 kilometers from town.

As Cambodia shut down for genocide, most foreigners left. Several embassies did stay open throughout the Khmer Rouge's rule of terror, though, amongst them Yugoslavia, Albania, Romania, North Korea, Vietnam, Laos, Cuba, and China. Pochentong Airport was closed to international flights, except to welcome occasional supply planes from Beijing, which continued to bankroll the Khmer Rouge revolution. By the end of 1975, Phnom Penh had ceased to exist as an urban community. Some 20,000 Communist Party members and factory workers were said to be living within the city limits for the next four years. On January 7, 1979, the Vietnamese army invaded, conquered, and liberated a virtually deserted Phnom Penh.

AROUND THE RIVERFRONT

For many visitors, the heart and soul of Phnom Penh lie around the banks of the Tonlé Sap River. Some of Phnom Penh's major sights jostle for attention with an astounding number of restaurants, cafés, and bars. In the evenings, thousands of Khmer cruise up and down Sisowath Quay, socializing from the back of their motorcycles, as travelers and the occasional Western film star rub shoulders with begging mine victims, while brightly lit river cruises slowly pass by on the river.

The Royal Palace and Silver Pagoda Complex

Both the Royal Palace and the Silver Pagoda are located in the same riverfront complex, surrounded by high walls 500 meters by 800 meters long and fronted by a large square. The palace complex was built in the 1850s. Its full Khmer name is Preah Barom Reachea Vaeng Chaktomuk, and it currently serves as the home of King Norodom Sihamoni, who was crowned in the palace in 2004, as well as his father, former King Norodom Sihanouk. Nevertheless, most of the palace grounds are open to the public.

The construction of the palace complex started after King Norodom had abandoned the temporary capital of Oudong and moved back to Phnom Penh. It was built, over more than a decade, on the grounds of the old citadel Banteay Kev, which had been constructed by King Ang Chan in 1813 and was later

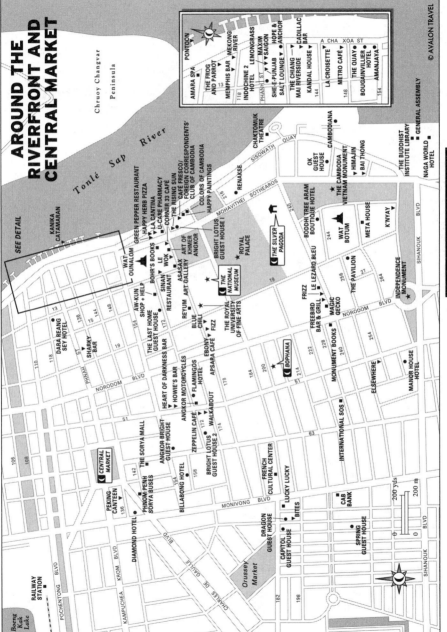

© AVALON TRAVEL

PHNOM PENH

AROUND THE RIVERFRONT AND CENTRAL MARKET

Chruoy Changvar Peninsula

Tonlé Sap River

SEE DETAIL

KANIKA CATAMARAN

DETAIL

PONTOON

AMARA SPA
THE FROG AND PARROT
MEMPHIS BAR
INDOCHINE 2 HOTEL
PHANH ST
MAXIM
SHE-E-PUNJAB
SALT LOUNGE
MEKONG RIVER
LEMONGRASS
HOPE & ANCHOR
SAIGON
THE CHIANG MAI RIVERSIDE
CADILLAC BAR
KANDAL HOUSE
A CHA XOA ST
LA CROISETTE
METRO CAFÉ
THE QUAY
BOUGAINVILLIER HOTEL
AMANJAYA

13
118
144
148
154

GREEN PEPPER RESTAURANT
HAPPY HERB PIZZA
U-CARE PHARMACY
LA CANTINA
CORNER 33 CAFÉ
THE RISING SUN
CAFÉ FRESCO/
FOREIGN CORRESPONDENTS' CLUB OF CAMBODIA
COLORS OF CAMBODIA
HAPPY PAINTINGS

WAT OUNALOM
BOHR'S BOOKS
LE WOK
ART OF KHMER ANGKOR
ASASAK
AW-KUN SHOP + HELP
SINAN RESTAURANT
REYUM ART GALLERY
THE LAST HOME GUEST HOUSE
BLUE CHILI
FIZZ
EBONY APSARA CAFÉ
HEART OF DARKNESS BAR
HOWIE'S BAR
FLAMINGOS HOTEL
ANGKOR MOTORCYCLES
WALKABOUT
ZEPPELIN CAFÉ
BRIGHT LOTUS GUEST HOUSE 2

BRIGHT LOTUS GUEST HOUSE
THE NATIONAL MUSEUM
THE ROYAL UNIVERSITY OF FINE ARTS
ROYAL PALACE
THE SILVER PAGODA
BOPHANA

CHAKTOMUK THEATRE
RENAKSE
SISOWATH QUAY
MOHAVITHEI
SOTHEAROS

BODDHI TREE ARAM BOUTIQUE HOTEL
THE CAMBODIA VIETNAM MONUMENT
WAT BOTUM
META HOUSE
K'NYAY
FRIZZ
LE LEZARD BLEU
FREEBIRD BAR & GRILL
MAGIC GECKO
THE PAVILION
MONUMENT BOOKS
ELSEWHERE
MANOR HOUSE HOTEL
INDEPENDENCE MONUMENT

OK GUEST HOUSE
CAMBODIANA
HIMAJIN
BAI THONG
THE BUDDHIST INSTITUTE LIBRARY
GENERAL ASSEMBLY
NAGA WORLD HOTEL

SISOWATH
NORODOM BLVD
SIHANOUK BLVD

DARA REANG SEY HOTEL
SHARKY BAR
THE SORYA MALL
CENTRAL MARKET
ANGKOR-BRIGHT GUEST HOUSE
BILLABONG HOTEL
PHNOM PENH SORYA BUSES
PEKING CANTEEN
DIAMOND HOTEL
FRENCH CULTURAL CENTER
LUCKY LUCKY
BITES
DRAGON GUEST HOUSE
CAPITOL GUEST HOUSE
SPRING GUEST HOUSE
CAB BANK
INTERNATIONAL SOS

RAILWAY STATION
Boeng Kak Lake
Oussey Market
POCHENTONG BLVD
KAMPUCHEA KROM BLVD
CHARLES DE GAULLE BLVD
MONIVONG BLVD

200 yds
200 m

110
118
136
142
144
148
154
158
172
174
175
178
182
184
196
198
200
206
214
216
222
228
232
240
244
254
256
264
13
15
19
27
51
63

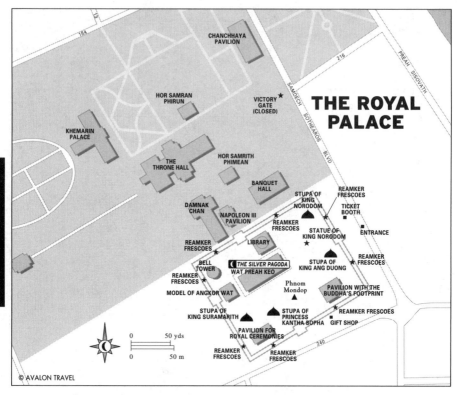

THE ROYAL PALACE

destroyed by Siamese troops in 1834. Within the palace walls, numerous royal buildings stand in a well-maintained tropical garden that seems light years away from the urban commotion beyond the palace walls. The layout of the complex changed numerous times between 1866 and 1970 and many of the older buildings have been replaced.

The palace complex is divided into three compounds: the throne hall compound; the walled enclosure of the Silver Pagoda; and the Khemarin Palace area, today's royal residence, which is separated from the rest of the buildings by a wall and is not accessible to the public.

There's a souvenir shop near the ticket booth at the main entrance on Sothearos Boulevard, which sells CDs, postcards, books, videos, and objects of kitsch. Visitors

are allowed daily 8 A.M.–5 P.M.; entrance costs US$3, and there are additional charges for still cameras (US$2) and video cameras (US$5). The use of cameras is not allowed inside the Throne Hall or the Silver Pagoda, and flash photography is prohibited altogether. English-speaking guides wait near the ticket booth, and it's worth hiring one if you are interested in Khmer culture and architecture. Rates are negotiable, but US$5 is appropriate. A tour of the royal compound should take about two hours.

CHANCHHAYA PAVILION

While the complex's main entrance is located near the Silver Pagoda, visitors generally first head for the Chanchhaya Pavilion, to the north of the Throne Hall area. The front of the palace complex faces the Tonlé

the Chanchhaya Pavilion

Sap River across a wide square and is dominated by the Preah Thineang Chan Chhaya, a rectangular building complete with golden spires and usually a giant image of the king looking out over the wide square directly in front of the palace walls. The open-air pavilion is the only building clearly visible from outside the palace walls. It is occasionally used for dance performances, and is also a perfect platform for members of the royal family to watch processions marching past on Sothearos Boulevard. The current pavilion was constructed in 1913, replacing an earlier wooden structure.

THE THRONE HALL

The Throne Hall does indeed contain two thrones, as well as busts of Cambodia's former kings. In Khmer, it is called Preah Thineang Dheva Vinnichay, which means "Sacred Seat of Judgment." It was built in 1915 and inaugurated by King Sisowath in 1919, replacing an older wooden hall. From here, the royal household once carried out its duties and directed policies. The ceiling frescoes depict scenes from the *Reamker,* the Cambodian retelling of the *Ramayana.* Its central spire is 59 meters high.

OTHER BUILDINGS IN THE THRONE HALL COMPOUND

Several smaller buildings are of note, especially the **Napoleon III Pavilion,** the first structure to be erected within the palace compound. The pavilion was originally built in 1869 for Empress Eugenie of France, wife of Napoleon III. Fortunately, the royal "N" of the Napoleons on the doors of the building did not have to be removed when the pavilion was gifted to King Norodom in 1876.

The building is made entirely of iron and houses a small museum presenting royal memorabilia. **Hor Samran Phirun** is a small former royal guesthouse that now houses gifts from foreign heads of state. **Hor Samrith Phimean** contains royal regalia and dress.

Two other larger structures, the **Damnak Chan,** which houses the administration of the Royal Palace, and the **Villa Kantha Bopha,**

PHNOM PENH

© AROON THAEWCHATTURAT

the Throne Hall

a 1950s Western-style villa built for foreign guests, are closed to the public.

(THE SILVER PAGODA

The impressive Silver Pagoda is named for the silver tiles that cover its floor, laid during King Sihanouk's pre–Khmer Rouge reign. There are more than 5,000 tiles, each weighing more than a kilo.

The Khmer name for the temple is Preah Vihear Preah Keo Morakot, the "Temple of the Emerald Buddha." The original temple was constructed from 1892 to 1902 and was made from wood and stone; the current building, built from concrete and Italian marble, hails from 1962 and uses the same design as the original.

Wat Preah Keo houses a great collection of national treasures, including Cambodia's Emerald Buddha, a 17th-century baccarat crystal Buddha. Even more impressive is a near life-size golden Buddha, dressed up in royal regalia and encrusted with more than 9,500 diamonds and commissioned by King Sisowath. Most of the other more than 1,500

objects are Buddha statues made from gold, silver, and bronze, some inlaid with diamonds, as well as objects used in Buddhist ceremonies. These were donated to the temple by the king, his family, and various dignitaries. The Silver Pagoda also contains what are said to be ashes of the Buddha, brought from Sri Lanka in the 1950s. No monks live here, but Wat Preah Keo is used by the king to listen to monks' sermons as well as for some royal ceremonies.

In addition to the temple building, several smaller structures—including a library, several stupas, and *chedis* and galleries covered in frescoes depicting the *Reamker*—were constructed in the late 19th and early 20th centuries. The library contains a collection of sacred Buddhist texts and a collection of Buddha statues. During the Khmer Rouge rule, many of the treasures were looted, while King Sihanouk and members of his family were kept within the palace grounds as virtual prisoners, forced to grow their own vegetables. There's also a small concrete model of Angkor Wat on the Silver Pagoda grounds.

◖ The National Museum

The National Museum (daily 8 A.M.–5 P.M., US$3), on the corner of Street 178 and Street 13 behind the Royal Cremation Ground, houses the world's greatest collection of Khmer art. The museum was designed by French archaeologist George Groslier and constructed between 1917 and 1920. During the Khmer Rouge years, the museum was looted and its director murdered. In the 1990s, this stunning Khmer-style terracotta structure of several open galleries, all linked via a picturesque central courtyard, was threatened by bats in the roof, but these pests were contained by the installation of a second roof during extensive renovations in 2002.

Today, more than 5,000 objects are exhibited and many more remain in storage. The museum primarily houses artifacts from the Angkor period, but there are also large collections of pre-Angkorian objects as well more recent items on display.

As you come in, the East Gallery contains a giant 10th-century sandstone statue of Garuda.

On display here are also numerous Buddha statues made from sandstone, copper, and bronze, dating as far back as the 6th century, as well as practical items such as bowls, candleholders, and elephant bells. Another highlight in this section is the Reclining Vishnu, a huge 10th-century bronze of which only the head, arms, and torso survive. This statue, which was found in the Western Mebon, is most likely the same one that was described by Chinese traveler Chou Ta-Kuan, who visited Angkor in the 13th century, as having been inlaid with countless precious stones, gold, and silver. The far right corner of the East Gallery contains a small collection of prehistoric objects.

More impressive is the South Gallery, with its pre-Angkorian Buddha statues, as well as statues of celestial dancers with narrow waists, full breasts, and wide hips. The highlight is an image of Vishnu, standing three meters tall, from the 7th century. The rest of the South Gallery is given over to stunning examples of Angkor-era artworks up the 11th century, including part of a wall from Banteay Srei.

© AROON THAEWCHATTURAT

the terracotta building of the National Museum

The West Gallery houses artifacts from the late Angkor period, including a famous statue of god king Jayavarman VII from the 12th century. There's also a sculpture of his head, with the faint and infamous *sourir Khmer,* the smile of the Khmer, as the French called it, both cruel and compassionate, on its lips.

Finally, the North Gallery presents more recent objects. Besides collections of firearms and canons, the wooden cabin of a royal barge, dating back to the 19th century, bedecked with fine carvings, is a highlight. King Norodom's funerary urn, made of wood and precious metals is, at three meters in height, equally impressive.

In the museum's courtyard, the giant statue of the Leper King, taken from the terrace of the same name in Angkor Thom, is another highlight of this fantastic museum.

Apart from being a great exhibition space, the National Museum is also the last safe refuge for many Angkor-era artifacts. Looting continues unabated at many temples and, no doubt, many of the objects on display here would have long disappeared into private collectors' vaults had they been left in their original locations. Perfect examples of this are two magnificent wall panels showing a multi-armed Lodestar, which were stolen from Banteay Chhmar in 1998. The panels were pried from the temple structure and smuggled into Thailand, where the smugglers were caught by police, who eventually returned the panels to Cambodia.

Photography is allowed only on the grounds and around the central courtyard. A souvenir stall inside the museum sells books and postcards. Competent English-speaking guides can be found around the ticket booth. Expect to pay US$5 and be sure to negotiate a price prior to embarking on a tour.

There's such an overwhelming amount of artifacts on display that it's easy to lose yourself for a couple of hours. If you can't make it to Angkor, the National Museum is the best place to get at least a small insight into Cambodia's magnificent past. If you do intend to visit Angkor or have already been, then the collection will deepen your understanding of the incredible cultural creativity of the Angkor period.

Wat Botum

The Temple of the Lotus Blossoms is a large pagoda complex located at Street 7, near Sihanouk Boulevard, and was founded in 1422 by Ponhea Yat, the Khmer king who moved the capital from Angkor to Phnom Penh. Wat Botum (daily 7 A.M.–5 P.M., free) got its name from its original location on an island in the center of a pond. The temple received its current name only during the French period, and has been rebuilt numerous times, most recently in 1937.

As the temple is the seat of the Thammayut sect of Buddhism, which was introduced by Thailand and is said to be close to the aristocratic establishment and the monarchy, numerous dignitaries' and royals' ashes have been interred in *stupas* here. The walls of the pagoda are covered in frescoes depicting the life of the Buddha. Though entry is free, a small donation is appreciated.

Wat Ounalom

The seat of Cambodian Buddhism and most important active temple in Cambodia, Wat Ounalom (daily 7 A.M.–5 P.M., free) is situated along Sisowath Quay on the riverfront, 300 meters north of the Royal Palace. Founded in 1443, the temple compound is massive and contains more than 40 buildings.

In 1975, the Khmer Rouge killed the abbot and many of the monks. Some of the buildings were vandalized, but restoration started as soon as the Vietnamese invaded in 1979 and the temple has since been rebuilt to its former glory. Cambodia's supreme patriarch lives here, and there's a *stupa* containing an eyebrow of the Buddha, as well as schools and a library. A small donation is appreciated.

The Cambodia Vietnam Monument

Remembering the liberation of Cambodia from the Khmer Rouge by the Vietnamese, this rather austere communist-style monument, dominated by a stone carving of gun-toting troops, was constructed in 1979. Today it's a popular meeting point for locals. The park

VANN MOLYVANN: PHNOM PENH'S VISIONARY

Contemporary Phnom Penh was built by the French, but its modern character is due mostly to one man. Vann Molyvann, born in 1926 in Kampot, studied first law and then architecture in Paris in the 1940s. He was taught by Le Corbusier and returned to Cambodia in 1955 to be appointed by King Sihanouk as the country's chief national architect. The post-independence years were heady days for Cambodia, the country was at peace, the king was a dynamic man and had dynamic plans for his people. His far-reaching cultural vision was perfectly represented by Molyvann's building style, called New Khmer Architecture, which sought to marry traditional Khmer and modern aesthetics and succeeded in creating a unique architectural style.

Molyvann's monuments for an independent Cambodia integrated well with the older colonial cityscape. His most prominent structures include the Independence Monument, the Olympic Stadium (now the National Sports Complex), the Institute of Foreign Languages at Phnom Penh University, and the Capitol Cinema. Molyvann left Cambodia in 1972, but returned in 1993 and became Minister of Culture, Fine Arts, Urban and Country Planning. Sadly, many of his buildings, including the National Theatre and the Council of Ministers, have recently been demolished to make space for more modern buildings. Molyvann has published a book called *Modern Khmer Cities*.

around the monument, located on Sothearos Boulevard a couple of hundred meters south of the Royal Palace, features a fountain light show, which attracts hundreds of people in the early evenings.

AROUND CENTRAL MARKET
The Olympic Stadium

You're right in thinking that the Olympic Games never took place in Cambodia. Yet, there's an Olympic stadium of Olympic proportions, nowadays called the National Sports Complex, located in the west part of the city, a little north of Sihanouk Boulevard. The complex was built in the early 1960s, following designs by renowned Cambodian architect Vann Molyvann, in order to host the Games of the New Emerging Forces (GANEFO), a sports initiative thought up by the Chinese. The games took place just once, in Cambodia, in 1966. Eighteen countries participated and Cambodia won 13 gold medals.

During the Khmer Rouge years, the lawn in the stadium was turned into a cabbage field. Buildings include the stadium, which seats 84,000; a hall for boxing, which seats 10,000; and an Olympic-size swimming pool. Following years of neglect, the complex has

now been restored. The halls and courtyards are used for political events and concerts. KA Tours (www.ka-tours.org), which offers architectural tours around the city to highlight Cambodia's recent architectural heritage, organizes regular trips to the stadium. Of course, it's perfectly possible just to drop in by yourself and watch Cambodian sports enthusiasts train.

SOUTH OF SIHANOUK BOULEVARD

Largely residential, the area called Boeung Keng Kang—located south of Sihanouk Boulevard, east of Monivong Boulevard, and west of Norodom—has always been considered the foreigners' quarter. It forms the heart of today's wealthy expat community, with many NGOs, embassies, and international companies based around here. Plenty of middle-class and wealthy Khmer live here, too. There are some excellent mid-range hotels and restaurants in the area, especially on Street 278.

The Independence Monument

The Vimean Ekareach, or Independence Monument, is located at the intersection of

PHNOM PENH

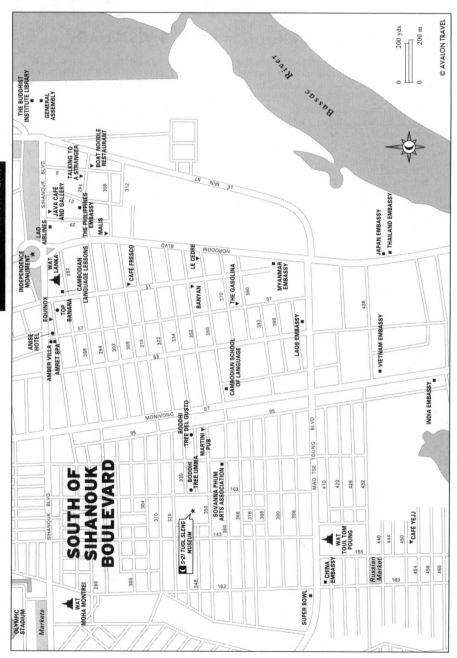

SOUTH OF SIHANOUK BOULEVARD

© AVALON TRAVEL

200 yds
200 m

Bassac River

THE BUDDHIST INSTITUTE LIBRARY
GENERAL ASSEMBLY
SIHANOUK BLVD
TALKING TO A STRANGER
BOAT NOODLE RESTAURANT
LE MIN ST
6
294
308
312
JAVA CAFÉ AND GALLERY
THE PHILIPPINES EMBASSY
MALIS
29
LAO AIRLINES
INDEPENDENCE MONUMENT
WAT LANKA
CAMBODIAN LANGUAGE LESSONS
282
CAFÉ FRESCO
NORODOM BLVD
LE CEDRE
JAPAN EMBASSY
THAILAND EMBASSY
51
BANYAN
THE GASOLINA
370
380
MYANMAR EMBASSY
EQUINOX
TOP BANANA
57
302 306 310 322 334 352 360
392 398
57
LAOS EMBASSY
ANISE HOTEL
AMBER VILLA
AMRET SPA
288 294
83
CAMBODIAN SCHOOL OF LANGUAGE
436
VIETNAM EMBASSY
MONIVONG ST
95
INDIA EMBASSY
BODDHI TREE DEL GUSTO
MARTINI PUB
95
MAO TSE TOUNG BLVD
SIHANOUK BLVD
304
330
BODDHI TREE UMMA
SOVANNA PHUM ARTS ASSOCIATION
103
410 420 428 432
310 320
350
368 376 386
390 396
S-21 TUOL SLENG MUSEUM
143 360
WAT TOUL TOM POUNG
155
CHINA EMBASSY
CAFÉ YEJJ
WAT MOHA MONTREI
280
300
348
163
Russian Market
440 444 450
163
454 456 460
OLYMPIC STADIUM
Markets
SUPER BOWL

Norodom and Sihanouk Boulevards. Built in the late 1950s, the structure, designed by renowned Cambodian architect Vann Molyvann, takes the shape of a lotus-shaped stupa, and is reminiscent of similar building elements used in Angkor Wat.

Today, the monument commemorates Cambodia's independence from foreign rule and the country's war dead. During important national holidays, a flame is lit on the interior pedestal by a royal or high-ranking government official, and the steps are covered in floral tributes. The green space stretching down towards the river used to be a notorious red light district, but has been rehabilitated. These days, food vendors set up their carts in the evenings, when the monument is lit up in red, blue, and white (the colors of Cambodia's flag).

Wat Moha Montrei

One of the most visited of the more than 20 pagodas in Phnom Penh is Wat Moha Montrei (daily 7 A.M.–5 P.M., free). King Monivong bestowed the temple's name (which means "The Great Minister") after one of his ministers had taken the initiative to start its construction in the 1930s. The pagoda walls are covered in frescoes depicting the life of the Buddha. The murals inside the main hall date from the 1970s; they also show the life of the Buddha, but are known for their modern touches, such as *apsara* dancers in place of angels and depictions of men in modern uniforms. During the Khmer Rouge years, Wat Moha Montrei was used as a granary. The temple lies just south of the Olympic Stadium at the turn-off for Street 123 from Sihanouk Boulevard.

◖ S-21 Tuol Sleng Museum

In August 1975, four months after the Khmer Rouge had taken control of Phnom Penh, the Tuol Svay Prey High School, south of Sihanouk Boulevard on Street 350, was converted into Security Prison 21, an interrogation and torture center, also called Tuol Sleng. Between 1975 and 1979, an estimated 17,000 people—men, women, and children—were imprisoned

the Independence Monument

© AROON THAEWCHATTURAT

here. Many of them, especially in later years, were themselves members of the Khmer Rouge who had been accused of betraying the party in an ever-expanding cycle of internal purges. Even high-ranking members of the Cambodian communists were incarcerated and tortured. A few foreigners, mostly caught at sea, were also sent to S-21.

All prisoners were photographed and forced to tell their life stories, from childhood memories to the moment of their arrest. They were then assigned their cells and systematically tortured in order to force a confession that suited the interrogators. Food was virtually nonexistent and any challenge to the guards or failure to obey the myriad of rules of S-21 resulted in severe, often deadly beatings. Prisoners were hung, electrocuted, and suffocated with plastic bags, and waterboarding was routinely applied to inmates. The confessions extracted usually contained the names of all the people prisoners knew. Often, those named were then also arrested and tortured. Most importantly, interrogators

A bust of Khmer Rouge leader Pol Pot sits next to rows of iron shackles with which prisoners used to be tied, inside the former interrogation center S-21 Tuol Sleng.

pried confessions of secret service conspiracies out of the prisoners, a reflection of the regime's paranoia. Inmates confessed to either working for the CIA or the KGB. Few, if any, of the inmates were likely to have done any such thing.

Initially, prisoners who had been killed were buried in the schoolyard, but as more space was needed, those inmates who had been "processed," were taken to Choeung Ek, executed, and buried in mass graves. More than 1,700 people worked at the prison, many of them teenagers. They were led by Comrade Duch, real name Kang Kek Iew, a former schoolteacher who had been imprisoned and tortured in 1967 by King Sihanouk's security services for his affiliation with Cambodia's fledgling communist movement. Prior to the Khmer Rouge takeover in 1975, Duch established torture centers in the communist-controlled provinces and developed his interrogation techniques. When Phnom Penh fell, he set up several prisons in the capital, which were amalgamated into one large center, S-21, in 1976.

When the Vietnamese liberated Phnom Penh in 1979, Duch fled with other Khmer Rouge cadre, too hurried to destroy the meticulous files kept on inmates. Nevertheless, he did take the time to execute the few remaining prisoners. Duch, who became a schoolteacher once more in refugee camps in Thailand, distanced himself from the Khmer Rouge after the movement's collapse in 1997. He became a Christian and worked for World Vision, a nongovernmental organization. He was eventually recognized by photojournalist Nic Dunlop and arrested in 1999. In 2007, Duch was indicted on charges of crimes against humanity by the Cambodia Tribunal. His trial began in February 2009, and in the face of witness statements, the former S-21 commander broke down and admitted his guilt while claiming he acted under orders.

Very few people survived S-21, amongst them Vann Nath, a Cambodian artist who was spared, because he painted portraits and created busts of Khmer Rouge leader Pol Pot. Since 1979, Vann Nath has painted the crimes of the Khmer

THE KHMER ROUGE UNITED NATIONS TRIAL

The trial of the former senior Khmer Rouge leaders has been underway since 1997, when the Cambodian government requested the United Nations to assist the country in the setting up of what's commonly known as the Cambodia Tribunal. In 2001, the Extraordinary Chambers in the Courts of Cambodia for the Prosecution of Crimes Committed During the Period of Democratic Kampuchea (Extraordinary Chambers or ECCC) was created through laws passed by the National Assembly.

Right from the outset, the international dimension of the crimes committed by the Khmer Rouge has been excluded from the tribunal's responsibilities. Neither China, which bankrolled the genocide, nor the United States, which conducted massive bombing campaigns that killed hundreds of thousands of Khmer civilians and drove thousands more into the hands of the radical communists, have any interest in the examination of their policies and actions relating to the Khmer Rouge's rise. The Cambodian government, too, is keen to limit the scope of the trial – since many of today's leading politicians are tainted by the country's past.

In 2003, after years of wrangling, mostly over influence and money, the Cambodian government reached an agreement with the United Nations about how the trial was to be conducted – with both Cambodian and international judges – and despite reports of massive pre-trial corruption. All through its creation, the court has been beset by funding problems, but finally, in 2006, Kofi Annan, then secretary general of the United Nations, appointed seven judges. Shortly after, the Cambodian justice minister announced the appointment of 30 Cambodian and United Nations judges to preside over the tribunal.

Between July and December 2007, five suspects, all of them elderly and frail, were indicted. Khieu Samphan, Nuon Chea, Ieng Sary, Ieng Thirit, and Duch have been arrested on charges of crimes against humanity, including genocide. It is unlikely that further indict-

ments will follow, as the Cambodian judges are keen to limit the case to the top Khmer Rouge echelon. Hearings started in February 2008, while the tribunal was still looking for millions of dollars in funds. In February 2009, the actual trial started with Duch as the first defendant. While facing survivors on the witness stand in June 2009, the former commander of the S-21 interrogation center broke down and admitted his guilt while claiming he had acted under orders from above.

In 2009, an internal report commissioned by the United Nations pointed out corruption inside the court and was subsequently suppressed. Prime Minister Hun Sen has repeatedly said he'd rather the international judges went home and let Cambodians continue with their trial, while at the same time questioning the wisdom and legitimacy of the trial altogether. Efforts to bring further defendants to the court have been blocked by Cambodian judges, not least because some members of Cambodia's current government were part of the Khmer Rouge regime. Continued budget problems and the internal and hardly transparent machinations of the court have called its usefulness into question.

The tribunal has had a mixed response among ordinary Cambodians who lived through decades of hardship and terror. According to the *New York Times*'s Seth Mydans, Cambodia's young people, more than 70 percent of the population, have little or no knowledge of the horrors their parents lived through: schoolbooks omit the Khmer Rouge years and, incredibly, many young Khmer do not believe the genocide ever took place. But the survivors of Cambodia's darkest period may find some kind of closure if the trials lead to transparent convictions. If the trial collapses or remains tainted by backroom deals between the United Nations and the Cambodian government or judiciary, the international community will have failed Cambodia yet again. There's no capital punishment in Cambodia.

Rouge. Many of his paintings, depicting life at S-21, are on exhibition at the museum. Vann Nath wrote a memoir of his time at Tuol Sleng, entitled *A Cambodian Prison Portrait: One Year in the Khmer Rouge's S-21 Prison,* which is widely available in Phnom Penh.

The torture center was discovered by Vietnamese war photographer Ho Van Thay. It has been partly preserved the way the Vietnamese found it, initially as a propaganda tool to show the world why it had been necessary to invade Cambodia. Some cells have been left undisturbed, while others are now lined with thousands of photographs of inmates. It also contains a large collection of photographs of the damage the Khmer Rouge wrought on Cambodia, the paintings by Vann Nath, as well as shelves of skulls of some of the victims of S-21.

A visit to the S-21 Tuol Sleng Museum (no phone, daily 8 A.M.–5 P.M., US$2) is a heart-wrenching experience, and visitors may ask themselves why they should confront so much horror. Yet, in order to understand Cambodia's recent tragic history and the country it is today, a visit to a site of Khmer Rouge atrocities is extremely helpful.

Many of the English-speaking guides waiting in the reception area lost family members in S-21 and a tour is highly recommended. Rates are negotiable, but expect to pay US$5–10. It's hard to put a price on an experience like this.

A souvenir stall on the premises sells photocopied books on Cambodian history. *S-21: The Khmer Rouge Killing Machine,* a 2003 feature documentary by renowned Cambodian director Rithy Panh, follows artist Vann Nath and another survivor back to S-21, where they confront some of the prison's former guards.

Wat Lanka

In the 13th century, Buddhist monks from Sri Lanka who had come to Cambodia as teachers and quasi-missionaries introduced monastic education and became advisors to the Cambodian monarchy. Wat Lanka, Cambodia's first center for the study of Theravada Buddhism, is located to the southwest of the Independence Monument and was established in 1422 by King Ponhea Yat. Since its founding, the temple has served as a meeting place for Sri Lankan and Cambodian monks. For this reason, it's called Wat Lanka. The temple was used as a warehouse by the Khmer Rouge, and hence escaped total destruction.

Wat Lanka (daily 7 A.M.–5 P.M., free) has been restored under the supervision of King Sihanouk's wife. Colorful wall frescoes recount the life of the Buddha on the ground and first floor of the pagoda. For meditation courses, call 023/721001.

◖ Bophana

Bophana (64, Street 200, tel. 023/992174, www.bophana.org, Mon.–Fri. 8 A.M.–6 P.M., Sat. 2–6 P.M., free) is an audiovisual resource center, founded by renowned Cambodian film director Rithy Phan and open to the public. It's set up to archive images and sounds of the Cambodian memory and to make them available to a wide public. It also trains Cambodians in the audiovisual professions by welcoming foreign film productions, and through its own artistic projects. The center offers visitors the opportunity to view many hours of digitized film footage, from hundred-year-old French reels to the movies of King Sihanouk. For those who'd like to get a glimpse of what life before the Khmer Rouge was like in Cambodia, the center's growing collection of footage is the best and most easily accessible starting point.

Bophana hosts exhibitions in its downstairs reception area. Films can be searched and watched at individual screens upstairs. The archive is continually expanding, and archive consultation is available Tuesday–Friday 2–6 P.M.

Entertainment and Events

NIGHTLIFE

Take care in any of the city's upscale Khmer nightclubs—a few rich kids like to exploit the fact that they are above the law and sometimes direct their aggression towards foreigners.

Boeng Kak and Wat Phnom Area

BARS

Well worth a visit is **The Elephant Bar** inside the Raffles Le Royale Hotel (Street 92, tel. 023/981888), if only to check out the history of this fantastic luxury hotel. It's a great place to watch Cambodia's high society relax to the tunes of a lounge pianist below a ceiling covered in murals depicting, yes, elephants. Cocktails are not cheap, but if you drop by during happy hour (daily 4–8 P.M.), it's not too painful. Forget about your wallet for a second, close your eyes, and just think of all the celebrities, from Jackie Kennedy to Angelina Jolie, who have pulled into this history-laden watering hole over the past decades.

In recent years, a number of nightspots have opened up on tiny Street 104 and the choice of venues, from sleazy hostess bars to upmarket bistros, is somewhat eclectic. Not bad is the little **Velkommen Inn** (23, Street 104, tel. 092/177710), which is under Norwegian management. It serves Scandinavian beverages and food and offers lodging in five very clean rooms. The **Pickled Parrot** (4–6, Street 104, tel. 023/986722, www.tonlesapguesthouse.com), another bar-cum-hotel, is somewhat more lowbrow, but offers an international menu with Australian steaks for around US$10. Most importantly, the Pickled Parrot is open 24/7, and has a pool table and Wi-Fi for guests.

KHMER NIGHTCLUBS

One of Phnom Penh's longest-running discos, the **Casa Nightclub** (5, Street 47, daily 7 P.M.–2 A.M.) has a reputation for raucousness and is rarely visited by foreigners, but makes for an interesting night out. Expect live music and dodgy techno.

PHNOM PENH FOR GAY TRAVELERS

A number of bars and hotels in the capital welcome gay travelers, though they tend not to be exclusively gay hangouts. Among them are the **Manor House Hotel** (21, Street 262, tel. 023/992566, www.manorhousecambodia.com), the **Salt Lounge** (27, Street 136), and the **Blue Chili** (36, Street 178). The latter establishment puts on cabaret shows on the weekend. Oh yes, and the infamous **Heart of Darkness Bar** (26, Street 51) is also gay-friendly.

Around the Riverfront

BARS

Pontoon (on the river, near Street 108, tel. 012/889175, daily 4 P.M.–4 A.M.) has a great atmosphere. For starters, this trendy bar, which regularly features local DJs, is located on a boat moored to the banks of the Tonlé Sap River. Add to that a Kubrickian interior, an extensive cocktails menu, and the river breeze, and you have got one of the best late-night hangouts in Phnom Penh. There are special parties on weekends and occasionally there's a ferry service across the river to Maxine's. The international food's not bad, either. The Pontoon sunk during a particularly wild party in 2008, but was re-launched a couple of weeks later.

Sharky Bar (126, Street 130, tel. 023/211825, www.sharkysofcambodia.com, daily 4 P.M.–2 A.M.), Phnom Penh's oldest rock-and-roll bar, appears to have it all—great hamburgers and Tex-Mex dishes, pool tables, scores of hostesses, big-screen TV for sports events, and draft beer. The atmosphere is somewhere between raucous and desperate, a kind of Hooters with loud music, and is probably not for everyone. Nevertheless, or perhaps exactly for this reason, Sharky Bar pulls in patrons every night and

© AROON THAEWCHATTURAT

view from the Foreign Correspondents' Club of the Tonlé Sap riverfront

weekends, especially, are packed. Occasionally, live bands put in a performance.

The **Cadillac Bar** (219 Sisowath Quay, tel. 011/713567, daily 8 P.M.–1 A.M.) is a great slice of Americana right on Phnom Penh's riverfront. The bar's motto is "Just Rollin' on the River," and besides ice cold beers and cocktails, there's a fine selection of food including burgers, salads, and pasta dishes from US$3–10. Expect loud classic rock and very friendly, hassle-free service.

LIVE MUSIC

The Memphis Bar (3 Street 118, tel. 012/871263, daily 5 P.M.–4 A.M.), probably Phnom Penh's longest-running live music venue, is close to the riverfront. The cover bands that rock the house (or play blues) from Tuesdays to Saturdays are pretty good.

CASINOS

Yes, Phnom Penh has long been a gambler's paradise. Numerous casinos, from huge gambling complexes to small poker clubs, are dotted around the city. The largest of the pack

is the **Naga World Hotel** (tel. 023/228822), right on the banks of the Tonlé Sap, south of Sihanouk Boulevard. Casual dress is okay, but you shouldn't turn up in shorts and flip-flops. The hotel, which opened in 2009, offers more than 500 international standard, if identical, air-conditioned rooms, all with Internet access; if you book via the Internet, room prices start at US$100, though the hotel does not have a website of its own. The roulette tables are separated by small water channels running through the casino hall, at the foot of an *Indiana Jones* reject fiberglass mountain. It's a jungle in there.

Around Central Market
BARS

Howie's Bar (32, Street 51, daily 7 P.M.–6 A.M.) is a small hole in the wall next to the Heart of Darkness, run by a young and friendly Khmer who returned from the United States a few years ago. This is a no-thrills filling station offering loud rock music, air-conditioning, a pool table, friendly service, cold beer, and sports on the TV. It's not a bad place to finish off the night.

The **Walkabout** (corner of Street 174 and Street 51, tel. 023/211715, www.walkabouthotel. com) is an Australian-style pub on Street 51 that serves beer around the clock. The bar food isn't bad, and there's a pool table, large-TV screen, and hostesses. The Walkabout is also a hotel with clean and reasonably priced rooms, ideal if you want to stay right in the heart of one of Phnom Penh's most vibrant nightlife areas.

Right next door to the Walkabout, the **Zeppelin Café** (109, Street 51, tel. 012/881181, daily 5 P.M.–4 A.M.) is run by Mr. Jun, who is surely the man with the largest collection of vinyl records in Cambodia. Mr. Jun's musical tastes are firmly anchored in the 1970s. Expect progressive rock, heavy metal, punk, and, of course, Led Zeppelin. There's occasional live music, cold beers, and Chinese snacks. The place keeps moving, so check for its current location.

An altogether different option is **Elsewhere** (175, Street 51, tel. 023/211348, Wed.–Mon. 10 A.M.–4 A.M.), a bar and restaurant set in a garden compound with comfortable couches around a pool. The atmosphere is mellow during the week and it can be hard to meet other people when it's not packed; however, parties on the weekend, sometimes organized by NGOs, can be good fun. People invariably end up in the pool.

KHMER NIGHTCLUB
The **Heart of Darkness Bar** (26, Street 51) is Phnom Penh's most legendary nightspot. This venue borrows its name from a Joseph Conrad novel set in Africa, but the bar actually started off as a kind of shrine to Tony Poe, a CIA operative in Laos, who served as the template for Colonel Kurtz in Francis Ford Coppola's 1979 movie *Apocalypse Now*. The Heart, as the locals call it, opened in the late 1990s, and has evolved from Phnom Penh's dingiest expat hangout to one of the trendiest nightspots in Southeast Asia. While marijuana-laden bowls no longer line the bar and most expatriates now go elsewhere, the atmosphere remains raucous, if not edgy—besides backpackers and taxi girls and boys (sex workers), young, rich, and spoiled Khmers occasionally like to prove their

immunity from the law on the dance floor; several shootings have occurred on the premises in recent years as a consequence. It's the Wild East all right. You have been warned. It's best to drop by after 11 P.M., and the place stays open until the last man/woman goes home.

South of Sihanouk Boulevard
BARS
Not far from the Independent Monument, quite a few bars and restaurants have opened on Street 278. One of the most relaxed is **Equinox** (3A, Street 278, daily 11 A.M.–very late), close to the corner with Street 51, which also doubles as an art gallery, putting on photo exhibitions. Food can be ordered from Setsara, a Thai and French restaurant next door. Besides friendly service, there's Wi-Fi, table football (possibly the only one in Phnom Penh), a pool table, a long cocktail list, and even some trendy clothes for sale.

Talking to a Stranger (21b, Street 294, daily 5 P.M.–very late) is a sedate hangout and garden bar with an extensive wine list and regular live events. It's popular with expatriates.

The Gasolina (56–58, Street 57, Tues.–Sun. 10 A.M.–4 A.M.) is another great garden bar. It's popular with the NGO crowd on the weekends, and hosts occasional live events and parties.

KHMER NIGHTCLUBS AND DISCOS
"Bored . . . , lonely . . . , hungry . . . ?" reads the advertisement for **Martini Pub** (45, Street 95, www.martini-cambodia.com, daily 7 P.M.–3 A.M.), a kind of multipurpose club left over from the UNTAC days. Martini can be pretty rough, or entertaining, depending on your point of view—with scores of hostesses vying for customers. There's a bar, an open-air food-court, a pool table, and an ice-cold indoor disco.

The Rock Entertainment Centre (468 Monivong Blvd., daily 6 P.M.–4 A.M.) is the city's largest disco, a huge cavernous place that features live DJs, bands, and canned techno and attracts the city's young and well-to-do. Entry is free, but the drinks are a bit pricey (beers around US$3).

Across the River

Upriver from the Chruoy Changvar Bridge, on the eastern shore of the Tonlé Sap River, a long strip of restaurants have set up along the water's edge. Most of these open-air places feature live music that can verge on the gaudy. The food is generally not bad, though there isn't always an English menu. Bring mosquito repellent and your own transportation or have the *motodup* wait outside.

BARS

Maxine's is a quiet bar just a little south of the Chruoy Changvar Bridge, on the eastern side of the river. Snow, the Australian owner, has been around Cambodia for more than 15 years and shone brightly in a short but memorable role as a debauched "sex-pat" in Matt Dillon's movie *City of Ghosts*. In real life, Snow is a quiet and humble gentleman who paints scenes from the *Remkar* in a unique style reminiscent of Aboriginal dot paintings. Some of his work is exhibited here. Maxine's, located in a wooden house that appears to be sinking into the Tonlé Sap River, is a beautiful getaway from the bustle on Sisowath Quay. It opens in the late afternoon (until 11 P.M., closed Mon.) and is a great place to watch the sunset. Ask any of the *motodups* or tuk-tuks along the riverfront for a lift.

THE ARTS
Art Galleries

The popular **Art Café** (84, Street 108, tel. 012/834517, www.artcafe-phnom-penh.com, daily 11 A.M.–11 P.M.) hosts regular exhibitions and musical performances of Khmer and international artists in an upscale bohemian environment. It serves Alsace-Palatinate cuisine, along with a selection of wines from around the region.

The smart and relaxed **Java Café and Gallery** (56 Sihanouk Blvd., tel. 023/987420, www.javaarts.org, daily 7 A.M.–10 P.M.), close to the Independence Monument, puts on regular exhibitions of Khmer and foreign artists (openings are often packed). Its first floor balcony location with views across the park; a great menu of coffees, teas, and sumptuous snacks (including great sandwiches and vegetarian dishes from US$4); free Wi-Fi; and a regular expat crowd have also made the Java Café a popular breakfast and lunch spot. Check the website for events.

Theater and Performance

Located right on the river, the **Chaktomuk Theatre** (tel. 023/725119) hosts occasional culture performances. Call for details.

The **Sovanna Phum Arts Association** (111, Street 360, tel. 023/221932) puts on traditional performances, including dance and shadow puppetry every Friday and Saturday.

Cinemas

There are numerous cinemas scattered around the city, usually showing home-grown horror flicks or badly dubbed Thai and Hollywood movies.

The **Mekong River Restaurant** (tel. 023/991159), on the corner of Sisowath Quay and Street 118, shows two documentaries every day. *Pol Pot: The History of Genocide* is on at 11 A.M., 2 P.M., 7 P.M., and 9 P.M. A film on land mines is always shown an hour later. Entrance costs US$3.

Cultural Centers

Meta House (6, Street 264, tel. 023/224140, www.meta-house.com) is Phnom Penh's first art, media, and communication center, offering a forum for artists from around the world. The center hosts exhibitions and workshops and puts on regular events, including film shows. The rooftop terrace has a restaurant, where the films are screened; it's a great place to hang out and connect with local and expat artists. Check the website for events. Films generally start at 7 P.M.

The **French Cultural Center** (214, Street 184, tel. 023/721383) organizes regular film events, often showing vintage French movies. The center's movie schedule is published in the *Phnom Penh Post*.

Shopping

MARKETS
◖ Central Market

This attractive art deco structure (daily 7 A.M.–5 P.M.) is locally known as Phsar Thmey, which actually means New Market. This ochre-colored dome-like structure is one of the city's most prominent landmarks. The market stands on a former swamp area, which was drained by the French in 1935. The building was completed in 1937. Around the main entrance you are likely to be accosted by mine victims selling photocopied books. They can be persistent, but keep in mind, that this is the only way they can make a living. Also around the entrance, numerous vendors are selling T-shirts with slogans such as "I survived Cambodia," alongside a bewildering variety of cheapish souvenirs and curios. The bootleg bookstalls sell decent maps of Cambodia, as well as beautifully simple, hand-drawn greeting cards, produced with watercolors and featuring traditional Cambodian themes.

All around the market building, a little city of covered stalls sells mostly fresh food. Simple food stalls offer noodles and fresh coffee. Inside the cavernous building, hundreds of small shops sell fake watches and sunglasses, cheap electronics, brand-name clothes and DVDs, also fake, as well as fresh meat, which is definitely real. Numerous money-changers ply their trade here; if you are after riel, they offer roughly the same rates as the banks and it's quicker. Sometimes, blind musicians, guided by street children, pass through the market area, singing somber tunes while playing the *tro,* a two-stringed fiddle-like instrument whose sound-box is covered in snakeskin.

Phsar Thmey is at the eastern end of Kampuchea Krom Boulevard, about a five-minute walk along Street 130 from the riverside. At the time of writing, the main building was being renovated and many of the vendors were forced to temporarily move outside.

PHNOM PENH

© AROON THAEWCHATTURAT

inside the art deco Central Market

The Russian Market

During the Vietnamese presence in the 1980s, Russians often came shopping here for Western goods they could not get elsewhere, hence the name. In the late 1990s, it was also possible to purchase large quantities of marijuana as well as AK-47s here, but the bad old times are long gone. Known as Phsar Toul Tom Poung in Khmer, the Russian Market (daily 7 A.M.–5 P.M.) has no architectural finesse—and, in the summer, the narrow aisles between the stalls crammed with products can seem like the inside of a microwave—but the market does retain a very special atmosphere. The choice of curios and souvenirs is much more varied here than at Central Market. Decent-quality silk, as well as silver, gold, precious stones, large wooden carvings, and opium pipes are also on display. The Russian Market has the largest selection of bootleg CDs and bootleg DVD movies in the country. Most shops let customers test the discs prior to purchase. Other sections of the market specialize in machine tools and other local products and there are numerous food vendors and coffee stalls both inside the area and in the surrounding streets. Located in the far south of the city, off Mao Tse Tung Boulevard, the Russian Market is best visited after a trip to nearby Tuol Sleng.

Old Market

Phsar Chas (daily 7 A.M.–5 P.M.), also known as Old Market, is definitely worth a visit, though it's not a tourist market. Located near the riverfront between Streets 108 and 106, the various stalls sell mostly fruits and vegetables, which makes for a rather fermented atmosphere on hot days. In the late afternoon, this market is crowded with thousands of shoppers and becomes a great place for photographs.

Orussey Market

This general market (daily 7 A.M.–5 P.M.) used to be located in the middle of the road on the northern side of the Olympic Stadium, but it's since been moved into a concrete building on Street 182. Orussey is worth a visit for the sheer

tightly packed stalls in the Russian Market

variety of products on offer, though none of it is particularly geared towards tourists. Expect food, clothes, and household goods.

The Night Market

A night market, selling curios, clothes, and souvenirs is held every weekend (Friday to Sunday) between Streets 106 and 108, just off Sisowath Quay. Popular with locals and tourists, more than a hundred stalls offer clothes, souvenirs (not all of them made in Cambodia), and a huge selection of food. Be sure to haggle.

SHOPPING MALLS
The Sorya Mall

Phnom Penh's first shopping mall, located on Street 63 near the Central Market, comes complete with an escalator, ridden with fascination and respect by out-of-towners. It's filled with the usual bootleg products—everything from video games, computer software, DVDs, and handbags. Somewhat more genuine are branches of BB Burgers and the Pizza Company, which offer familiar-looking fast food, prepared for Asian palates. On the roof, a cinema, a roller-skating rink, and a games arcade are very popular with the city's teenagers. Views across the city are spectacular.

The Paragon Mall

Some Cambodians can afford to buy sofas for US$3,000 a pop. The Paragon Mall on Street 214, near the Independence Monument, is proud to be the most ostentatious shopping space in the capital and the country—until the day a larger mall opens, of course. The rapidly growing number of middle-class Cambodians make this mall profitable, while a third of the population continues to survive on US$0.50 a day. But the Paragon is more than a place full of stuff for people who already have everything: There's a large supermarket on the ground floor as well as a good food court.

CRAFT AND BOOK SHOPS

Street 178 has been dubbed Gallery Street. Running alongside the National Museum,

the road was initially home to family workshops that churned out garish paintings of Angkor Wat. Many of these shops are still operating and some of the colors on the huge canvasses are positively psychedelic. In recent years, a number of galleries and boutiques selling contemporary art and crafts have joined the more traditional artists and have created a small but vibrant scene that hosts regular exhibitions and has begun to publish books on modern Khmer art and architecture. A number of NGO craft shops are also found in the area.

Reyum (47, Street 178, tel. 023/217149, www.reyum.org) is the most notable gallery. It regularly shows the work of Cambodia's most cutting-edge artists, runs its own publishing house, and sells a wide variety of books on Asian art. Books published include nonfiction works on art, but the company also puts out Khmer language books for children. Profits are reinvested in publishing additional titles. Besides exhibitions, Reyum presents lectures and music performances. The Reyum Institute, a Cambodian NGO, runs a free arts school for Cambodian children. Visiting artists from the United States, Canada, France, Japan, and other Asian countries introduce students to new artistic techniques.

Asasax Art Gallery (192, Street 178, tel. 023/217795, www.asasaxart.com.kh) is another exhibition space worth a visit. Mr. Asasax is a well-established Cambodian artist who sells his original work (paintings from around US$25), which often feature traditional motifs executed with contemporary techniques.

Stephane Delapree, a French-Canadian cartoonist, paints extremely colorful canvasses with Cambodian scenes. The artist calls his work Happy Paintings (www.happypainting.net) and even former King Sihanouk has praised Delapree for his contribution to contemporary Cambodian art. Stef's paintings can be viewed in his gallery on Sisowath Quay, underneath the FCC and next to Café Fresco.

For traditional Khmer sculptures made from wood, bronze, and sandstone, visit

Art of Khmer Angkor (29, Street 178, tel. 012/555450). This is the workshop of Chan Sim, who was a professor at the Royal Art University before the Khmer Rouge years and has since resumed teaching. Small pieces start at around US$10.

Colors of Cambodia (373 Sisowath Quay, tel. 023/217974), around the corner from Street 278, offer a wide variety of handicrafts from around the country. All the crafts are supplied through NGOs in order to assist in generating income for small local businesses. Products are made from silk, leather, and wood, and include handbags, clothes, cooking utensils, and pottery. Beautiful handbags made from natural fibers cost around US$10.

Nearby, on Street 172, Active Help Cambodia (tel. 098/701428, www.active-helpcambodia.com) runs the **Aw-Kun Shop + Help.** The shop sells handicrafts (such as silk and cotton scarves), coffee, and fruit wine in order to help vulnerable women around Phnom Penh. Street 240 also has a fair number of resident art and crafts shops (as well as great bars and restaurants). Drop by the **Magic Gecko** at #87 for silk products, some of them geckos, and the upmarket **Le Lezard Bleu** at #61 for high-quality Khmer art, both traditional and contemporary.

Monument Books (111, Norodom Blvd., tel. 023/217617) is Phnom Penh's largest (and, unfortunately only) outlet for new books. Having no competition, Monument's prices are high. Nevertheless, there is a wide selection of regional and international titles. Travel guides and run-of-the-mill thrillers are especially well stocked, as is a great deal of academic background on the region. There's also a small branch at the airport.

For a great selection of used books, visit **Bohr's Books** (5 Sothearos Blvd., tel. 012/929148), near the National Museum. Unlike in many shops in the city, books are clearly ordered and easy to find, and the owner, Chea Sopheap, is a genuine bookseller—he knows what people read. Bohr's Books buys and exchanges secondhand titles and prices are very reasonable.

Sports and Recreation

SWIMMING
Numerous Phnom Penh hotels have swimming pools; the largest hotel pools are at the **InterContinental** (296 Mao Tse Tung, tel. 023/424888, www.intercontinental.com) and **Le Royal** (Street 92, tel. 023/981888, www.raffles.com/EN_RA/Property/RLR). For a cheaper alternative, check out the pool at the Olympic Stadium, which has the only Olympic-size pool in town.

The **Phnom Penh Water Park** (tel. 023/881008, daily 9:30 A.M.–6 P.M., US$3 weekends, US$2 weekdays), on the Airport Road, is extremely popular with Cambodians, who flock here on the weekends to enjoy water slides and a wave pool. It's pretty quiet on weekdays, when the large slides are closed, and is least crowded in the mornings.

BOWLING
Phnom Penh's only bowling alley is **Super Bowl** (113, Mao Tse Tung Blvd., daily 10 A.M.–very late). Sessions cost US$6–9 an hour, depending on the time of day.

CYCLING
Many of the cheaper guesthouses rent bicycles for around US$3 a day.

GOLF
Phnom Penh's 18-hole golf course, the **Cambodia Golf and Country Club** (Office 56, Street 222, tel. 023/363666), lies 35 kilometers south of the city along Route 4.

GO-CARTS
Kambol Go-Karting (daily 9 A.M.–6 P.M.) has a kilometer long track off Route 4, seven

kilometers past the airport. It's US$10 for a 10-minute race.

SHOOTING RANGE

In the same area as Kambol Go-Karting, Phnom Penh's shooting range offers visitors the opportunity to shoot an AK-47 (US$30 for 30 rounds) or throw a hand grenade. The range has been threatened with closure by a government keen to avoid promoting violence.

HORSE RIDING

If you fancy learning to ride in Cambodia, contact the **Cambodia Equestrian Centre** (tel. 012/231755), an international standard riding school located at Northbridge School on Northbridge Road.

MOTORBIKE RENTAL

One of the cheapest places to rent a motorbike in Phnom Penh is **Lucky Lucky** (413 Monivong Blvd., tel. 023/220988). A better option—with more reliable bikes for rent—might be **Angkor Dirt Bikes** (www.toursintheextreme.com).

TRADITIONAL MASSAGE AND SPA

Cambodia has its own traditional massage technique. There are plenty of massage places in Phnom Penh, some more traditional than others. Recently, several boutique spas have opened around town. The swankiest is the **Amara Spa** (tel. 023/998730) on the corner of Sisowath Quay and Street 110. Also popular is the **Amret Spa,** south of Sihanouk Boulevard (2, Street 57, tel. 023/997994). For Thai- and Balinese-style massage, head to **O'Spa** (4B, Street 75, tel. 012/852308).

GYMS

Most of the gyms in Phnom Penh are located in international hotels. Head for the **Amrita Spa** (tel. 023/981888, daily 6 A.M.–10 P.M.) at Le Royal or the **Clark Hatch Fitness Center** (tel. 023/424888, ext. 5000, weekdays 6 A.M.–10 P.M., weekends and holidays 8 A.M.–8 P.M.) in the InterContinental. Early in the morning, locals exercise on the square in front of the Royal Palace.

KHMER LANGUAGE COURSES

If you are going to spend some time in the country, you might want to learn some Khmer. There are several language schools in town; call **Cambodian Language Lessons** (19, Street 282, tel. 012/345858) or **Cambodian School of Language** (46, Street 360, tel. 012/552532), for schedules and rates.

ARCHITECTURAL TOURS

KA-Tours (www.ka-tours.org), an NGO promoting and documenting modern Khmer architecture, offer tours around the city that take in Phnom Penh's architectural landmarks from the 1960s, including the Olympic Stadium.

RIVER CRUISES

Numerous boat operators offer short and long river journeys. Short hops along the Tonlé Sap River are best at sunrise for views of Phnom Penh's skyline. Boats can be found along the riverfront between Street 130 and Street 178, as well as near the pier at Street 104. Outings should be around US$10 an hour. Day trips and longer excursions are offered by **Satra Boat** (tel. 012/432456).

Accommodations

Phnom Penh offers accommodations for every budget, from cheap flophouses where a double room costs a few dollars to exquisite boutique and luxury hotels that will set you back hundreds of dollars a night. All room rates are for double occupancy in high season, but, given Cambodia's currently booming economy, expect prices to rise, especially at the lower end of the market.

BOENG KAK AND WAT PHNOM AREA
Under US$15
The area to the west of the Boeng Kak Lake is Phnom Penh's backpacker ghetto, for now. Right next to the city's largest mosque, a strip of cheap guesthouses and cafés cater to low-budget travelers. Plans to fill in the lake and turn it into a residential area became a reality in late 2008; flooding of some parts of Phnom Penh was the immediate result. No one, least of all the guesthouse operators in the area, knows if and when the area will close.

Among the best of the cheapies is **Number 9 Guest House** (9, Street 93, tel. 012/424240, US$5), which offers small, box-like rooms with fan directly on the water. The wooden terrace on the water's edge is a great place to enjoy a beer and while away lazy afternoons in a hammock. Number 9 has Internet, a travel agency, and a restaurant serving all the backpacker standards, from banana shakes to pancakes.

Right next door to Number 9 is the **Lake Side Guest House** (10, Street 93, tel. 012/725032), which offers similar facilities at similar prices. Small doubles are US$3, rooms with air-conditioning cost US$8. A boat that serves as a bar is moored to the hotel's wooden terrace.

Set back from the lake, the **Grand View Guest House** (4, Street 93, tel. 023/430766, www.grandview.netfirms.com, US$10) has decent rooms with air-conditioning and a rooftop restaurant, but lacks the nice lakeside vibes. There's a travel agent and Internet café attached.

Simon's Guest House (10, Street 93, tel. 012/608892, US$15) offers air-conditioned rooms, as well as an extensive breakfast menu.

US$25-50
L'Auberge des Jardins d'Orient (35, Street 75, tel. 012/413825, www.phnom.penh.biz/jardinsdorient, US$26) is a delightful hotel in a stunning and well-restored 1960s villa located in an attractive garden setting. Rooms are simple but clean and have air conditioning, hot shower, and TV. The hotel has a good French restaurant that serves a variety of Mediterranean dishes. L'Auberge des Jardins d'Orient is lively and a good place to meet people, and Street 75 is very quiet and relaxed.

US$50-100
Excellent fully furnished and serviced rooms, especially suitable for business travelers and expatriates, can be rented, either per night or long term at the swish **Colonial Mansion** (1A, Street 102, tel. 012/958619, www.colonial-mansion.com). Located close to Wat Phnom, this residential building offers studios, and one-, two-, and three-bedroom apartment packages, which include the use of a large pool, Wi-Fi, a gym, laundry service, drinking water, and car parking. Small units cost US$70 a night, US$700 a month; larger units are US$100–300 a night, US$1,000–1,600 a month.

Over US$200
The foremost address for colonial style and international luxury is **❰ Le Royal** (Street 92, tel. 023/981888, www.raffles.com/EN_RA/Property/RLR, US$260 doubles, up to US$2,000 suites), located in its own well-kept tropical gardens off Monivong Boulevard. In the late 1960s and 1970s, this handsome building served as a base for foreign media and featured heavily in Roland Joffe's movie *The Killing Fields* (though the Railway Hotel in Hua Hin in Thailand served as a stand-in for Le Royal in the film). This Raffles hotel has been restored to

its former glory. Expect first-class service along with plenty of old world charm and history. A large swimming pool and gym are open for guests. For those who can afford it, it's a great place to experience the capital. For those who can't, it's still worth a visit. Drop by for a drink and marvel at the splendor.

AROUND THE RIVERFRONT
Under US$15
🄲 **The Last Home Guest House** (21, Street 172, tel. 016/307134, last_home_gh@yahoo.com) is a budget hotel right in the heart of Phnom Penh. Less than a stone's throw away from the National Museum, and just a few minutes' walk from Sisowath Quay and the Royal Palace, the Last Home has long been a favorite with travelers and expats. Owner Sakit promises "real food" and "real people," and she means it. The Last Home, besides offering clean, decent-sized rooms with TV and shower from US$7, as well as larger rooms with air-conditioning and big windows to the street at US$20, serves excellent home-cooking (both Western dishes and a selection of Asian favorites). The guesthouse also arranges Chinese, Vietnamese, and Thai visas, and is a reliable place to book your onward tickets or arrange for local transport. The Last Home has good security, a definite bonus in the city center.

The **OK Guest House** (5, Street 258, tel. 023/986534), in a side street opposite the Cambodiana, is just that: OK. With its tiny cell-like rooms (with attached bath), it's not much of a holiday, but at US$4–6 a night for a double, US$10–15 with air-conditioning, there's nothing to complain about. What's more, the OK has a decent backpacker restaurant that seems to show the latest Hollywood movies back to back and a good notice board with travel advice. The staff can be moody and jaded, but is efficient enough.

US$15-25
The Indochine 2 Hotel (28–30, Street 130, tel. 023/211525, www.indochine2hotel.com, US$15–25) is relatively characterless, but it's reliable and clean—and in an excellent location close to the riverfront. Popular with tour groups, the hotel also has a restaurant and bar that never seems to close, but with so many attractive nightspots in walking distance, it's hardly of note. Double rooms have attached bath and air-conditioning, and the larger rooms also come with a window.

The reliable **Bright Lotus Guest House 1** (22, Street 178, tel. 023/990446, US$18, US$22 with balcony) offers large, simple but clean rooms with high ceilings. All rooms feature TV, air-conditioning, and hot water.

Comfortable air-conditioned rooms—some with a balcony—can be found at the clean and basic **Dara Reang Sey Hotel** (45, Street 118, tel. 023/428181, www.darareangsey.com, US$20). Guests who stay more than seven days get free Internet access, otherwise it's US$1 an hour. The in-house restaurant serves decent Khmer dishes for around US$3. The hotel can arrange for visas, transportation, and city tours.

The **Velkommen Inn** (23, Street 104, tel. 092/177710, US$20–40), which is under Norwegian management, offers five very clean rooms. The larger rooms are great, offering simple old world style with modern amenities—hot shower, bathtub, mini-bar, safe, and air-conditioning.

US$25-50
One of the most delightful hotels in Phnom Penh is the **Renakse** (40 Sothearos Blvd., tel. 023/215701, US$40 doubles, US$60 triples, including breakfast), a former royal guesthouse located in a stunning French villa in its own well-kept gardens directly opposite the Royal Palace compound. The rooms are basic and clean, and the hotel is a little threadbare, but the ambience is great. Unfortunately, the Renakse closed temporarily in 2009 and has allegedly been sold by the CPP to a private company, though this is being contested in court.

The **Hope & Anchor** (21, Sisowath Quay, tel. 023/991190, www.hopeandanchor-cambodia.com, US$20–45) is a British-style riverfront pub that offers cold beer, Wi-Fi, and pub grub, including a number of pasta dishes. Upstairs, it has 15 decent, air-conditioned rooms. The smaller rooms are windowless and a bit cramped. Larger rooms have great river views and are a better value.

US$50-100

The very green **Boddhi Tree Aram Boutique Hotel** (70, Street 244, tel. 012/565509, www. boddhitree.com, US$78) is submerged in potted palm trees and situated next to the residence of the British ambassador. This delightful small hotel has a terrace restaurant and rooms are well designed, clean, and bright. Rates breakfast and free Wi-Fi access. Note that the same owners have opened two more Boddhi Trees around town.

Located in a stunning colonial villa, surrounded by high protective walls and just around the corner from the Royal Palace, **(The Pavilion** (227, Street 19, tel. 023/222280, www.pavilion-cambodia.com, US$55–70) is one of the nicest mid-range places in town. The main building has smart and bright rooms with hardwood floors, some with a balcony looking out on the swimming pool and garden. A 1960s villa next door serves as an adjunct with equally fine rooms. The staff is friendly and efficient and there's free Internet for guests and a poolside bar.

The smart **(Bougainvillier Hotel** (277 Sisowath Quay, tel. 023/220528, www.bougainvillierhotel.com, US$81, US$113 riverside) offers large, beautiful rooms filled with lovely wooden furniture in a careful blend of modern boutique and old world styles. The higher-priced rooms have a riverside view with a balcony, while the others have windows out the back. The hotel restaurant serves very good Khmer cuisine, as well as great steaks.

US$100-200

One of the most luxurious addresses in Phnom Penh is the **Amanjaya** (1, Street 154, tel. 023/219579, www.amanjaya-pancam-hotel. com, US$155–250), an exquisite boutique hotel. ultramodern suites have subtle lighting, hardwood floors, and contemporary interiors influenced by Cambodian designs. All suites have air-conditioning, a safe, TV, Wi-

Fi, and a minibar. The equally well-designed ground-floor restaurant, K-West, is also recommended and serves a wide variety of Asian and European dishes.

One of Phnom Penh's modern upmarket hotels, the **Cambodiana** (313 Sisowath Quay, tel. 023/426288, www.hotelcambodiana.com, US$160–360) is right by the river and is a short tuk-tuk ride from the Royal Palace. It offers all the usual international-standard amenities, including a swimming pool, a gym, shops, and several restaurants. The huge in-house Q-Ba nightclub and casino is one of the city's trendiest nightspots, with live music, a huge drink selection, and regular party events. Rates include a breakfast buffet.

Right on the riverfront, **The Quay** (277, Sisowath Quay, tel. 023/224894, www. thequayhotel.com) is one of Phnom Penh's finest boutique hotels. Opened by the people behind the FCC, The Quay is a futuristic experience. Everything is white, with decor reminiscent of *A Clockwork Orange,* and the rooms are simple but luxurious. The windowless doubles (US$70) out back are a bit claustrophobic, but the front suites (US$120), with hardwood floors, spacious bathrooms, and balcony views of the Tonlé Sap are fantastic.

AROUND CENTRAL MARKET
Under US$15

The somewhat run-down **Capitol Guest House** (154A, Street 182, tel. 023/217627) is one of Phnom Penh's longest established cheapies. Rooms are cramped, but alright at US$5—though the US$14 charged for air-conditioned rooms is not quite justified. The Capitol offers reasonably priced day trips to numerous destinations outside the city. A decent backpacker restaurant is attached.

Diagonally across the road from the Capitol, the French-run **Dragon Guest House** (238, Street 107, tel. 012/239066, US$5) offers slightly brighter rooms. Guests can relax in the nice balcony restaurant that has good travelers' ambience. The menu is extensive and includes Khmer, Indian, and international favorites.

Also very nice is the **Spring Guest House**

(24, Street 111, tel. 023/222155, US$9 with fan, US$13 with a/c). The front looks like the entrance to a DIY shop, but the small and simple rooms are clean and bright. Long-term stays are welcome.

The **Bright Lotus Guest House 2** (76, Street 172, tel. 023/365640, US$7 with fan, US$14 with a/c) is a clean budget hotel that offers medium-sized rooms with attached bath. The guesthouse offers bicycle and motorbike rentals, but has no restaurant.

US$15-25
A step up from the rock-bottom cheapies is the well-maintained **Angkor Bright Guest House** (84, Street 63, tel. 023/221162, US$17–22). Large and simple rooms have wood paneling and air-conditioning.

US$25-50
Very attractive and comfortable, modern, air-conditioned rooms can be found at the small **Billabong Hotel** (5, Street 158, tel. 023/223703, www.thebillabonghotel.com), which also has a swimming pool framed by coconut palms, a great restaurant that serves a wide variety of Thai dishes, and a 24-hour poolside bar. Airy doubles with views over the pool cost US$39.

A little tacky, but a good value nevertheless, the **Flamingos Hotel** (30, Street 172, tel. 023/221640, www.flamingos.com.kh, US$25) is a Chinese-style, mid-range hotel with air-conditioned rooms. There's an in-house ATM, a pool table, a bar, a restaurant that serves Asian and international dishes, and a great rooftop bar. Foot reflexology, body massages, and a sauna are also on offer.

US$50-100
Yet another fine 1960s Cambodian villa is home to the **Manor House** (21, Street 262, tel. 023/992566, www.manorhousecambodia.com, US$38–60), a gay- and straight-friendly bed-and-breakfast with a decent pool, located in a leafy, private courtyard. Rooms are not large, but they're smart and very quiet, and there's free Wi-Fi.

The **Juliana** (16, Street 152, tel. 023/880530, www.julianacambodia.com, US$70–95), a Chinese-style inner-city resort hotel has more than a hundred well-kept rooms, a large pool, sauna, massage, and even a hair salon for guests. The in-house Vanda Restaurant serves good Western and Asian cuisine, while a second restaurant, the Shark's Fin, unfortunately offers what its name suggests. Nevertheless, the rooms are a good value and include breakfast. (With the superior rooms, lunch or dinner is also thrown in.) A free pick-up service from the airport is also included, if you book ahead.

The **Diamond Hotel** (172–184 Monivong Blvd., tel. 023/217221, www.diamondhotelpnh.com, US$60) is a good hotel for business travelers, offering large and clean mid-range rooms—some with balconies facing Monivong Boulevard. A Khmer and Thai restaurant serves decent main courses at US$3. Breakfast is included in the room rate (US$5 for nonguests).

SOUTH OF SIHANOUK BOULEVARD
Under US$15
One of the few real cheapies around Street 278, the friendly **Top Banana** (corner of Street 51 and 278, tel. 012/885572, www.topbanana.biz), is on the second floor of a Khmer townhouse. The common area is relaxing, but the rooms are a bit dark. It's US$5 for a box with a bed and a fan, or US$14 for a large, air-conditioned room. There's an attached restaurant offering standards and a travel service.

US$15-25
If you don't mind staying directly opposite the Tuol Sleng Museum, then the **Boddhi Tree Umma** (50, Street 113, tel. 012/565509, www.boddhitree.com, US$15–48) is a good choice. Smartly turned-out rooms in an airy contemporary style are located in a well-restored traditional Khmer house. The restaurant isn't bad, either, with plenty of healthy choices like salads and fruit juices. Service is prompt, if not particularly friendly.

US$25-50

There are two good mid-range choices on Street 278. The **Anise Hotel** (2C, Street 278, tel. 023/222522, www.anisehotel.com.kh, US$40–70) is a simple but clean and stylish hotel, with lots of traditional Khmer paintings on the walls and pleasant outdoor seating. The 20 air-conditioned rooms are large, spotless, and convenient. The larger rooms also feature a safe and a DVD player. The downstairs restaurant serves superior Asian food and international fare.

Across the road from the Anise Hotel, the **Amber Villa** (1A, Street 57, tel. 023/216303, www.amber-kh.com, US$45) is more traditional Khmer in its choice of decor. The property is professionally run, offering air-conditioned rooms with a safe, TV, DVD player, and an Internet connection. Some rooms have a kitchen. Breakfast, laundry, and newspaper are also included.

The intimate **Boddhi Tree Del Gusto** (43, Street 95, tel. 023/998424, www.boddhitree. com, US$70–90) is located in a colonial villa with a shady forecourt under rose apple and mango trees. It has just eight rooms, which are bright, airy, and air-conditioned, and there's a great café for meeting people.

Over US$200

One of Phnom Penh's top hotels and part of the international chain, the **InterContinental** (296 Mao Tse Tung, tel. 023/424888, www. intercontinental.com) has everything a business traveler or high-end tourist might desire. The InterContinental offers large, air-conditioned rooms and suites with modern amenities, a swimming pool, a nightclub, a gym, and conference facilities. Breakfast is included in the room rate and there's a decent spa and sauna. Standard walk-in rates for a double room are around US$250, with suites for up to US$3,000, but rooms are available from US$130 if you book online. Wi-Fi access costs a whopping US$25.

Food

Phnom Penh offers a vast culinary range and new restaurants seem to open every week. Besides food served at markets, there are countless Khmer restaurants—some of them roadside stalls, others fully air-conditioned diners. Food from the region is also present, with Thai, Japanese, and Indian restaurants to choose from. Finally, the selection of international eateries in the capital is simply astounding. If you're looking for a pizza, a steak, pasta, or a good piece of cake, and you won't have to go far. Most restaurants are very good value by U.S. standards, with dishes usually ranging US$3–6.

BOENG KAK AND WAT PHNOM AREA
Street Cafés and Bakeries

Among the cluster of guesthouses around Boeng Kak Lake, the **Lazy Gecko Café** (tel. 012/912935) offers a large menu of typical backpacker fare. There's comfortable downstairs seating as well as a number of private movie rooms. Guests can choose from over 400 (mostly Hollywood) movies for US$3 a showing.

The smart **Garden Center Café** (60–61, Street 108, tel. 023/997850, www.gardencentercafe.com, Tues.–Sun. 7 A.M.–10 P.M., US$5–15) has great ambience and an extensive menu of Asian, Mexican, and vegetarian dishes, as well as great fresh coffee. Located in an old terraced townhouse a few minutes from the river, the walls of the café are covered in reprints of 1950s Hollywood movies and pre-WWII French and British posters praising colonial efforts. There's even a strange photograph of a nun smoking a bong above the sink out back. Guest can choose between the bright and airy inside or curbside seating amongst tropical vegetation and a small fountain. A second Garden Center Café at 4, Street 57, offers a similarly extensive menu.

a baguette sandwich being prepared at a roadside stall in Phnom Penh

Khmer

The **Bopha Phnom Penh Restaurant and Titanic Lounge** (US$5–15) is everything it promises. Located on Sisowath Quay, next to the ferry dock for boats to Siem Reap, this multi-cuisine restaurant, in the shape of a ship, is very popular with Khmers. There's a long chrome bar inside and plenty of outdoor seating by the riverbank. Besides standard Khmer and international meals, vegetarians have a large choice, and there are also some pretty exotic main courses, such as stir-fry water buffalo with pumpkin. Occasionally, live performances by Khmer pop groups almost make the ship sink.

Asian

The friendly **Kabab Shop** (1, Street 104, tel. 023/992104, Sun.–Wed. 11 A.M.–10 P.M. and Thurs.–Sat. 5 P.M.–2:30 A.M., US$3–6) serves a wide variety of decent Indian and Pakistani dishes, including plenty of vegetarian fare (US$3 for a vegetarian *thali*).

A couple of doors down from the Kabab

Shop, on the same side of the road, **Monsoon** (17, Street 104, tel. 012/247832, daily 6 P.M.–2 A.M.) offers great modern ambience and more high-quality Pakistani food in a cozy but swish setting. Comfy couches, cool ambient sounds, and an appropriate wine list make this a favorite of the young NGO set.

International

Tell (13, Street 90, tel. 023/430650, daily 11 A.M.–10:30 P.M.) is Phnom Penh's most established German restaurant. Expect generous portions of international standards, especially German and Swiss dishes, served in a typically cozy yet smart atmosphere. The *Eisbein mit Sauerkraut* (grilled pork leg with fermented cabbage) is popular. Main courses generally cost around US$10–15, but there's also a large selection of Asian standards at more modest prices.

The excellent Italian restaurant **La Volpaia** (20–22, Street 13, tel. 023/992739) is located on the beautiful post office square and serves great pizzas, pasta dishes, steaks, and other Italian specialties. The restaurant is smart, air-conditioned, and comfortable, and it's also possible to sit outside and watch the bustle on the square. La Volpaia is open only for lunch during the week, but on weekends it stays open until 10:30 A.M.

AROUND THE RIVERFRONT
Street Cafés and Bakeries

Café Fresco (ground floor, FCC, tel. 023/217041, daily 7 A.M.–9:30 P.M.) offers excellent international delicatessen fare. Deli sandwiches with all imaginable toppings and great health juices battle for your stomach and wallet with freshly baked cakes—either to enjoy in a comfortable air-conditioned atmosphere, sold over the counter to go, or available for home delivery. There's a second branch on the corner of Street 51 and Street 306.

Just around the corner from Café Fresco is **The Rising Sun** (20, Street 178, tel. 012/970719, daily 7 A.M.–11 P.M.), a British-style pub that serves massive breakfasts all day—a popular hangover cure. There's nice retro-pop decor, curbside seating, friendly service, and a wide variety of magazines and papers to read.

Also close by is the upmarket **Corner 33 Café** (33 Sorthearos Blvd., daily 7 A.M.–late), a futurist coffee hangout that has the atmosphere of an airline lounge, with great views of the Royal Palace. Use of the Internet, either with your own laptop or the in-house screens is free, but the snacks and wide selection of international food served here are not cheap—expect to pay US$10 for a main course.

Khmer

The **Sinan Restaurant** (166, Street 13, daily 11 A.M.–9 P.M.) is a real hole in the wall just down the road from the National Museum. It offers extremely friendly service, cheap beer, and decent Khmer and Western food. Most dishes are under US$2: Loc lak is US$2, and steaks cost US$1.50, so don't hold your breath…but the chicken salad is excellent. There's an Internet café next door.

The **Kanika Catamaran** (tel. 012/848802) is docked on the riverfront at Street 136 and offers high-tea river cruises (daily 4–6 P.M.) and dinners (daily 6–9 P.M.). Proceeds go to an educational NGO.

Asian

The Chiang Mai Riverside (tel. 011/811456, daily 10 A.M.–10 P.M.) has been around for years and is located on the ground floor of a small shop house at 227 Sisowath Quay. Customers can sit inside the air-conditioned restaurant or curbside. The menu is extensive and prices are moderate (from US$4). The food is pretty authentic and not too spicy (though you can always ask for additional power). Vegetarians will also be happy here and the restaurant runs a delivery service.

Excellent fusion food is served at **Le Wok** (33, Street 178, tel. 092/821857, daily 8 A.M.–11 P.M.), a smart, modern, air-conditioned eatery on Phnom Penh's gallery street. It serves Asian and European dishes, including excellent green curries and a number of seafood concoctions at around US$10–15 for a main course; it also offers an extensive wine list from France and Chile. Le Wok is a great place for a romantic and quiet dinner.

The **Green Pepper Restaurant** (daily 10 A.M.–2 P.M. and 4–10 P.M.) is what I'd call cozy, and the extensive menu of standard Thai and Khmer dishes is pretty complete. The food tastes good too, though the cook is conservative with chili and spices. Main dishes are around US$4. Located opposite Bohr's Books at 6F Sothearos Boulevard, this is a good place for lunch or an early dinner.

The very chic **Metro Café** (tel. 023/222275, daily 10 A.M.–11 P.M., US$10–15), right on the corner of Sisowath Quay and Street 148, looks like a postmodern sushi bar, but actually serves great salads, sandwiches, steaks, and original and strange Asian snacks—like grilled squid with lychee and chili jam. The Metro has a take-away service and offers Internet access to customers.

Lemongrass (14, Street 130, tel. 012/996707, daily 10 A.M.–10 P.M., US$3–5) serves reliable Thai and Khmer standards, including a number of vegetarian dishes and great

Thai dips and salads. It's a relaxed, modern atmosphere, just a few meters off the riverfront.

Right next door to Lemongrass is the equally reliable but altogether different **(She-E-Punjab** (16, Street 130, tel. 023/992901, daily 10 A.M.–10 P.M., US$3–5). As the name suggests, the food is predominantly Punjabi, but many Indian favorites, from chicken tikka to lamb korma, are available. There are also quite few vegetarian options on the menu. A second branch has opened at 72 Sothearos Boulevard.

If you hunger for Vietnamese cuisine, try the modern **Maxim Saigon** (4, Street 130, tel. 012/868531, daily 8:30 A.M.–9:30 P.M.), which serves excellent *pho* (soup) for US$3.50, as well as a wide selection of other Vietnamese dishes.

A number of restaurants have opened along Street 240. Among them, the small and elegant **Frizz** (67, Street 240, tel. 023/220953, www. cambodia-cooking-class.com, daily 7 A.M.– 10 P.M., US$3–5) serves *chhnang phnom pleung* ("Cambodian Volcano Pot," a local version of a Korean-style BBQ), as well as a wide variety of good Khmer dishes, including several vegetarian courses that use local ingredients. Delivery is available daily 11 A.M.–9 P.M., and Frizz also organizes one-day cooking classes (US$20).

International

(Kandal House (239 Sisowath Quay, tel. 023/986203, daily 10 A.M.–midnight) is a friendly hole-in-the-wall eatery on the riverfront. It seems to play mostly 1980s rock music, serves excellent freshly oven-baked pizzas, and has a free Internet terminal for guests. Kandal House has indoor and sidewalk seating and serves a wide variety of cocktails.

For those who like their food and beer with a little bit of grunge, **The Frog and Parrot** (175 Sisowath Quay, tel. 017/494806, daily 6 A.M.–2 A.M.), a Welsh-run pub and restaurant, might be the ticket. This small place serves British pies, burgers, and a long list of Khmer and Thai favorites, all at around US$5, with curbside seating and friendly staff.

With its arty ambience (a large painting of American writer Hunter S. Thompson graces one wall), great international dishes,

a fruit vendor's cart

© AROON THAEWCHATTURAT

and Khmer standards **(La Croisette** (241 Sisowath Quay, corner of Street 144, tel. 023/220554, daily 7 A.M.–midnight, US$5– 10) is the perfect place for a sumptuous dinner. There are roadside tables and smart indoor seating, and eclectic music and a good wine list round out this reliably excellent restaurant. What's more, there's free Wi-Fi access.

One of the best places to watch the hustle and bustle on Sisowath Quay is the Mexican joint **(La Cantina** (347 Sisowath Quay, Sun.–Fri. 7 P.M.–midnight), run by Hurley, an eccentric but agreeable American who has been in Cambodia since the UNTAC days. The little bar-cum-restaurant is only open in the evenings and serves a wide variety of Mexican dishes (meals around US$10), cocktails, and beers. Customers usually gather after sunset when tables and chill sounds spill out onto the sidewalk. La Cantina is also an exhibition space and Hurley has managed to persuade the legendarily moody American photographer Al Rockoff (played by John Malkovich in *The Killing Fields*) to exhibit his finest work here. Stark and iconic black-and-white images of the fall of Phnom Penh have lost none of their harrowing effect, but the somber mood is tempered by excellent stills from Matt Dillon's film *City of Ghosts,* by equally renowned photographer Roland Neveu.

A couple of doors down the road from La Cantina, the long-established **Happy Herb Pizza** (345 Sisowath Quay, tel. 023/362349, daily 8 A.M.–11 P.M.) is nothing like your local Pizza Hut. Toppings include not just mushrooms, olives, and pineapple, but also generous helpings of marijuana. Do you want it happy, very happy, or extremely happy? By the way, the trusty weed has always been an integral part of the Khmer cuisine, long before Cambodia discovered pizzas.

A great vantage point to watch the sunset over the Tonlé Sap River is the ◖ **Foreign Correspondents' Club of Cambodia** (363 Sisowath Quay, tel. 023/724014, www.fcccambodia.com, daily 7 A.M.–midnight), better known as the FCC. Established in 1993 and long famous as a hangout for journalists, film stars, expats, and tourists, the FCC is located on the second floor of a beautifully restored colonial building. It hosts regular photo exhibitions and occasional live music events. Wood-fired oven pizzas are delicious, if pricey, but what you really pay for is the excellent ambience.

As much a great hangout as a restaurant, Phnom Penh's most established American Bar, the **Freebird Bar & Grill** (69, Street 240, tel. 023/224712), is a good place to drink a cold beer, meet people, and consume generous portions of excellent American and Mexican food in a gentle biker-style ambience. The Freebird Bar seems to have been teleported in from the United States, lock, stock, and barrel. Decor, music, food, free home delivery, and friendly service make it feel just like home. The humongous Freebird Burger is US$6.50, while steaks are around US$10.

AROUND CENTRAL MARKET
Khmer
K'nyay (25K, Street 268, tel. 023/225225, www.knyay.com, Tues.–Fri. noon–9 P.M., Sat.

7 A.M.–9 P.M., Sun. 7 A.M.–3 P.M.), which is Khmer for "ginger," is a modern place with a nice, cool ambience specializing in Khmer and vegan cuisine. Jackfruit and banana curries will set you back US$4. Try the carrot cake with soy ice cream for US$3.

Another good Khmer restaurant is the **Ebony Apsara Café** (42, Street 178, tel. 012/581291, daily 11 A.M.–midnight), which touts itself as a late-night eatery and serves a wide variety of Khmer and Asian dishes. The *tom yam* soup is not bad at US$2.50.

The Khmer bistro **Fizz** (42, Street 178, tel. 012/554421, daily 10 A.M.–10 P.M.) sports teen-friendly decor and serves Khmer and Thai dishes, as well as fresh fruit juices. It's a favorite hangout for affluent youngsters.

The **Café Mondulkiri** (84, Street 63, tel. 023/221162, daily 10 A.M.–10 P.M.) downstairs in the Angkor Bright Guest House, is a buzzing, smart restaurant. It's very popular with the lunchtime office crowds in the area, and serves Khmer delicacies, including pig's brain and black chicken.

Asian
The ◖ **Pyongyang** (400, Monivong Blvd., tel. 023/993765) is a truly unique dining experience. This restaurant is owned and run by the government of North Korea, a kind of advert for North Korean culture. The food, including *kimji* (fermented cabbage, a standard Korean dish), is great, but the main attraction is the cultural show put on by the all-female staff halfway through the evening. It's all very prim, proper, and socialist, with dance routines, a violinist who unleashes a sonic inferno on diners, and the ubiquitous karaoke numbers. The staff, trained in China, all speak English and are happy to converse about their country, given that they are cultural ambassadors. Expect to pay around US$15 a meal. The culture shows supposedly start around 8 P.M., but the timing can be erratic. Call ahead for details. The existence of the Pyongyang probably owes much to former King Sihanouk's friendship with North Korea's leader Kim Jong-Il. There's a second

branch in Siem Reap. Americans are welcome and they even sell Coke.

A row of small restaurants has settled on Sothearos Boulevard, just south of the Royal Palace. Popular among these is the **Himajin** (84 Sothearos Blvd., tel. 023/216641), a small Japanese eatery. Head here for reasonably priced sushi and sake. Not far away, the **Bai Thong** (100–102 Sothearos Blvd., tel. 023/211054, daily 10 A.M.–10 P.M.) has the stylish ambience of an upscale, family-orientated restaurant and serves excellent Thai dishes with a contemporary twist. Most amazingly, it's not expensive, with main courses around US$6.

Bites (240B, Street 107, tel. 012/856567, daily 7 A.M.–10 P.M.), a small but reasonably smart Khmer-Malaysian halal restaurant, serves a wide variety of dishes from the region, including curries and banana roti. It offers delivery and take-away service.

The **Peking Canteen** (93, Street 136, daily 11 A.M.–10 P.M.) is located on a small road between the Diamond Hotel and Central Market. It's in a row of several small Chinese eateries. Unlike the others, the Peking Canteen has an English menu.

SOUTH OF SIHANOUK BOULEVARD
Street Cafés and Bakeries

A branch of the delicatessen **Café Fresco** (tel. 023/224891, daily 7 A.M.–7 P.M.) is located on the corner of Street 51 and Street 306 and offers deli sandwiches, fruit juices, and cakes—much like its sister operation at the FCC. You can choose between the rooftop terrace or indoors with air-conditioning. A delivery service is available.

The small and very smart **Café Yejj** (170, Street 450, tel. 012/543360) is an excellent getaway after cruising the hot and dusty aisles of the nearby Russian market. There's a great selection of coffees, along with pasta dishes and cakes.

Khmer

The long-established **[Boat Noodle**

Restaurant (8B, Street 294, tel. 012/774287, daily 7 A.M.–10 P.M., US$5–10) is a few minutes away from the riverfront. This simple but atmospheric eatery, located in a traditional wooden house, overgrown by vegetation, is worth a visit. All the Khmer standards, as well as a decent list of Thai dishes, are on the menu and the dining experience is enriched by a group playing traditional Khmer music.

If you want to experience some of the best Cambodian cooking in the country, head for **[Malis** (136, Norodom Boulevard, tel. 023/221022, www.malisrestaurant.com, daily 7 A.M.–midnight), a first-class Khmer restaurant in its own delightfully upscale compound on Norodom. Guests sit among pools and vegetation, and can choose from an eclectic menu of contemporary and traditional Khmer dishes. Since it's open all day, you could indulge in scallop dumplings (US$2.20) for breakfast, frogs' legs with curry paste and palm wine (US$6.80) for lunch, and a baked goby fish with mango dips (US$10) for dinner. Naturally, there's an extensive wine list.

Right next door to the Rock Nightclub on Monivong Boulevard is the **Good Dream Restaurant** (daily 6 P.M.–midnight), a truly authentic and very popular Cambodian open-air eating experience. The Good Dream is moderately priced, with steaks, served with a peppery lemon sauce, for US$4.

Asian

The **[Banyan** (245, Street 51, tel. 012/850065, daily 7 A.M.–10 P.M., US$10) serves a wide variety of fantastic Thai cuisine in a relaxed candlelit setting—customers can choose whether they want to dine at a table or lounge on comfortable cushions on the floor.

A bit remote but well worth a visit is the **[Man Han Lou Restaurant** (456 Monivong Blvd., tel. 023/721966, daily 5 P.M.–midnight) in the far south of the city. This bright and gaudy Chinese restaurant not only serves great food—try the excellent dim sum or seafood salads, all around US$5 a plate—but also brews its own beer. To be precise, the Man Han Lou serves a blonde beer, a red beer, and a green beer, which has seaweed in it. The beer is made in huge copper vats on the premises.

International
The only Lebanese restaurant in Phnom Penh, **Le Cedre** (1, Street 360, tel. 023/997965, daily 11 A.M.–2 P.M. and 5–10 P.M.) offers plenty of Middle Eastern standards—including great *mezze*, with possibly the best hummus in town, as well as grilled meats, traditional sweets, and a substantial wine list that features Lebanese bottles. A set menu with more than you can eat is US$12 per person.

Information and Services

TOURIST INFORMATION
Phnom Penh's tourist office keeps moving and appears to serve no tangible cause. The best sources of information on the sights of the city are the widely distributed and free visitors' guides published by CanBy Publications (www.canbypublications.com). There are also a number of small pocket guides published regularly, focusing on the city's vibrant nightlife, as well as Phnom Penh's increasing dining and shopping possibilities. These publications live off the advertising revenue of the businesses they feature, so don't expect objective opinions, but as a source for sights and contacts, they are useful. Most hotels and restaurants stock copies.

LIBRARIES
The National Library
The National Library (Street 92, tel. 023/430609, Mon.–Fri. 8–11 A.M. and 2–5 P.M.) is located in a stunning and well-restored French colonial building dating from 1924. During the Khmer Rouge years, members of the Pol Pot regime used the building as lodging and destroyed many of the books. The library reopened in 1980 and now holds more than 100,000 titles in several languages. Special collections, including numerous palm leaf manuscripts, which can be seen on microfilm, have been established in recent years.

The Buddhist Institute Library
Located in a magnificent group of buildings adjacent to Hun Sen Park and the Naga World Hotel, the Buddhist Institute, founded in 1930, houses a large library (tel. 023/212046, daily 7:30–11 A.M. and 2:30–5 P.M.), which documents Cambodian culture and religion. The Kampuja Surya Bookstore, which sells a wide variety of books on Buddhism, is also on the grounds.

MONEY
Banks, usually with ATMs attached, can be found all over central Phnom Penh and usually open Monday–Friday 8 A.M.–3 or 4 P.M., and sometimes on Saturdays until 11:30 A.M. All ATMs, including those at the airport, dispense U.S. dollars. Money-changers can be found all over the city, and they offer a marginally better rate for riel than the banks. Large ripped dollar notes will not be accepted by Cambodian businesses. Credit cards (especially Visa, MasterCard, and JCB) are widely accepted, but businesses usually charge a few percent commission on transactions. Travelers' checks are accepted at most banks, at some hotels, and by some money-changers. Some banks with foreign-exchange facilities include CAB (439 Monivong Blvd., tel. 023/220000) ACLEDA Bank (61 Monivong Blvd., tel. 023/998777), ANZ Royal Bank (20, Street 114, tel. 023/726900), and Canadia Bank (265–269, Street 114, tel. 023/215286).

HEALTH AND EMERGENCIES
If you become seriously ill or sustain injuries in a traffic accident, then have yourself evacuated as quickly as possible to Bangkok or Singapore. For less-serious emergencies, visit International SOS (161, Street 51, tel.

023/216911 or 012/816911, www.internationalsos.com). This clinic also has a dentist and can assist with evacuations. Also recommended for minor injuries is the American Medical Center (tel. 023/991863), which has a doctor licensed in California and operates out of the Cambodiana Hotel.

Note that ambulances may or may not show up if you have an accident, and that emergency numbers (tel. 119 from 023 phones or 023/724891) often go unanswered.

The main local hospital is Calmette (3 Monivong Boulevard, tel. 023/426948), though it's not at all recommended. Also avoid all other hospitals in the capital. Cash or credit card payment is always expected prior to treatment.

Avoid buying antibiotics or other serious medications over the counter at small pharmacies, as many are fake. U-Care Pharmacy (tel. 023/222499), on the corner of Sotheoras Boulevard and Street 178, sells a wide selection of genuine medicines.

INTERNET ACCESS

Phnom Penh has scores of Internet cafés, from small hole-in-the-wall operators crammed with videogame-playing schoolchildren to high-tech outfits around the riverfront, from where you can make international Internet phone calls, Skype, and upload documents and pictures. All of them are pretty fast, as the days of dial-up are thankfully gone. Rates in the purpose-built-for-tourists places are around US$1 an hour. Numerous restaurants and bars now also offer Wi-Fi access to customers.

POST OFFICE

Phnom Penh's main post office is one of the best places to mail anything important from Cambodia. Located on its own square near Wat Phnom, it's open Monday–Saturday 6:30 A.M.–9 P.M.

TRAVEL AGENTS

Most hotels and guesthouses in Phnom Penh offer reliable travel services and can procure visas for neighboring countries. The few dollars extra you are likely to pay for boat, plane, bus tickets, and visas can save you lots of time and hassle. The Capitol Guest House (154A, Street 182, tel. 023/217627) is not a great place to stay, but it offers reliable and cheap trips around the Phnom Penh region and has its own regional bus service.

LAUNDRY

Virtually all hotels, from budget flophouses to first-class boutique hotels, offer a laundry service.

Getting There and Around

GETTING THERE

Phnom Penh is one of two transportation hubs in Cambodia (Siem Reap being the other). Regular buses and taxis travel to virtually all destinations in Cambodia from the capital.

Air

From Pochentong International Airport, it's a 20-minute drive to downtown Phnom Penh, a trip that costs US$9 in a taxi and US$2 with a *motodup* (motorcycle-taxi).

There is currently only one domestic route in operation, from Phnom Penh to Siem Reap.

Only one airline offers regular flights: Siem Reap Airways (65, Street 214, tel. 023/720022, www.siemreapairways.com), which flies several times a day.

Airports in the northeast and in Sihanoukville are currently being redeveloped and flights from Phnom Penh to these destinations may recommence in 2010.

AIRLINE OFFICES

Phnom Penh has the following airline offices:

- **Air Asia:** Sydney Supermarket, Kampuchea

Krom Boulevard, tel. 015/456001 or 017/908066, www.airasia.com

- **Bangkok Airways:** 61A, Street 214, tel. 023/722545, www.bangkokair.com

- **China Southern Airlines:** 53, ground floor of Phnom Penh Hotel, Monivong Boulevard, tel. 023/430877, www.csair.com

- **Dragon Air:** 168, Monireth Boulevard, tel. 023/424300, www.ce-air.com

- **Lao Airlines:** 58B, Sihanouk Boulevard, tel. 023/222956, www.laoairlines.com

- **Silk Air:** 219B, Himawari Hotel, tel. 023/426808, www.silkair.net

- **Thai Airways:** 294, Mao Tse Toung Boulevard, tel. 023/214359, www.thaiair.com

- **Vietnam Airlines:** 41, Street 214, tel. 023/990840, www.vietnamairlines.com

Train

The train system in Cambodia is dilapidated, the rolling stock is in terrible condition, and speeds average 20 kilometers per hour, so a train ride is only an option if you have lots of time on your hands. Two routes currently operate: Phnom Penh–Battambang takes more than 12 hours and costs around US$4. It departs just once a week, on Saturdays, between 6:20 A.M. and 7 A.M. It returns about the same time on Sundays. The second line runs every second day from the capital to Sihanoukville via Kampot at between 6:40 A.M. and 7:15 A.M. Journeys to Kampot take up to nine hours, and to Sihanoukville a leisurely 13 hours.

Keep in mind that you'll get there by bus or taxi in less than half the time. The schedules are likely to change as the railway system is about to be restored to pre–Khmer Rouge standards. It's possible to ride on the roof of the wagons, but be careful, as the tracks are wobbly.

Bus

Phnom Penh does not have a central bus station, so buses leave and arrive at different points in the city. Phnom Penh Sorya Buses

(tel. 023/210359) arrive and depart opposite the southwest corner of Phsar Thmey and offer services to Siem Reap, Sihanoukville, Kampot, Battambang, Kompong Cham, Tbeng Meanchey, Kratie, Stung Treng, Banlung, Sisophon, Poipet, and the Lao border. Mekong Express (87 Sisowath Quay, tel. 023/427518) has deluxe buses going to Siem Reap and Sihanoukville. Paramount Angkor (24, Street 102, tel. 023/427567) runs buses to Siem Reap, Sihanoukville, Battambang, Sisophon, and Poipet. Several other bus companies, most of them also leaving from around the Central Market area, offer similar services.

Most hotels and guesthouses can save you the hassle of booking your own ticket. Prices vary widely. Fares to Siem Reap range US$3.50–10. Buses to regional destinations generally leave between 7 A.M.–noon.

It's also possible to travel directly from Phnom Penh to Bangkok and Saigon. Sorya Buses have a direct connection to Bangkok, leaving daily at 6 A.M. for US$15. You have to change buses at the Thai border. Sorya Buses, Mekong Express, and a couple of other companies run buses to Ho Chi Minh City (Saigon) between 7 A.M. and 2:30 P.M. for US$10–15. Make sure you have a visa for Vietnam.

Boat

Due to improved road conditions, many boat services have been canceled in recent years, but it's still possible to reach Siem Reap via the Tonlé Sap Lake. Ferries depart daily at 7 A.M. from the boat landing on Sisowath Quay near Street 104. Journeys take 4–6 hours and cost around US$30. If you're planning to sit on the roof, wear strong sun block. Most hotels and guesthouses can save you the hassle of booking your own ticket.

A far more luxurious alternative is a three-day trip on a traditional wooden riverboat with Companies Fluevial Du Mekong (tel. 012/240859, www.cfmekong.com).

Taxi

Taxis ply many regional routes, either as private hire or share taxis. Share taxis cost about as much as buses, but are extremely cramped, unless you buy yourself two seats. Share taxis generally leave from around Phsar Thmey (Central Market). The fare to Siem Reap is 50,000 riel in a share taxi, and to Sihanoukville it's 30,000 riel. In a private taxi, these routes cost around US$70 and US$50, respectively. It's slightly faster, but arguably more dangerous, to travel by taxi than by bus. Rising petrol prices keep these fares in flux.

GETTING AROUND

Most sights lie relatively close together in Phnom Penh and much of the city can be explored on foot. Phnom Penh does not have a public bus system. Regular metered taxis were introduced in 2008 (and you should insist on using the meter), and there are also on-call taxi services. Try Taxi Vantha (tel. 012/855000). A taxi from the airport into town costs US$9.

If you have lots of time, then grab a cyclo, which should cost 2,000–4,000 riel for short rides. The most common form of transport in Phnom Penh is the trusty *motodup,* the motorcycle-taxi. Drivers can be recognized by their baseball caps. Short rides cost the same as on a cyclo; for a full-day rental, expect to pay about US$8.

Alternatively, numerous tuk-tuks, which are safer and slightly more expensive, ply the roads of the capital. These motorcycle-trailers seat 4–6 people and are more comfortable than

THE CYCLOS

A distinctive feature of Phnom Pen traffic are cyclos – cycle-rickshaws, steered, for the most part, by grinning old-timers who slowly move through the city streets on the lookout for a fare.

Cyclos are not really suitable for long distances, but in the daytime, they are great for short hops or sightseeing trips around the riverfront. Expect to pay 1,000–4,000 riel for a short distance, US$6 for a half-day fare, though you'll probably be sick of the traffic before your time is up. Agree on a fare before you embark. It's not recommended to use cyclos at night.

motodup. Short trips should be US$1–2; for a full-day rental, expect to pay US$15.

If you feel that you must brave the Phnom Penh traffic by yourself, plenty of shops rent motorcycles (100cc–250cc), though the heavier bikes are hard to maneuver in city traffic. Only experienced riders should attempt to drive in Phnom Penh. Always wear a helmet, drive on the right side of the road, and keep in mind that medical facilities are lacking in Cambodia. Try Angkor Motorcycles at 92, Street 51 (tel. 012/722098) or Lucky Lucky at 413 Monivong Boulevard (tel. 023/212788). Both businesses also offer visa services.

Vicinity of Phnom Penh

Several attractive if low-key day trips can be undertaken from the Cambodian capital. The former capital of Oudong lies to the northwest of Phnom Penh on the way to Kompong Chhnang. The temples of Phnom Chisor and of Tonlé Bati can be covered in a day, with a stopover at the Phnom Tamau Zoological Gardens and Wildlife Rescue Center thrown in. The killing fields of Choeung Ek are close to town and tuk-tuk drivers often take

visitors there from S-21, the genocide museum in town.

◖ CHOEUNG EK KILLING FIELDS

Following the victory of the Khmer Rouge in 1975 and the construction of S-21, the torture center in Phnom Penh, prisoners—men, women and children—were brought to this site of a former Chinese graveyard and executed. In order to save ammunition, the guards forced prisoners to kneel next to freshly dug graves, into which they were beaten with shovels, hammers, and wooden spikes, before being quickly buried. An estimated 17,000 people were killed at Choeung Ek.

In 1980, following the Vietnamese liberation of Cambodia, 129 mass graves were dug up. Some of the skulls and bones of the victims found here are on display in a mausoleum in the shape of a stupa, though many graves were left undisturbed.

The site is open daily 8 A.M.–5:30 P.M.; entrance is US$3. Visitors can walk among the opened, overgrown pits near the mausoleum. For a better understanding of what happened here, you can hire a guide at the ticket office for about US$5.

In 2005, the city authorities signed the killing fields over to a Japanese company on a 30-year lease in order to promote the tourist potential of the site. The company is planning to build a visitors center and substantially increase entrance fees. So far only the road to the site has been upgraded.

Choeung Ek lies 15 kilometers southwest of Phnom Penh. Many *motodups* and tuk-tuk drivers know the way. Expect to pay around US$6–10 for a round-trip.

◖ OUDONG

Cambodia's forgotten capital, Oudong rises from the flat expanse of paddy fields north of Phnom Penh like a fairy-tale castle. A city here served as Cambodian capital from the early 17th century until 1866, when the government moved, for the last time, to Phnom Penh. There's nothing left to indicate that this was once a population center, but several stupas, temples, and shrines cover three hills, which have spectacular views across the surrounding paddies.

The main stairway to the highest outcrop takes about 10 minutes to climb. Here, on a broad terrace, stand three large stupas. The first, painted in ochre, is called **Chet Dey Mak Proum** and contains the remains of King Monivong, who reigned in Phnom Penh from

1927 to 1941. The middle stupa, **Tray Troeng,** contains the ashes of King Ang Duong, who reigned at Oudong from 1845 to 1859. The third stupa, **Damrei Sam Puan,** contains the ashes of Oudong's founder, King Sorypor, who reigned from 1601 to 1618.

A number of other structures can be found around the hillsides, including the remnants of several temples, all of them blown up by the Khmer Rouge. Some new shrines have been built in recent years. At the base of the hills, picnic pavilions have set up; it gets really busy here, especially on the weekends.

The base of the hill is also the site of a killing field, which is commemorated with a stupa containing victims' skulls. The area was heavily bombed by U.S. and government forces after 1970—and the temple was blown up by Khmer Rouge troops in 1977, and was fought over fiercely by Khmer Rouge and invading Vietnamese troops in 1979. The second stairway leads past murals illustrating Khmer Rouge atrocities. Entrance to the site is free.

Just below the hills of Oudong and in walking distance, **Prasat Nokor Vimean Sour** is a concrete replica of Angkor Wat, huge in proportion, playful in its interpretation of the nation's most important building.

Oudong lies 40 kilometers to the northwest of Phnom Penh on Route 5. The hills are clearly visible on the left side of the main road and there are several small roads leading though rice fields to the monuments. It's best to take a taxi to get there (for around US$15).

THE TEMPLES OF TONLÉ BATI

Tonlé Bati is probably best known for its lake, a popular picnic spot surrounded by small pavilions where locals like to relax, especially on the weekends. On the road to the lake, two Angkor-era temples, **Ta Prohm** and **Yeay Peau,** can be visited. Don't expect massive ruins as in Siem Reap, though Ta Prohm is quite impressive. Entrance is free.

To get there, take a bus from Sorya Transport (tel. 023/210359) headed for Takeo along Route

2. At the Kilometer 35 road marker, get off and grab a *motodup* to the temples.

THE TEMPLE OF PHNOM CHISOR

Perhaps more impressive than Tonlé Bati is Phnom Chisor, a mountaintop temple also near Takeo. The views from this isolated hill are stupendous, the 11th century temple is well preserved, and, best of all, you will have it virtually to yourself. Few visitors make it here. The climb to the top of the hill, 500 steps in all, will make you sweat. Entrance is free.

To get there, take a bus from Sorya Transport (tel. 023/210359) headed for Takeo along Route 2. At the Kilometer 52 road marker, a big sign will point you in the right direction.

PHNOM TAMAU ZOOLOGICAL GARDENS AND WILDLIFE RESCUE CENTER

This zoo is really more of a safari park. Tigers, leopards, bears, and elephants are kept in large enclosures, but predatory birds sit around in tiny cages. The animals on show here have been rescued from traffickers by wildlife NGOs. A ruined 11th-century temple sits on top of Phnom Tamau nearby. The facility is open daily 8 A.M.–5 P.M.; entrance is US$5.

The zoo is 39 kilometers south of Phnom Penh on Route 2. Take a taxi (US$30) or hop on a bus from Sorya Transport (tel. 023/210359) headed for Takeo and tell the driver where you want to get off.

PHNOM PENH

THE COAST

The Cambodian coast stretches 430 kilometers from the Thai border at Koh Kong in the west to the Vietnamese border at Ha Tien in the east. Much of the coast is lined with dense and inaccessible mangrove forests, sparsely populated, and bordering on the impenetrable jungles of the Cardamom Mountains.

Only four towns lie along the coast. The best beaches are found on the many forested islands that lie in the Gulf of Thailand. While some of these islands have become popular destinations for day trips, others continue to be off-limits due to the activities of smugglers, pirates, and the military. Still others are being sold to investors and developers and the next few years should see an explosion of island casinos, resorts, and eco-lodges.

The main port town of Cambodia, Siha-noukville, also known as Kompong Som, offers the country's best developed beaches. Two national parks are not too far from the city. Farther along the coast to the east, the sleepy French town of Kampot invites visitors with peaceful Conradian vistas. Kep-sur-Mer, commonly known as Kep, offers a truly surreal sight: a hundred ruined villas and holiday homes of Cambodia's 1960s high society lingering in the jungle. It's like the former Cannes of Cambodia. Beyond Kep Beach, the Elephant Mountains are home to the stunningly beautiful Bokor National Park and its eerie French hill station and numerous caves. To the west and the border with Thailand, Koh Kong is just emerging from years of isolation and offers some exciting adventure trips to waterfalls and jungles.

HIGHLIGHTS

◖ Phnom Chhnork and Phnom Sorsia Caves: Spectacular mountain views and caves containing Buddha shrines and bat populations make for an interesting day trip out of Kampot (page 164).

◖ Bokor National Park: Visit one of Cambodia's most spectacular national parks and trek to the remote French hill station with its eerie casino (page 164).

◖ Ghost Villas of Kep: Walk through spooky, ruined holiday villas of Cambodia's former elite in a slowly reawakening beach resort (page 167).

◖ Koh Tonsay: The locals call it Rabbit Island, as it apparently looks like a rabbit from the air. Once a prison for political undesirables, Koh Tonsay offers one great beach, some beautiful walks, and very basic accommodation (page 171).

◖ Caves of Kompong Trach: Secret tunnels, ancient Buddha shrines, and jungle vegetation make these caves beyond Kep a great adventure destination (page 172).

◖ Angkor Borei: Reached via a magical boat ride in the rainy season, these remote Angkor-era ruins see few visitors (page 173).

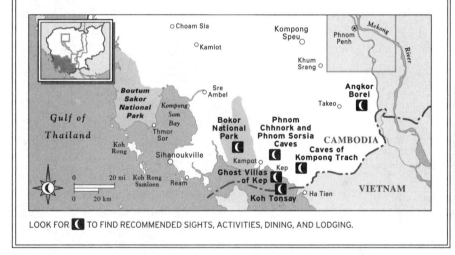

LOOK FOR ◖ TO FIND RECOMMENDED SIGHTS, ACTIVITIES, DINING, AND LODGING.

PLANNING YOUR TIME

The beaches around Sihanoukville are the main draw—and are an excellent place to relax after traveling the dusty Cambodian roads. In the far east of Cambodia, close to the Vietnamese border, Kep, Kampot, and Bokor provide enough distractions to spend a week. Koh Kong, near the Thai border in the west, is only just starting to develop, but with interesting jungle treks and two dive shops, a few days stop here before crossing into Thailand can make for great adventure. A nice side-trip could be the Kirirom National Park, a surprisingly temperate mountain region 120 kilometers northeast of Sihanoukville.

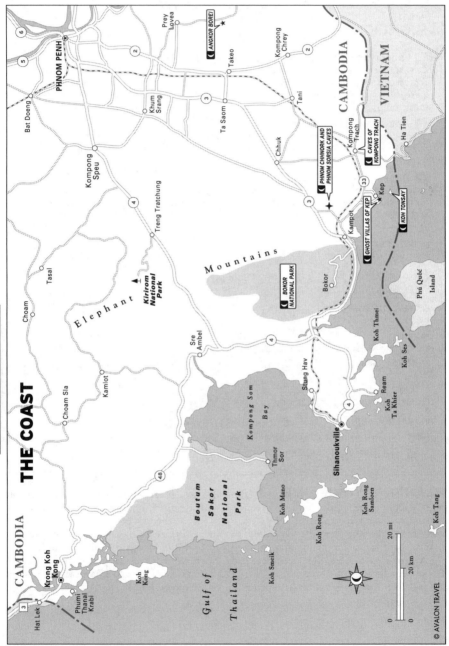

THE COAST

Sihanoukville (Kompong Som)

Sihanoukville is Cambodia's most modern city. It lacks colonial flair, and while a few examples of New Khmer Architecture from the 1960s survive, today's downtown area looks like any medium-sized Asian town. The port has reopened (it is closed to the general public though) and serves primarily as a container port, while cruise ships berth regularly as well. Commercial activities may well expand considerably once the railway line from Phnom Penh has been fixed.

Sihanoukville has no real sights. The main attractions are the beaches. Visitors should bear in mind that the trade-off for deserted beaches is an at times down-at-the-heels vibe. Sihanoukville's *motodup* drivers are the most aggressive in Cambodia and gangs of children roam some of the beaches, so there's a real danger of having one's bags ripped off. What's more, much of the nightlife is sleazy. There's no better word for it, unfortunately.

HISTORY

Sihanoukville is Cambodia's premier beach town, but its origins have little to do with tourism. The town's beginnings lie in the late 1950s. At the time, both the newly independent Cambodian government and several foreign powers vying for political influence felt it advisable for Cambodia to have a real port city in order to increase trade and create a better connection to the outside world. French engineers and thousands of Cambodian workers (called coolies, or kulis, at the time) toiled for several years to build the port, while the money for the road from Phnom Penh, the so-called American–Khmer Friendship Highway, came from the United States. Materials were partly imported from South Vietnam, and in 1960, the port of Sihanoukville, the country's only deep-water port, was inaugurated by Louis Jacquinot, the then French Minister of State.

As international airfares became more affordable in the late 1950s, more and more tourists from Europe and the United States arrived in Cambodia; while most visitors came for the temples, the off-white sand beaches of Sihanoukville soon proved to be a major attraction. Numerous villas and the luxurious Independence Hotel, now restored to its former glory, attracted international jet-setters; early travelers also began camping on the beaches near town.

When General Lon Nol toppled Sihanouk in 1970, the town got its original name back—Kompong Som—which persisted under Vietnamese rule. But the beach paradise was short lived and when the Khmer Rouge came to power in 1975, all the fun, and trade, came to an end. Recovery only started in the late 1990s and now, 10 years later, the town has big plans in store, aspiring to become Asia's Acapulco—while risking ending up as Cambodia's Pattaya. Nowadays, Kompong Som is Sihanoukville once more, though locals use both names. For more information on the history of the town, try to get hold of a copy of Robert Philpotts's excellent booklet *A Port of Independence,* published by Blackwater Books in the United Kingdom in 2006.

SIGHTS

Sihanoukville has got few sights as such, but for a great view of the city, visit Sihanoukville Mountain, three kilometers out of town. It's all of 132 meters high and has an active pagoda, Wat Chotynieng, on top.

BEACHES

The main draw of the beaches around Sihanoukville, in comparison to nearby beach destinations in Thailand, is the lack of crowds. It's still easy to find a quiet stretch of beach. During the weekends, some beaches get crowded with visitors from the capital, but on a weekday it's pretty tranquil.

Some of the beaches have been partly redeveloped, and, since 2007, quite a few have been sold to foreign investors. Some local businesses—bars, restaurants, and

THE COAST

THE COAST

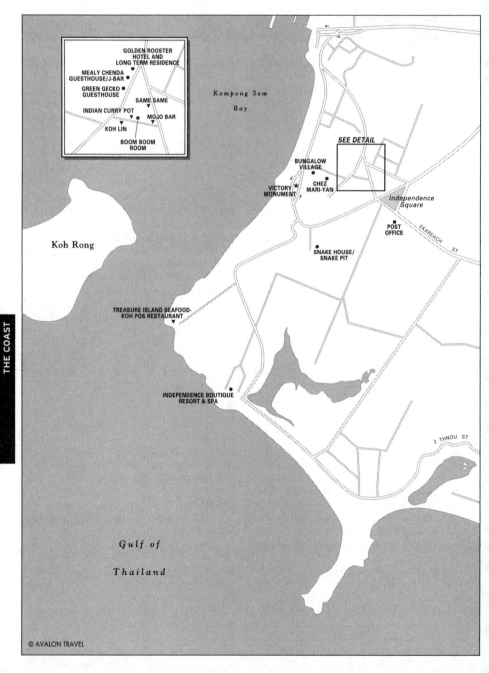

GOLDEN ROOSTER
HOTEL AND
LONG TERM RESIDENCE
MEALY CHENDA
GUESTHOUSE/J-BAR
GREEN GECKO
GUESTHOUSE
SAME SAME
INDIAN CURRY POT
MOJO BAR
KOH LIN
BOOM BOOM
ROOM

Kompong Som
Bay

SEE DETAIL

BUNGALOW
VILLAGE
CHEZ
MARI-YAN
VICTORY
MONUMENT

*Independence
Square*

POST
OFFICE

EKAREACH ST

Koh Rong

SNAKE HOUSE/
SNAKE PIT

TREASURE ISLAND SEAFOOD-
KOH POS RESTAURANT

INDEPENDENCE BOUTIQUE
RESORT & SPA

2 THNOU ST

Gulf of

Thailand

© AVALON TRAVEL

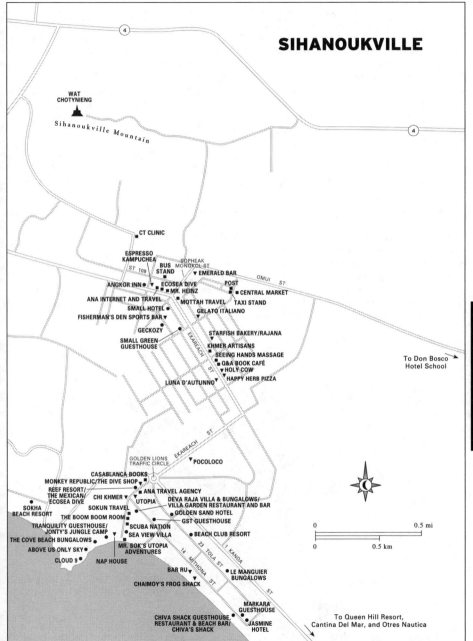

SIHANOUKVILLE

WAT CHOTYNIENG

Sihanoukville Mountain

THE COAST

CT CLINIC

ESPRESSO KAMPUCHEA
SOPHEAK MONGKOL ST
BUS STAND
ST 109
EMERALD BAR
OMUI ST
POST
ANGKOR INN
ECOSEA DIVE
MR. HEINZ
CENTRAL MARKET
ANA INTERNET AND TRAVEL
TAXI STAND
MOTTAH TRAVEL
SMALL HOTEL
GELATO ITALIANO
FISHERMAN'S DEN SPORTS BAR
GECKOZY
STARFISH BAKERY/RAJANA
SMALL GREEN GUESTHOUSE
KHMER ARTISANS
EKAREACH
SEEING HANDS MASSAGE
Q&A BOOK CAFÉ
HOLY COW
ST
LUNA D'AUTUNNO
HAPPY HERB PIZZA

To Don Bosco
Hotel School

EKAREACH ST

GOLDEN LIONS
TRAFFIC CIRCLE
POCOLOCO

CASABLANCA BOOKS
MONKEY REPUBLIC/THE DIVE SHOP
REEF RESORT/
THE MEXICAN/
ECOSEA DIVE
ANA TRAVEL AGENCY
CHI KHMER
UTOPIA
DEVA RAJA VILLA & BUNGALOWS/
VILLA GARDEN RESTAURANT AND BAR
SOKHA BEACH RESORT
SOKUN TRAVEL
THE BOOM BOOM ROOM
GOLDEN SAND HOTEL
GST GUESTHOUSE
TRANQUILITY GUESTHOUSE/
JONTY'S JUNGLE CAMP
SCUBA NATION
SEA VIEW VILLA
BEACH CLUB RESORT
THE COVE BEACH BUNGALOWS
ABOVE US ONLY SKY
MR. SOK'S UTOPIA
ADVENTURES
CLOUD 9
NAP HOUSE
14
23
TOLA ST
MITHONA ST
KANDA ST

BAR RU
LE MANGUIER BUNGALOWS

CHAIMOY'S FROG SHACK

0   0.5 mi
0   0.5 km

MARKARA GUESTHOUSE

CHIVA SHACK GUESTHOUSE,
RESTAURANT & BEACH BAR/
CHIVA'S SHACK
JASMINE HOTEL

To Queen Hill Resort,
Cantina Del Mar, and Otres Nautica

guesthouses—have been closed and some beaches may be off-limits to visitors. Whether the foreign investors build luxury resorts on their properties or whether the land was simply bought as investment remains to be seen. The same goes for several of the islands off the coast of Sihanoukville—at least one of which has already been turned into an exclusive US$3,000-a-night hotel/casino, a remote James Bond–type lair for Russian jet-setters. In 2008, the Cambodian government announced that investors who failed to build a business on their land within seven years would forfeit both the land and the money they'd paid for it. Development is likely to continue in this vein.

Victory Beach

Victory Beach lies at the bottom of Weather Station Hill, a couple of kilometers from the downtown area. Numerous resorts and bungalow operations have set up here, including some real cheapies. Despite the laid-back backpacker feel of Weather Station Hill, Victory Beach is Sihanoukville's most developed beach, with a new pier (called Russian Pier by the locals) and views of the port. Extensive development is likely to continue here at a rapid pace. An old Russian Antonov plane, mounted on poles in its own custom-built hangar, opened in 2009 as a bar and restaurant, squarely aimed at Russian visitors. The far north of the beach is called Port Beach, due to its proximity to Sihanoukville's harbor.

Lamherkhay Beach

This small, laid-back beach, also called Hawaii Beach, is south of Victory Beach and divided from it by a headland. The beach is dotted with a few bars and restaurants (but no accommodations) and you can while away the afternoons in deck chairs.

Independence Beach

Independence Beach, about four kilometers southwest of downtown Sihanoukville, is a beautiful curved bay with a thin sliver of sand. Unfortunately, this beach is private and off-

© TOM VATER

The decorated front of a fishing boat, at Victory Beach in Sihanoukville, honors spirits.

THE INDEPENDENCE HOTEL

The history of the Independence Hotel is a reflection of the fortunes and misfortunes of Cambodia in the late 20th and early 21st century.

Designed by French architects in the New Khmer style and helped along by the aesthetic touches of King Sihanouk himself, the Independence Hotel was the place to be in the 1960s, providing you were rich. Rock bands played by the ornamental pool, one of the few unrestored parts of the hotel today, and waterskiers zipped up and down Independence Beach, which backed onto a well-kept tropical garden with small fountains and mythical statues. With the Khmer Rouge takeover, the hotel closed and, in the late 1990s, functioned as a brothel ruin.

In 2008, the Independence Hotel finally reopened, now called the Independence Boutique Resort & Spa. The towering, at once futuristic and retrospective building has been beautifully restored, with carefully redesigned rooms and 1960s period furniture. The hotel is worth a visit for a drink, even if you don't plan to stay.

limits to the public. The western half of the beach is part of the Independence Hotel, while the eastern half was sold to a Korean company that has yet to develop anything here. Behind the beach, an old garden with statues and fountains survives from the 1960s. The road along the beach is open to everyone.

Sokha Beach

The swish Sokha Beach Resort, a couple of kilometers east of Independence Beach, gives this attractive kilometer-long white-sand crescent its name, but the beach is open to the public. The bars and restaurants on the beach are connected to the resort and, accordingly, are pricey. At the southern end of the beach, the giant tail of a *naga* snake emerges from the headland above the sand. Locals come cruising by on motorbikes in the evenings to enjoy the sunset.

Serendipity Beach and Ochheuteal Beach

Serendipity and Ochheuteal, no more than a couple of kilometers from the downtown area, are the two most lively beaches around Sihanoukville and flow into one another.

As you approach the sea on the bumpy road from the Golden Lions Traffic Circle, Serendipity is to the right as you face the Gulf of Thailand. It offers some of the best beach accommodations in Cambodia, with a handful of small, simple, and smart bungalow and hotel operations for small to moderate budgets, all located on a rocky headland. Serendipity Beach is the only beach in Sihanoukville with accommodation located right by the water's edge.

Ochheuteal Beach, to the left as you face the Gulf, is a long white-sand arc stretching almost into infinity, with several small islands rising out of the placid water in the distance. Accommodations are set back from the beach here, while the sloping sand is dotted with bars and restaurants. Banana boats and Jet-Skis are a real hazard, so beware if you're swimming far out from shore. A large part of Ochheuteal Beach is currently closed and is waiting for resort-style development. The road from the Golden Lions Traffic Circle to the beaches is the place to party at night, and is lined with numerous bars and budget to midrange resorts.

Otres Beach

Otres Beach, some four kilometers from town, is the most remote and—for the time being—least developed beach near Sihanoukville. Lined with casuarinas rather than palms, the beach is quite narrow. As there are barely any accommodations and just a small collection of restaurants, the atmosphere is very low-key and most visitors drop by on day trips from town. A few simple bungalow operations have set up shop here, but Otres Beach is waiting

THE COAST

© TOM VATER

Serendipity Beach

for development; it's reasonably likely that all the existing businesses will one day in the not-too-distant future be thrown out to make way for luxury casinos and the like. First a road has to be built—in the rainy season, it can still be challenge to get here. For now, it's enough for most people to laze around in the surf, eat excellent barbecued seafood, and have a cocktail for the sunset before heading back to the party on Serendipity or Ochheuteal Beach.

SHOPPING

Shopping options are more limited in Sihanoukville than in Phnom Penh or Siem Reap. Several small supermarkets stock most things visitors might need. In January 2008, Sihanoukville's Central Market, Phsar Leu, burned to the ground. Some vendors have moved into the streets around the former market, which has now been rebuilt.

Craft and Book Shops

Rajana (tel. 012/789350), downtown, above the Starfish Café, is an NGO outlet that sells arts and crafts from around the country. **Khmer Artisans** (Ekareach St., tel. 012/615111) offers silks, silver, and carvings. **The Boom Boom Room** offers a massive selection of downloadable music MP3s and trendy club wear, just like its successful cousin in Siem Reap. There are two branches: one at Weather Station Hill and one on the unpaved bit of road to Serendipity Beach.

For decent selections of secondhand books, check out **Mr. Heinz** (Ekareach St.) or **Casablanca Books** at Mick & Craig's, a restaurant near the Golden Lions Traffic Circle. Also worth checking out is the friendly **Q&A Book Café** (96 Ekareach St.), which has a wide range of Asian titles that can be rented or purchased. Vietnamese, Khmer, and Western food is served throughout the day, and the café also rents bicycles.

SPORTS AND RECREATION
Diving

Compared to neighboring Thailand, Cambodia's dive industry is still in its infancy. What's more, widespread dynamite fishing, limited infrastructure, and long journeys to the best dive sites have so far prevented an expansion of the small dive community. On the plus side, reefs in Cambodia are uncrowded and the type of factory diving prevalent in neighboring Thailand is entirely absent here.

Around Sihanoukville, a number of dive sites—some reachable in day trips, many others as overnighters—are worth checking out. Visibility is 10–25 meters October–June, and worse during the rainy season. The water in the Gulf of Thailand is 27–30°C year-round.

The best close-by dive sites lie off the islands Koh Rong Samloen and tiny, adjacent Koh Kon, which have decent reefs. Farther afield, Koh Tang and Koh Prins offer the best dives in the area, but require an overnight stay. Generally, visibility, sea life, and coral growth are better around Koh Tang and Koh Prins than closer to the mainland—and dives tend to be deeper, all the way down to 40 meters.

The last battle of the American war in Southeast Asia took place around Koh Tang, to the southwest of Sihanoukville, where Khmer Rouge forces hijacked a U.S. container ship, the S.S. *Mayaguez*. U.S. forces attacked the small island, bombed several installations in Sihanoukville and suffered significant casualties, though the ship was eventually freed. Traces of the battle are still visible on the island, as are the remains of a couple of people of unknown origin that have been left there much more recently. Koh Prins has two dive sites featuring shipwrecks.

Two fun dives during a one-day trip cost US$60–85, while PADI Open Water courses are usually just under US$300. All outfits listed here offer PADI courses, as well as snorkeling trips. All dives are led by experienced Divemasters.

Scuba Nation (Mohachai Guesthouse, on the road to Serendipity Beach, tel. 034/933700, 012/604680, 023/211850, www.divecambodia.com) has its own custom-built liveaboard and offers day trips as well as longer excursions. **EcoSea Dive** (225 Ekareach St., or near Serendipity Beach, tel. 012/654104, www.ecoseadive.com) also offers courses, day trips, and liveaboard dive trips and has its own simple

bungalows on Koh Rong Samloen. **The Dive Shop** (on the road to Serendipity Beach, tel. 012/161-5517 or 034/933664, http://diveshop-cambodia.com) offers similar packages to the other two outfits and is engaged in a number of social projects to help the community.

Boat Trips and Trekking Tours

If you're interested in a snorkeling trip, fishing, or a trekking tour in a national park, many guesthouses and hotels can make arrangements. For one-day trips, you can hire a tourist boat directly at the beaches. The following tour operators all offer a variety of trips, as well as rental vehicles, ticketing, and reconfirmation.

Sokun Travel (on the road to Serendipity Beach, tel. 012/965079) is one to try. **Ana Travel Agency** (downtown, on the road to Serendipity, tel. 012/915301, www.anainternet.com) also offer visa services. **Mottah Travel** (Ekareach St., tel. 012/996604) offers Internet services and makes travel arrangements. At the end of the road that leads to Serendipity Beach, **Mr. Sok's Utopia Adventures** (tel. 016/309464) offer boat trips to Otres and Ream Beaches, as well as to some of the islands.

If you're up for an island adventure, check out **Jonty's Jungle Camp** (tel. 092/502374, www.jontysjunglecamp.com). Jonty's runs trips to Koh Takeo, where you can spend a night or two in a hammock in the middle of the jungle.

Water Sports

Otres Nautica (tel. 092/230065, otres.nautica@yahoo.com), on Otres Beach, is a small, well-run sailing club. Small sailing dinghies cost US$10 an hour, or US$30 for a half-day. A kayak that can hold up to three paddlers can be rented for US$4 an hour, or US$10 for a half-day. Note that the islands should not be approached in sailboats, as they might cause damage to what little coral is left around there. A nearby Navy base should also be avoided.

Several businesses offer Jet-Skis for rent (US$50–100/hour). The most professional operator with the safest machines is the **Sokha**

THE COAST

Beach Resort and Spa (tel. 034/935999, www.sokhahotels.com). There have been several accidents due to reckless riding, so swimmers should be careful off Serendipity and Ochheuteal Beaches.

Sailing Trips

If you're looking for a few days of serious sailing among the islands, check out **Sailing Cambodia** (tel. 016/450964, www.sailcambodia.info), which offers one-day, overnight, and week-long excursions.

Fishing

If a day out catching big and small fish appeals to you, check out **Fisherman's Den Sports Bar** (tel. 034/933997), located downtown. This Australian outfit organizes day trips for groups of 6–12 people for US$34 per person. Trips leave at 8 A.M. and return around 5:30 P.M. The cost includes all the fishing tackle you need, tea, coffee, and lunch. Following the trip, the day's catch is prepared, cooked, and served with fries and salad at Fisherman's Den (also included in the trip cost).

Massage

Seeing Hands Massage, an NGO with blind masseurs and masseuses, is located on Ekareach Street at the eastern end of town. One-hour sessions are US$5. For the only real luxury spa in Sihanoukville, head to the **Sokha Beach Resort** (tel. 034/935999, www.sokhahotels.com), where you can enjoy massages, aromatherapy, body wraps and scrubs, a whirlpool tub, and a swimming pool.

ENTERTAINMENT
Bars
DOWNTOWN SIHANOUKVILLE AND WEATHER STATION HILL

The nightlife is somewhat limited downtown, so most visitors head for the beach bars in the evening. But even in town, a cold beer is never far away.

The friendly sports bar **Fisherman's Den** (tel. 034/933997), located on a small road south of Ekareach Street, is open late. A pool table,

darts, and a large TV showing rugby, soccer, Formula One, and other sports on request keep the customers happy. Organize your fishing trips here or come for a late-night drink.

Live bands and hostesses are not to everyone's taste, but that's what's on offer at numerous sleazy bars-cum-hotels around town. Most of these places also serve burgers, *lok lak,* and other fast-food dishes.

If you're looking for a standard Irish bar, look no further than the **Emerald Bar** (daily 10 A.M.–late), a somewhat dingy place on Sopheak Mongkol Street with a pool table, pub grub, cold beer, and even a few rooms for rent.

The **Mojo Bar** is an agreeable little corner spot in the center of Weather Station Hill. It offers cold beers, great music, and nice people, and stays open late.

The **J-Bar** (daily 6 A.M.–late), on the rooftop of the Mealy Chenda Guesthouse on Weather Station Hill, is one of the best places for a sunset drink. It's got great, uninterrupted views of the Sihanoukville coast.

The Russian-owned **Snake Pit** (daily 8 P.M.–late), above Victory Beach, is an adjunct to the bizarre Snake House. It features not only dancing girls and swimming girls, but also a pit of crocodiles (US$10 fine if you feed the reptiles). There's also a pool table and a vast selection of drinks, including many types of vodka. It surely is not everyone's cup of tea, but its jungle location, and well, lots of reptiles in and out of the water, can make for an interesting evening.

SIHANOUKVILLE BEACHES

Monkey Republic, the bungalow operation on the road to Serendipity Beach, has one of the most happening bars in Sihanoukville that does not cater to Western men looking for Khmer hostesses. The crowd is young and trendy and it's a great place to meet people. The pool table, loud music, and friendly management make this place a winner. The bar closes when the last guests stumble out, usually 1–2 A.M.

For those who never sleep, love to party, and care nothing about constant noise, **Utopia** (tel.

034/934319, www.utopiagathering.com), a night and day club, on the road to Serendipity and Ochheuteal Beaches, is the place to be and stay. Dorm beds, and that's all there is, cost just US$2 in the high season—and are free in the low season.

Right in the middle between Serendipity and Ochheuteal Beaches, **Nap House** is usually packed with party heads till 1 A.M. A variety of dance and rock music, a pool table, and a wide range of cocktails keep the crowds coming. The dance floor sometimes fills up with the resident lady-boy community, which makes the place all the more cosmopolitan and interesting.

Chiva's Shack is probably the liveliest bar on Ochheuteal Beach. The crowd here is young and likes to party nonstop, and the bar and restaurant are open around the clock. Chiva's also offers some very simple rooms without bath (US$5).

Another late-night place on Ochheuteal Beach is **Chaimoy's Frog Shack,** which organizes parties on Mondays and Thursdays. It sells the dreaded "Mekong buckets" (a small bottle of rum, a can of Red Bull, and a can of Coke)—deadly every time.

Discos

Pocoloco is an open-air disco-cum-bar on Ekareach Road (coming from downtown, it's just 100 meters ahead of the Golden Lions Traffic Circle). Expect rock music and hostesses, though it's a step up from the sleaze pits in town.

ACCOMMODATIONS
Downtown Sihanoukville and Weather Station Hill
UNDER US$15
The **Angkor Inn** (Sopheak Mongkol St., tel. 016/896204, US$6–15) is an old-style, Khmer-run guesthouse in town. It lacks flair, but it's clean enough and some rooms have air-conditioning, private baths, and TV. The restaurant menu includes a number of interesting vegetarian dishes and there's Internet access for 3,000 riel an hour.

The **Small Green Guesthouse** (tel. 034/399052, US$15) is located downtown in a fluorescent green building. This friendly Swedish-run place offers spacious, clean, simple rooms, all with air-conditioning, TV, hot water, and minibar, though the ceilings are a bit low. The restaurant serves Western dishes and Scandinavian specialties.

Geckozy (tel. 012/495825, www.geckozy-guesthouse.com, US$4–7), also downtown, is an old-school wooden guesthouse with small, cheap rooms in an adjacent concrete building, set in a garden. The restaurant is run by a Frenchman and offers predominantly German food.

The **Bungalow Village** (tel. 012/490293), on Weather Station Hill about 100 meters up from the beach, is situated in a lush and overgrown hillside rock garden overlooking the sea. Very basic bungalows (US$5) with mosquito nets are a throwback to the grand days of hippie-dom, but the larger huts (US$10–15) are pretty smart and have great ambience. All huts have spacious verandas to while away your lazy afternoons. The restaurant serves predominantly Asian food, as well as Western-style breakfasts.

The **Green Gecko Guesthouse** (tel. 012/560944, www.greengeckocambodia.com), a classic backpacker cheapie right next door to the Mealy Chenda Guesthouse on Weather Station Hill, has small, clean rooms lacking any kind of style. That said, the views across the bay from some of the rooms are fantastic—and there's a pool table, Internet, a TV lounge, travel agent, and motorbikes for rent (US$4–5 a day). And it's hard to complain about fan rooms for US$5 and air-conditioned rooms for just US$10. If you're on a budget, this place isn't bad.

US$15-25
The **Small Hotel** (tel. 012/716385, US$15–20) is a friendly Scandinavian-owned place downtown. The large, very clean rooms have thoughtful decor. The restaurant serves Western, Asian, and, of course, Scandinavian dishes.

A little above Bungalow Village on Weather Station Hill, **Chez Mari-yan** (tel. 012/916468, US$5–30) offers pretty basic but quite smart wooden bungalows in a garden compound. Some of the huts are linked by wooden walkways. Several rooms have air-conditioning, but most have so far stuck to fans. The atmospheric restaurant, located in a large wooden house, has excellent views across the Gulf of Thailand.

Also on Weather Station Hill, the **Mealy Chenda Guesthouse** (tel. 012/670818) is one of Sihanoukville's largest guesthouses. The countless clean rooms include cheap, cell-like rooms for just US$3–5. Larger, airier rooms, with reasonable decor and air-conditioning, cost US$20 and are often fully booked. Motorcycles are available for rent from US$4–5.

US$25-50

It's probably not for everyone, but the **Don Bosco Hotel School** (tel. 012/919834, www. donboscohotelschool.com) is not only a fine hotel, but also an interesting experience. Staying here also contributes to the economic improvement of the local community. Started in 2007, this compound teaches local youth all aspects of hotel management, including reception duties, restaurant management and cooking, food and beverage service, and housekeeping. In 2008, the school had 74 students. The rooms are a very good value and have beautiful bathrooms. Standard rooms for two are US$40–45, while the large and plain but well-designed deluxe rooms are just US$60. This includes breakfast, Internet, free pick-up and transfer to the beaches, and a good-sized swimming pool. All the staff are students at the school and do their very best to keep guests happy. The downside is the hotel's location, between town and Otres Beach, stranded in a wasteland that can look muddy and forlorn in the rainy season. So far, virtually all the guests have been members of the NGO community from Phnom Penh, which might lead observers to suppose the entire enterprise was embarked upon for the benefit of jaded missionaries—but

let's hope that tourists will avail themselves of this beautiful place one day as well.

US$50-100

Definitely not built by missionaries, the Russian-owned **Snake House** (tel. 012/308426, www.snake-house.com), just off Weather Station Hill and above Victory Beach, is completely unique—and reminds visitors that Cambodia is a country where things that would be unthinkable elsewhere in Asia can still happen. Really, there's nothing else quite like it. Smart and tastefully decorated concrete bungalows (from US$25) in Khmer building style stand clustered around a jungle-like dense garden, which is dotted with ponds. The larger rooms (US$80) have a somewhat faux–Imperial Russian flair. The restaurant is furnished with numerous terrariums inhabited by poisonous snakes and various lizards. An artificial tide pool in the center of the restaurant adds extra strangeness. So does the food, which includes red caviar sandwiches (US$15), shashlik (pork, liver, and chicken skewers, US$9), and goulash (US$7). The adjacent Snake Pit Bar features dancing girls and swimming girls—yes, there's a pool, as well as a pool table. Ostentatious, vulgar, over the top, and very 21st century, this place is almost a tourist site (and for those merely curious, it's US$3 to get in).

For a much more sedate and conventional vibe, head to the **Golden Rooster Hotel and Long Term Residence** (tel. 012/617943, US$50–75), not far from the Mealy Chenda Guesthouse. The large rooms feature heavy wooden furniture and, for the most part, great ocean views. All rooms are air-conditioned and have a TV and DVD player. The restaurant serves international cuisine, and a large swimming pool and a bar with a pool table round out the picture.

Sihanoukville Beaches
UNDER US$15

On the road down from the Golden Lions Traffic Circle to Serendipity Beach, **Monkey Republic** (tel. 012/490290, US$7) is a trendy little operation run by three young and enthusiastic British guys who thrive on their guests having a good time. The rooms are small, simple, clean, and functional, and there's a safe in each room. As the rooms are close to the bar, don't come here for solitude or quiet. The restaurant serves decent, typical backpacker fare at very reasonable prices. Asian dishes, such as tofu with noodles, are around US$2.50.

Chiva Shack Guesthouse, Restaurant & Beach Bar (tel. 012/360911, US$5) on Ochheuteal Beach has simple rooms (no attached bathrooms) in a wooden longhouse. It's okay for party-hardened types, but there are better options along the beach. That said, the restaurant is popular and serves dishes from US$2. Deckchairs line the beach in front of the bar and the views to the islands are great.

GST Guesthouse (tel. 034/933816) is one of the cheapies on Ochheuteal Beach. It has a staggering 100 rooms, all of them located in wooden longhouses. The rooms are small and clean, and cost just US$5–8 with fan, US$12 with air-conditioning and TV—but you might hear your neighbors snore. Motorbikes can be rented for US$4.

Run by a laconic Frenchman, **Le Manguier Bungalows** (tel. 034/933801, US$10) is set back from Ochheuteal Beach (about a two-minute walk). Eight smallish, bright green bungalows offer no great comforts, but are fine for the price. Motorbikes are US$6 per day; 250cc dirt bikes are US$13. The bar-cum-restaurant has a pool table.

US$15-25

A number of new and smart accommodation choices have sprung up on Serendipity Beach, the area's nicest beach. **Tranquility Guesthouse** (tel. 017/595191, www.tranquilityguesthouse.com, US$10–35) is not fantastic, but it's in a great location right at the start of Serendipity Beach. Rooms are located in a kind of wooden longhouse and some have air-conditioning. The boats for Jonty's Jungle Camp (tel. 092/502374, www.jontysjunglecamp.com) leave from here. The restaurant sells the usual international traveler's fare.

Farther along the beach, **The Cove Beach Bungalows** (tel. 012/380296, US$15–25) offers very comfortable, small wooden bungalows, located in a wonderful garden on the headland with great views of the beach. All huts have balconies and the view from the restaurant is great, too.

Managed by a friendly German woman, the popular ◖ **Cloud 9** (tel. 012/479365, www.cloud9bungalows.com, US$20–35) has a warm-hearted, family-friendly atmosphere. It offers just seven wooden bungalows on a steep hillside. All rooms have mosquito nets, spacious balconies, and fantastic sea views. The restaurant has a variety of Asian and European dishes, including good salads, from around US$5.

The **Jasmine Hotel** (tel. 012/761868, US$10–25), off Ochheuteal Beach, has decent rooms located in a large, modern Khmer-style building—all have TV and hot water, and either fan or air-conditioning, and some come with a view of the beach. The restaurant makes the usual international standards from US$5. In the same area, the **Markara Guesthouse** (tel. 034/933611) is almost budget. Clean and simple rooms in a concrete longhouse set in a garden come with fan (US$7) or air-conditioning (US$25), TV, and hot water. There's Internet access, a travel agent, and motorbike rental.

Located high above the beaches on the shady headland between Ochheuteal Beach and Otres Beach, the **Queen Hill Resort** (tel. 012/482418, www.queenhillresortbungalows.com) is a cluster of simple bungalows with fantastic views across the water. Fan rooms are US$15, while those with air-conditioning cost US$30. There's free Internet and the restaurant is a couple of minutes down the hill on Otres Beach.

US$25-50

On the bumpy track that leads down to Serendipity Beach, the **Sea View Villa** (tel. 092/759753, www.sihanoukville-hotel.com) has very smart, modern rooms with air-conditioning and a careful design. Some rooms

THE COAST

have no windows and are US$20, while absolutely huge rooms with windows (some with sea views) are US$30. Opened in 2008, the Sea View Villa is about two minutes from the beach.

Right in the center of Serendipity Beach, ◖ **Above Us Only Sky** (tel. 089/822318, www.aboveusonlysky-cambodia.com, US$35) has bungalows (new in 2008) well above the waterline, with fan, hot water, and fridge. Despite the lack of air-conditioning, which the owners plan to install soon, the huts are worth the price. There's no restaurant, but a small friendly bar at the water's edge will keep you from strolling too far.

The **Deva Raja Villa & Bungalows** (tel. 017/409395, www.devarajavilla.com, US$30) is a gay-friendly, family-oriented (no, there's no contradiction here) hotel behind Ochheuteal Beach. Rooms are very nicely furnished with plenty of attention to detail and great bathrooms with tubs and hot water. The American owner is keen to keep the area around his hotel clean, and the restaurant, which serves some interesting pan-Asian concoctions, is also recommended.

The **Beach Club Resort** (tel. 034/933634, www.beachclubcambodia.com), also opened in 2008, is set back from Ochheuteal Beach and offers clean, simple, modern rooms from US$25 with air-conditioning, TV and DVD player, Wi-Fi, safe, and minibar. Large triples and family rooms (US$65) are also available. The food in the hotel restaurant is Western-oriented and guests can book in-house massage. The highlight, though, is the decent-sized swimming pool.

US$50-100

The ◖ **Reef Resort** (tel. 034/934281, www.reefresort.com.kh) is located on the approach road between the Golden Lions Traffic Circle and Serendipity Beach. This smart, contemporary hotel has well-decorated and comfortable rooms facing a small pool. Standard rooms (US$42), all with air-conditioning and Wi-Fi, are well worth it. And if you'd like to indulge, larger rooms are US$80.

Off Ochheuteal Beach, the **Golden Sand Hotel** (tel. 034/933607, www.goldensand.com. kh) is perhaps the shape of things to come on the beaches. A multi-story, family-oriented place with heavy Khmer wood furnishings and more than 100 rooms faces a large swimming pool and the appropriately named Club Slotmachine. There's an in-house ATM and free Wi-Fi for guests. The rooms (US$35), all air-conditioned and with TV, are large, bright, and reasonably stylish. The suites (US$70) are huge and have tubs.

OVER US$100

The legendary Independence Hotel is now the ◖ **Independence Boutique Resort & Spa** (tel. 034/934300, www.independencehotel. net), by far the most stylish place to stay anywhere on the Cambodian coast at the moment. This unique place first opened in 1963 and was a popular watering hole for the global jet-set for almost a decade. The hotel closed in the 1970s and reopened in 2008. The extensive restoration has done wonders, and today the rooms are attractive, spotless, and furnished with period pieces from the 1960s that add real flair, especially in the suites. The staff is friendly and attentive. Rooms are not cheap at US$150–170, though they do include breakfast. The huge President Suite goes for US$750 a night, but it will make you feel like a president, with its tasteful furniture arrangement and great sea view. A large swimming pool and a private beach with a bar, a restaurant, and a forest-style garden full of monkeys complete the amazing picture. It's worth coming down here to take a look, even if you are not staying at the hotel.

More modern in style, but with less of it, the **Sokha Beach Resort** (tel. 034/935999, www.sokhahotels.com, US$200–1,000) looks slightly clunky with its sprawling Khmer design, but, for your creature comforts, this is the best place in town. The Sokha has everything you might expect from an international first-class hotel, including its very own private beach and a large swimming pool.

FOOD
Downtown Sihanoukville
STREET CAFÉS AND BAKERIES

Espresso Kampuchea, diagonally opposite the Angkor Inn on Sopheak Mongkol Street, is a small and amiable hole-in-the-wall joint that serves a wide variety of coffee and juices, snacks, and Western breakfasts with a jazz/blues soundtrack.

Staffed by students of the Don Bosco Hotel School near Otres Beach, **Gelato Italiano** (tel. 012/919834, daily 7:30 A.M.–9:30 P.M.) on Makara Street offers superior ice-cream, a large choice of fresh coffees, as well as good sandwiches. There's also a bar that serves cocktails and cold beer. Proceeds go towards the Don Bosco Project.

The **Starfish Bakery** (tel. 012/952011, www.starfishcambodia.org, daily 7 A.M.–6 P.M.), located down an unpaved dirt road in town, is part of another NGO, which trains young people to work in the catering business. In addition to fine cakes and healthy snacks, it also offers massage and Internet.

ASIAN

The **Indian Curry Pot** (tel. 034/934040, daily 7 A.M.–late) on Weather Station Hill serves reliable curries from around US$3. There are plenty of vegetarian choices and there's a buffet on weekends. This large restaurant also has a pool table, a large screen that shows sports events, and a few simple rooms that cost just US$4.

A little below the Independence Monument on Ekareach Street, **Same Same** (tel. 012/968882, US$5, daily 9 A.M.–10 P.M.) has a largely Vietnamese menu, as well as a handful of Thai and French dishes. Try the excellent *pho* (soup) for breakfast, or enjoy a dinner of *tom yum* (a spicy Thai soup) and stuffed squid.

Located in the center of the main bar and restaurant strip on Weather Station Hill, **Koh Lin** (tel. 012/489421, daily 9 A.M.–midnight) is a small and reliable Vietnamese/Khmer restaurant, though several European dishes are also available. Try a decent selection of seafood dishes and excellent crèpes for dessert. The Koh

Lin is popular with foreign residents, not least because of its very reasonable prices.

The restaurant and rooftop bar of the **Mealy Chenda Guesthouse** (tel. 012/670818, www.mealychenda.com) on Weather Hill Station afford great views across the bay. This is a good place to sample a large variety of Khmer dishes, handily photographed for the menu, as well as a range of seafood. All dishes come in small, medium, and large portions and start around US$2. On Thursdays and Sundays, there's an all-you-can-eat barbecue buffet for US$5.

INTERNATIONAL

The thoughtfully decorated and smart ◖ **Holy Cow** (tel. 012/478510, US$3–7), on Ekareach Street towards Ochheuteal Beach, offers a wide variety of Western dishes—sandwiches on homemade bread, salads, and other vegetarian and vegan dishes. Handicrafts are also on sale and the management is professional and friendly. It's highly recommended for its upscale ambience and food.

Happy Herb Pizza (tel. 012/632198) is part of a chain of decent pizza joints with branches in Phnom Penh and Siem Reap. The food—Italian, Khmer or otherwise—is reliable, and you may be asked just how "happy" you want your pizza—which can be prepared with marijuana as a topping. There's a second local branch off Ochheuteal Beach.

Luna d'Autunno (tel. 034/934280, daily 10:30 A.M.–10:30 P.M., US$10) is a smart Italian eatery located in a beautifully lit building on Ekareach Street. There are pizzas and pasta, with an excellent wine list; dining in town does not get much better than this. Guests may choose between air-conditioning indoors and a rooftop terrace.

Sihanoukville Beaches
KHMER AND ASIAN

Set in a beautiful tropical garden off the road between the Golden Lions Traffic Circle and the beaches, **Chi Khmer** (tel. 012/728901, daily 5–10 P.M., US$6) serves traditional Khmer standards such as *lok lac* and fish

THE COAST

amok, as well as Royal Khmer cuisine. Credit cards are accepted.

If you're in the mood for an upscale Khmer-Chinese meal, head for the **Treasure Island Seafood-Koh Pos Restaurant** (tel. 016876618, daily 10 A.M.–10 P.M.), located on a private strip of sand between Hawaii Beach and Independence Beach. Lobsters, prawns, clams, crabs, and fish can be picked right out of tanks, only to materialize on your plate a few minutes later. Open-air covered seating overlooks nearby Koh Pos Island.

INTERNATIONAL

The **Villa Garden Restaurant and Bar** (tel. 017/409395, www.devarajavilla.com/fooddrink. php, US$6–10), part of the Deva Raja Villa, has an eclectic menu of Asian-global fusion dishes. Try Indian-style Baja fish tacos, Kerala curries, or some of the other seafood dishes, or enjoy the nightly barbecue in the garden.

Bar Ru is a relaxed beach shack/bar/restaurant in the heart of Ochheuteal Beach, right by the water's edge. You can lounge in deckchairs on the beachfront while drinking cheap beers and indulging in the nightly seafood barbecue, which starts at 7:30 P.M.

The Mexican (tel. 012/315338, US$6–8), at the Reef Resort on the road from the Golden Lions Traffic Circle to the beaches, is smart and clean. It serves a wide variety of international food, though it specializes in Mexican fare, such as burritos, fajitas, and tacos. Visa and MasterCard are accepted. The more down-to-earth **Cantina Del Mar,** on Otres Beach, also serves competent Mexican dishes and cold beer. It's an offshoot of the well-known expat hangout in Phnom Penh.

INFORMATION AND SERVICES
Money

The U.S. dollar is the most commonly used currency in Sihanoukville, though of course everyone also accepts Cambodian riel. Some hotels and restaurants also take Thai baht. Plenty of banks have exchange facilities and ATMs. Some upscale hotels and restaurants accept credit cards. Note that neighboring Koh Kong has only one ATM, which only accepts Visa cards, though the village of Hat Lek on the Thai side of the border has an ATM that accepts all major international cards.

Health and Emergencies

There are no recommended hospitals in Sihanoukville. For minor injuries and illnesses, **CT Clinic** (47 Borei Kamakor Street, tel. 034/934222) is your best bet. They are open around the clock, sometimes have a European doctor in attendance, and can advise on evacuation. In case of a serious accident, travel to Phnom Penh or to Thailand as quickly as possible.

Internet Access, Telephone, and Post Office

Numerous guesthouses, hotels, and bars now offer Wi-Fi or broadband Internet access. Internet cafés are dotted around town. These usually offer the best international telephone rates, around 500–1,000 riel a minute to most countries. The best of the lot is the friendly **Ana Internet and Travel** (tel. 012/372018), on Ekareach Street next to Eco Sea Dive. A small and laid-back restaurant is attached, and boat trips, all manners of bus tickets, and visas can be arranged here.

Sihanoukville's main post office is on Ekareach Street. A second branch is opposite Phsar Leu, the town's biggest market.

Vietnamese Consulate

The Vietnamese Consulate (tel. 034/349 33 669, www.vietnamconsulate-shihanoukville. org), on Ekareach Street on the way to Weather Station Hill, issues visas for Vietnam. Note that you cannot enter Vietnam from Cambodia without a visa.

GETTING THERE
Air

While Sihanoukville Airport has the longest functional runway in Cambodia, no airline currently offers regular flights here—though this is likely to change in the future.

Train

At press time, no passenger trains were commuting between the capital and Sihanoukville, following the derailment of a train in 2008. Irregular cargo trains ply the route, and you may be able to jump one of those and ride hobo-style. Be warned, it takes all day. It's rumored that regular passenger services will resume following the restoration of the tracks, allegedly in 2010, but don't hold your breath.

Boat

A daily ferry from Sihanoukville to Koh Kong leaves at 9:30 A.M. From Koh Kong, the ferry leaves at 8 A.M. Boats take four hours and cost US$25. In the rainy season, ferries are often cancelled. Having to compete with a good road and increased frequency of buses, it is quite possible that this service may cease in the near future. Like other boat services in Cambodia, the ferries plying this route do not conform to international safety expectations.

Regional Road Transport

It's 230 kilometers from Phnom Penh to Sihanoukville and National Route #4 is in

excellent condition. Air-conditioned buses ply the route several times a day from 7 A.M. until early afternoon and cost US$5–7. The trip takes 4–6 hours. Bus companies include Sorya Transport (tel. 023/210359), which leaves from a stop near the Central Market; Mekong Express (tel. 023/427518), which leaves from 87 Sisowath Quay; and Capitol Guesthouse Tours, which leaves from the Capitol Guesthouse. In Sihanoukville, all buses leave from the central bus stand downtown.

Taxis make the trip a little faster. A seat in a share taxi will set you back about 25,000 riel. To rent a taxi all by yourself, expect to pay at least US$50.

GETTING AROUND

The trusty *motodup* is your first option. Rides around town cost 1,000–2,000 riel, and to the beaches it's at least US$1. At night, the prices are higher. Be aware that the *motodups* in Sihanoukville have the reputation of being the most rapacious operators in Cambodia's free-wheeling transport business. Always agree on a fare before going anywhere and insist on going directly to your destination, without detours.

THE COAST

© AROON THAEWCHATTURAT

water traffic along the coast

Tuk-tuks are more comfortable, but expect to pay double the *motodup* rates. Alternatively it may be possible to rent a motorbike (US$4–6 for a 100cc, US$8–12 for a 250cc dirt bike).

At times there appears to be a rental ban for foreigners in place, much like in Siem Reap, but this rule seems to be more flexible in Sihanoukville.

Taxis can be hired at the bus and taxi station. Expect to pay about US$25 for a day in the area, or around US$5 for trips around town.

Numerous guesthouses rent out bicycles for US$1–3 a day. The roads in Sihanoukville are hilly and some are unsurfaced.

VICINITY OF SIHANOUKVILLE
Kirirom National Park
Located in the Damrei Mountains, the Kirirom National Park lies at an altitude of some 600 meters. It's significantly cooler than the lowlands and the coast, which brings in the daytrippers from Phnom Penh on weekends. The park is covered with forest and contains a temple (Wat Kirirom), lakes, and several clusters of ruins, including an old royal palace, long destroyed by the Khmer Rouge.

Locals say that Prince Sihanouk had the tropical vegetation removed and replaced with temperate forest. Others claim that the area was denuded by U.S. bombing and then replanted by Sihanouk. Both theories seem outlandish, but whatever the truth, don't expect dense tropical jungle here. Animal sightings are rare, except for a variety of birds, but the odd bear might cross your path, especially if you are exploring the park on foot. It's possible to climb a small mountain, Phnom Dat Chivit, for great views across the surrounding area.

Buildings and lakes are far apart, so the best way to get around the park is by car or motorcycle. The main road through the park is surfaced. Entry is US$5, to be paid at the ticket booth at the entrance. Guides for walks can be arranged at the ticket booth for around US$5. Visitors experiencing problems inside the park should call 012/540981 or 016/574471.

ACCOMMODATIONS
The **Kirirom Guesthouse** inside the park is very basic and unreasonably pricey at US$20 for a very simple room. Food is sometimes available, sometimes not, and should cost around US$5.

The garish **Kirirom Hill Resort** (tel. 016/590999, www.kiriromresort.com) seems squarely aimed at local tourists with its castle-like entrance, landscaped garden, and dino-park. Prices range from US$25 for a decent room to US$160 for a VIP suite bungalow. There's also a VIP villa for US$220. Nicely kept and large bungalows are around US$60 a night. The resort has a booking office in Phnom Penh (15, Street 214, tel. 023/216471) and special packages can be booked via the website. Note that prices vary with the number of occupants and that this place charges foreigners more than Khmer.

A homestay organized by **M'lup Baitong** (tel. 023/214409, www.mlup.org), a local NGO, might be the best lodging option in the area. The project center is in Chambok, some 10 kilometers from the park. Simple village accommodations are US$3 per person, and food and handicrafts are available for sale. Walks to nearby waterfalls are possible with or without guides.

GETTING THERE AND AROUND
Kirirom National Park lies some 20 kilometers west of Route 4, about halfway between Phnom Penh and Sihanoukville. The turn-off is posted. If you have your own wheels, it's pretty straightforward to get to and around the park. If you don't, grab a bus from Sihanoukville to the turn-off and then catch a ride on a *motodup* (US$7). It's also possible to get the *motodup* to take you around the park for the day, but make sure you bargain hard for a decent rate. Otherwise, you can explore some sights on foot or rent a bicycle to get around.

Ream National Park
Ream National Park, also known as Preah Sihanouk National Park, has a bit of everything. Visitors can take boat trips to two

islands, Koh She and Koh Thmei, which have decent beaches and some coral growth; a riverboat trip up the Prek Tuk River to view wildlife and traditional fishing villages; or arrange for jungle walks. There's quite a variety of resident wildlife here, including macaques, dolphins, and more than 150 species of birds. Sightings of pangolins and sun bears are rare.

Tours (US$10–20) are best organized at the park office (tel. 012/875096, daily 7 A.M.–5 P.M.), just 23 kilometers north of Sihanoukville. The park office can also arrange basic lodging (US$5) on Ream Beach, where there are also a couple of seafood stalls and it's possible to hire a guide. Hotels and guesthouses in Sihanoukville also offer day trips to the park.

The park office is located 23 kilometers north of Sihanoukville. Turn off Route 4 after 15 kilometers on the road to Sihanoukville Airport. It's a 30-minute ride by motorbike and the road is paved all the way.

THE SOUTH COAST ISLANDS

Tourism on the islands off the Cambodian coast is currently either very basic or extremely exclusive. For now, the extremely basic prevails on most islands, while many others have no accommodations at all and are best visited on day trips. This is changing as many of the islands are being sold to foreign investors. While huge potential for ecotourism is present, some locals fear that more and more islands will become off-limits to everyone but those with huge amounts of cash.

Sun-Tours (tel. 023/990460, www.sun-tours-cambodia.com) offers island cruises. The boat leaves from the Russian Pier at 9 A.M. (upon booking) and trips include snorkeling, visiting several islands (including Koh Rong, Koh Rong Samloen, and Koh Kon), and a barbecue. The large wooden yacht is a beautiful ship with a large sundeck and eating area, as well as cabins for overnight trips. Transport to all the islands can be arranged on Ochheuteal Beach with several operators. Try **Mr. Sok's Utopia Adventures** (tel. 016/309464), located across the road from Nap House.

Koh Rong

Koh Rong, a little northwest of Sihanoukville, is the largest island in the area. So far, there's been very little development, though there's a great beach as well as coral gardens popular with divers on Koh Rong's west side. There's no dive shop on the island, nor is there electricity.

Currently, the best place to stay on Koh Rong is **Lazy Beach Bungalows** (tel. 016/214211, www.beachcambodia.com, US$15), which offers simple huts with attached bathrooms and balconies with a sea view; its restaurant is equipped with hammocks and a bar. Enjoy the solitude, as this type of uncomplicated beach tourism is a rarity in Southeast Asia nowadays.

Koh Rong Samloen

Koh Rong Samloen is a little smaller than Koh Rong and slightly to the south; many of the dive courses out of Sihanoukville take place on its reefs. At the time of writing, several small bungalow operations were in the process of setting up shop on the island. Two of Sihanoukville's dive shops offer basic accommodations on the island for their students and customers on fun dives.

Tiny **Koh Kon,** just north of Koh Rong Samloen, is another good dive site in the area.

Koh Dek Koul

Local expatriates call this the Island of Dr. No, but that could just be jealousy. Tiny Koh Dek Koul is almost entirely covered by the Russian-owned **Mirax Resort** (tel. 012/966503, www.miraxresort.com). According to its advertising, it's a place where life is beautiful—offering ultimate privacy, royal pampering, and breathtaking adventure. Rooms and suites range US$300–3,000.

Koh Pos

A tiny islet in front of Victory Beach, Koh Pos is also known as Snake Island. A Russian investor had planned to build a resort on this island, but was deported after being charged with having sex with a minor. Development is to continue soon with a new investor.

Koh Russei

Koh Russei is also known as Bamboo Island. The beaches are hassle-free and wonderfully quiet. Several modest bungalow operators have set up businesses here. Stay at **Bim Bamboo Bungalows** (tel. 017/500485, www.bamboo-island.com, US$12), which has simple beachfront huts with attached bathrooms—and a bar.

Other Islands

It's possible to organize boat trips to several other islands off the coast. Dive operators regularly head for Koh Tang and Koh Prins, farther out in the Gulf of Thailand. Closer to shore, Koh Kteah, Koh Ta Kiew, and several other islands can be reached with short boat trips, even in a sailing dingy or kayak. Check with **Otres Nautica** (tel. 092/230065, otres.nautica@yahoo.com) on Otres Beach.

Koh Kong

Koh Kong lies about 10 kilometers east of the border to Thailand on the banks of the Ka Bpow River. It has long been a transit point for travelers between Thailand and Cambodia. I crossed the Thai–Cambodian border here in 1995, without visa or passport, and visited the town in a speedboat. In those days, Koh Kong was a smugglers' nest, offering cheap sex and drugs and not much else.

But things have changed a little and the small town is slowly becoming a tourist destination in its own right, promising access to some of the most remote jungles, coastline, and coral reefs the country has to offer. A good selection of budget and mid-range accommodations and the possibility of ecotourism adventures and dive trips await visitors. And while there's no colonial architecture to see, making Koh Kong a bit nondescript, the town does have a genuine, remote, border feel. Add some decent beaches and spectacular waterfalls and Koh Kong has all the makings of a new coastal destination. Close to the border, casino hotels cater to gambling addicts from neighboring Thailand.

SIGHTS
The Market

With no real sights in Koh Kong, the market (daily dawn–dusk) is the most interesting place to see. But don't expect souvenirs and handicrafts. Koh Kong Market, a large open hall

and collection of rickety stalls in the center of town, has everything local people need—from numerous fruit stalls to vendors selling household goods, clothes, and mobile phones. The glass counters of money-changers are clustered around the market.

Koh Kong Safari World

On the road to Thailand, just 500 meters before reaching the border, this mini-zoo (tel. 016/800811, daily 8 A.M.–5 P.M.) will probably appall some Western visitors. Orangutan boxing matches, crocodile feedings, dolphin shows, and birds riding small bicycles are not likely to be to everyone's taste. Besides, tigers, bears, and ostriches linger in cages. This dubious enterprise is connected to the Koh Kong International Resort Club, a casino hotel near the border. Entrance for foreigners is US$12.

ENTERTAINMENT
Bars

Bob Bar is a hole-in-the-wall, Australian-owned bar, serving cold beer and basic Western dishes. There's a pool table and the clientele appear to be predominantly local expatriates and former residents of Pattaya. The **Dive Inn,** connected to Impian Divers next door, is a British-style pub on the riverfront road, diagonally opposite the Champa Koh Kong Guesthouse. There's cold beer and a small menu of British pub food on offer. Travelers often congregate here. The **Sunset Lounge** is a small shack behind the Dive Inn on the riverfront road. You can get a cold beer here and arrange boat trips along the coast.

The **Barracuda Beach Bar** on Koh Yor Beach, some eight kilometers from town towards the border, offers fine seafood, cold beer, and good music. It's closed in the rainy season. Note that this beach has allegedly been sold to investors and that redevelopment may soon take place and replace current businesses.

SPORTS AND RECREATION
Diving

Diving is in its infancy in Koh Kong, with just two dive businesses that opened in 2008. dives close to shore are not spectacular, but some of the sites farther out into the Gulf of Thailand—such as Shark Island, Marlin Point, and Condor Reef—are worth the trip. There are regular sightings of black tip, white tip, nurse sharks, and grey reef sharks as well as turtles and some decent coral gardens at these sites. Besides, you are virtually guaranteed not to meet other divers in the water.

Located next to the Koh Kong Guesthouse on the riverfront road not far from the bridge, **Koh Kong Divers** (tel. 017/502784, www.kohkongdivers.com) is the town's only dive center. It offers trips around all the main dive sites and PADI courses—as well as island tours and trips to nearby waterfalls. Koh Kong Divers is run by a young, enthusiastic British guy who is keen to discover new sites along the coast. For now, divers are taken out in a long-tail, but a custom dive boat is under construction. Full-day dive excursions cost 3,000 baht, and PADI Open Water courses are 9,800 baht. The shop is a good place to meet other tourists.

Impian Divers (tel. 035/393912 or 099/707434, www.impiandivers.com), next to the Dive Inn on the riverfront road, opened in late 2008 and offers snorkeling trips to all the main sites around Koh Kong. Owned by a Welshman, this small center operates its own comfortable boat.

THE COAST

© TOM VATER

fishing boats moored off Koh Kong's riverside road

Bike Tours and Jungle Treks

The British-run outfit **Jungle Cross** (tel. 35/393937, www.junglecross.com) offers dirt-bike and Jeep tours into the Cardamom Mountains. The owners have years of experience in off-road biking and organize well-designed tours with overnight stays in the middle of nowhere. They currently offer the only way to get deep into this very remote region. Interested parties should bear in mind that these adventure trips go beyond mere holiday outings, require some driving skills, and lead into areas where poachers and illegal loggers operate. That said, owners Nick and Coralie have run countless day trips and overnighters into the jungle and are well connected to local trackers. Day trips in the Jeep cost around $100 for up to four people; on dirt bikes provided by Jungle Cross, it's US$60 per person plus gas. That may seem rather expensive, but these adventures take riders to some of the most off-the-beaten-track corners in the country. The Jungle Cross shop is in the town center, not far from the bridge.

Fishing

The German-run **Blue Marlin** (tel. 016/489523), a small bar in town, organizes fishing trips into the Gulf of Thailand—and serves pizzas.

ACCOMMODATIONS
Under US$15

The **Cham-Pa Koh Kong Guesthouse** (tel. 016/450333, US$9–15) is a Khmer-style drive-in motel on the riverfront road, some five minutes' walk south of the bridge. It has well-appointed, clean rooms, some with air-conditioning, all with hot water. Western-run and with friendly staff, this is one of the most appealing addresses in town.

The **Dugout Hotel** (tel. 035/936220, 300–500 baht), on Street 3 near the main roundabout in town, has probably seen better days, but it does have a small swimming pool, as well as free Internet access. All the rooms are air-conditioned.

Otto's (Street 7, tel. 012/924249, ottoskoh-kong@yahoo.com, US$3–10), on a small road leading from the river into the center of town, is a long-established guesthouse and restaurant located in a large wooden house. The rooms are so-so, most with fan, some with air-conditioning. There's plenty of information on the surrounding countryside, as well as travel information. The restaurant serves a wide variety of Western dishes, including German specialties.

Neptune Guesthouse (tel. 011/984512, US$4–6) is southeast of the traffic circle in town, a few minutes' walk from the river. It offers simple, small rooms in a traditional, brightly painted wooden house. A beer garden out the back borders on a small pond and the German owner organizes boat tours and charters. Dirt bikes are available for rent.

The equally simple and attractive **Koh Kong Guesthouse** (tel. 016/286669, US$5) is located in a wooden building on the riverfront road, next door to Koh Kong Divers. The restaurant area is very tastefully done and the predominantly Thai menu is interesting—but the rooms are tiny.

The **Bopha Koh Kong Hotel** (Street 6, tel. 035/936073) has rooms with fans for US$7, as well as air-conditioned rooms for US$13. Popular with backpackers, it's clean enough, though rooms are on the small side and can be damp in the rainy season.

US$15-25

The **Asean Hotel** (tel. 012/936667, US$15–20), on the river road just south of the bridge, is one of the best Khmer-run places in town, offering large, clean, and airy rooms with air-conditioning, minibar, and TV. The rooms to the front might be a bit noisier, but they have river views and a small balcony. The **Koh Kong City Hotel** (tel. 035/936777, http://kkchotel.netkhmer.com), opposite the Asean Hotel, has clean, spacious—if nondescript—rooms with TV and air-conditioning for the same price.

The █ **Oasis Resort** (tel. 016/551556,

http://oasisresort.netkhmer.com, US$20–30) is located a kilometer north of the bridge and offers the best accommodations in the area. Just five spacious bungalows—with air-conditioning, cable, DVD player, and hot water—in a nice garden arranged around a decent-size swimming pool make for a relaxing stay. Oasis is a family-oriented place and offers excursions into the jungle and along the coast. The restaurant, complete with pool table, offers Western, Thai, and Khmer dishes, but is for guests only. The British owner organizes trips to several waterfalls and islands in the area.

For something completely different, try the idyllic **Rainbow Lodge** (tel. 099/744321, www.rainbowlodgecambodia.com), some 20 kilometers outside of Koh Kong. Located on a riverbank, with the jungle looming in, this eco-friendly resort relies on solar power for most of its electricity. The resort offers bungalows and full board, as there are no other facilities in the area. Two people sharing a room pay US$50 a day. For four people, it's US$60–80. The British owner organizes trips into the jungle, including overnight camping excursions. Kayaks and rowboats are free for guests and it's possible to swim right by the resort.

Over US$25

If you like the idea of staying in a casino hotel near the border, check out the **Koh Kong International Resort Club** (tel. 011/364336, www.kohkonginter.com, US$25–250), which offers bungalows, rooms, and suites for an astounding range of budgets. Besides, good rooms, a swimming pool, fitness center, sauna facilities, and free entry to the adjacent safari park might keep you away from the roulette tables long enough to defer bankruptcy to another (gambling) day.

FOOD

Once the sun sets, several small local restaurants around the traffic circle fill up quickly. Pots with ready-cooked dishes are lined up on a table outside, so you can just pick and choose; most dishes start at about US$1 (depending on size of serving). A little off the circle heading north, a sandwich stall on the left sells good paté, chili paste, and fermented salad baguettes from US$1.50.

On the main road through town, north of the traffic circle, **Baan Peakmai** offers a decent range of moderately priced Thai food in a nice garden setting in the center of town. Expect to pay about US$2.50 for a main dish. **Otto's** (Street 7) probably has the best selection of Western dishes in town. The menu includes burgers, schnitzel, salads, and fruit shakes. Main dishes are around US$4.

A little out of town and across the river, the **Rock Garden Restaurant** offers a great sunset and good Khmer food, including some seafood dishes.

Out on Koh Yor Beach, eight kilometers from town, the **Barracuda Beach Bar** offers a small selection of good dishes, mostly seafood, but is open only in the dry season. A Khmer family has also set up a small no-name restaurant there and offers seafood year-round.

INFORMATION AND SERVICES
Money

ACLEDA bank, on the north side of the market, has an ATM (which only accepted Visa cards at press time) and cashes travelers checks. Money-changers are clustered around the market. The Thai baht is the common currency in Koh Kong, though you should be okay with U.S. Dollars, and, of course, with Cambodian riel.

Health and Emergencies

There are no recommended doctors or hospitals in Koh Kong. In case of an accident or illness, go to Thailand immediately. Trat, 90 kilometers inside Thailand, has a reasonable provincial hospital.

Internet Access

The Asean Hotel and the Dugout Hotel provide Internet access. A reliable Internet café can be found just south of Bob's Bar.

THE COAST

GETTING THERE
Air

Nearby Sihanoukville has a modern airport, but at the moment, no regular flights go there. This makes Trat in neighboring Thailand the nearest airport. Trat Airport, about 100 kilometers from the border and Koh Kong, was built and is operated by Bangkok Airways, which flies Bangkok–Trat twice a day. Tickets cost around 2,500 baht one-way. Trat Airport levies a 200 baht departure tax. The airport is 40 kilometers from Trat town. Minibuses and taxis ply the route and meet incoming flights. Frequent minibuses from Trat to the Hat Lek border crossing take 90 minutes and cost 120 baht. There's nothing much to see in Hat Lek, except for a small market along the road. Coming from Thailand, a motorcycle taxi from the border to Koh Kong will set you back 50–70 baht. The Thai–Cambodian border at Cham Yaem is open daily 7 A.M.–8 P.M.

Boat

A regular ferry runs from Koh Kong to Sihanoukville for most of the year. Boats depart daily at 8 A.M., take four hours, and cost US$25. The return trip from Sihanoukville leaves at noon. With recent improvements in road connections, it's doubtful whether this service will be able to survive. Neptune Resort (tel. 011/984512) offer daily speedboat trips, via immigration offices at the border, to the Thai islands of Ko Mak and Koh Kud from October to April, weather permitting. Phone for prices and availability.

Regional Road Transport

A daily bus from Virak Buntham Express Travel (tel. 012/322302) leaves Phnom Penh (Street 106, near the riverfront) for Koh Kong at 7 A.M. From Koh Kong, the same bus leaves from the bus stand at 8 A.M. Travel time is 5–7 hours, depending on the season. Tickets cost US$13. From Sihanoukville, you can grab a daily Virak Buntham Express Travel bus, which leaves at 7 A.M., takes 4–5 hours and also costs US$13. From Koh Kong, a bus travels daily at 8 A.M. from the bus stand back

to Sihanoukville. There's also a later bus, at 9 A.M., but the vehicle is not in great condition. A private taxi from Phnom Penh to Koh Kong costs US$100–150, so anything but a dire emergency will probably eliminate this mode of transport for most travelers. A seat in a share taxi can be had for around 60,000 riel.

GETTING AROUND

Koh Kong is small enough to walk around, but as there are no sights as such, you may want to opt for a *motodup* to get you to where you want to go. *Motodups* charge 500–1,000 riel around town. To the Cham Yaem border crossing, 12 kilometers from town, it's 80–100 baht. For the same price, several guesthouses will rent you a small motorbike. Dirt bikes can also be rented in Koh Kong at Jungle Cross. A minivan or taxi to or from the border costs 600 baht. On the Thai side, minivans leave for Trat every 30 minutes, take 90 minutes, and cost 120 baht. Several buses leave Trat for Bangkok in the morning; tickets are 200 baht. In Koh Kong, you can hire a *motodup* for the day for around US$7.

VICINITY OF KOH KONG
Koh Kong Island

The huge Koh Kong Island is barely inhabited—there's a small village on the southern tip and an army post on the northern shore—but it does have six attractive beaches on its western side. Beach Number 3 is possibly the best, with a lagoon behind it. Several outfits in town, including Neptune and Oasis Resort, organize occasional day trips, but periodic problems between Thailand and Cambodia make this difficult at times. Foreigners are forbidden to go inland, where there are said to be attractive waterfalls.

Koh Yor Beach

The most accessible and developed beach near Koh Kong is across the river, back towards the border. Developed is perhaps too grand a term for this fine strip of white sand, dotted with beach shack restaurants. Visitors can relax at the Barracuda Beach Bar, owned by Koh Kong Divers; it offers excellent seafood, but is only open in the dry season. A no-name restaurant shack offers basic dishes and beer year-round. During the rainy season, piles of flotsam wash up on the sand and, unfortunately, no one makes the effort to clean up. Apparently, the beach has been sold to private investors and big changes are just around the corner.

Other beaches between Koh Kong and Sihanoukville are more picturesque, but can only be reached by boat. Ask at Neptune Resort or Oasis Resort for details.

To get to Koh Yor Beach, cross the bridge towards the border and take a dirt road to the left until you get to a sign post for the beach, some eight kilometers from town. A *motodup* will take you for US$1.

Sre Ambel

Sre Ambel is a former smuggler's nest that's now a small town at the turn-off from Route 48 to Route 4 (the road from Phnom Penh to Sihanoukville). There's nothing much to do or see here, but there's gasoline, several restaurants, and a few cheap guesthouses.

Kampot

East of Sihanoukville, the coast fronts the Elephant Mountains, still largely covered by forest and topping out at 1,000 meters high. Set between mountains and sea, Kampot, the laid-back and pretty capital of Kampot Province, is a great place to relax for a few days. Kampot is the largest town between Sihanoukville (105 kilometers away) and the Vietnamese border, but visitors will be pleasantly surprised by the slow, small-town pace of the place.

There are no sights as such, but a few blocks of attractive French colonial architecture along

THE COAST

© AROON THAEWCHATTURAT

a street scene in Kampot, with a colonial building in the background

THE COAST

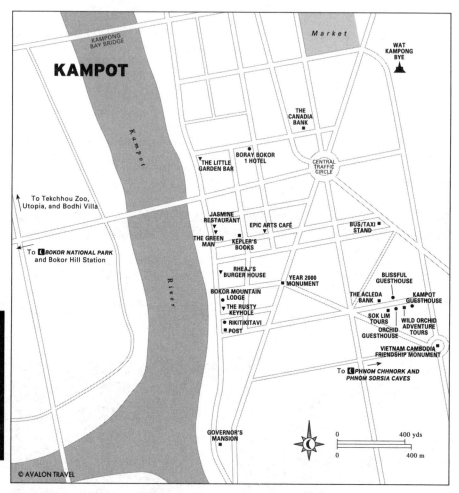

KAMPONG BAY BRIDGE

KAMPOT

Market

WAT KAMPONG BYE

THE CANADIA BANK

BORAY BOKOR 1 HOTEL

▼ THE LITTLE GARDEN BAR

CENTRAL TRAFFIC CIRCLE

Kampot

To Tekchhou Zoo, Utopia, and Bodhi Villa

To **C** BOKOR NATIONAL PARK and Bokor Hill Station

JASMINE RESTAURANT ▼

EPIC ARTS CAFÉ

BUS/TAXI STAND ■

THE GREEN MAN

KEPLER'S BOOKS

River

■ RHEAJ'S BURGER HOUSE

YEAR 2000 MONUMENT

BLISSFUL GUESTHOUSE

BOKOR MOUNTAIN ● LODGE

● THE RUSTY KEYHOLE

THE ACLEDA BANK ■

KAMPOT GUESTHOUSE

SOK LIM TOURS ■

WILD ORCHID ADVENTURE TOURS

● RIKITIKITAVI

■ POST

ORCHID GUESTHOUSE

VIETNAM-CAMBODIA FRIENDSHIP MONUMENT

To **C** PHNOM CHHNORK AND PHNOM SORSIA CAVES

GOVERNOR'S MANSION
■

0   400 yds

0   400 m

© AVALON TRAVEL

the broad Kampong Bay River that form the center of town, dominated by the handsome Governor's Mansion and the large market square, make for great morning or afternoon walks. There's also a good range of attractive accommodations, restaurants, and bars, plus a great bookshop. Kampot Province produces the country's best pepper, for sale in many of the town's guesthouses. All that and a small but fascinating choice of day trips around Cambodia's southernmost province make Kampot well worth a visit. Once you are here,

you just might get sucked into blissful holiday apathy for a few days.

ENTERTAINMENT
Bars

The Rusty Keyhole (daily 8:30 A.M.–midnight), a friendly Western-run bar and restaurant, is a good hang-out on the riverfront road. It has indoor and outdoor seating, and serves a decent menu of Western food (British pub grub, steaks, and burgers) and Asian dishes, as well as draft beer. A little closer to the old bridge, but also on the riverfront, Kampot's only Irish bar, **The Green Man,** no longer has an Irish owner, but it's a late-night hangout in a town that pretty much goes to sleep after 10 P.M. And they do have bottled Guinness.

SPORTS AND RECREATION
Trekking Tours
Treks to Bokor Mountain can be arranged through the guesthouses and hotels in Kampot. At times it is possible to get to Bokor independently; at others, it's US$40 for a round-trip. Ask at your guesthouse for current conditions.

Boat Trips
Several travel agents in town offer sunset river cruises, as well as trips to nearby salt fields. Try **Sok Lim Tours** (tel. 012/801348, www.soklim-tours.com), which also organizes trips to Bokor and Rabbit Island near Kep. Or check out **Wild Orchid Adventure Tours** (tel. 092/226996), based at the Orchid Guesthouse. Besides the stunning scenery, the main attractions upriver are the local villages, while downriver and into the estuary, the fishing fleet is worth a look.

Massage
Massage by the Blind (tel. 012/662114) can be found on the riverfront road and offers traditional Khmer massage and Anma Shiatsu–style massages from Japan. Sessions start at US$4 per hour.

ACCOMMODATIONS
Under US$15
The laid-back **Blissful Guesthouse** (tel. 012/513024, US$3–6) lies on a wide, quiet street not far from the 2000 Monument, which is in the center of a small traffic circle. It has small rooms with fans, a popular backpacker restaurant, and a friendly atmosphere. There are some books for sale, and you can rent bicycles here or join tours to Bokor National Park. On the same lane, diagonally across the road, **Orchid Guesthouse** (tel. 033/932634, orchidguesthouse@yahoo.com, US$4–15) offers a series of small bungalows with fans or

air-conditioning. The older huts, sitting next to a lotus pond, are rustic, while the new concrete ones are smart. A restaurant serves Asian and Western standards, including seafood. The guesthouse rents motorcycles, bicycles, and boats to guests. If these two places are full, try **Kampot Guesthouse** (tel. 012/512931), on the same lane. Located in several refurbished 1950s villas, the rooms are clean, if impersonal and lackluster—but at US$3–7 with bathroom and fan, or US$10–15 with air-conditioning, it's hard to complain. There's a decent backpacker restaurant attached.

The **Boray Bokor 1 Hotel** (tel. 092/978168, US$15) is one of the largest hotels in town. The air-conditioned rooms are clean, but the place lacks style, a restaurant, and Internet access. Nevertheless the Boray Bokor 1 is popular with groups and lies just a minute away from the riverfront. The Boray Bokor 2 is an old pile, badly refurbished, by the traffic circle.

For all traveling party-people, the ▐ **Bodhi Villa** (tel. 012/728884, http://web.mac.com/houstonair/web, US$10) is the perfect place to chill out, drop off, or tune in. Located a couple of kilometers outside of town on the Western bank of the Kampong Bay River, this basic backpacker resort has it all—floating bungalows that are basically open to the river, basic rooms with fans, and a couple of huts in the forest-like garden. Accommodations and a restaurant, serving cheap Asian and Western standards, are clustered around a small 1960s villa, making for a unique and carefree ambience.

US$15-25
On the Western side of the Kampong Bay River, some eight kilometers north of Kampot, the reclusive and quiet **Utopia** (tel. 017/742681, www.utopiakampot.com) offers US$3 dorms, basic rooms with low ceilings for US$6 (shared bathroom), and smart bungalows for US$25. This small resort lies on a quiet stretch of the river, bordered by brush. It has something of a Conradian Inner Station feel, not least because of its Kurtz-like German owner. The restaurant serves seafood at reasonable prices. Utopia is a place to get away from it all for a

KAMPOT PEPPER

One of Cambodia's best known exports prior to the Khmer Rouge revolution was pepper, grown for the most part around Kampot. Chou Ta-Kuan, the Chinese envoy who visited Cambodia in the 13th century made mention of pepper in his book *The Customs of Cambodia* as part of a list of remarkable Cambodian products. He recommended pepper be consumed when it's fresh and blue-green in color.

Major production started in the late 19th century and pepper was soon exported all over the world. In France, Kampot pepper soon became a household name. By 1900, production had reached 8,000 tons a year. In 1960, there were more than a million pepper poles in Kampot Province. The Khmer Rouge put an end to this, but many surviving farmers returned to their fields in the 1980s and some have begun to grow pepper again.

Because most small-scale farmers live more or less hand to mouth, the pepper vine, which needs to mature for three years before it starts producing any harvestable

pepper corns, has been slow to return. And yet, the plant is a good long-term investment. It reaches full maturity after six years and can be harvested for as long as 15 years. Several hundred farmers are now working with NGOs and foreign investors to rebuild the industry.

In Kampot Province, pepper is grown just once a year and harvested between September and April, depending on the type of pepper. The region produces fresh green pepper, black pepper, white pepper, and red pepper. Sometimes it's possible to purchase bird pepper, which, as the name suggests, has been digested and expelled by birds. Bird pepper is said to have aphrodisiac powers.

Angela Vestergaard (kampotpepper@ yahoo.com), of FarmLink, is an excellent source for further information about Kampot pepper. This Danish businesswoman has set up a cottage industry with more than 100 local farmers. For tours to the plantations, enquire at Angela's guesthouse in Kampot, the **Blissful Guesthouse** (tel. 012/513024).

few days—and a lot of Phnom Penh–based expatriates agree, using this resort to relax from city life.

US$25-50

Bokor Mountain Lodge (tel. 033/932314, www.bokorlodge.com, US$40–45), located in an attractive colonial corner building on the riverfront, offers reasonably smart air-conditioned rooms, an international menu, an extensive wine list, and Wi-Fi (as well as ordinary Internet access).

Possibly the nicest accommodation in Kampot is the **Rikitikitavi** (tel. 012/235102, US$30–35), which offers just a handful of boutique rooms on the riverfront. Rooms are nicely furnished and spotless, and all have air-conditioned and have a TV and DVD player. Breakfast is included in the room rates. The upstairs restaurant could be the best eatery in Kampot.

FOOD

Most guesthouses and hotels in Kampot have their own restaurants; the best among them is the riverfront **Rikitikitavi** (US$6), which serves Asian and Western standards.

The tiny, NGO-managed **Epic Arts Café,** next to the old art deco market, offers breakfasts, snacks, and cakes in a laid-back atmosphere. The *mezze* (US$3.75) is recommended. It's open in the daytime, and sometimes puts on small events, like exhibitions.

Jasmine Restaurant serves good Asian and Western dishes in a smart riverfront location. It's got a great wine list, a nice ambience, and sunset views.

Rheaj's Burger House (daily 7 A.M.–midnight) has an attractive location on the riverfront and a Christian vibe. It sells, yes, you guessed it, burgers, and pizzas, sandwiches, shakes, and fruit juices are also served.

Just north of the bridge on the river road, **The Little Garden Bar** (daily 7 A.M.–midnight) is run by a friendly German-Australian couple and serves excellent Western dishes, including salads and pizzas as well as Khmer standards from around US$3.

INFORMATION AND SERVICES
Bookshop
Kepler's Books, near the riverside on the north side of the market, is run by the brother of the owner of the excellent Bohr's Books in Phnom Penh. It offers a broad selection of Cambodia-related titles, as well as several shelves of secondhand books. The shop also rents bicycles and sells bus tickets.

Money
The Canadia Bank in Kampot has a 24-hour ATM and a currency-exchange service, and accepts VISA cards. ACLEDA Bank offers Western Union services. Around the market, several money-changers have set up shop.

Internet Access and Post Office
A couple of cheap Internet cafés operate on the road between the old bridge and the traffic circle. It's possible to make Internet phone calls from these places. The post office is on the riverfront road and offers EMS parcel service.

GETTING THERE
Train
In 2008, a cargo train derailed on the Phnom Penh–Kampot line. There's currently no passenger train service, but services may resume in 2010.

Regional Road Transport
Buses (US$8) run by Phnom Penh Sorya depart from near Central Market in Phnom Penh at 7:30 A.M. and reach Kampot around 1:30 P.M. Buses leaving Kampot at 7:30 A.M. get into Phnom Penh about 12:30 P.M. Other bus companies make a similar run. If you only want to go as far as Kep from Kampot, take the Phnom Penh bus for US$2. The cheapest way to get from Kampot to Sihanoukville is with Outback Tours (tel. 012/1707857), which run a daily minibus out of Sihanoukville at 8:30 A.M. The bus leaves from Kampot for Sihanoukville at 11 A.M. Tickets are US$7.50. A shared taxi seat is US$5 per passenger; to rent the entire vehicle costs US$40. Taxis from Phnom Penh are about US$8 for a seat in a shared vehicle or US$50–70 if you rent the entire vehicle. Back from Kampot to Phnom Penh, you might be able to find a slightly cheaper taxi.

GETTING AROUND
Both *motodups* and tuk-tuk drivers will welcome you with open arms and broad smiles when the bus from Phnom Penh arrives in Kampot, hoping to take you to a guesthouse or hotel of their choice in exchange for commission. Rides in town are 1,000–2,000 riel, or a dollar for a short ride in a tuk-tuk. Some guesthouses rent bicycles for US$2–4 a day. A number of small places rent motorcycles. Expect to pay US$5 for a 100cc, US$10–15 for a 250cc dirt bike.

Even in sleepy Kampot, the traffic can be hair-raising and the police love fining people for taking turns down one-way streets that are not always clearly signposted. Always negotiate the fine.

THE COAST

Vicinity of Kampot

◖ PHNOM CHHNORK AND PHNOM SORSIA CAVES

A number of caves near Kampot are worth visiting, though those around Kompong Trach, a little farther afield and best reached from Kep, are more spectacular. Nevertheless, Phnom Chhnork, a small hillock north of Kampot, is worth a visit, as it contains a well-preserved 7th-century brick temple—which is very, very slowly being enclosed by stalactites and stalagmites. A monk at the pagoda ahead of the caves will collect US$1 entrance fee, while local children can be hired as guides here. It's possible to climb to the top of Phnom Chhnork for great views across the surrounding paddy fields.

A little farther up the road, Phnom Sorsia, another hillock, also on the road towards Kep, features several more caves that can be entered. A garish pagoda about one kilometer from the main road is the gateway to these caves. Entrance is free. The most spectacular cave, Phnom Sasear (the White Elephant Cave), is named after a characteristic limestone outcrop vaguely resembling an elephant. Nearby, another cave is filled with bats. The small mountain is home to a band of monkeys and affords great views over the coast and the island of Phu Quoc in the distance. Definitely bring your walking boots and a flashlight and be prepared to do a little climbing to make the most out of these locations.

Phnom Chhnork is some 10 kilometers from Kampot on the main road to Kep. The turn-off to the cave is signposted. Phnom Sorsia is farther along the road to Kep, 15 kilometers from Kampot. Turn left off the main road when you see the temple gateway to Phnom Sasear; from here, it's barely a kilometer.

The caves are easily reached in 20 minutes if you have your own transport or catch a ride with a *motodup*. Expect to pay US$7–10 for a return trip to the caves, including waiting time.

TEKCHHOU ZOO

Some eight kilometers north of Kampot on the road running on the western side of the Kampong Poy River is the small and very modest Tekchhou Zoo (no phone, daily 8 A.M.–5 P.M., US$4). If you'd like to get your wedding photography done here, it's US$25. Yes, there are tigers, lions, and monkeys, but their living conditions are sad.

Another kilometer down the road, you'll have to pay US$1 at a gate if you'd like to visit the river rapids nearby. On weekends, local people flock here to have picnics, but it's pretty quiet during the week.

If you don't have your own wheels, a *motodup* is likely to charge you US$5–8 for a round-trip (including waiting time).

◖ BOKOR NATIONAL PARK

One of the most remarkable sights in Cambodia, **Bokor Hill Station** and the surrounding national park are located on a 1,000-meter-high plateau above Kampot. A rough road up leads from the coast to the plateau through dense jungle. There are stunning views across the plateau—which is covered in boulders, colonial ruins, and gnarled trees—as well as over a sheer cliff face down to the coast.

A weather-beaten casino standing on the edge of the cliff is often clouded in fog and gives the park an eerie ambience. Its adjacent buildings were once a community of more than 500 souls.

Numerous walks are possible from the park headquarters, some 40 kilometers into the park on top of the plateau. Apparently, the area is not mined, but you should stick to the paths anyway—there are stories of a three-legged tiger living near the active pagoda on the plateau. Sometimes, a map is handed out at the entrance gate. About 10 kilometers before reaching the hill station area, travelers come across the so-called Black Villa, a former royal retreat right by the roadside, now just a stone shell. Servants' quarters are hidden in the surrounding bushes. Most of the other remaining buildings are located within walking distance of the

THE SPOOKIEST BUILDING IN THE WORLD: THE BOKOR CASINO AND THE CONSTRUCTION OF BOKOR HILL STATION

Once Cambodia's most luxurious colonial hideaway, Bokor Hill Station had it all: hotels and dance halls, a church, a royal villa, restaurants, servants' quarters, a prison, and a water tower that appears to have walked straight out of a 1950s sci-fi picture. It must have made for an incredibly exclusive ambience in an incredibly remote location.

The crowning glory of this community in the clouds was the casino, **Le Bokor Palace,** constructed in the 1930s on a plateau overlooking the sea below – a towering monument to France's vain glory. The construction of this most unusual holiday resort came at a price – more than 2,000 Cambodians are said to have died during the building of the road up from the coast, which snakes through 40 kilometers of dense, forbidding jungle. After just 15 years in business, the casino closed in the 1940s, when Khmer Issarak rebels threatened the security of the area. The hill station reopened in the 1950s, King Sihanouk built a second royal villa, and for a while the plateau had as many as 500 inhabitants. Following General Lon Nol's takeover, the casino closed once more in the early 1970s and was the site of some fighting between the Khmer Rouge and the Vietnamese in the 1980s.

The buildings have long fallen into disrepair.

The casino, especially, often hidden in thick fog that seeps through windows and doors, looks like the perfect location for a horror movie. No wonder then that several films, including Matt Dillon's atmospheric *City of Ghosts* and a Korean fright flick, have been made in and around the casino.

Bokor is now a national park and precious jungle surrounds the former hill station. This should protect the area from commercial exploitation, but the redevelopment of the casino, which started in 2008, will perhaps put an end to nature's recovery. The reconstruction of the road, the building of a second road, yet to be carved through the jungle, and plans for an 18-hole golf course will have a significant impact on this wilderness area. There's even talk of a dinosaur park. Given that the potential clientele will be made up of well-heeled Asian golfers and high-rolling gamblers, the quietly lingering French charm is likely to disappear. That and the ghosts of war, as well as the jungle, may soon make way for the 18th hole and the blackjack table. Construction of the new developments is supposed to be completed by 2010, but delays are expected. It's uncertain what kind of access visitors will have to the site once the golf course and resort have opened.

THE COAST

© AROON THAEWCHATTURAT

front view of Le Bokor Palace, one of Asia's most haunted buildings

ranger station, the casino is about 15 minutes away. The two-kilometer walk to the prison is particularly attractive; it starts behind the ranger station and leads across several streams of rust-colored water. The prison building is overgrown and stands in a gully on the edge of a former tea plantation. It's also possible to trek farther afield to a waterfall. Be sure to take a ranger to guide you on longer treks.

Entry to the park is US$5, and at the ranger station, a comfortable bed in a dorm room is US$5. A few rangers and military families live here and a small exhibition by Wild Aid, an NGO, illustrates the challenges that rangers face from loggers. Be sure to bring warm clothes and a flashlight. The park rangers sell a little food—such as instant noodles, beer, and biscuits. If you plan to stay more than one night to explore the area, bring some food of your own, as there is a kitchen that guests can use. It's not possible to book advance accommodation at the park headquarters, but the location, for now, is too remote for the dorms to ever fill up.

Until 2008, most visitors drove up to the hill station on dirt bikes or pick-up trucks organized by guesthouses in Kampot. Since redevelopment of the site has begun, the road is sometimes open to individual travelers, at other times blocked. At times it's only possible to travel to the hill station in a truck with a guide. These regular day trips cost US$20. Sometimes a boat ride is also included on these tours. It's also possible to walk up to Bokor Mountain. Ask in Kampot guesthouses for guides. It's either a long one-day hike up and down (with little time to see the ruins up top) or a slower trek that requires an overnight stay. It's 37 kilometers from Kampot to the entrance gate of the park, and another 40 kilometers up to the plateau from there.

Kep

The French first discovered Kep for themselves and built a few administrative buildings on this sparsely populated stretch of coast east of Kampot in the late 19th century. In the 1950s and 1960s, as Cambodia enjoyed independence under King Sihanouk, Kep became the weekend hangout for the chattering classes from Phnom Penh, who built a couple hundred villas and holiday homes here. During this period, waterskiing and rock bands were par for the course. As there was no natural beach, sand was shipped in from Sihanoukville. King Sihanouk had his own island off the coast, where he threw private parties.

In the early 1970s, with the Khmer Rouge closing in, the resort town was abandoned. The houses were locked up and left in the hands of local caretakers. Soon after, the Khmer Rouge moved all of the town's inhabitants out into the countryside and Kep stood empty for a few years. Many locals were taken to killing fields in the mountains and never seen again.

Following the liberation by the Vietnamese, those who returned stripped the villas down to their walls, in the hope of finding scrap to sell. In the 1980s, roofs caved in, stairways collapsed, and the jungle began to claim back its space. Roads were soon overgrown by weeds, and streetlamps were replaced by towering coconut palms. Since the 1990s, many buildings have been occupied by the area's homeless people. With most of the original owners dead and documents lost, it's been a slow rebirth.

During my first visit in 2001, Kep was little more than a bizarre collection of ruins lurking in thick undergrowth. Property after property, home after home, along with the infrastructure one might expect from a beach resort, had fallen victim to the ravages of time and gave Kep the air of a sad, but fascinating open-air museum. This has changed somewhat—some properties have been sold, a few have been redeveloped, and a number of attractive guesthouses and resorts have set up in their midst. While many of the original properties were modest by today's vacation home standards,

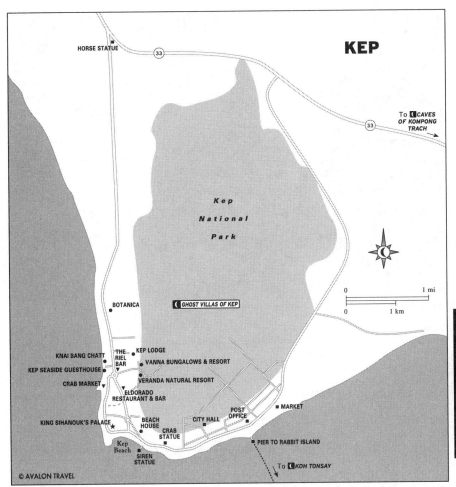

KEP

HORSE STATUE

33

To **CAVES OF KOMPONG TRACH**

33

Kep National Park

0   1 mi
0   1 km

BOTANICA

GHOST VILLAS OF KEP

KEP LODGE
THE RIEL BAR
KNAI BANG CHATT
VANNA BUNGALOWS & RESORT
KEP SEASIDE GUESTHOUSE
CRAB MARKET
VERANDA NATURAL RESORT
ELDORADO RESTAURANT & BAR

POST OFFICE
MARKET
CITY HALL
KING SIHANOUK'S PALACE
BEACH HOUSE
CRAB STATUE
Kep Beach
SIREN STATUE

PIER TO RABBIT ISLAND

To **KOH TONSAY**

© AVALON TRAVEL

THE COAST

some ostentatious buildings—with modernist architectural features in tune with the prevailing Vann Molyvann–type designs—remain impressive.

SIGHTS
Ghost Villas of Kep
All along the main beach road that leads through Kep, villas built in the 1950s and 1960s stand on their own spacious properties. Some are still fenced in by brick walls and ostentatious gates, simply forgotten and overgrown by jungle. Stairways lead straight into the sky, and first- and second-floor levels have holes in the floor large enough to drop a small car through. A few buildings are older, such as a royal villa east of Kep Beach, a handsome structure in a large, well-maintained garden; there are rumors that it will be turned into a boutique hotel. Set back from the beach, the formerly paved, wide roads can still be made out.

If you enjoy wandering (there are said to be no mines in Kep) among this strange archaeological site, there are more properties

THE COAST

© AROON THAEWCHATTURAT

a dilapidated administrative building in Kep

hidden in the growth towards the Elephant Mountains. Quite a few buildings are occupied by squatters, while others are being demolished or renovated.

King Sihanouk's Palace

Located on a headland above Kep Beach and easily reached via a short tarmac road, this palace, built in the late 1960s, has all the grace of a sports gym. It was never used. Perhaps out of respect for Cambodia's former monarch, the building largely escaped vandalism. A number of small viewing pavilions just below the main building offer great views of the Gulf of Thailand. Sometimes the palace is open, but there's nothing much to see inside.

ENTERTAINMENT
Bars

The Riel Bar (www.kep-riel-bar.com) is Kep's premier nighttime venue. Run by Marcel, a friendly Dutch guy, this trendy and welcoming place right in the center of Kep offers a wide range of drinks, healthy Western food

(a real rarity in these parts), a pool table, and great music. It also serves as a venue for occasional film showings, music performances, and readings—so it's a veritable oasis of culture. If you pay with Cambodian riel instead of U.S. dollars, it's 10 percent cheaper. Check the website for upcoming events or just drop by.

SPORTS AND RECREATION
Trekking Tours

Trekking tours to Bokor National Park can be organized by some resorts in Kep, though it's best to get up-to-date information from hotels or travel agents in Kampot.

Snorkeling Tours

Several hotels and guesthouses offer snorkeling trips around the islands off of Kep. Full-day trips are usually US$25, for a minimum of two people, including snorkels and masks. The water here can be murky, so you'll want to check conditions first. For more details, ask at **Vanna Bungalows** (tel. 012/755038, www.vannabungalows.com).

ACCOMMODATIONS
Under US$15
The **Kep Seaside Guesthouse** (tel. 012/684241, US$5–10), not far from the crab market, has an unbeatable location right on the water's edge (though there's no beach to speak of here). Simple, no-frills rooms, some with air-conditioning, and small pavilions by the oceans make this a good option.

The friendly **Botanica** (tel. 016/562775, www.kep-botanica.com, US$8–10), a couple of kilometers outside of Kep on the road to Kampot, has just five small and clean en-suite fan bungalows set in a great overgrown garden. Bicycles and a pool table are free for guests.

US$15-25
A smart choice is (**Kep Lodge** (tel. 092/435330, www.keplodge.com, US$23), which offers just seven rooms on a property at the foot of the Elephant Mountains, some two kilometers from Kep on the road to Kampot. The nicely decorated bungalows have fans, and there's a small pool and a restaurant with Wi-Fi access and pool table. You'll need transportation to get into Kep from here.

Possibly the best budget place in Kep is the friendly and low-key (**Vanna Bungalows & Resort** (tel. 012/755038, www.vannabunga-lows.com, US$10–20), up on the hillside above the municipal buildings. Great ocean views—on a clear day you can see all the way to Bokor Mountain—are best enjoyed from the patios or balconies of the small but smart rooms. Rooms, some with air-conditioning, are located in several wood or stone bungalows, and set in a tropical garden. The restaurant serves decent backpacker fare. Best of all, this place is really quiet. You won't want to leave.

US$25-50
The highly recommended (**Veranda Natural Resort** (tel. 012/888619, www.veranda-resort.com) is next door to Vanna Bungalows & Resort, but is more upmarket and busier. Spacious, comfortable bungalows are reached via an attractive wooden walkway on stilts in a huge tropical garden. The terrace restaurant has the best sunset dinner views in Kep, as well as a great menu of Asian and Western dishes and cocktails. The old bungalows (US$25) are a bit overpriced for what they are, but the newer rooms (US$30–40) are extremely attractive and private and have beautiful bathrooms. A villa with two bedrooms can be rented for US$200 a day and makes for an ideal family retreat. Veranda currently offers the only public Internet access in Kep and has Wi-Fi for guests in its restaurant.

Right in the heart of Kep, the **Beach House** (tel. 012/240090, www.thebeachhousekep. com, US$35–50) is a handsome white building above Kep Beach. Rooms are spacious, modern, and bright, and have air-conditioning and TV. There's a pool, spa, bar, and restaurant serving good Asian and Western dishes.

Over US$50
If you are looking for luxurious privacy, then **Knai Bang Chatt** (tel. 012/349742, www. knaibangchatt.com) is the place for you. The resort claims to be not a hotel, but a private residence for rent on an exclusive basis. As such, it's a great place for a family reunion or a small business conference. Situated directly on the shoreline in Kep, this boutique resort offers 11 beautifully and thoughtfully decorated rooms in two spectacularly restored villas, as well as a new building constructed in the typical 1960s modernist style of so many ruined buildings in the area. An excellent restaurant is attached, and management and staff go out of their way to make you feel comfortable. The fact that the staff doesn't speak English and the (foreign) management is somewhat haughty barely distracts from the beauty of the place. Rooms are around US$160, and it costs about US$1,000 to rent the entire property.

FOOD
The Crab Market
The crab market is really just a collection of stalls in front of a row of abandoned ruined

THE COAST

steamed crab, a local delicacy, at the crab market in Kep

© AROON THAEWCHATTURAT

villas. One day, this small lively bay will be gentrified, but for now, the small restaurants facing the sea offer excellent crab, which you order by the kilo. The grilled squid is also recommended. During weekends and public holidays, it's packed and the prices for crab shoot through the roof.

Restaurants

When the Belgian chef is in attendance, the **Botanica** (tel. 016/562775, www.kep-botanica.com) kitchen serves Algerian, Peruvian, and Belgian food, as well as other world cuisines.

A great place to eat, drink, and socialize is the **Eldorado Restaurant & Bar,** an ingeniously designed and crafted Hungarian eatery on a garden property not far past the Riel Bar on the back road through Kep. Beautifully located in front of a mountain overgrown with jungle, this is where to enjoy wood-fired pizzas (US$8), a number of excellent Hungarian dishes (like delicious lamb sausage, US$6), and a full bar run by the amiable Hungarian chef.

INFORMATION AND SERVICES
Money

There are currently no banks, ATMs, or money-changers in Kep. The nearest bank or ATM is in Kampot. Some resorts might be able to change money for you, but don't expect a competitive rate.

Health and Emergencies

There are no recommended doctors or hospitals in Kep. In case of an accident, go to Phnom Penh as quickly as possible.

Internet Access

No Internet cafés have yet opened in Kep, but you can check your email at Veranda Natural Resort and Kep Lodge if you have your own laptop.

GETTING THERE

Buses run by Phnom Penh Sorya depart from near Central Market in Phnom Penh at 7:30 A.M. and reach Kep around 12:30 P.M.

Buses leaving from Kampot at 7:30 A.M. pass through Kep an hour later. Other bus companies may make a similar run. If you only want to go as far as Kep from Kampot, take the Phnom Penh bus for US$2. A taxi from Phnom Penh is about US$50–70 and takes around four hours.

Motodups make the run from Kampot for around US$8 round-trip, while tuk-tuks are likely to be US$15.

GETTING AROUND

It's possible to rent a bike or motorbike in Kep to explore the area, though businesses in Kampot may be more reliable for renting motorized vehicles.

Vicinity of Kep

◖ KOH TONSAY

Koh Tonsay sits a few kilometers off the coast of Kep and has the feel of a real desert island refuge, or perhaps a place where a pirate might have been dropped off and forgotten. The island is called Rabbit Island in English (from the air, it apparently has the shape of a rabbit).

At one time the island served as a prison, at another as a retreat for King Sihanouk. There are few traces of its past but for a few bunkers, which may have once held Khmer Rouge troops

guarding against Vietnamese invasion. Rabbit Island is still largely overgrown by tropical jungle, though coconut trees have made some inroads. Mangroves and rocks ring much of the island. There is no coral growth. It's possible to visit a couple nearby islands with local fishermen.

The island's fishermen and their families eke out a precarious existence and offer very basic but popular accommodations on the island's largest beach, a rocky bay with fine sand, lined with coconut trees facing the Gulf of Thailand.

THE COAST

© AROON THAEWCHATTURAT

beach on Koh Tonsay, called Rabbit Island in English

Simple bamboo huts (just two have bathrooms) go for US$5 a night. A handful of basic restaurants serve excellent seafood but little else (main dishes US$3), making the island a good excursion for two or three days. None of the island's basic accommodations and restaurants have names or phone numbers.

A narrow path rings most of the island and makes for a half-day trek. Several old concrete bunkers lurk in the undergrowth on the way. It's also possible to climb its highest peak—though you should take a guide from one of the beach restaurants.

It's rumored that Koh Tonsay was sold in 2008, though neither its inhabitants nor local authorities knew to whom—or what this might mean to the fledgling tourism on the island.

Boats from the Koh Tonsay boat dock in Kep cost US$15 for a round-trip. Tourists often end up paying more, however, as you're supposed to return on the same boat you arrived on—and if that boat is not around, you have to take another boat. And pay again. The crossing takes around 30 minutes. Book your tickets through your guesthouse in Kep or at the Long Villa Restaurant at the pier, which also does decent seafood. In the rainy season, the sea is often too rough for the long-tails to cross, so you could find yourself stuck on Koh Tonsay longer than expected.

◖ CAVES OF KOMPONG TRACH

The caves around Kompong Trach, near the Vietnamese border, make for a great day trip in the Kep area. The small town is nothing to write home about, but the limestone caves in the nearby hillock of Phnom Sor are worth a visit. There are several caves fronted by temples, some of which are rather small. The roof of one large cave fell in eons ago and a small patch of jungle has grown in its interior. Stepping through a tunnel into this overgrown, magical opening is somewhat of a surprise, as if stumbling on a land that time forgot. There's a small temple with a large reclining Buddha here, which was rebuilt recently after being destroyed by the Khmer Rouge in the 1970s. More caves farther into the mountain can be reached from here. Entrance is US$1, and local children can guide you to the most interesting caves for a small fee. Bring a flashlight and strong shoes.

To get to Kompong Trach from Kep, head to the White Horse Monument on the road to Kampot and turn right there. From here, it's 20 kilometers to Kompong Trach. It's also possible to connect to this road by heading east through Kep, past the market. After seven kilometers, you'll get to a crossing and turn right. From here, it's another 17 kilometers to Kompong Trach. The unpaved road is in pretty good condition and a new road that passes Phnom Voar, a mountain that served as one of the last Khmer Rouge strongholds in southern Cambodia, leads through some beautiful stretches of countryside. If you get stuck in the area, a couple of simple guesthouses in Kompong Trach are passable in an emergency.

Takeo

Takeo, some 80 kilometers south of Phnom Penh, is one of those small provincial capitals that has seen very little change in recent years. It's not an unattractive place, but for visitors there's almost nothing to see and most people stop off only to visit the nearby temples of Angkor Borei. A large lake, larger still during the rainy season, lies north of town and the area around its shores is the most attractive part of the area. The market, housed in a new building, is crammed with goods from nearby Vietnam.

SIGHTS
Ta Mok's House

Given the shortage of tourist sites in Takeo, Ta Mok's house might be of some interest.

Ta Mok, Brother Number 5, was a notorious Khmer Rouge general who allegedly massacred thousands of civilians and party members before and during the reign of the Khmer Rouge. He died in prison in Phnom Penh in 2006. The house is a dilapidated villa on an island in the lake, but there's no documentation about Ta Mok or the Khmer Rouge here. Restoration plans are being bandied about, but the building, located about one kilometer north of town, is currently closed to visitors.

ACCOMMODATIONS

The **Boeung Takeo Guesthouse** (tel. 032/931306, US$5–10) has the best location in town, right on the lakeside promenade, and the better rooms have views of the lake and Ta Mok's house. Some rooms also have air-conditioning and cable TV. There's a shop downstairs selling toothpaste and beer, though the entire establishment has probably seen better days.

A newer alternative in the same area is the **Phnom Da Guesthouse** (tel. 016/957639, US$5–10), near the boat dock for Angkor Borei. It offers simple, clean rooms with TV, some with air-conditioning.

FOOD

Food options in Takeo aren't great. For basic snacks and simple dishes, try the stalls in Phsar Nat or around the Independence Monument. There's also a restaurant near the boat dock, but it doesn't have menus in English.

GETTING THERE

Passenger services on the southern train line between Phnom Penh and Sihanoukville have been suspended and are not likely to resume until 2010 at the earliest. Takeo lies some 90 kilometers south of Phnom Penh on National Route #2.

Several bus companies, among them Sorya Transport (tel. 023/210359), make the two-hour run from Phnom Penh to Takeo hourly 7 A.M.–4 P.M. Tickets are US$2–3. The buses pass Tonlé Bati, Phnom Chisor, and the Phnom Tamau Zoological Gardens and Wildlife Rescue Center. By share-taxi or minibus, it's more uncomfortable, but faster, and costs 10,000 riel. A private taxi costs US$30.

Onward travel from Takeo to Kampot along Route 3 is a bit more complicated, as you will have to head for the junction of Route 2 and Route 3, about 10 kilometers west of Takeo. From there, it's possible to catch a bus or share-taxi to Kampot in about an hour. Expect to pay 10,000 riel. A *motodup* or tuk-tuk will take you from Takeo to the road junction for US$2–4. It might also possible to catch a share-taxi from Takeo down Route 2, all the way to the border with Vietnam at Prek Chak/Ha Tien. Check with drivers in Takeo.

GETTING AROUND

Motodups can be hired for 500–2,000 riel around town. For day trips in the area, expect to pay US$6–8. Taxis around the area can be hired from local guesthouses for about US$25.

VICINITY OF TAKEO

Angkor Borei

The area around Angkor Borei is sometimes called the cradle of Cambodia and has been inhabited for some 2,500 years. Artifacts from the Neolithic period—as well as the Funan period and the Chenla and Angkorian eras—have been unearthed here, though there are no spectacular temples to see today. It's said that some remnants of these cultures were destroyed in recent memory by the local population in order to make space for the ever-increasing population.

The town of Angkor Borei has nothing to offer but an old wall surrounding it. Excavations have been taking place since the mid-1990s and a small museum (open daily, US$1) displays a collection of items found in the area.

More interesting is the nearby mountaintop temple of **Phnom Da** (US$2), just south of Angkor Borei. Several caves in the side of the hill have served as shrines for both Hindus and Buddhists, and there's a tower on top dating from the 6th or 7th century (and extensively restored in the 11th century). The tower, almost 20 meters high and built from laterite

THE COAST

and brick, has four imposing doorways, though only one of them really opens—the other three are blind. The sandstone pediments above the doorways are carved into *naga* snakes. The views across the paddy fields and canals, all the way to Vietnam to the southeast, are spectacular, especially in the rainy season when the land is partially flooded.

On a much smaller hill nearby, the 8th-century **Ashram Maha Rosei,** a small structure at the foot of the hill, is unique for its Indian architectural influences.

Angkor Borei can be done in a day trip from Phnom Penh, but to really appreciate the canals running through the countryside around the site, an overnight stop in Takeo is recommended. It's the journey from Takeo to the site that makes the trip interesting.

The best way to reach Angkor Borei, especially in the rainy season, is by boat. At the boat dock in Takeo, you can hire a speedboat for around US$30, or a slower, more agreeable boat for US$15. Initially, you may be quoted higher prices, so make sure you use your bargaining skills. The journey in the speedboat takes less than an hour. The boats follow a canal built by the French in the late 19th century and you'll see plenty of other boat traffic, especially traders bringing goods from Vietnam.

It's also possible to reach the two sites by motorbike, at least in the dry season. In the rainy season, you might have to load the bike on small ferries several times to cross submerged parts of the road. It's best to ride this route with a local *motodup* (US$10 round-trip).

THE TONLÉ SAP BASIN

If Angkor is Cambodia's spiritual and cultural heart, the Tonlé Sap Lake is the geographical heart of the kingdom, as well as Cambodia's nutritional life line. During the rainy season, the flood waters of the Mekong push into the Tonlé Sap River near Phnom Penh, reverse the flow of the river, and sweep its nutrient-rich waters into the lake, which expands seven-fold. After the Mekong waters have receded, the Tonlé Sap River changes direction again, and drains the lake back into the Mekong.

Prahoc, a pungent fish and chili paste that's eaten with virtually every meal and could be considered Cambodia's national dish, is almost entirely derived from fish caught in the lake. The soil around the lake is the best in the country and forms the country's rice basket. It was here that the farmers ruled by the builders of

Angkor could achieve two rice harvests a year, turning the Khmer Empire into an economic powerhouse. While the towns around the lake may not be spectacular in comparison to the temples, they do convey impressions of daily life in Cambodia, while a trip across the ever-changing waters of the Tonlé Sap is a highlight of a visit to Cambodia.

The provincial capital Battambang, south-west of the lake, is the most attractive town, with some fine colonial architecture, several temples and Khmer Rouge sites nearby, and a number of great-value hotels.

Kompong Chhnang, the small market town on the eastern side of the lake, is also an interesting stopover, with its fascinating commercial riverfront, a few small temples, and a bizarre Khmer Rouge airfield near town.

HIGHLIGHTS

◖ **Kompong Luong:** This sprawling Vietnamese floating village of some 10,000 inhabitants lies on the shores of the Tonlé Sap Lake (page 185).

◖ **Bamboo Trains:** Powered by water pump engines, these homemade platforms race up and down dilapidated railway tracks to get local produce and people from their homes to the markets in Battambang (page 188).

◖ **Wat Banan and Wat Phnom Sampeau:** These two spectacular hilltop

temples near Battambang make for an excellent day trip to soak up Cambodian country life (pages 194 and 195).

◖ **Koh Ker:** Little-visited and remote, this vast temple complex lies deep in the forests northeast of Siem Reap (page 206).

◖ **Preah Vihear:** This magnificent Angkor-era temple on a mountaintop cliff right on the border to Thailand received UNESCO World Heritage Site status in 2008 (page 208).

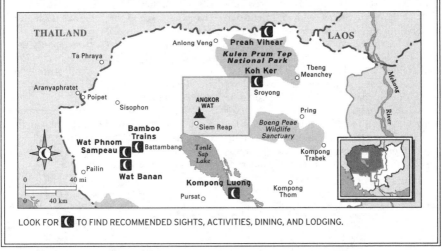

LOOK FOR ◖ TO FIND RECOMMENDED SIGHTS, ACTIVITIES, DINING, AND LODGING.

On the lake itself, numerous floating villages, inhabited, for the most part, by Vietnamese, present a truly unique way of life. The roads around the lake, Route 6 to the north and Route 5 to the south, have been surfaced and are among the best in the country, which has reduced traffic across the lake considerably and has made stops in the smaller towns around the lake a more attractive option. The two roads also form the main road link between Bangkok and Ho Chi Minh City, a journey that should become more straightforward in the next years, as the roads beyond the lake are slowly (very slowly) being upgraded.

Finally, some of Cambodia's most remote and spectacular temples are found in jungle pockets north of Tonlé Sap Lake. While these magnificent structures are still hard to access due to some of the worst roads in the country, temples like Preah Khan and Koh Ker should soon be on standard tourist itineraries.

PLANNING YOUR TIME

The best time to visit the area around the lake is in the dry season, as many of the roads away from the main highway around the Tonlé Sap are not surfaced. South of the lake, Battambang

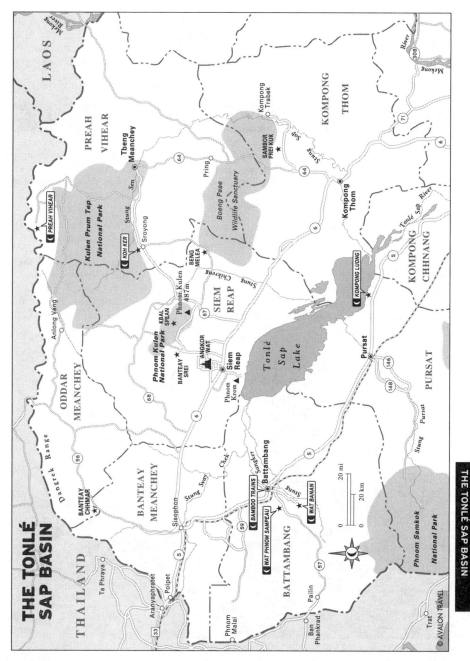

is the most interesting town and worth a three-day visit, while Pursat and Kompong Chhnang make great overnight stopovers. North of the lake, the remote temples of Koh Ker, Preah Khan, and Preah Vihear can be reached in adventurous day or overnight trips from Siem Reap or Kompong Thom. The best time to be on the lake itself is in the rainy season, but the floating villages can be explored in day trips year-round.

Kompong Chhnang

Traveling from Phnom Penh along Route 5, the first place of note is Kompong Chhnang, an attractive small riverside town, which lies at the point where the Tonlé Sap River meets the Tonlé Sap Lake, 90 kilometers northwest of the capital. The town center—with its bustling covered market—is lively, but the real action is by the riverfront, where hundreds of boats unload produce onto the banks of the river against a backdrop of a warren of stilt houses that reach out into the water. Fishermen cast their nets from rickety wooden piers while children play in the water between houseboats. Both Cambodians and Vietnamese crowd the riverfront, which is an excellent place to observe daily small town life. The town is well known for its plain but attractive pottery, which is made by hand and dried solely in the sun. Oxcarts are often seen slowly trundling towards Phnom Penh, loaded with vases and plates.

There's nothing much to do in Kompong Chhnang beyond sitting by the river, though there are a couple of great destinations for day trips. The river life can be explored by boat and there are several temples in the area, as well a fully functioning (but never used) airport built by the Khmer Rouge.

rush hour in a floating community on the Tonlé Sap Lake, near Kompong Chhnang

BIODIVERSITY AND THE TONLÉ SAP LAKE

The Tonlé Sap Lake is the largest natural freshwater lake in Southeast Asia. During the dry season, November–May, the lake drains into the Mekong River via the Tonlé Sap River. When the rains begin in June, the Tonlé Sap River reverses its flow and feeds the lake from the Mekong, which contributes over 80 percent of water to the lake. As a consequence, the lake expands from an area of 2,500 square kilome-

© AROON THAEWCHATTURAT

the Tonlé Sap Lake, Southeast Asia's largest body of freshwater

ters to 16,000 square kilometers; water depth increases from two meters to up to nine meters, providing breeding and feeding grounds for millions of migratory fish.

The influx of nutrients and sediment from the Mekong contribute to the Tonlé Sap's incredible productivity. The fisheries on and around the lake yield about 230,000 tons of fish per year, more than 50 percent of Cambodia's catch. The Tonlé Sap Lake provides more than half of the country's protein intake. Some 800 fish species have been identified, making it one of the world's richest fish habitats and a biodiversity hotspot. In 1997, UNESCO designated the Tonlé Sap Lake as a Biosphere Reserve in order to reduce biodiversity loss; to improve the livelihoods of people living around its shores; and to enhance social, economic, and cultural conditions for environmental sustainability.

Yet today, the Tonlé Sap Lake faces massive environmental degradation. Over-fishing, logging on the lakeshores, and construction projects (such as roads, bridges, dams, and dikes) around the lake all contribute to the loss of the abundance of fish – as well as to reduced fertility of its flood plains. In 2000, the govern-

ment passed a law to cut fishing by half and to contain illegal fishing. But the impact of construction is changing the balance of hydrology, fauna, flora, and seasonal variation.

The time, level, and duration of the annual floods affect the flora, as the water alone does not make the lake productive. Most importantly, the interplay between biosphere and floodwaters makes the Tonlé Sap the incredibly rich body of water it is. For example, tree trunks provide microorganisms such as algae to feed the fish, creating a food chain. Logging the trees kills the spawning and feeding grounds of the fish population. If the flow of the Mekong River, which brings in 87 percent of the migratory fish species, declines, a drastic change in the number of species found in the lake is likely to occur.

The consequences of upstream development, such as dam construction in China, are also likely to be severe: Floods could start later, their duration would decrease, flooded areas could decline, and less nutritious sediment is likely to be swept into the lake. As a result, the Tonlé Sap floodplain would be less fertile and fish stocks would go down, endangering the country's food supply.

THE TONLÉ SAP BASIN

SIGHTS
The Market
The main market is in the old part of town, away from the river. Don't expect souvenirs, as this is a bustling trade market that sells everything from dragon fruit to motorcycle parts.

The Port and River Market
The port is a steep concrete embankment crowded with hundreds of river vessels of all shapes and sizes and lined with stilt houses. From early morning, porters ferry produce up the steep climb to the market on the riverfront, which extends past the riverside pagoda, halfway back into town. Fried food smolders on barbecues, while huge mountains of chili are sorted, bagged, and loaded onto waiting pickups, all making for a lively atmosphere.

The Riverside Communities
If you hang around the riverfront for a little while, young Vietnamese women, with smiles half-hidden under conical hats, are likely to approach you to offer boat trips to the floating homes in the vicinity. Tourists are paddled out into the river in narrow wooden long-boats that sit three or four passengers. The floating community in this area is mostly made up of Vietnamese. The small family homes, some on stilts, others floating on the water, are, for the most part, anchored in straight lines. Some have floating gardens, and even floating pigsties, attached.

A sunset cruise among the homes and shops bobbing about in the water is a magical experience and an opportunity to watch these water-borne people go about their daily lives. Expect to pay US$5 an hour per boat. It may also be possible to stay overnight with a family if you ask around.

ACCOMMODATIONS
Coming into Kompong Chhnang from Phnom Penh, two of the town's best hotels are located on the right side of the road, just before the Independence Monument. The **Sovannphum Hotel** (tel. 026/989333, US$6–15) offers 30 clean and simple rooms, some with fan, others

THE TONLÉ SAP BASIN

© AROON THAEWCHATTURAT

pottery for sale in Kompong Chhnang

with air-conditioning. There's also Internet access, car rental, laundry, and currency exchange. Right next door, the **Asia Hotel** (tel. 026/988727) is very similar, if a little gaudier.

Along the second-to-last turn-off on the left before the Independence Monument, the recommended and long-running **Sokha Guesthouse** (tel. 012/762988, US$5–15), a traditional wooden house with several extensions, is located in a large garden. Some rooms have fans, while others are air-conditioned.

Past the market and on the road to the riverfront, the **Samrong Sen Hotel** (tel. 026/989011, US$6–15) is another clean and modern hotel. There are unfortunately no hotels directly on the riverfront.

FOOD

During the day, food stalls and fruit vendors set up around the market as well as along the riverfront. The most consistent restaurant in town appears to be the friendly **Metapheap Restaurant,** near the Independence Monument. Fried chicken with ginger is US$1.50, as are noodles with pork.

INFORMATION AND SERVICES
Tourist Information

The only concession to tourism is a big sign by the riverfront that reads Tourism Port. There's no tourist office in town.

Money

There are no ATMs in Kompong Chhnang. ACLEDA Bank/Western Union has a branch near the market and cashes travelers checks. Canadia Bank has a branch near the Independence Monument. Money-changers can be found around the market area and can be recognized by the class counters filled with money and small plastic signs with exchange rates.

Health and Emergencies

There's a provincial hospital near the Independence Monument, but should you fall ill or have an accident, try to head back to Phnom Penh immediately.

Internet Access

An Internet café (3,000 riel an hour) called KC Computers can be found in the long row of shops facing the river.

GETTING THERE
Boat

The Phnom Penh–Siem Reap ferry passes Kompong Chhnang and will stop on request. A riverboat will pick you up and take you into the port.

Train

There is currently only one train a week (leaving the capital on Saturdays at 6:20 A.M.) operating between Phnom Penh and Battambang, which stops in Kompong Chhnang after about four hours. The same train returns on Sundays from Battambang, passing through Kompong Chhnang in the afternoon. This excruciatingly slow ride is only recommended to hardened railway enthusiasts.

Regional Road Transport

Numerous buses ply Route 5 between Phnom Penh and Battambang, including Phnom Penh Sorya Buses (tel. 023/210359) and Paramount Angkor (tel. 023/427567) from 6:30 A.M. in either direction. Journey time from Phnom Penh is about two hours. Tickets from Phnom Penh to Kompong Chhnang cost US$3. From there to Battambang, it's US$5. Share taxis and minibuses also shuttle from the capital to Kompong Chhnang, at around 10,000 riel a seat, from Battambang 20,000 riel, and from Pursat 6,000 riel. A private taxi from the capital costs around US$25.

GETTING AROUND

Motodups charge 1,000–2,000 riel for rides around town. For day trips in the area, expect to pay US$8.

VICINITY OF KOMPONG CHHNANG
The Chinese Airport

Just a few kilometers northwest of Kompong Chhnang, the Chinese government

© AROON THAEWCHATTURAT

Farmers plant rice in front of a long-abandoned airport building near Kompong Chhnang.

constructed an airport in order to send sup-plies to the then ruling Khmer Rouge. Just before completion in 1979, the Vietnamese toppled the Pol Pot government and the air-port was never used. The huge runway and control tower remain, guarded by a handful of soldiers who are happy to let you climb onto the roof of the tower for a spectacular panoramic view over the area. The sight has an eerie, forlorn atmosphere, and is a well-pre-served remnant of Cambodia's darkest times. There's a guarded gate at the entrance to the complex. The soldier on duty is likely to de-mand a dollar or two as an entrance fee.

To get there, hire a *motodup* for around US$5 or drive yourself. Leave town in the direction of Battambang on Route 5. After about six

kilometers, a concrete road forks off to the left. The white, square control tower is soon visible among the rice-paddies. Turn right at the next junction and follow the road to the gate.

Prasat Srei

Prasat Srei is a small temple dating from the 6th–8th century. The building itself is not spectacular (nor are several other structures in the area from the same era), but the coun-tryside is stunningly idyllic, especially during and after the rains, when the rice paddies are full of water.

You have to cross the river to visit the tem-ple. If you hire a *motodup,* the round-trip will cost around US$6. Taking a motorbike on the ferry costs an additional US$2.

Pursat

Pursat is the largest town on the southern side of the Tonlé Sap Lake, though this provincial capital is actually more than 30 kilometers from the lake's shore. There's nothing particularly interesting to do in Pursat, but a few decent hotels, Internet access, and a bank make the sleepy town a good base for tours into the surrounding area. Pursat is well known for its marble sculptures of deities, animals, dragons, and god kings, popular among Khmer visitors. There are several workshops around town, but if you don't have the time to search these out, don't worry, as virtually every hotel sells plenty of statues.

SIGHTS
The Market

The market faces the Pursat River and sells almost everything that money can buy in Pursat. There's plenty of fresh fruit, as well as a number of stalls selling fried food. Money-changers can be found around the market. A little north of the market, a temple in the shape of a ship

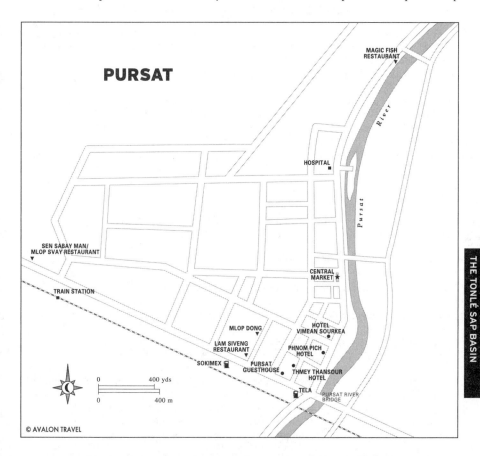

THE TONLÉ SAP BASIN

was being constructed on a small island in the river at the time of writing.

ACCOMMODATIONS

On the western side of the Pursat River, right on Route 5, the modern **Pursat Guesthouse** (tel. 012/682053) offers small and clean rooms with fans for US$5 (or with air-conditioning for US$15). Right next door and set back from the main road is the **Thmey Thansour Hotel** (tel. 012/962395). The rooms in the old building (US$3) are not particularly recommended, but the air-conditioned rooms (US$10) with TV in the new building are clean and are a good value. The new building also has communal balconies, good for sitting around in the evening, and the attached restaurant is one of the best in Pursat.

Right on the river, the **Phnom Pich Hotel** (tel. 052/951515) is probably Pursat's largest. It's a little rundown, but not bad, with cleanish rooms for US$7 (or US$15 with air-conditioning). The hotel has a small restaurant.

The **Hotel Vimean Sourkea** (tel. 052/951466), in an old ochre building across the road from the Phnom Pich Hotel, offers similar rooms for US$5 with fan and US$10 with air-conditioning.

FOOD

Besides food stalls around the market by the river, Pursat has a few eating options. The **Lam Siveng Restaurant** on Route 5 towards Battambang has an English-language menu and reliable Khmer standards for US$2–3. It also sells plenty of marble statues. The **Mlop Dong** in the alley behind the Lam Siveng has both indoor and garden seating (behind the main building). A little farther out of town along Route 5 towards Battamabang, the **Sen Sabay Man** and the **Mlop Svay Restaurant,** united by a generous parking area, have the ambience of a drive-in, complete with beer girls in the evenings. Dishes at all these places are similar in quality and price. Expect to pay around US$2–4 for a main dish.

The most atmospheric place to hang out and enjoy a decent meal is the **Magic Fish Restaurant,** on the western bank of the river beyond the hospital. This eatery is an excellent place to enjoy the sunset over the river and there's a menu in English with main dishes costing 4,000–20,000 riel.

INFORMATION AND SERVICES
Money

There are no ATMs in Pursat. ACLEDA Bank/Western Union has a branch next to the Lam Siveng Restaurant on Route 5 and cashes travelers checks. Money-changers can be found in the market.

Health and Emergencies

There's a hospital in along the riverfront in Pursat, but should you fall ill or have an accident, try to head back to Phnom Penh.

Internet Access

An Internet café (3,000 riel an hour) can be found in a long row of shops facing the river, just south of the market.

Post Office

The post office is also along the riverfront, but if you need to send anything important, Phnom Penh or Siem Reap are more reliable alternatives.

GETTING THERE
Train

There is currently only one train a week (on Saturdays at 6:20 A.M.) operating between Phnom Penh and Battambang, which stops in Pursat sometime in the early afternoon, after about eight hours. The same train returns on Sundays from Battambang, arriving around noon.

Regional Road Transport

Numerous buses ply Route 5 between Phnom Penh and Battambang, including Phnom Penh Sorya Buses (tel. 023/210359) and Paramount Angkor (tel. 023/427567) from 6:30 A.M. in either direction. Journey time is about two hours. Tickets cost US$3. Share taxis and minibuses also shuttle from the capital to Pursat, at around 16,000 riel a seat, from Battambang 15,000 riel, and from Kompong Chhnang 6,000 riel.

GETTING AROUND

Motodup rides around town are 1,000–2,000 riel. For day trips in the area, expect to pay US$8.

VICINITY OF PURSAT
🄲 Kompong Luong

This floating village is one of the largest waterborne communities on the Tonlé Sap Lake. A boat trip through this community, especially in the afternoon just before sunset, is a fascinating, at times otherworldly, experience. Most of the 7,000 inhabitants are Vietnamese, as is the case for similar villages on the lake.

Kompong Luong is really the rebirth of an old tradition, the Tonlé Sap houseboat, which had almost disappeared in the chaos that reigned in Cambodia for 30 years. Following persecution and massacres of Vietnamese

fishermen by the Khmer Rouge, the floating villages all but vanished after 1975 and only returned following Vietnamese liberation in the 1980s.

A short ride through wetland rice and floating bushels of morning glory takes visitors out to the first houses that bob gently in the shallow, muddy water of the lake. Kompong Luong is entirely waterborne, but the houses are not raised on stilts. The buildings float on bamboo platforms, gently bobbing in the waves made by passing boats. The houses, moored to the lake floor, are arranged in a proper town grid and support shops, a hospital, beauty parlors, gas stations, a church, video rental shops, karaoke bars, and family homes. At a central crossing, several ice factories lie clustered together.

It's about 40 kilometers from Pursat to the village of Krakor, the jumping-off point for Kompong Luong. Expect to pay a *motodup* US$8 round-trip for the journey. Once on the lakeshore, boats can be hired for US$10–15 per hour. The distance between Krakor and the floating village varies from season to season as

A farmer drives his buffaloes home in the afternoon, near Pursat.

the entire community moves with the expanding and retreating shoreline.

Phnom Aural National Park and Phnom Samkok National Park

These two wilderness areas lie south of Pursat, but are not yet easily accessible. At 1,764 meters, Phnom Aural is Cambodia's highest mountain. Roads into these areas are still treacherous and tourist infrastructure is nonexistent.

For a taste of the Cardamoms, hire a *motodup* and head for the O'da rapids, located deep in the forest about 60 kilometers south of Pursat. This once-popular picnic site has been abandoned in recent years. The road can be an adventure and you may have to drive through several shallow rivers and across some spectacular wooden bridges. Bring food and drink, as there are no facilities at the rapids, though you'll pass a small village along the route. It's best to have a local help you find the way. The utter remoteness of the site, the beautiful shallow riverbed (with pools to swim in), and the journey itself are hard to beat for a genuine soft adventure.

Battambang

Battambang is Cambodia's second largest city. This attractive and laid-back population center is 290 kilometers from Phnom Penh, on the southern side of the Tonlé Sap Lake. It's actually situated some 50 kilometers from the lake, connected by the year-round navigable Sangker River. Colonial as well as splendid modern Khmer architecture from the 1960s, numerous lively pagodas, and, above all, fantastic trips into the stunningly beautiful surrounding countryside make Battambang a great stopover between Phnom Penh and the temples of Angkor.

The history of Battambang has been nothing but turbulent. The region around the city was part of Siam (Thailand) from the 15th century until the early 20th century, when it was returned to Cambodia under the French colonial authority. The Thais returned in the 1940s, with the help of the Japanese, and held on until after Word War II, when the Allied Forces pressured Thailand to return the region to Cambodia. Battambang Province was Cambodia's economic powerhouse, producing much of the country's rice, until the Khmer Rouge takeover in 1975. With the Vietnamese invasion in 1979, Pol Pot's troops fled northwest towards the Thai border, and for the next 18 years, the province was engulfed in a vicious civil war, which has left the area dotted with thousands of landmines that are still being cleared today. During the civil war, Battambang served as the government army's headquarters. As recently as 1996, the Khmer Rouge operated close to the city, around Wat Banan.

Today, a little more than a decade later, Battambang is slowly becoming a center of local commerce again. It's perfectly safe now, and well-trodden paths have long been cleared of landmines and unexploded ordnance. It's wise to err on the side of caution in the countryside, however, and it's advisable to hire local guides to destinations out of the city, especially to rarely visited places.

ORIENTATION

Battambang stretches from north to south along both sides of the Sangker River. The main town center is on the western side of the river, which can be traversed on three bridges within the downtown area. Many of the most attractive colonial buildings flank both sides of the river, including the spectacular Governor's Mansion on Street 1, which unfortunately is closed to the public. Visitors coming from Phnom Penh along Route 5 will encounter a giant statue of Dambong, a giant guard holding the Bat Dambong, the "Disappearing Stick" from which the city takes its name.

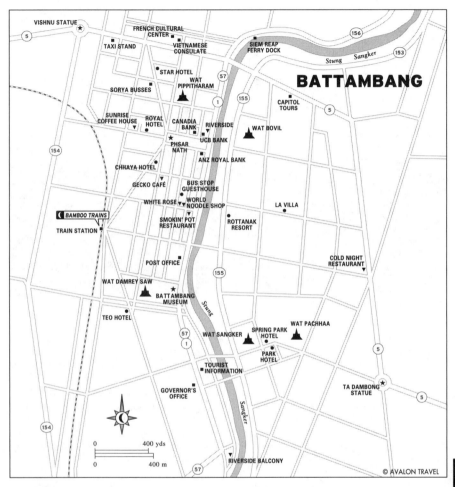

The map shows BATTAMBANG with the following labeled locations:

VISHNU STATUE · FRENCH CULTURAL CENTER · TAXI STAND · VIETNAMESE CONSULATE · SIEM REAP FERRY DOCK · 156 · 153 · Stung Sangker · STAR HOTEL · WAT PIPPITHARAM · 57 · SORYA BUSSES · 1 · 155 · CAPITOL TOURS · 5 · SUNRISE COFFEE HOUSE · ROYAL HOTEL · CANADIA BANK · RIVERSIDE · WAT BOVIL · 154 · UCB BANK · PHSAR NATH · ANZ ROYAL BANK · CHHAYA HOTEL · GECKO CAFÉ · BUS STOP GUESTHOUSE · WHITE ROSE · WORLD NOODLE SHOP · LA VILLA · BAMBOO TRAINS · SMOKIN' POT RESTAURANT · ROTTANAK RESORT · TRAIN STATION · COLD NIGHT RESTAURANT · POST OFFICE · 155 · WAT DAMREY SAW · BATTAMBANG MUSEUM · Stung · TEO HOTEL · 57 · WAT SANGKER · SPRING PARK HOTEL · WAT PACHHAA · 1 · PARK HOTEL · 5 · TOURIST INFORMATION · GOVERNOR'S OFFICE · TA DAMBONG STATUE · 5 · Sangker · 154 · 0 400 yds · 0 400 m · RIVERSIDE BALCONY · 57 · © AVALON TRAVEL

SIGHTS
The Market

Phsar Nath is located in a great-looking art deco structure right in the heart of town. Long narrow aisles run the length of the building, crowded with stalls offering mostly clothes and household goods. Around the outside of the market, countless stalls sell foodstuffs—from dragon fruit to smoked river fish. Phsar Nath is busy from early morning and there are several banks, with ATMs attached, as well as money-changers, located in the streets around the building.

Battambang is a regional center for rubies and sapphires, which are mined in nearby Pailin, and are cut and polished in the city. Numerous gem dealers are located around Phsar Nath. If you don't know anything about gemstones, beware: there's a good chance that you could end up with a fake.

Wats

Numerous Buddhist temples are dotted around town, many of them built in the early 20th century during the French occupation.

Phsar Nath, the central market in Battambang

Battambang Museum

Worth visiting is the Battambang Provincial Museum (tel. 092/914688, US$1) on Street 1, which is located in a handsome ochre Cambodian building on the riverfront. It contains a small collection of Angkorian and pre-Angkorian statues, lintels, and other artifacts. Many of the items on display appear to have been partly looted—statues are missing their heads more often than not. The museum is officially open daily 8–11 A.M. and 2–5 P.M., though actual hours of operation vary. Photography is not allowed inside the building.

◖ Bamboo Trains

The Bamboo Trains, also called Funny Trains, are a unique way to travel in the region. As Cambodia's railway system is barely functioning (though a major restoration program financed by Japan is in the works), people around Pursat and Battambang have set up their own train system—running little bamboo platforms, powered by engines meant for water pumps, up and down the tracks. It's well worth hitching a ride for a few kilometers just for the experience.

The Bamboo Trains, called Norry by the locals, zip along wonky rails at 30–60 kilometers per hour. They occasionally almost derail when there's a gap in the tracks, and they frequently stop to disassemble when there's on-coming traffic—another Bamboo Train, most likely. These very basic modes of transport carry up to 20 passengers at a time, as well as cows, pigs, and motorcycles. The Bamboo Trains have been around since 1980, when locals first built them with wooden wheels and powered them by hand. Later, tank or tractor wheels were added. A 35-kilometer ride is likely to cost around US$5–8, but for those with sensitive behinds, shorter journeys of just a few stops are recommended.

The *motodup* guides in Battambang take tourists to Ou Dambang, a small village some five kilometers from town, which serves as the main departure point for the Bamboo Trains. Semi-assembled Bamboo Trains linger in the shade of a bombed-out station building here,

THE TONLÉ SAP BASIN

The Bamboo Train provides local people with transport in the absence of regular trains or usable roads.

while the drivers, who have formed a kind of union of Norry operators to ensure equal earnings, sit in the shade, play cards, and wait for customers.

As the road network between outlying villages improves slowly, the Bamboo Trains will one day be obsolete. A ride on one of these contraptions is a truly amazing experience and gives great insight into the daily toil of ordinary Cambodians.

ENTERTAINMENT
Bars
The very agreeable **Riverside Balcony** lies on the western bank of the Sangker River, in the far south of the city and is the smartest place in town. This bar-cum-restaurant is located on the first-floor terrace of an old Khmer building. It has a pool table, a limited menu of French and Mexican dishes, and a large choice of drinks, including draft beer. Pizzas are around US$6. The pork fillet is great. In the evenings, foreign NGO staff congregate here.

Nightclubs
A few years ago, one could observe drunken policemen draw their guns on the dance floor of the **Bopha Thip,** a typical provincial Khmer nightclub, located a block south of the Governor's Mansion. These days, tempers ignite less frequently and a visit to one of these places can be a great cultural experience. Expect Khmer renderings of popular Thai and European club numbers, plenty of beer, and, for the local VIPs, bottles of whisky and dancing girls.

SPORTS AND RECREATION
Meditation
It's possible to embark on a Buddhist meditation retreat at the **Battambang Vipassana Centre** (tel. 012/870766, www.latthika. dhamma.org) at a temple some 15 kilometers south of the city. You can visit the website and apply via email. Ten-day retreats are free, but a donation is expected, as all the teachers are volunteers.

Cooking Classes
Sambath's Cooking School (tel. 012/639350) offers day-long cooking courses for US$10. Participants visit the market to purchase ingredients, learn to prepare a curry paste, then cook two dishes and take home a booklet containing the recipes. And of course, they get to eat what they've prepared. The courses take place at Sambath's family home in Battambang. Sambath will pick participants up at their respective hotels.

The **Smokin' Pot Restaurant** (tel. 012/821400, vannaksmokinpot@yahoo.com) also offers daily cooking courses, with a trip to the local market to buy ingredients and a chance to cook three different local dishes. Half-day courses start at 9 A.M. and cost US$8.

ACCOMMODATIONS
Since 2005, a whole range of hotels has opened around the city. In fact, there's now an oversupply of rooms in Battambang. That said, a lot of the long-established budget places are

THE TONLÉ SAP BASIN

pretty rundown, so the new kids on the block are more in tune with the boom and bustle of Cambodia's second city.

Homestays

Mr. Sambath (tel. 012/639350), an experienced tour guide, organizes homestays in villages around the city in order to give visitors an opportunity to experience genuine Cambodian country life and food. Stays cost US$10 per person per night and include a transfer from your hotel in Battambang to the villages. For more information, visit http://geocities.com/battambangvillagehomestay.

Under US$15

The **Royal Hotel** (tel. 016/912034, royalasia-hotelbb@yahoo.com), located in a side street off Phsar Nath, is one of Battambang's longest-running and most reliable budget guesthouses. It offers clean, no-frills rooms with TV and fan for US$5, or with air-conditioning and hot water for US$10. A rooftop restaurant serves international backpacker favorites as well as a selection of Khmer dishes. A small army of *motodups* hangs around outside, ready to take guests to the sights surrounding Battambang.

The **Bus Stop Guesthouse** (tel. 053/730544, www.busstopcambodia.com, US$7) on Street 2 is a simple and spotless British-run backpacker place. All rooms and the downstairs bar have Wi-Fi.

The **Chhaya Hotel** (tel. 053/952170, www.chhayahotel.com) on Street 3 is one of those worn-down budget places, with clean but dingy rooms (US$5 with fan, US$10 with air-conditioning). The hotel has long offered trips through the countryside (with one of the *motodups* working here). It also sells boat, train, and bus tickets; arranges for taxis; and has a free pickup service from the ferry dock or the bus stop.

The **Park Hotel** (tel. 053/953773), on the eastern side of the river, is a better option, a kind of almost-3-Star modern hotel that's really a budget place. Spacious rooms with fans are US$6, while the air-conditioned versions are US$12. Some rooms have hot water, TV, and fridge.

US$15-25

The **◖ Star Hotel** (tel. 053/953523, www.as-rhotel.com, US$15), owned by the same people as the Royal, opened in 2008 in the northern part of town. Large, spotless rooms with air-conditioning and TV are well worth the price, and the rooftop restaurant offers cold beer, good views, and a limited but decent menu. Fast Internet service (US$1/hour) is available in the lobby.

On the eastern side of the river near the new iron bridge, the **Spring Park Hotel** (tel. 015/789999, www.springparkhotelbtb.com) is a modern glass-fronted establishment for business travelers and tourists. Large, air-conditioned rooms with heavy wooden furniture are US$11, and a small suite with two en-suite bathrooms is a good value at US$30.

US$25-50

A long-running favorite with visiting NGO staff, the reliable **Teo Hotel** (tel. 012/857048, US$11–44), built in the 1960s, is located in the southern part of town. It offers clean, air-conditioned rooms with hot water and TV.

US$50-100

◖ La Villa (tel. 053/730151, www.lavilla-battambang.com, US$65) is as francophone an experience you are likely to have in Battambang. Located on the eastern bank of the Sangker River, this colonial mansion under French management offers seven incredibly well-restored, air-conditioned rooms furnished with wonderful art deco items. The small suites on the first floor are especially romantic, but the two rooms on top, with low-slanting roofs, are also great. The restaurant offers French cuisine and there's a small garden with a pool out the back. Single occupants get a slight discount on room rates.

Also delightful, yet completely different, is the **Rottanak Resort** (tel. 012/501742, therottanakresort@yahoo.com, US$66–88), in a walled compound on a quiet side street on the eastern side of the river. Smart and spotless bungalows with attached bathrooms that are partly open to the sky stand around a reasonably sized swimming pool, flanked by a chic restaurant and bar. The food is fusion French and Asian and most main dishes are around US$6–8.

FOOD
Numerous food and drink stalls set up along the western riverfront in the afternoon and evenings. Several large garden-style restaurants around town are crammed with beer girls and serve as the main entertainment venues for the male half of Battambang's population.

The **Sunrise Coffee House** (Mon.–Sat. 6:30 A.M.–5 P.M.), on the same street as the Royal Hotel, has a Christian vibe and offers cakes, sandwiches, breakfasts, a book exchange, and a chance to scrawl your name onto a wall or ceiling to join hundreds of others who have passed through before. On the menu, an entire page is dedicated to coffee.

The **White Rose,** set back from the river near the iron bridge, is a no-frills corner restaurant that offers reasonably priced Khmer and Thai standards. It's possible to sit by the roadside and watch life go by. Beef *lok lak* is US$2.

Two doors down from the White Rose, the simple **World Noodle Shop** (daily 6 A.M.–7:30 P.M.) is not signposted in English, but it does have an English menu. A bowl of beef soup with freshly made noodles is 5,000 riel.

For Vietnamese and Western dishes, head to the **Riverside** (daily 6:30 A.M.–8 P.M.), facing the river just north of Phsar Nath. It has a English-language menu with color photos, so you know exactly what you are ordering. Excellent Vietnamese coffee is 3,000 riel, while a beef steak will set you back US$4.

Right in the heart of town, the attractive ⬛ **Gecko Café** (daily 8 A.M.–10 P.M.) is located on the first floor of an old colonial corner building overlooking a busy intersection on Street 3 just south of the market. The balcony seating is great and there's a modest menu of good Western and Khmer dishes. Fish *amok,* a mild fish curry, is US$3.50. The café, owned by a friendly American, also offers a massage service and rents out motorcycles. There's a cheap Internet shop right underneath.

The **Smokin' Pot Restaurant** (tel. 012/821400, vannaksmokinpot@yahoo.com) is a small hole-in-the-wall restaurant near the river and across the road from the World Noodle Shop, with a phenomenally large menu of Khmer and Thai dishes, as well as a page of Western comfort food from US$2. The restaurant also offers daily cooking courses (US$8 for a half-day class).

Located on Route 5 on the eastern side of the river, the **Cold Night Restaurant** (tel. 012/994746, daily 6 A.M.–midnight) is another NGO hangout. It serves decent Western, Thai, and Khmer food, as well as a selection of cocktails and beers. And there's a pool table.

INFORMATION AND SERVICES
Tourist Information
Battambang's tourist information center, located in a small kiosk next to a French-era house on the western side of the Sangker River, is staffed by a large number of young and enthusiastic trainees. The friendly youngsters hand out a map of the province with some of the major sights.

Long-time Cambodia traveler and academic Ray Zepp has written a book called *Around Battambang* (US$10 in shops and hotels around town), which contains incredibly detailed cultural information on the entire province. All profits from the book go towards funding the German Christian NGO Evangelischer Entwicklungsdienst, which supports HIV-positive orphans and monks in raising AIDS awareness.

You can apply for visas at the Vietnamese Consulate (tel. 053/952894) in town. Apparently, it's less of a hassle here than in Phnom Penh. The consulate is in the north of Battambang on Street 3 and opens in the mornings 8–11 A.M. and again in the afternoons 2–4 P.M.

The French Cultural Center (tel. 053/952897, www.ccf-cambodge.org) can be found in the north of the city, just around the corner from the Vietnamese Consulate. Check the website for programs, such as exhibitions and movies.

Money

There are numerous banks and quite a few 24-hour ATMs in town. Canadia Bank, ANZ Royal Bank, and UCB Bank are located near Pshar Nath, change money and travelers checks, and have ATMs. The ACLEDA Bank/Western Union is located on the eastern side of the river. Money-changers can be found around the market and are easily recognized by the glass counters filled with bundles of different currencies.

Health and Emergencies

The Battambang Provincial Hospital cannot be recommended for anything but the most minor accident wounds. If you have a serious injury or disease, cross the border to Thailand as quickly as possible and seek medical attention there.

Internet Access

Numerous cheap Internet cafés can be found around town and many hotels also have Internet facilities. Expect to pay US$0.50–1 per hour. The Bus Stop Guesthouse has Wi-Fi.

Post Office

The newly restored post office is on the eastern side of the river. But don't send anything from here unless you have to. And if you have to, don't expect it to arrive.

GETTING THERE

Air

There are currently no flights to Battambang and the airfield is in a pitiful condition, but this is likely to change in the future.

Train

The train from Phnom Penh to Battambang takes more than 12 hours and costs around US$4. It departs just once a week, on Saturdays, between 6:20 A.M. and 7 A.M. The train returns about the same time on Sundays. This rather meager timetable may well change once the extensive railway restoration program is completed some time in 2010. Bear in mind that the same journey takes just five hours in

a bus. Cargo trains also move on to Sisophon. If you are determined to get there as slowly as possible, you might be able to talk yourself on board and ride like a hobo.

Boat

Boats for Siem Reap leave every morning at 7 A.M. from the ferry dock on the western side of the river, a little north of the new stone bridge. The journey takes 6–8 hours, depending on the water level. En route, the ferry passes numerous small villages along the river before joining the Tonlé Sap Lake. Passengers disembark in Phnom Krom, some 11 kilometers from Siem Reap, where they are accosted by hordes of touts. The tickets are a whopping US$20 and the boats do not meet international safety standards, though it is one of the most scenic river journeys one can undertake in Cambodia. At the height of the dry season, the journey can take much longer. There are no regular boats running from Battambang to Phnom Penh.

Regional Road Transport

Since Route 5 has been upgraded, numerous bus companies make the run from Phnom Penh to Battambang in about five hours. Early buses leave both cities from around 6 A.M. The last buses depart around 2:30 P.M. Tickets cost US$4–5. The Phnom Penh Sorya Transport buses (tel. 023/210359) leave from Route 5 on the eastern side of the river, near Wat Bo Knong. Capitol Tours (tel. 053/953040), Paramount Angkor (tel. 023/427567), and Neak Krorhorm (tel. 023/219496) have offices near the Star Hotel. Most hotels and guesthouses can arrange tickets. Share taxis to Phnom Penh are around 30,000 riel. Share taxis leave from the taxi stand on Route 5, on the way to Sisophon. Private taxis from Battambang to Phnom Penh (four hours) cost around US$50; to Siem Reap (3–4 hours), it's around US$40.

GETTING AROUND

The easiest way to get around town if you don't want to walk is the trusty *motodup*, who sits waiting for customers on virtually every street corner. Some of the hotels, especially the back-packer places, have a small army of drivers attached to their businesses. Rates around town should be 1,000–2,000 riel. If you want to hire a *motodup* for the day to see some of the sights outside of town, expect to pay US$6–10, depending on how far you are planning to go. Most hotels also offer taxi services. Around town, it's US$25 a day, and day trips around the area should be no more than US$40.

Vicinity of Battambang

The countryside around Battambang is stunning and easily accessible with the help of a *motodup*. Several attractive day trips through nearby small villages and rice fields are possible. The hilltop temples of Wat Banan and Wat Phnom Sampeau can be visited in a day. Wat Samrong and Wat Ek Phnom, both to the north of the city, are close enough to be seen in a half-day. The Kamping Poy Reservoir is a popular day-trip destination for the Khmer and especially at weekends a great place to interact with locals. Further afield, the frontier town of Pailin is, unless the road is in excellent condition, an overnight excursion.

WAT EK PHNOM

This 11th-century temple is not particularly spectacular in itself, as it's been looted, but it makes a nice excursion through the villages north of Battambang. There's a modern temple nearby.

The temple is situated among rice fields about 10 kilometers north of the city. Follow the river road (Street 1) pretty much all the way to the temple. A round-trip with a *motodup* should cost US$6–8.

WAT SAMRONG

Wat Samrong is located in a beautifully atmospheric compound to the north of Battambang. An old crumbling *chedi,* a prayer hall built during the French occupation, several stupas, and a new temple building stand among tall coconut palms.

During the Khmer Rouge years, more than 10,000 people were killed here and left to rot in

© AROON THAEWCHATTURAT

the prayer hall of Wat Samrong, a temple near Battambang where more than 10,000 people were killed during the reign of the Khmer Rouge

THE TONLÉ SAP BASIN

ditches around the temple compound. A stupa containing some of the bones of the victims was erected behind the temple in 2008. Frescoes in the walls of the building graphically relate the suffering of the people of Battambang during this time and are captioned in English. Behind the stupa, rice fields and palm trees make for a beautiful backdrop but the many ponds between the paddy still contain the bones of thousands of victims. The people living around the temple make sweet sticky rice, a popular and tasty local snack, which is sold by the roadside in bamboo tubes. Entrance to the temple and stupa is free.

Wat Samrong is eight kilometers north of downtown Battambang. It's best to hitch a ride with a local *motodup*. A round-trip should cost around US$5.

◖ WAT BANAN

The *motodups* in Battambang usually offer a ride to the Angkor-era hilltop temple Wat Banan and the modern temple of Wat Phnom Sampeau as a combined day trip through the countryside around Battambang. Wat Banan, constructed in the 11th century, sits on top of a hill surrounded by a vast expanse of paddy fields. Near the food stalls at the bottom of the hill, you will be accosted by tourist police who demand US$2 to enter the temple grounds. A broad and well-restored stairway takes about 10 minutes to climb. There are five intact towers on the hilltop and the views across the plains are spectacular. Many of the carvings have been destroyed by looters. The figures of elegant *apsaras* are still there, but their heads are missing.

Make sure you stay on the paths. There may still be plenty of small caliber ammunition, spent and rusty, lying around—and parts of the steep forested ravines of the hill may still be mined.

Drink sellers have assembled their stalls at the foot of the hill as well as up by the temple. Keep the receipt, as this payment entitles you to visit Wat Phnom Sampeau as well.

The temple mountain is about 20 kilometers south of Battambang. Follow the road on

the main tower of the hilltop temple Wat Banan

© AROON THAEWCHATTURAT

THE TONLÉ SAP BASIN

the western bank of the Sangker River (Route 154) until you see Wat Banan on the right side of the road. A dirt road leads directly to the mountain. There's a shortcut through beautiful paddy fields and villages to Phnom Sampeau, but it's hell for a bike in the rainy season and a struggle in a car any time of year. A round-trip, which also takes in Phnom Sampeau, should cost around US$15.

◖ WAT PHNOM SAMPEAU

This temple sits on a forbidding forest-covered limestone rock protected by steep cliffs. A local legend tells of a crocodile that loved the beautiful Rumsay Sok. The crocodile's love went unanswered, so it smashed the ship Rumsay Sok and her fiancé, a local prince, were traveling on and killed the couple. In revenge, the local villages drained the sea and the crocodile perished. Phnom Sampeau is thought to be the sunken sailing boat while another nearby hillock represents the crocodile. Fighting between government forces dug in on Phnom Sampeau and the Khmer Rouge dug in on Crocodile Mountain continued until 1997.

The more than 700 steps to the top are a strenuous affair, but there is a new road, which takes around 20 minutes on foot. Wat Phnom Sampeau, like so many temples, was used as a killing site during the Khmer Rouge years. Prisoners were led to the mouth of a deep cave shaft, pushed down and then machinegunned. It's possible to climb down into two caves where small shrines with bones remind visitors of the atrocities committed here. Old women try to encourage tourists to buy candles and the atmosphere is appropriately somber. A metal cage, which is locked for fear of theft, contains human remains. A man sitting at the top of the stairs might charge you US$1 to enter. The modern temple contains some garish murals. The views from the top of the rock across the perfectly flat plain towards Thailand are impressive.

Just below the temple, a couple of old artillery pieces (one's a Soviet cannon from 1944) linger in the forest. On the side of the rock mountain, a giant face of the Buddha has been carved into the rock face. Drinks sellers can be found at the foot of the hill, as well as up by the temple. A new temple with the same name was constructed at the foot of the hill in 2008.

Phnom Sampeau is about 15 kilometers south of Battambang along Route 57 to Pailin. A round-trip, which also takes in Wat Banan, should cost around US$15.

KAMPING POY RESERVOIR

This large reservoir, flanked by an eight-kilometer-long dam, was one of the Khmer Rouge's many engineering disasters. Thousands are said to have died during the dam's construction, despite Pol Pot's declaration that under his watch the Khmer people would build like the great master-builders of Angkor—something of a delusion as the Khmer Rouge had killed all the engineers. Today, the area is a popular picnic place and swimming hole for locals, who arrive in great numbers during the weekend. Vendors selling drinks and fruit ply their trade along the water's edge.

The reservoir is sign-posted on the left on Route 57 about 15 kilometers south of Battambang. From this turn-off, it's another 15 kilometers along a road flanking a canal. A *motodup* ride costs around US$10.

PAILIN

Famous Cambodian singer Sim Sisamuth wrote several songs about Pailin and the region south of Battambang is rich in folklore—but Cambodia's long wars have seen to the gradual and almost total decline of Pailin's fortunes. It was in this area, in nearby Samlot, where peasants first rose against the Sihanouk government in the 1960s. And Pailin was among the places that the Khmer Rouge fled following Vietnamese liberation and from where they conducted the vicious guerilla war of attrition that was to last another 18 years—until 1996, when Hun Sen, leading the government forces, cut a deal with Khmer Rouge leader Ieng Sary, to absorb his fighters into the Cambodia army. In exchange, Ieng Sary and his comrades crawled under the rock called Pailin and struck it rich with gems and logging. The plundered

ANGELINA JOLIE: CAMBODIA'S HONORARY CITIZEN

There's little need to introduce Angelina Jolie. She is one of Hollywood's top-earning actresses and is constantly in the headlines – not just for the roles she plays, but also for her marriage to Brad Pitt, her numerous children (both biological and adopted), and her long-term humanitarian commitment to Cambodia.

In 2001, Jolie starred as the video game heroine Lara Croft in the movie *Lara Croft: Tomb Raider*, which was partly shot in Cambodia. The film utilized some of the Angkor temples (most notably Ta Prohm) as exotic backdrops for ultraviolent cartoon shoot-outs between Jolie and an array of bad guys and mythical monsters. While the movie was corny and received bad reviews, it did make Jolie an international superstar. And as the first major Hollywood movie production in Cambodia since the 1960s, the film seemed to be part of the country's re-emergence from obscurity.

While in Cambodia, Jolie became aware of humanitarian issues, most notably the curse of the countless landmines still lying dormant across the country. This led to her interest in other regions in crisis, such as Afghanistan, Tanzania, and Darfur. Since August 2001, Jolie has been a Goodwill Ambassador for the UNHCR (the office of the United Nations High Commissioner for Refugees). Of her work, Jolie has said:

> We cannot close ourselves off to information and ignore the fact that millions of people are out there suffering. I honestly want to help. I don't believe I feel differently from other people. I think we all want justice and equality, a chance for a life with meaning. All of us would like to believe that if we were in a bad situation someone would help us.

Since 2001, Jolie has continued her humanitarian work all over the world, while lobbying for her political causes in Washington. In 2002, she was back in Cambodia to adopt her first child, seven-month-old Maddox Chivan Jolie-Pitt, out of an orphanage in Battambang.

In 2003, the actress pledged several million dollars to help establish a wildlife reserve near Pailin, the former Khmer Rouge stronghold in the western part of the country. Money was also set aside to help rehabilitate former Khmer Rouge fighters in the Samlot region near Pailin, where Jolie owns a house. In 2005, King Sihamoni signed a decree awarding Cambodian citizenship to Jolie in recognition for her conservation work in the country.

resources were sold off to Thailand for the most part and Khmer Rouge generals soon owned sumptuous villas in Thai provinces bordering Cambodia. Following the death of Pol Pot in 1998, many of the other Khmer Rouge leaders retired to Pailin and the town became a semi-autonomous zone within Cambodia, de facto ruled by the Khmer Rouge. Until 2001, there was even a border crossing into this absurd free state.

In the late 1990s, Pailin was a boomtown and people from all over Cambodia moved there, having heard that one could become rich overnight. Few did and the gemstones ran out. Most of the trees in the area were logged and

sent west. The town was left with brothels and destitute inhabitants, some of them Khmer Rouge, others perhaps their victims. The grand communist vision had finally gone to the dregs. As late as 2002, I saw Khieu Samphan, the Khmer Rouge's Brother No. 2, strolling around the streets of Pailin with impunity. But with the gemstones gone, the locals forced into working on monoculture plantations controlled by Thais, and the Khmer Rouge leaders finally in jail awaiting trial (though Ieng Sary's son is the town's governor), Pailin has turned from a fiefdom of mass murderers into a dusty urban slum with no redeeming features.

What's perhaps most amazing is that the

Khmer Rouge were so concerned about destroying all aspects of decadent Western influence in Cambodia society. Yet, under their watch, Pailin became as perfect an expression of debauched decadence and rot as one might never wish to see. For a while even, there were organized boxing matches between people with disabilities.

With much of the area still saturated with landmines (never leave well-trodden paths!), only people really interested in Cambodia's recent, dark past are likely to get any mileage out of this town. There's a dusty market where it's possible to buy flip-flops made from car tires, a nod to the Khmer Rouge's glorious past (the movement made much of their cheap and effective rubber footwear). The only half-decent hotel in town is often closed. Behind the massive government hall, a tourist office awaits visitors, but I suspect a true demand for such a service is still some years off.

The only interesting sight is **Phnom Yat,** a temple mountain, which affords great panoramic views over the town and the denuded hills beyond. This temple is amazingly gaudy and features a representation of hell, in which life-size human figures are tortured in various terrible ways.

The Chrork Prum international border crossing to Thailand (daily 7 A.M.–8 P.M.) lies 22 kilometers beyond Pailin. On the Thai side, public transportation is available.

Accommodations

Since Pailin's glory days are a thing of the past, the choice of accommodations in town is limited. A number of fleabag hotels, where rooms can be rented by the night or the hour, can be found around the market, but the best hotel in town is the **Hang Meas** (tel. 053/640763, US$15), a somewhat rundown affair near the market with a karaoke restaurant and rather worn, air-conditioned rooms that seems to be open only sporadically.

A better alternative is the **Bamboo Guesthouse** (tel. 053/405818, US$10–15), which is outside of town on the road to the border. It offers smart bungalows with air-conditioning. In the evenings, local military and police sometimes congregate at the restaurant for drinking binges.

On the Cambodian side of the border, several casino hotels have been carved out of the dusty tired soil and offer decent rooms with air-conditioning for around 500 baht.

Food

Pailin is no culinary paradise. Your best bets in town are a number of cheap eateries around the market. For decent Thai food, try the little **Heineken Beer Garden** in the parking lot in front of Caesar's Palace by the border. Dishes are around 100 baht.

Getting There

Route 57 is terrible, all the way from the outskirts of Battambang to downtown Pailin. Potholed, deeply rutted, and virtually impassable in the rainy season, the drive to Pailin is a bone-jarring experience. Several bridges en route are also in appalling condition.

Two regular buses run from Battambang to Pailin; one leaves at 7:30 A.M., the other at noon. Share taxis are around 25,000 riel. A private taxi is around US$50–60. Only consider this route on a motorbike if you have off-road and Cambodian driving experience. Depending on your mode of transport, the journey takes about 3–5 hours. In the rainy season of 2008, it took 13 hours by taxi. The road from Pailin to the border is just as bad as Route 57.

THE TONLÉ SAP BASIN

Sisophon

Sisophon is the provincial capital of Banteay Meanchey. This province has moved back and forth between Thailand (Siam) and Cambodia for centuries. Once an integral part of the Angkor Empire, the Siamese absorbed it in the 17th century. At the beginning of the 20th century, the Siamese lost the province, along with Battambang and Siem Reap, to the French. Following the reign of the Khmer Rouge, the province was fought over by their remnants and the Cambodian government army for years.

Today, the small town of Sisophon has no obvious redeeming features. It lies halfway between Poipet, on the Thai border—a place most people want to leave as quickly as possible—and Siem Reap, a place most people would like to reach as quickly as possible. Hence hardly anyone stops here. The only attractions, the temples of Banteay Chhmar and Banteay Top, lie about 50 kilometers north of town; though they have been plundered repeatedly, these sites are worth a visit.

As Sisophon sits at the crossing of two of Cambodia's most important highways, its role as a regional transport hub is likely to grow, especially if/when the road from the border to Siem Reap is fixed. In early 2009, the whole town was a construction site, with major roadworks removing entire blocks.

ACCOMMODATIONS

In the heart of town, the only place worth trying is the **Golden Crown Hotel** (tel. 054/958444), a bright yellow modern building. Rooms with fans are US$7, and air-conditioned rooms, which include hot water, cost US$15.

At the western end of town on the road to Poipet, a couple of hotels were just about to open at the time of research. The **Bottom Hotel** looks like a bit of a drive-in, while the **Phnom Sway Hotel** next door appears to be going for delusions of grandeur with its rather expansive facade. Both places promise to have similar facilities as the Golden Crown Hotel.

FOOD

The best place to eat may be the **Phkay Preuk Restaurant,** next to the Bottom Hotel, which serves Cambodian standards as well as some Thai dishes from US$2. Otherwise, try your luck in the market area, where a number of cheap Khmer eateries cook up Cambodian dishes from US$1.

INFORMATION AND SERVICES

Money

There are a couple of banks in town; they cash travelers checks, as well as offering cash advances and currency exchange. ACLEDA Bank as a 24-hour ATM that accepts Visa cards.

Internet Access

There are a few Internet places around town, two of them on the opposite side of the road the Golden Crown Hotel is on (one is directly opposite, the other a few doors down).

GETTING THERE

Sisophon is served by buses from Phnom Penh, including Capitol Tours (tel. 053/953040) and Neak Krorhorm (tel. 023/219496), for US$10–12. From Siem Reap, some 100 kilometers to the east, it's possible to catch a morning bus for US$5. Moving west to Poipet and the Thai border, some 50 kilometers away, it's an hour by bus and costs just US$2. Buses to Battambang are US$3. More frequent are the share taxis and pickups that congregate in the bus station and go in either direction when they are full. A taxi from Siem Reap is US$25. Buses, pickups, and share taxis leave from the central bus station in town near the market, but this will change with the completion of a new bus terminal on the edge of town not far from the road to Poipet.

GETTING AROUND

Sisophon is quite spread out and not nearly attractive enough to invite a stroll. *Motodups* charge around 1,000 riel to get around town.

VICINITY OF SISOPHON
Banteay Chhmar

Not many visitors make it to the temple of Banteay Chhmar. This is not so much because access is difficult, but because this Angkor-era temple, built during the reign of the great god king Jayavarman VII, has been looted heavily in recent years. Nevertheless, the trip, especially just after the rainy season, is rewarding.

The temple complex, surrounded by a moat, has many similarities to the royal city of Angkor Thom, including a causeway lined by stone guards (only two remain) holding *naga* snakes. Beyond the causeway and past a *dharamshala* (rest house for pilgrims), which is in reasonable state, an arched gate opens into the inner courtyard containing Bayon-style towers, complete with smiling faces of the *bodhisattvas* and huge trees, creating a remote forest ambience reminiscent of Beng Melea or Ta Prohm. Despite the looting, some impressive carvings remain, including lintels and *apsaras,* though most of these heavenly dancers have had their heads cut off. On the temple's western wall, a 32-armed carving of Vishnu and another deity with 22 arms were once part of a group of eight such carvings. The other six were chiseled off, loaded onto trucks and driven to Thailand in 1998. Luckily, the trucks were intercepted at the border. Several temple walls are covered with vivid scenes of warfare, both on land and on the water, between the Khmer and the Cham. Local kids will point out all the highlights to you. Numerous smaller temples lie strewn around the vicinity of the main complex. Entrance is US$5, collected by local military.

On a bumpy trail that forks off (signposted) the road some 15 kilometers south of Banteay Chhmar, the small temple of Banteay Top, also called the army's citadel, is a ruined site amongst rice paddies. Dating from the same era as the much larger complex to the north, Banteay Top is worth a visit if you are in the area, not least for its isolated ambience. No extra fees are levied at this quite-abandoned location.

Note that the province of Banteay Meanchey, in which the temples lie, is still heavily mined in parts. Never leave well-traveled paths.

Banteay Chhmar lies some 60 kilometers from Sisophon on Route 69, which continues to the small dusty town of Samroeng and the border at O'Smach. There's no public transportation between Sisophon and the temples, but a *motodup* will take you for US$20 round-trip. The journey takes less than two hours in the dry season. From Siem Reap, the journey can be done in about four hours on a motorbike. At the time of writing, several simple guesthouses were being built near the temple.

Poipet

Poipet is easily the worst place you could find yourself stranded in Cambodia, if not in most of Southeast Asia. It's also a town that has seen more than its fair share of tragedy.

Casinos line the border and draw in the crowds from the neighboring kingdom of Thailand, where gambling is illegal. Beyond the casinos, dusty slums crammed with desperate Cambodians selling everything and everyone grow like a cancer. At night, scores of skid row brothels bring in loads of customers, including some foreigners. Nevertheless, Poipet is the most important overland border crossing into Cambodia and lies on the preferred route of tour buses from Bangkok's backpacker ghetto, the Khao San Road.

During the civil war, which dislodged the Khmer Rouge in 1979, following liberation at the hands of the Vietnamese, Pol Pot's troops retreated to Cambodia's western border, mined it heavily, and dug in. At the same time, thousands of refugees fled west from all parts of the country in order to reach Thailand. Those who did manage to get past the Khmer Rouge ended up in refugee camps, many located around Poipet, ostensibly run by Thai military, but often in fact ruled by the Khmer Rouge. When the refugee crowds crossing the border became too large, the Thai military drove them back into Cambodia, often into certain death in minefields or Khmer Rouge troops waiting to exact revenge on what they perceived as traitors to the cause. Khmer Rouge cadres joined the refugees in the camps and used them as mules to ferry arms and other supplies back to their camps inside Cambodia. Many thousands died this way in minefields or skirmishes.

Travelers should note that the Cambodian authorities in Poipet engage in numerous scams. While the official visa fee is US$20, the immigration officials may demand 1,000 Thai baht instead, more than US$30. There's no easy way to get around this, as refusal to pay results in non-admittance or long delays. Numerous touts hang around the immigration office on the Cambodian side. Don't believe anyone at the border who tells you that you need a health certificate or yellow fever certificate to enter; it's another scam.

Leaving Cambodia through Poipet is no problem and the Thai authorities play things straight. On the Thai side, traffic connections are excellent—numerous buses depart from Aranyaprathet for Bangkok daily 7 A.M.– 10 P.M., and there's a much slower train at 1:55 P.M. The ATMs, convenience stores, clean roads, and the bustling market can feel a bit strange, if welcome, after the limited facilities of Cambodia.

ENTERTAINMENT
Casinos
The only thing Poipet has got going for itself are the casinos. As soon as you've passed Thai Immigration, these giant edifices to the dollar rise out of the parched soil and the slums beyond, making for a pretty surreal sight. The casino scene is likely to thrive as long as gambling remains illegal in Thailand. Thai military and well-connected businessmen allegedly own some of the casinos—and Thai gamblers don't have to pass through Immigration, as the casinos are in a no-man's-land between the two immigration posts.

ACCOMMODATIONS
Staying at one of the casinos is not expensive and it's safer than anywhere else in Poipet. The owners bank that you'll spend the money you saved on the room at the roulette tables. If you do need a room or fancy a night at the tables, check out the **Grand Diamond Casino Hotel** (tel. 054/967345, US$30) or the **Star Vegas International Resort** (tel. 018/487785, US$30), both located in the no-man's-land between the Thai and Cambodian immigration posts.

If you must stay in Poipet itself, though there really is no reason to do so, try the impersonal **Huy Kea Hotel** (tel. 012/346333), about 500 meters before the border, which has decent-enough, air-conditioned rooms for 500 Thai baht. There's a small supermarket opposite and an Internet place diagonally across the road. Right by the traffic circle before the casinos, the **Orkiday Angkor Hotel** (tel. 012/767676) offers clean rooms with air-conditioning and hot water for 600 Thai baht.

There's plenty of decent accommodation in the Thai market town of Aranyaprathet, so if you are stuck at the border, the Thai side is definitely more attractive.

FOOD
The casinos all offer buffets, and you can take your pick between Western, Chinese, and Japanese food. Poipet has numerous small eateries along its main road leading away from the border.

INFORMATION AND SERVICES
Health and Emergencies
If you have an accident or get sick in or near Poipet, go to Thailand immediately and seek medical help there. Aranyaprathet has a decent provincial hospital.

Money
The most commonly used currency in Poipet is the Thai baht, followed by the U.S. dollar and the Cambodian riel. There are a couple of banks in town, which cash travelers checks and

offer cash advances and currency exchange. There are no ATMs in Poipet, but there are plenty of banks on the Thai side, with ATMs right by the 7-Eleven near the border post. Avoid changing money near the border or at the bus station.

Internet Access

Poipet has several Internet shops along Route 5.

GETTING THERE

All buses leave from the Poipet bus terminal (which can be reached in a free shuttle bus from the border). The Sorya Bus Company runs buses from Poipet to Phnom Penh, leaving at 6:45 A.M. and 7:30 A.M. In Phnom Penh, Sorya Buses (tel. 023/210359) arrive and depart opposite the southwest corner of Phsar Thmey at 6:30 A.M. Alternatively, Neak Krorhorm Buses (tel. 023/219496) leave Poipet for the capital at 6:30, 9:30, and 10:30 A.M. Their buses for Poipet leave from the corner of Sisowath Quay and Street 108 in Phnom Penh at 6:30, 7:30, and 8:30 A.M. The Capitol Bus Company also has a daily bus to and from Poipet, leaving from the guesthouse of the same name in Phnom Penh. Note that buses between Poipet and the capital do not go via Siem Reap, but turn off in Sisophon and travel south of the lake along Route 5 through Battambang.

A frequent bus from Poipet to Siem Reap leaves when it's full and costs US$10. Coming from Siem Reap, the bus is the same price but considerably faster. Share taxis, which can be found either just past Immigration or around the bus station, run to Sisophon (US$3), Siem Reap (US$6), or Battambang (US$6), and are a good option if the buses have gone. Pickups also do the run to Sisophon for a little less money and a lot less comfort.

The best way by far to get from Poipet to anywhere else in Cambodia is by private taxi. The run to Siem Reap costs around US$40, to Battambang US$25. A taxi from the border all the way to Phnom Penh will set you back about US$80–100.

GETTING AROUND

Numerous *motodups* around town will offer their services as soon as you stand still. Expect to pay 1,000–2,000 riel for a short ride. They might also offer all sorts of things, including hard drugs and sex with minors. Sadly, they might just be able to deliver.

Anlong Veng

The small town of Anlong Veng, close to two Thai–Cambodian border crossings in the north of Oddar Meanchey Province, is famous for being the last stronghold of the Khmer Rouge. It was here that Pol Pot, Nuon Chea, Khieu Samphan, and Ta Mok lived until 1998, when Cambodian government forces finally took control of the area. This was made possible by the final disintegration of the Khmer Rouge leadership. Pol Pot and other Khmer Rouge leaders had lived in eastern Thailand for years, until the Vietnamese withdrew from Cambodia in 1989. With the Vietnamese out of the picture, the Khmer Rouge leadership returned to Cambodia and settled in Anlong Veng, from where they continued to fight the Cambodian government (which had been installed by the Vietnamese and then elected under the supervision of UNTAC in 1992).

In June 1997, Pol Pot had his longtime lieutenant Son Sen killed, along with 11 members of his family, because his former confidante had been seeking a settlement with the Cambodian government. Officially, Pol Pot had handed power over to Son Sen years before and had suffered a stroke in 1995, but behind the scenes, the enigmatic Khmer Rouge leader still held the strings. Following the murders, Pol Pot fled, but was arrested by other Khmer Rouge cadres and put on trial. The show trial, held not for the benefit of Cambodia or the world, but for internal political reasons of the

THE TONLÉ SAP BASIN

Khmer Rouge, took place at Ta Mok's house in Anlong Veng. Pol Pot was sentenced to life-long house arrest.

On April 15, 1998, 23 years to the day since the Khmer Rouge invaded Phnom Penh and unleashed its reign of terror on Cambodia, the Voice of America announced that the remaining Khmer Rouge leadership had agreed to hand over Pol Pot to an international tribunal. The same night, Pol Pot died, according to his wife, in bed in Anlong Veng and his body was cremated before an autopsy could be undertaken. Ta Mok claimed that his erstwhile leader had died from heart failure. Many people, including a Thai general stationed at the border, have subsequently claimed Pol Pot was murdered. Whatever the truth, in April 1998, Anlong Veng was integrated into the rest of Cambodia and a road linking the town to the south was built. Nuon Chea and Khieu Samphan left to live in Pailin, the second Khmer Rouge stronghold in western Cambodia. Both men have since been arrested and are charged with crimes against humanity at the United Nations tribunal in Phnom Penh.

Anlong Veng did not have much of an infrastructure prior to being the Khmer Rouge base, and the communists did little to improve the lot of local people. When the Khmer Rouge were finally put out of business, there was only one school in town, which was barely functioning. In 2001, Prime Minister Hun Sen issued a directive to the Ministry of Tourism to cooperate with local authorities and other relevant institutions to transform Anlong Veng into a national region of historical tourism. At the time, support for the Khmer Rouge was still strong and locals proudly showed me the hospital, filled with tuberculosis patients and very little else, claiming it had been built by Pol Pot or Ta Mok. Precious few of these government initiatives have materialized and Anlong Veng remains a dusty backwater with a few sights dating back to the final days of the Khmer Rouge.

Sympathies for the erstwhile revolutionaries remain strong here. Nhem En, a Khmer Rouge member from age 11, who took more than 5,000 photographs of Khmer Rouge victims at S-21 in Phnom Penh and remained with the Khmer Rouge until 1995, is now a local politician and plans to open a museum presenting images he took of Khmer Rouge leaders in Anlong Veng. Hopefully the international community will refrain from funding this project.

If you have a strong interest in recent Cambodian history or want to leave the country by the border crossings in this area, the town is worth a visit; otherwise there's little reason to come here. Note that the area around town may still be mined and that the area along the border is definitely still mined. Never ever leave the well-trodden paths.

SIGHTS
Ta Mok's House
Ta Mok's house (no phone, open daily, US$2) lies two kilometers north of town on a hillside overlooking a lake. The house itself is not particularly special, but it is the best-preserved building formerly owned by a Khmer Rouge leader. No doubt luxurious in its time, the building just looks like a family home. Several walls on the ground and first floor are covered in gaudy murals of Angkor Wat and wildlife scenes. The furnishings have long gone.

Ta Mok, which just means Grandfather Mok, is also called The Butcher by Cambodians, and was sometimes known as Brother Number 5. His real name was Chhit Choeun. He allegedly fought the French and Japanese in the 1940s and 1950s and then joined the Khmer Rouge sometime in the 1960s. Eventually he became a Khmer Rouge general and a darling of Pol Pot's, who made him leader of the national army of Democratic Kampuchea. Ta Mok, who lost one of his legs to a landmine, is believed to have orchestrated massacres and party purges from the early 1970s until the end of Democratic Kampuchea in 1979. He was arrested in Anlong Veng market in 1999 by government forces. He died in prison in Phnom Penh in 2006 and thus escaped the judgment of the United Nations trial.

Ta Mok's Lake

Always having the welfare of his people on his mind, Ta Mok flooded a stretch of forest near town and created an artificial lake. The dead tree trunks sticking out of the water like skeletal fingers make for an eerie atmosphere, but many locals are enamored by the lake, and indeed Ta Mok.

ACCOMMODATIONS

The **Monorom Hotel** (tel. 012/900726), 300 meters north of the Dove of Peace Monument in the center of town, offers clean rooms with fans and baths for US$7, or for US$15 with air-conditioning. The hotel has a passable restaurant. The **Bud Oudom Guesthouse** (tel. 012/779495, US$15), 200 meters west of the monument, has large air-conditioned rooms with TV. Both guesthouses have *motodups* attached who can take visitors to the sights around town.

FOOD

The guesthouses offer basic dishes. Otherwise, try your luck at the market stalls. The **Chuom No Tro Cheak Restaurant,** directly by the lake, has no English menu, but offers Cambodian standards for around US$3, as well as game like deer and wild boar.

INFORMATION AND SERVICES
Health and Emergencies

Forget about the glorious Ta Mok Hospital; it's sadly just a place to die. In case of accident or sickness, cross into Thailand as quickly as possible and check into a hospital in Ubon Ratchasima or in Bangkok.

Money

Anlong Veng has an ACLEDA Bank, which cashes travelers checks, and numerous money-changers operate around the market.

GETTING THERE

Anlong Veng lies 125 kilometers north of Siem Reap and most visitors either travel from there or come from the nearby Thai border. The road from Siem Reap to Anlong Veng is not surfaced (except for the first 30 kilometers), but is generally in good condition and is likely to improve in coming years, as there's plenty of construction going on. There's one regular bus a day operated by GST. The bus leaves at 1:30 P.M. from Siem Reap and takes about four hours. From Anlong Veng the bus leaves at 7 A.M. Tickets are US$5. A share taxi from Siem Reap is US$4 and slightly faster than the bus. Note that during the rainy season, travel times are considerably longer and the bus may not go. A private taxi is US$60.

It's also possible, via an unsurfaced but reasonable road, to journey east from Anlong Veng to the border temple of Preah Vihear. While there's no bus, pickups do the journey in three hours and cost US$5 outside or US$8 inside the cab. A share taxi, if you can find one in Anlong Veng, is US$10 a head. A private taxi is US$60. Only attempt this route if you are prepared for seriously rough roads during your onward travel from the temple, as it is not possible to cross from Preah Vihear into Thailand.

VICINITY OF ANLONG VENG
The Grave of Pol Pot

Pol Pot's final resting place is not a fancy affair. Shortly after the Khmer Rouge leader died under unresolved circumstances in 1998, he was cremated on burning car tires. A few years later, locals put a metal roof over the cremation site. Souvenir hunters have been fishing bones out of the ashes and it's suspected that local children replace these with new bones. Despite its low-key atmosphere, this is an eerie and depressing place to visit. Never leave the path from the road to the grave, as landmines might still be buried in the vicinity. The grave is very close to the border, just a few hundred meters away.

The grave lies a few kilometers out of town towards the Dangrek Mountains, and is usually visited in conjunction with a trip to the vacation homes of the Khmer Rouge.

The Kbal Tonsoung Homes of the Khmer Rouge

Some 20 kilometers from Anlong Veng in the

THE TONLÉ SAP BASIN

Dangrek Mountains and just a few kilometers from the Thai–Cambodian border, the leading lights of the Khmer Rouge had a series of modest vacation homes built in the jungle. Khieu Samphan, Nuon Cheah, Ta Mok, Sen Son, and Pol Pot chose this remote stop not just for the idyllic jungle location, but as a place from where escape across the border would be easy.

The houses themselves were never spectacular and are in ruins now. The attraction of the place is the terrible history associated with it—and the great views. The Tourism Ministry in Anlong Veng has plans to restore about 15 buildings in the area, but for now, former Khmer Rouge soldiers guide tourists around the structures. Note

that there might still be landmines in the ground. Never leave well-trodden paths. The Dangrek Mountains are also rife with malaria and dengue fever and protection against mosquitoes is essential.

Near Ta Mok's house (not to be confused with the Butcher's other home in Anlong Veng), visitors can stay at the **Khnong Phnom Dangrek Guest House** (tel. 012/444067) with basic rooms for US$5—perfect for those who want to spend a night in a truly creepy place.

The former vacation homes of the Khmer Rouge leaders are spread across a wide forested area. *Motodups* from Anlong Veng charge about US$10–15 to drive up here and visit the various sites.

Tbeng Meanchey

Tbeng Meanchey is the provincial capital of Preah Vihear Province, but aside from being the jumping-off point for trips to the temples of Koh Ker and Preah Vihear, there is absolutely no reason to come here. A dusty town with a couple of main roads, a bank, and a handful of hotels and restaurants, Tbeng Meanchey has no sights or attractions and sees few foreign visitors but for a small number of NGO staff based here.

In 2008, it was announced (amid great publicity and controversy) that Preah Vihear would become a UNESCO World Heritage Site. The town may well develop in the next years as better roads are likely to be built to make the temples in the province more accessible to visitors. On the other hand, if the main road to Preah Vihear is constructed from Anlong Veng to the west, Tbeng Meanchey is likely to retain its current status as an insignificant backwater. Preah Vihear Province is very poor and infrastructure is limited. Much of the area is home to magnificent tropical forests, though these are being logged quickly.

Note that parts of Preah Vihear Province are still mined. Never leave well-trodden paths.

ACCOMMODATIONS

At the far end of town, the **Happiness Guesthouse** (tel. 017/409822, US$5–17), called Sopheak Meangkol in Khmer, is one of the best cheapies. It has simple and sort of clean doubles, and a couple of rooms have air-conditioning. The Sabay Sabay Drink Shop is next door.

In town, the **27th May Guesthouse** (tel. 011/905427, US$7–8) has equally simple and almost clean small rooms, some with bathrooms. The **Heng Heng Guesthouse** (tel. 092/262261, US$17) is the first place you reach on the road from Kompong Thom. Clean, simple rooms have air-conditioning and hot water. Slap bang in the middle of town, the **Monyroit Guesthouse** (tel. 012/789955, US$16) is pretty similar and offers doubles with air-conditioning.

FOOD

The **Mlop Dong Restaurant,** next to the Monyroit Guesthouse, serves Khmer standards from US$2. The swankier **Dara Reah** is near the pagoda on the main road and serves better versions of the same food from US$3. Both places close around 9 P.M.

INFORMATION AND SERVICES
Health and Emergencies
Tbeng Meanchey does have a provincial hospital; in case of accident or serious illness, return as quickly to Phnom Penh as possible. If you are somewhere in the province near the Thai border, your best bet is to seek medical attention in Thailand.

Money
Tbeng Meanchey has an ACLEDA Bank, which cashes travelers checks, as well as numerous money-changers around the market. It also has an ATM that accepts Visa cards.

Internet Access
There are no public Internet places in Tbeng Meanchey, but in an emergency you could ask at one of the NGO offices around town.

GETTING THERE
A daily bus leaves Phnom Penh for Tbeng Meanchey at 7 A.M., takes around seven hours, and passes through Kompong Thom around 10 A.M. A taxi from Kompong Thom costs around US$50.

VICINITY OF TBENG MEANCHEY
Preah Khan
Preah Khan, called Prasat Bakan by locals, is the largest temple complex in Cambodia—and, in fact, is the largest temple area constructed during the Angkor Empire. The entire complex stretches over five square kilometers and includes a *baray* (reservoir), which is three kilometers long. The island temple of Prasat Preah Thkol stands in the center of the reservoir. At the *baray's* western end, Prasat Preah Stung is the most impressive temple and sports the enigmatic faces of Jayavarman VII (similar to those on the Bayon), who is said to have lived here. The famous head of Jayavarman VII (which graces thousands of images and statues in souvenir shops in Cambodia) was found here, followed by, a few years later, the body. Both are now on display, reunited, at the National Museum in Phnom Penh. At the *baray's* eastern end, Prasat Damrei, the temple of the elephants, has lost its outer walls, but its central and quite small pyramid structure is still standing.

It is uncertain when exactly construction of temples began in this area, but some structures are said to go back to the 9th century. The main structure of Preah Khan was probably built by Suryavarman I (1010–1050) and was originally a Hindu temple, like Preah Vihear to the north, although Suryavarman I was a Buddhist. He made Buddhism the state religion, but did not force people to convert from Hinduism. Suryavarman II, the god king who built Angkor Wat, also lived here, which suggests that the site was a significant second imperial city in its time. Jayavarman VII undertook large-scale additions and reconstruction in the late 12th and early 13th centuries, during a time when Angkor was occupied by the Cham. The temple of Preah Khan itself was once surrounded by a giant moat, similar to the one around Angkor Wat, though little of that is visible today and the *naga* snakes on the bridges have long gone. Inside the moat, a *dharamshala* (guesthouse), built by Jayavarman VII, survives. Many of the temple towers in this central enclosure have collapsed and the entire compound looks a bit like a battlefield.

For now, Preah Khan is rarely visited, partly because it's a long way from the Angkor Archaeological Park, partly because the roads to the temple are not in great shape—and partly perhaps because it has been looted so many times. The history of looting Preah Khan is almost as complex as that of the temple itself. The Frenchman Louis Delaporte, in charge of the first expedition exploring the temples, stole significant parts, which are now on display at the Musée Guimet in Paris. Despite this, the central area was still intact in the mid-1990s. But as Cambodia's civil war was drawing to a close, gangs with drills and diggers moved in and took everything they managed to pry from the walls. It's thought that many of the towers collapsed for this reason.

In Preah Khan's heyday, tens of thousands

of people lived around the temples in order to support the royal elite. A hundred-kilometer highway used to connect Preah Khan with Angkor Thom via the jungle temple of Beng Melea. Remnants of this road can be found in the forests to the west of Preah Khan, including some bridges with *naga* heads. The temple area has been cleared of landmines, but as always in Cambodia, it's safest to stick to well-trodden paths. Entry to temple should be around US$5.

GETTING THERE

There is no need to travel all the way up to the provincial capital of Tbeng Meanchey to access Preah Khan. The best way to get there is from Kompong Thom, first along Route 6 towards Siem Reap to the turn-off of Route 64, a few kilometers west of town. Route 64 snakes north for about 65 kilometers and is in such appalling condition that it is unlikely to be passable in the rainy season. Turn left off Route 64 after the village of Phnom Daik. The temple is clearly signposted. Follow a narrow unsurfaced road, also very bad and sandy in places, for another 60 kilometers until you reach Prasat Preah Stung, the first of the temples.

There's a village on the way, where water and gas can be purchased. It's also possible to stay with a local family here, which is easy to arrange if you're traveling with a *motodup*. Expect to pay US$5 for a bed and dinner.

No regular transportation comes up here, so renting a motorbike is unavoidable. A round-trip with a *motodup* from Kompong Thom costs US$50. Taxis cannot make this journey, as the road is too rough. Some *motodup* drivers also offer a three-night, four-day round-trip from Kompong Thom via Preah Khan, Koh Ker, and Preah Vihear. Before embarking on this circuit, be sure to have the stamina to sit on a bike without suspension on the worst roads in the world for days on end.

◖ Koh Ker

Koh Ker is an experience. As recently as 10 years ago, the only way to get to this vast temple complex, which served as Angkor's capital from A.D. 928 to 944 was by helicopter. Even today, the area around the temples remains heavily mined and it is imperative that visitors avoid strolling more than a hundred meters away from the buildings and stay on well-trodden paths. But this should not deter you, because Koh Ker, which currently sees very few visitors, more than compensates for the trouble of getting there and the small risks of being there.

Almost 100 structures, around 40 of them of note, are spread across a forested area of some 35 square kilometers. The main temples are so spread out that you will need a car or bike to travel between them.

Truly impressive is Prasat Thom, the largest temple. Reached via a number of gates and corridors lined with large, partially collapsed pillars, the main temple structure is some 40 meters high and overgrown with weeds. It's reminiscent of an ancient Central American pyramid, made all the more remarkable by the open area around it, which in turn is surrounded by a striking but crumbling wall. The stairway to the top is precarious and closed to visitors, but the views from up high over the surrounding forest are fantastic.

Prasat Pram, near the entrance to the complex, is made up of five towers, all heavily overgrown by vegetation, with two buildings slowly being strangled by the roots of a ficus tree. Prasat Krahom, the second-largest temple group, has a somewhat eerie and forlorn atmosphere—a jumble of broken towers, doorways subsumed in the undergrowth, huge pillars, and the finely carved window columns so familiar from Angkor. Huge stone linga can be found inside several smaller towers, including Prasat Thenng and Prasat Leung. Many smaller temples lie on a circuitous road through the forest.

Tickets for the Koh Ker complex (US$10) must be purchased at the tollbooth entrance to the area. If no one is manning the tollbooth, employees of APSARA, the ministry in charge of Koh Ker, will catch up with you

Prasat Thom, Koh Ker's spectacular principal temple structure, is a 40-meter-high sandstone-faced pyramid with seven tiers.

in one of the temples. The temple complex is open daily 7 A.M.–5 P.M.

ACCOMMODATIONS AND FOOD

The best place to stay in the vicinity of Koh Ker is the **Mom Morokod Guesthouse** (tel. 012/865900, US$8) near the tollbooth. It offers huge rooms in a concrete building with nothing in them but comfortable double beds—though there are attached bathrooms. There's electricity in the evenings. Alternatively, there are a number of cheap guesthouses in the nearby village of Srayong. Try the **Ponloeu Preah Chan Guesthouse** (tel. 012/498058, US$5), which has tiny rooms with fans in a wooden house, with bathrooms downstairs.

A number of decent food stalls with basic menus in English in front of Prasat Thom are open till about 7 P.M. In Srayong, several small food stalls and restaurants can be found around the market.

GETTING THERE

There are two ways to get to Koh Ker. The most comfortable journey is by car or motorbike from Siem Reap, some 120 kilometers to the southwest, via the temple of Beng Melea. Expect to pay US$80 for a taxi, US$20 for a *motodup*. Follow Route 6 towards Phnom Penh and take a left in the village of Dam Dek, 35 kilometers south of Beng Melea. From Beng Melea, it's another 60 kilometers to Koh Ker. The road is not bad, because it's private and there's a toll to pay—US$2.50 for cars and US$1 for motorbikes—each way.

The more adventurous, but far more arduous, way to get to Koh Ker is from Kompong Thom, via Tbeng Meanchey. The first part of the trip, some 160 kilometers, is mostly awful. From Kompong Thom, it's US$150 for a taxi, US$100 for a *motodup*—with an overnight stay to allow for enough time to see the temple complex. Count on about six hours for the entire journey. The 70-odd kilometers of unsurfaced road from Tbeng Meanchey to the tollbooth of the temple complex are not too bad, at least in the dry season. A taxi takes around two hours one way for this stretch and should be around US$70, while *motodups* charge US$15 for a round-trip. Some *motodup* drivers also

THE TONLÉ SAP BASIN

offer a three-night, four-day round trip from Kompong Thom via Preah Khan, Koh Ker, and Preah Vihear for US$150. Being fearless helps on this journey.

☾ Preah Vihear

The Hindu temple of Preah Vihear offers some of the most breathtaking views in Cambodia. This large complex sits on top of a 700-meter-high cliff that drops sharply down to the Cambodian plains to the south. Climbing up from the base of the hill and the border via an ancient stairway will leave you out of breath, but lets you appreciate the amazing location all the more.

Preah Vihear was probably built during the reign of Suryavarman I (1010–1050) and dedicated to Shiva, creator and destroyer of the universe. Successive kings added to the complex, including Suryavarman II (1113–1150). Inside the temple, several stone pavilions, so-called *gopuras,* in varying states of collapse and decorated with detailed and beautiful carvings, are arranged around several courtyards. The *gopuras* are linked by causeways, some lined with *naga* snakes. This makes the temple complex almost 800 meters long. The third *gopura* contains a carving of the churning of the ocean around Mount Meru. A more sophisticated and famous rendition of this story is a highlight of the bas relief galleries around Angkor Wat. The main sanctuary of the temple is the best-preserved structure and sits right at the edge of the cliff.

The temple's recent history is as dramatic as the views across the plains below and at the time of writing Cambodia and Thailand still have hundreds of troops stationed in the region. Note that the area around the temple is still heavily mined—never step off the well-trodden paths in the area. Several soldiers sustained terrible injuries from landmines in 2008 and 2009, during the recent spat between Thailand and Cambodia, and Cambodia's prime minister even threatened Thailand with war if the neighboring kingdom did not pull back its troops.

For years, virtually all tourists visiting the temple came from Thailand and paid 400 Thai baht to the Thais for entering the area (a so-called national park) and another US$10 to the Cambodians to enter the temple. There is no official border crossing at Preah Vihear and visitors from Thailand have to be back across the border by 5 P.M. Due to the military and political deadlock between the two countries over the temple, access from Thailand has been impossible since mid-2008, though this is likely to change once border issues have been resolved. Other, smaller Khmer temples line the border all the way back to Anlong Veng, but these can only be visited from Thailand.

From the Cambodian side, entry to the temple is US$10. It's open daily 7 A.M.–5 P.M. if the military situation permits.

ACCOMMODATIONS AND FOOD

The village at the foot of the mountain has a couple of cheap and cheerless guesthouses with rooms for US$3. Don't expect anything much. As the road is likely to improve, it's expected that tourist infrastructure around the temple will be established soon. Some stalls selling snacks and drinks have spring up around the temple, and you will be able to find basic food in the village.

GETTING THERE

The easiest way to get to Preah Vihear is from Thailand, if the border is open. The nearest town with accommodation in Thailand is Kantharalak, which is the best place to access the temple from the Thai side. If and when border demarcation issues have been resolved, it will no doubt be possible again to enter Prasat Preah Viharn, as it's called by the Thais, this way.

In the meantime, hardy and adventurous travelers will have an interesting time braving the bumpy roads inside Cambodia that lead to the temple. And with so much attention currently focused on Preah Vihear, access may well improve in coming years—and there's even talk of constructing a cable car to improve access from the base of the Dangrek Mountains.

For now there are two difficult routes to get

PREAH VIHEAR: WHOSE TEMPLE IS IT ANYWAY?

The magnificent temple of Preah Vihear, which straddles the Cambodian-Thai border, has been a bone of contention as well as a political tool hampering relations between the two countries for half a century. Listed as a UNESCO World Heritage Site in 2008, this remote temple has become a symbol not of peace, but of small-minded nationalism and petty internal and foreign politics. The conflict surrounding the site continues to contribute significantly to the prejudices and misconceptions that have existed amongst the populations of both nations for decades, if not centuries.

The border between Thailand and Cambodia was first drawn up by the French in 1907, who put the temple in Cambodian territory. The Thais did not protest, but in 1954, shortly after France's exit from Indochina, invaded the temple with a military force and claimed it as their own. In 1959, Cambodia went to the International Court of Justice in order to protest Thailand's occupation. The court focused on the legality of the earlier French demarcation and Thailand's reaction to it and decided in favor of Cambodia. Mass demonstrations against Cambodia and the International Court followed in Thailand. In a gesture of generosity, Prince Sihanouk, Cambodia's leader at the time, offered Thais free access to the temple and assured his neighbors that they could keep any artifacts they had already carted away from the monument.

In 1975, the temple was the last site in Cambodia to fall to the Khmer Rouge, and in 1998, Preah Vihear was the last site to be given up by the Khmer Rouge fighters. In the following years, it was accessible from the Thai side only, until the Cambodians built a road in 2003. But the squabbling between the two Buddhist kingdoms over this ancient sacred site was far from over.

Cambodia applied for UNESCO World Heritage status for the temple; inclusion of the site was debated, and, following renewed Thai protests, deferred in 2007. Soon after, Thailand changed its mind and supported Cambodia's proposal to have the site formally inscribed on the World Heritage List. Yet a few months later, Thailand withdrew that support again because of protests playing on patriotic sentiment, launched by a non-parliamentary ultra-nationalist movement in Thailand. At the same time, Cambodian Prime Minister Hun Sen used the territorial squabble over the temple to win more votes in his country's general election in 2008. Thailand promptly massed troops around the temple.

Despite official Thai protests, Preah Vihear finally became a World Heritage Site in July 2008 and the Cambodians swiftly introduced their own troops into the area, making for a highly volatile stand-off between the two countries. Several skirmishes ensued and both sides suffered casualties. Some parts of the temple were damaged in the fighting and access from Thailand has been closed ever since. In the months following the military encounters, the conflict widened to other, smaller temples along the two kingdoms' border. A joint commission has been set up to diffuse the situation and to finally demarcate the border. Perhaps an eventual result in the negotiations will once and for all lay the Preah Vihear issue to rest.

to the temple from the Cambodian side. Most straightforward is access from the provincial capital of Tbeng Meanchey, 110 kilometers south of the temple. This road suffered enormously in 2008, when heavy military hardware was dragged up to the temple during the conflict with Thailand. But due to its strategic as well as economic importance, this is likely to change very soon and perhaps significant improvements will take place during the lifetime of this book. There's no bus yet, but a share taxi costs US$12 and takes four hours in the dry season. A private taxi costs some US$100 round-trip.

Alternatively, there is a gravel road from Anlong Veng to the west. While there's no bus, pickups do the journey in three hours and cost US$5 outside or US$8 inside the cab in the dry-season. A share taxi, if you can find one, is US$10 a head. A private taxi is US$60. Some *motodup* drivers offer a three-night, four-day round trip from and to Kompong Thom via Preah Khan, Koh Ker, and Preah Vihear for US$150. In a taxi, the round-trip, minus Preah Khan, which can only be accessed by motorbike, takes two nights and three days and costs around US$200. Make sure you arrange in advance who pays for the driver's bed and food, as well as parking fees and road tolls.

Kompong Thom

Kompong Thom, the capital of the province of the same name, lies on Route 6 about halfway between Phnom Penh and Siem Reap. Due to its strategic location as a halfway point on the country's busiest road, the town is quite prosperous and lively, in contrast to some smaller provincial capitals.

The town itself is not particularly remarkable as a tourist destination, but it's the jumping-off point to several interesting temple sites in the area. Roads are paved, so it's not dusty, and there are decent facilities and accommodations for those planning a trip into the countryside. It's worth visiting the market and there are a few colonial traces along the Stung Sen River as well, though these don't warrant a visit.

SIGHTS
The Market
Phsar Thmey, right in the center of town, is a good place to hunt for local fruit, or, for those with more eccentric tastes, fried grasshoppers.

grilled chicken for sale in front of Kompong Thom's central market

Wat Kompong

The town's main temple, with a pagoda that was reportedly built in the 17th century, lies west of the bridge. Some of the younger monks speak a little English. The main prayer hall was closed when I visited, but it's said that there's a bizarre mural in the hall that depicts the funeral of the Buddha, with King Sihanouk and some 1960s world leaders in attendance.

ACCOMMODATIONS
Under US$15

The towering **Arunras Hotel** (tel. 062/961294) has the strategic advantage of standing right by the bus stop a stone's throw from the central market—hence, it attracts many of the tourists staying overnight. Many bus companies break here for lunch, so the hotel's restaurant is periodically flooded by hordes of passengers before getting back to its usual quiet self. The hotel is not a bad value, offering clean rooms with TV and bathtub for US$8. Rooms with air-conditioning, bathtub, and fridge cost US$15. Avoid the fourth floor, which has karaoke rooms that will be noisy at night. The adjacent guesthouse of the same name has simpler rooms from US$4. Behind the Arunras Hotel, on a quiet backstreet, the **Vimean Sour Guesthouse** (tel. 012/620009, US$5) provides clean and simple rooms. No English is spoken here, but the owners are friendly.

The **Mittapheap Hotel** (tel. 062/961213) at the bridge on the western side of the Stung Sen River, is another mid-range hotel. It offers clean and comfortable rooms with fan for US$7, with air-condtioning for US$15.

US$15-25

The most popular place in town appears to be the **Stung Sen Royal Hotel** (tel. 012/309495, US$20 doubles, US$30 triples), which offers spacious, air-conditioned rooms. This hotel is a little bit worn-down, but tour groups and NGO staff stay here. A restaurant next door serves standard Khmer dishes from US$3.

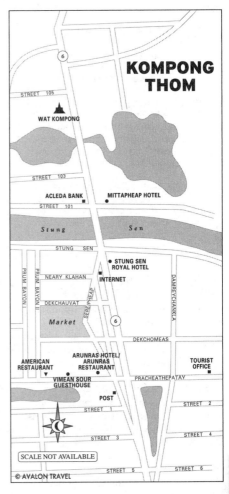

FOOD

The restaurant in the Arunras Hotel serves Khmer and Chinese dishes, and it isn't bad. For a few items of comfort food, head around the corner to the **American Restaurant** (tel. 092/579410), an ice-cream parlor and hamburger restaurant run by an American-Khmer couple, which is open until around 9 P.M. The ice cream is homemade and it's really great.

THE TONLÉ SAP BASIN

THE CASHEW NUT

Cambodia produces some 50,000 tons of raw cashew nuts per year. Almost the entire harvest is exported to Vietnam. The present cultivation areas are in Kompong Cham, Kompong Thom, and Ratanakiri Province. At the moment, the country has only one processing factory that takes care of just 3 percent of the country's annual produce. Cambodia urgently needs more processors in order to add more value to its products and generate more jobs for local people. Some farmers are slowly turning to organic farming as the price for organic cashews is 30 percent higher than the price for conventional cultivation.

INFORMATION AND SERVICES

The tourist office in Kompong Thom is housed in a wooden building on a lane across the road from the Arunras Hotel and has a brochure with information about the province. A little English is spoken.

Health and Emergencies

Kompong Thom has a provincial hospital, but, in case of accident or serious illness, return as quickly as possible to Phnom Penh or Siem Reap.

Money

Kompong Thom has an ACLEDA Bank, which cashes travelers checks and has an ATM that accepts Visa cards. Numerous money-changers are located around the market.

Internet Access

There's an Internet place in a lane opposite the Stung Sen Hotel.

GETTING THERE

Kompong Thom lies about halfway between Phnom Penh and Siem Reap on Route 6. Frequent buses make this journey, and all of them stop in Kompong Thom. The journey from the capital takes just three hours. To Siem Reap, it's another couple of hours. Buses cost US$4 from the capital, another US$4 to Siem Reap. By share taxi or minibus, the journey is a bit faster; seats cost US$6. A private taxi will cost US$25–30 to Phnom Penh or Siem Reap.

Mr. Hem John (tel. 012/1857385) is an excellent local driver who speaks English well and knows the province like the back of his hand.

GETTING AROUND

Plenty of *motodups* hang around the hotels and the market and will take you anywhere in town for 1,000–2,000 riel.

VICINITY OF KOMPONG THOM
Sambor Prei Kuk

This large temple complex just north of Kompong Thom town and about 125 kilometers east of Siem Reap was built in the 7th century and was part of Isanapura, the pre-Angkorian capital of the Chenla Empire. Isanapura, which was Hindu and spre ad over several square kilometers, had its heyday 500 years before Angkor, but the site remained active for hundreds of years.

Three groups of temples lie in light forest, each with a central tower amid smaller structures, ponds, and broken walls. It's a short stroll between each of the groups. **Prasat Sambor,** the structure closest to the road, was dedicated to a reincarnation of Shiva. Some brick carvings on the crumbling outer walls remain. Across the road from Prasat Sambor, a small shrine is slowly exploding as the roots of an old banyan tree work their way into the brickwork. One tower in this group contains a headless statue of Durga, while another houses a statue of Harihara, an amalgamation of Shiva and Vishnu. Both these figures are replicas; the originals are housed in the National Museum in Phnom Penh.

The **Prasat Yeai Poen** group lies in denser forest. It features an interesting wall with four circular carvings, so-called medallions, one of which depicts Shiva surrounded by monkeys.

Prasat Tao, the temple of the lion, has two original stone lions guarding its main structure. The lions were smashed up by the Khmer Rouge but have been well restored.

Aside from the main tower, the smaller shrines around this complex have been badly damaged. The temples were bombed by the United States in the early 1970s and later vandalized by the Khmer Rouge. Despite the damage, a visit is well worth it (especially if you have not been to Angkor yet)—not least because you will have the temples to yourself. Well almost. Small groups of persistent young girls follow visitors from temple to temple, selling colorful scarves. Several drinks and food stalls have set up shop around the temples. Local guides, most of them teenage boys with a surprising amount of knowledge on the area, charge US$3 to take tourists around all three temple groups.

Beyond the three main groups of temples, many more ruins lie half-buried in the undergrowth in the area—all in all, it's said that there are 280 structures. Archaeologists continue to work around the site. Although Sambor Prei Kuk has been de-mined, visitors should not leave well-trodden paths while exploring smaller structures.

The entrance fee is US$3, collected at a toll bridge a kilometer before the temples. Allow at least a couple of hours to explore the temple complex. It's open daily 7 A.M.–5 P.M., though no one is likely to stop you if you arrive earlier.

The temples are just 35 kilometers north of Kompong Thom town. If you are driving yourself, the journey, on unsurfaced but clearly signposted roads, should not take more than an hour. Head east from town for about five kilometers until the turn-off for Tbeng Meanchey on Route 64. Follow this potholed stretch of road, which leads through rice paddies and small villages, for 10 kilometers to the turn-off on the right to the temples, which are another 12 or so kilometers away. A round-trip with a *motodup* should cost around US$10.

Phnom Santuk

This temple mountain is worth the trip for the great views alone, but there are a number of interesting temples as well as reclining Buddhas on this hillside. On top, an active pagoda welcomes visitors. From the base of the mountain, a stairway guarded by *naga* snakes with almost 1,000 steps leads to the top. For those too lazy or tired to clamber up here (and pay the US$1 entrance fee), there's a trail to the left of the steps around the mountain that can easily be done on a dirt bike.

On the way to Phnom Santuk from Kompong Thom, the small village of Samnak produces stone carvings, many of which are for sale by the side of the road. All sorts of traditional items are produced here, from elephants to god kings, including huge replicas of the famous Jayavarman VII statue that was found at Preah Khan.

Phnom Santuk stands some 20 kilometers west of Kompong Thom and can easily be visited on a day trip from town. Follow Route 6 back towards Phnom Penh for 15 kilometers to a signposted turn-off on the left. From here, it's less than five kilometers to the base of the mountain. It's possible to hire a *motodup* for the trip. Expect to pay US$7, which should include the waiting time at the foot of the mountain.

THE TONLÉ SAP BASIN

NORTHEASTERN CAMBODIA

If the Tonlé Sap Lake is the heart of Cambodia, then Southeast Asia's largest river, the mighty Mekong, which flows almost 4,350 kilometers from China, through Laos, Thailand, Cambodia, and Vietnam into the South China Sea, is the kingdom's lifeline. The Mekong crosses from Laos into Cambodia and flows for 450 kilometers through the country. Rapids just inside Cambodia, and farther south, between the river outposts Stung Treng and Kratie, make serious shipping impossible. From the lower rapids, the Mekong flows through Kompong Cham to Phnom Penh, where it crosses paths with the Tonlé Sap River, before meandering south through Kandal Province and into Vietnam.

The soil along the river is extremely nutritious and many sections of the riverbanks are densely populated. Boat journeys are possible and riverside towns have a quiet, remote charm. Rustic markets and Cambodian country food, including excellent fish dishes, as well as a general sense of time standing still may tempt visitors to hang out longer than planned.

East of the Mekong, Cambodia's two northeastern provinces, Ratanakiri and Mondulkiri, border on Vietnam and are among the most remote and inaccessible regions of the country. Neither province has a paved road yet. The provincial capitals of Banlung and Sen Monorom are the jumping-off points for all excursions in the two provinces.

Mondulkiri is Cambodia's largest province, offering miles and miles of dense jungles that are teeming with animals such as tigers, elephants, and leopards, and possibly some species

HIGHLIGHTS

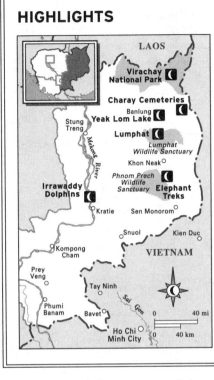

Irrawaddy Dolphins: Hop in a boat and explore the banks of the Mekong around Kampi to catch a glimpse of endangered Irrawaddy dolphins (page 226).

Yeak Lom Lake: This ancient crater lake near Banlung is calm and clear, making it the perfect place to take a dip (page 238).

Charay Cemeteries: These eerie graves with intricately carved totems lurk in the jungle near the Tonlé Se San River (page 239).

Virachay National Park: Multi-day treks through this barely explored national park are led by park rangers and include village homestays (page 239).

Lumphat: A bombed-out area of ruins from the not-too-distant past comprise this lost city on the Ho Chin Minh Trail (page 241).

Elephant Treks: For the ride of a lifetime, board an elephant and enjoy being guided by a Bunong *mahoot* (page 245).

LOOK FOR **(** TO FIND RECOMMENDED SIGHTS, ACTIVITIES, DINING, AND LODGING.

we have yet to identify. Attractions include waterfalls and gem mines.

The northeastern part of Cambodia is also home to the Khmer Loeu, or Chunchiet, Cambodia's indigenous hill tribes. In Ratanakiri, 12 ethnic minorities live in villages spread across the province. The Bunong, the major population group in Mondulkiri, keep domesticated elephants and have recently started offering treks on their pachyderms. Bombed flat by American B-52 bombers in the 1960s, Cambodia's northeast has very little in the way of infrastructure. This situation was made worse in the 1970s when the Khmer Rouge, who had been holed up in Ratanakiri in the 1960s during their struggle against the government in Phnom Penh, returned and killed more than half of the indigenous people.

The remoteness of Ratanakiri makes the province ideal for off-road motorbike tours. The road between the two provincial capitals of Banlung and Sen Monorom, the legendary Death Highway, is one of the most bone-shaking and remote routes in the country, but should only be attempted by experienced riders.

In recent years, the Cambodian government has awarded large land concessions to foreign companies in both Ratanakiri and Mondulkiri. Primary jungle is being logged widely. Environmental issues take a backseat in the cash-strapped kingdom and so much of the wilderness in the province—one of the largest, virtually undisturbed areas in Southeast Asia, and home to some of the region's last herds of wild elephants—is likely to be reduced to monoculture plantations and large-scale mining projects in the coming years. What's

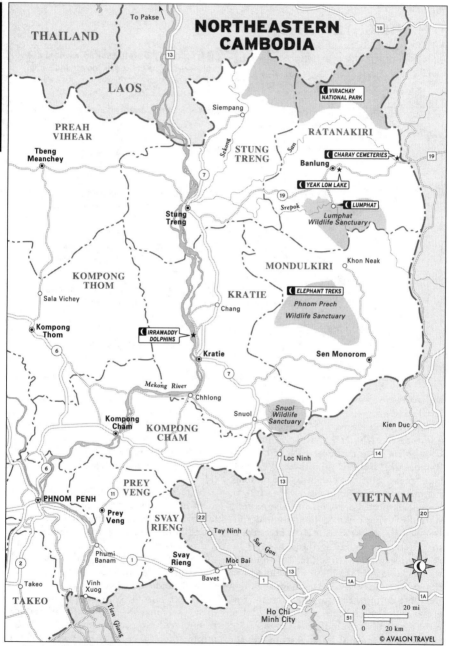

NORTHEASTERN CAMBODIA

more, facilities for locals remain extremely limited. Besides bad roads, there are virtually no schools or health posts. Villages, for the most part, do not have electricity. The influx of ethnic Khmer, the ever-increasing scramble for land, and the unregulated establishment of businesses is pushing the Khmer Loeu slowly to the margins. A number of foreign NGOs are trying to establish limits to this exploitation, with limited success. Nevertheless, the northeastern part of Cambodia remains a wild place, remote and hard to move around in, and a journey out of one of the provincial capitals can seem like a trip back in time.

PLANNING YOUR TIME

Most visitors who travel along the Mekong north of Phnom Penh are on their way to the northeastern provinces or the Lao border. There are no spectacular sights along this route, but a two-day stopover in laid-back Kratie to see the rare Irrawaddy dolphins is worthwhile. Because of the northeast's relative remoteness and the long travel times, most visitors only make it to either Ratanakiri or Mondulkiri. Each destination can easily be explored in 3–4 days, but attractions are spaced far apart, especially in Ratanakiri, and with Banlung as a relaxing base, a week or ten days need not be boring. River trips, visits to minority villages, and a beautiful lake are the main attractions around the capital. In Mondulkiri, activity options are more limited, but elephant treks with the Bunong minority, lasting from one day to a week, are definitely a highlight of a visit to Cambodia.

Kompong Cham

Kompong Cham is the first town that spreads along the Mekong north of Phnom Penh. The town derives its name from the Cham people, who fled here in great numbers following the collapse of the Champa kingdom, after invasions by the Vietnamese. While the province of the same name, Cambodia's most populated, lives by the seasonal rhythms of the agriculture almost everyone is engaged in, the provincial capital of 50,000 is unassuming and most visitors simply change buses here to head to Kratie and towards the northeast region. During the French occupation, rubber was grown here in large plantations and there are efforts to revive

© TOM VATER

Kompong Cham, along the Mekong River

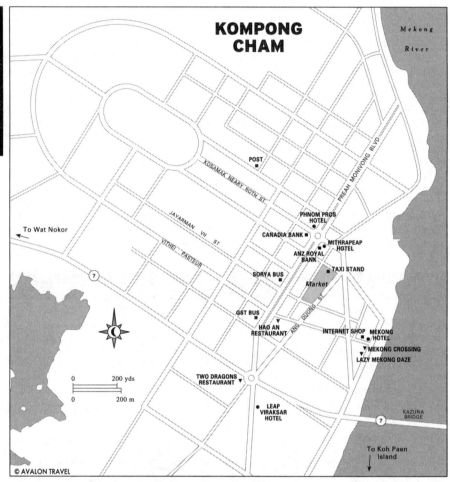

the business. A few blocks of crumbling but attractive French architecture survive in town and it's not a bad place to stop off for a night and spend the afternoon on the banks of the Mekong. Oh, and Prime Minister Hun Sen comes from Kompong Cham.

SIGHTS
Koh Paen Island
This small island lies in the middle of the Mekong a few hundred meters south of town. It's reached via an impressive bamboo bridge, which is built by hand anew every year. The island is dotted with a few pagodas and tobacco fields.

The Lighthouse
The old French lighthouse by the bridge on the opposite side of the Mekong has been restored and can be climbed. Entrance is free.

SHOPPING
The *krama*, Cambodia's all-purpose scarf, is mostly produced in this region. Beyond that,

there's nothing special to buy in Kompong Cham, but you can still check out the central market.

ACCOMMODATIONS

The enormous, yellow **Mekong Hotel** (tel. 042/941536, US$6–12), right by the Mekong, is not too bad as mid-size hotels go—though it could do with some refurbishment and a good cleaning. Rooms are large, and some have air-conditioning, TV, and hot water. Breakfast and travel information are available. A little farther away from the river, the **Phnom Pros Hotel** (tel. 042/941444) belongs to Prime Minister Hun Sen's nephew. It's a better value than the Mekong Hotel, though it has smaller rooms. The rooms on the top floor seem to be in the best condition. Choose between fan (US$7) or air-conditioning with hot water (US$12). There are karaoke nightclubs attached to both hotels.

If these two establishments are full, the **Mithrapeap Hotel** (tel. 042/941565) is nearby and offers rather worn downstairs fan rooms

for US$6 and slightly better rooms upstairs with air-conditioning for US$10.

The best place to stay in town, though, is the new annex of the **Leap Viraksar Hotel** (tel. 042/941239, US$15), which has small but comfortable and clean rooms with air-conditioning and TV. The old building next door looks tired, perhaps because it has karaoke going on at night.

A couple of really cheap guesthouses along the Mekong, just to the south of the two expat bars, offer dingy rooms for around US$3; if you arrive in Kompong Cham almost broke, head there.

FOOD

Stalls selling snacks and beer and excellent sugar cane juice set up by the riverfront near the bridge in the afternoon. Also along the riverfront, a couple of amiable expatriates run restaurants. **Mekong Crossing** (tel. 012/427432) is run by an American and serves decent Asian dishes as well as Western comfort food such as salads and burgers. The owner is a good

© TOM VATER

an ox-cart transporting rice from a paddy field in Kompong Cham

RUBBER PLANTATIONS ALONG THE MEKONG

Rubber was first introduced to Cambodia by the French in the 1920s and farmed on a large scale, mostly by Vietnamese workers. Following independence, the trade continued under successive Cambodian governments until the Khmer Rouge took over.

In more recent times, the Cambodian government has awarded huge land concessions to a Vietnamese business conglomerate in Kompong Thom, Kratie, and Mondulkiri. Some private, locally run plantations continue to operate on a much smaller scale. The intense logging that preceded the French plantation efforts and, more recently, the setting up of new plantations, has changed the climate and affected the lifestyle of the local population who were – and are – unfortunately paid a pittance for working the rubber trees.

source of information on the area. A little farther down the road, **Lazy Mekong Daze** (tel. 099/569781), run by a friendly French guy, has a pool table. Kitchens in both places close at 10 P.M., but the beers keep flowing into the night when NGO staff, missionaries, and travelers congregate in both spots.

The **Hao An Restaurant** is popular with Khmer, but Western tour groups also eat here. The menu of Khmer and Chinese dishes is vast and all orders come in three sizes; large portions are enough to feed a family. Prices start from 8,000 riel for small portions to 30,000 riel for the family-size plates. For absolute exotica, try the fried eel for US$3.50–6, or boiled and fried pig intestines for US$4.50–7. For more conventional fare, chicken with cashew nut is US$4.50–7.

The **Two Dragons Restaurant** is a smaller alternative at the traffic circle near the bridge and offers good value Cambodian standards from US$1 a plate.

Across the bridge, a row of restaurants

serves good Khmer dishes (though menus are not in English), accompanied by singers or karaoke. Similar eateries can also be found as you leave Kompong Cham on the road towards Phnom Penh.

INFORMATION AND SERVICES

Your best bet for information on local sights and events is the restaurant **Mekong Crossing** (tel. 012/427432) on the riverfront. It has produced a few pages of information to the sites around town, tagged to its menus.

Health and Emergencies

The hospital in Kompong Cham is inadequate. If you have an accident or fall ill, try to get to Phnom Penh as quickly as possible. The health posts in the area will not be able to provide even the most basic treatment.

Money

There are several banks in town that cash travelers checks, as well as offer cash advances and currency exchange. Most of them also have ATMs that accept Visa cards.

Internet Access

Kompong Cham has a number of Internet shops. The most reliable is diagonally across from Mekong Crossing, clearly signposted, on a small side road from the river into town. This place closes at 9 P.M.

GETTING THERE

Kompong Cham is 120 kilometers from Phnom Penh. The Sorya Bus Company (tel. 023/210359) and GST (tel. 023/335199) have frequent buses leaving for Kompong Cham from the southwest corner of Phsar Thmey (Central Market) in Phnom Penh 6:30 A.M.–4 P.M. From Kompong Cham back to Phnom Penh, departure times and frequency are the same. Buses leave from just north of the roundabout on the bridge road. It's two hours and US$6 a ticket. Share taxis and minibuses for Kompong Cham leave from the southwest corner of Phsar Thmey (Central

Market) in Phnom Penh. It's US$5 a seat. A private taxi from Phnom Penh to Kompong Cham is US$25. The taxi stand in Kompong Cham is north of the market. Moving north, several buses pass through Kompong Cham from Phnom Penh on their way to Kratie and Stung Treng. Sorya and Huan Lin pass around 10 A.M., while GST pass at 1:15 P.M. To Kratie, it's four hours.

If you are driving yourself, there are three options to move on to Kratie. One is to follow Route 7, surfaced all the way, via Snuol, the same way the buses go. This circumambulating route takes more than four hours, but the road is in excellent condition. Alternatively, you can follow a small scenic road along the Mekong, though this should only be attempted in the dry season. Finally, go down Route 7 towards Snuol for about 40 kilometers until the turn-off onto Route 73, just past a huge rice depot with a blue roof. From here, it's about 60 kilometers to the interesting French plantation town Chhlong, before reaching Kratie after another 30 kilometers. This last stretch of this road, just before Kratie, can also be rough in the rainy season.

GETTING AROUND
Kompong Cham is small enough to walk around, but if you're in a hurry, a *motodup* will charge 1,000 riel and up for a ride around town.

VICINITY OF KOMPONG CHAM
Wat Nokor
Wat Nokor is an 11th-century temple with an active, modern pagoda as well as an interesting local legend. Together with a side trip to the hill temples of Phnom Srei and Phnom Proh, Wat Nokor makes an interesting day trip from Kompong Cham. The original temple is small but relatively intact, fronted by a row of stone lions. There are even a couple of carvings visible in the entrance gate. Note that the local police charge US$2 to enter the old part of this large pagoda complex. It's open daily.

To get there, follow the road to Phnom Penh

© TOM VATER

the entrance to Wat Nokor, an 11th-century Angkor-era temple outside Kompong Cham

THE LEGEND OF WAT NOKOR

Once upon a time, a man in Kompong Cham left his baby unattended under a tree. When he checked on his child, the young boy was covered in bird droppings, so the man took him to the banks of the Mekong to be washed. Somehow, though, the man slipped and the baby fell from his hands and was promptly swallowed by a huge fish. The man did not manage to catch the fish and died shortly after of heartbreak.

The fish swam down the Mekong and into the Gulf of Thailand and from there into the South China Sea, until it was caught by a fisherman. When the fisherman cut the fish open, he found the baby boy, alive and well. Believing he was witnessing a miracle, he took the boy to the emperor, who adopted the child.

As the boy grew up, he often wondered where he had come from. Upon reaching maturity, the emperor offered him a boat with a crew of 5,000 men to sail off and look for his homeland. The boy did just that, and eventually sailed up the Mekong in search of his home. But none of the people he asked en route could remember a story of a baby being swallowed by a fish. Eventually the boy reached Kompong Cham. Here, too, no one had heard of the story, but the young man liked the place and decided to stay for a while. His crew of 5,000 stayed along with him. He met a very attractive woman, a little older than him, and the two decided to marry. One day, the young man's wife noticed a birthmark on her husband's forehead and asked him about it. The young man related the story of the fish to his wife and his wife told him the story of how her first husband had died. They were both shocked to discover that that they were in fact mother and son. The mother ordered her son to become a monk and to construct a temple in her honor, which he did. She also told him to erect a statue of himself paying respect to his mother.

Chinese-Cambodians have been visiting the statue ever since to pay their respects. The original statue was destroyed by the Khmer Rouge, but was rebuilt in 1979.

out of town. At the first traffic circle, turn left at a large signpost for the temple and follow the road for another kilometer. A round-trip ride with a *motodup* should cost US$2.

Phnom Srei and Phnom Proh

The two hillside temples Phnom Proh (Mountain of Man) and Phnom Srei (Mountain of Woman) are magnificent collections of gaudy *chedis* and statues. The central prayer hall of Phnom Proh has demons and gods all around pulling the *naga* snake to dislodge the nectar of immortality. The area is also sadly known for the atrocities the Khmer Rouge committed in the area. A killing field where some 500 people are buried lies between the two temples, with a concrete structure housing the victims' bones.

To get there, take the road to Phnom Penh past the traffic circle at the end of town. From there it's about three kilometers to the turnoff on the right. The temple mounts are clearly visible from the main road. A round-trip ride with a *motodup* should be about US$5.

The Longest Airstrip in Cambodia

Just outside of Kompong Cham, the U.S. military built what is assumed to be Cambodia's longest runway. Apparently, B-52 bombers took off from here in their efforts to destroy the Ho Chi Minh Trail. No plane has landed at this airfield for many years. There are great views from a small bunker on a hill, but there's nothing much to see except the runway and a broken control tower in a rice field nearby.

To get there, take the road to Phnom Penh past the traffic circle. The small turnoff for the airfield is opposite a garment factory, about two kilometers out of town. A round-trip ride with a *motodup* should be about US$5. There's no signpost, but the factory is unmistakable; it's a huge sprawling complex behind high walls.

THE SPIDERS OF SKUON

The best tarantula in the world is deep-fried in garlic and salt. Shiny black on the outside and gooey on the inside, the tarantulas, known as *a-ping* in Cambodia, should be served hot. They taste a bit like crickets. Or grasshoppers. Or bamboo grubs. Or chicken. The best way to eat *a-ping* is to pull the legs off first; these are usually crispy, like French fries. Then just split open the body and devour the soft flesh inside.

When visitors get out of the taxi in the small town Skuon between Kompong Cham and Phnom Penh, they are accosted by a small army of friendly Khmer women, their heads wrapped in *kramas*, who carry huge trays loaded with the town's premier delicacy – fat, black, hairy, venomous spiders.

A popular myth tells us that the Khmers first consumed spiders in the days of the Khmer Rouge killing fields in the 1970s. In those days, *a-ping* were vital sustenance as there was little else to eat. These days, the spiders are bred in the ground in nearby villages, so there should be ample supplies for years to come.

The ladies of Skuon do the hard sell, but readily admit that foreigners rarely stop, and when they do, they never purchase more than one or two spiders. Spiders can be purchased alive or dead. The live ones are taken home and put into bottles of rice wine, which is said to be a good remedy for aches and pains. Traditional medicine has been around in Cambodia for hundreds of years; under the Khmer

© AROON THAEWCHATTURAT

fried spiders, a Skuon specialty

Rouge in the 1970s, when there were no medical facilities left in the country, there was a real renaissance of products with alleged medicinal properties. Snake wine is popular, too, and bottles, filled with a little wine and a lot of snake, are for sale in Phnom Penh. A bottle of spider wine sells for up to US$3.

Skuon

Skuon is an unassuming small town and at first glance nothing more than the crossroads where Route 6, which leads farther north to Kompong Thom, meets Route 7, which veers to the east and towards Kompong Cham. But if you take a break at the market, directly by the main road, you will quickly discover the town's gourmet specialty: fried spiders. The arachnids are popular with Cambodians passing by, and the vendors, most of them women, know a scared foreigner when they see one. Expect some spidery offers.

Skuon lies some 85 kilometers north of Phnom Penh on Route 6, and every bus and taxi heading north from the capital will pass through this small town. If you drive yourself, count on about 90 minutes of journey time from the capital, or 40 minutes from Kompong Cham.

Kratie

Kratie is perhaps the best place to break up the journey along the Mekong towards Laos and northeastern Cambodia. The small, laid-back provincial capital is more interesting than Kompong Cham to the south and less dusty and forlorn-looking than Stung Treng to the north. The remnants of French architecture and tree-lined streets, the market, and the rare and endangered dolphins that can be seen nearby make Kratie a great place to linger for a couple of nights.

Cruises up and down the Mekong offer travelers great views of traditional life along the banks of one of Asia's major rivers, undisturbed by industry, development, or, most of the time, other tourists. The nearby town of Chhlong also offers some interesting French architecture and one colonial mansion-turned-upscale-hotel to luxuriate in.

The province straddles the Mekong, but besides picturesque villages, there's not much to see. A few Khmer Loeu, members of Cambodia's indigenous minorities, live in the area.

SIGHTS
The Market
Kratie's bustling market lies in a square of mostly French buildings and is a pretty run-down affair, quite muddy in the rainy season. Nevertheless, it is the small town's heart and soul, and in the mornings and late afternoons, the narrow roads around the market are packed with shoppers. Vendors from the villages set up small stalls outside the market building or simply display their vegetables or fish on the ground.

Koh Trong
Right by Kratie in the middle of the Mekong River, this island is slowly becoming a tourist destination. Visitors can observe fishermen, visit a local temple, find rare turtles, and go for long walks through bamboo groves. The island has a 14-kilometer bicycle track along its banks, but you'll need to bring your own bike from Kratie. Day trips to the island, offered by

young guides around the riverfront, cost around US$10 per person. For details on guided ecotours, check www.becambodia.com.

River Cruises
While no regular boats arrive in or leave from Kratie anymore, it is possible to hire boats at the small port in the center of town. With high gas prices, this is not cheap; boats charge around US$15 an hour, more if you want to travel all the way up to Kampi to see the dolphins.

ACCOMMODATIONS
The **Santepheap Hotel** (tel. 072/971537, US$7–15), directly facing the Mekong, is Kratie's longstanding standard hotel. It was recently refurbished and offers simple, clean rooms with no frills (except air-conditioning and hot water in some rooms). There are plenty of parking spaces and passing tour groups tend to stay here.

Just a few doors down the riverfront road from the Santepheap, the **Riverside Hotel** (tel. 012/242914) offers much the same deal—with slightly more worn rooms with fans for US$6, or US$12 for rooms with hot water, air-conditioning, and TV. The **Oudom Sambath Hotel** (tel. 072/971502, US$15), a more modern version of the Santepheap, is a few doors down and offers simple but clean rooms, some with air-conditioning and hot water.

Right at the southern edge of town on the riverfront road, the **Sun Set Bar and Inn** (tel. 012/725032) is possibly the best cheapie in town. Rather small and dark but clean rooms are US$3–5 with fan, or US$12 with air-conditioning and hot water. A small common area balcony is a good spot to watch the Mekong drift by and the bar downstairs can rustle up a cold beer or two.

Right in town, on one of the roads leading from the riverfront to the market, the **You Hong Guest House II** (tel. 012/957003) is a very good value. Rooms are spotless and smart (US$5 with fan, US$13 with air-conditioning and hot water). The You Hong also offers a ticket service, information on the area, and Internet. It's possible to rent bicycles for US$2 a day or motorbikes for US$5.

Facing the market, the long-running **Star Guest House and Restaurant** (tel. 011/777269, US$4–6) doesn't look like much from outside, but the cheap and cheerful rooms aren't bad.

FOOD

The (C **Red Sun Falling,** run by a friendly and erudite American expatriate, is a restaurant, bar, and secondhand bookshop on the riverfront. It offers the most consistent breakfast in town, as well as a decent dinner menu of Khmer and Western dishes, including some good salads for US$3. Red Sun Falling is closed for lunch, but provides the only notable entertainment in the evenings and stays open till 11 P.M.

The **Mekong Restaurant,** next to the Sorya bus company office, is good for a coffee and a quick plate of food before you hop on a bus. The restaurant attached to the **Star Guest House,** near the market, has a decent selection of Asian and Western dishes. Tasty sandwiches cost around US$2.50, and pasta is US$3.50. Service can be a bit chaotic, but it does all turn up eventually. Otherwise, the cozy restaurant at the **You Hong II Guest House** serves travelers standards from US$3.

For more traditional Khmer cuisine for about US$3 a dish, try the **Heng Heng Restaurant,** a large old place on the riverfront.

INFORMATION AND SERVICES

Joe, the owner of **Red Sun Falling,** is a good source for local travel information and can help arrange river cruises as well as trips to Koh Trong.

Health and Emergencies

Health services in Kratie, such as they exist, are not adequate. If you have an accident or fall ill, try to get to Phnom Penh as quickly as possible. The health posts in the area will not be able to provide even the most basic treatment.

Money

There's an ACLEDA Bank in Kratie, which cashes travelers checks and changes dollars to riel. It also has an ATM, which only accepts Visa cards at this time. Money-changers around the market offer a competitive rate for your dollars.

Internet Access

The Internet place between the You Hong II Guest House and the Star Guest House, clearly signposted, is fast and reliable (until 9 P.M.). The You Hong II Guest House also provides Internet access.

GETTING THERE

Passenger boats no longer ply the Mekong from Kratie. Cambodians prefer to travel by road. Buses from Kratie to Phnom Penh leave two times a day, at 7:30 and 9:15 A.M., go via Kompong Cham, and take about seven hours. Tickets are US$6.50 (US$5.50 to Kompong Cham). The Sorya Bus Company (tel. 023/210359) has buses leaving for Kratie from the southwest corner of Phsar Thmey (Central Market) in Phnom Penh at 7:15 and 8 A.M. There's one bus from Kratie directly to Siem Reap, which leaves at 7:30 A.M., takes nine hours, and costs US$12. A bus for Battambang also leaves at 7:30 A.M., takes 10 hours, and costs US$12. Heading north, a bus leaves for Stung Treng and the Lao border at 8 A.M. It's US$6 and three hours to Stung Treng, US$9 and five hours to the border. A pick-up to Banlung leaves at 1:30 P.M., takes six hours, and costs US$11. Heading east into Mondulkiri, a pickup from Kratie for Sen Monorom leaves daily at 8 A.M. costs US$12, and takes six hours—longer if it's been raining. A bus also leaves for Kompong Thom at 7:20 A.M., takes eight hours, and costs US$11. A share taxi from Kratie to the capital takes six hours (US$12.50).

GETTING AROUND

Kratie is very much a walking town. There's really nowhere very far away, but if you are feeling lazy, then the town's *motodups* are happy to take you to any place in town for 1,000 riel.

VICINITY OF KRATIE
◖ Irrawaddy Dolphins

The Irrawaddy dolphins are teetering on the verge of extinction and remain only in a few isolated pockets of the Mekong in Laos and Cambodia, and in the Irrawaddy, the main river in Burma. Little more than a hundred of these animals are said to survive today. Locals call the dolphins *payapee,* which means "man-fish." Some people believe the dolphins are reincarnations of people.

River traffic has virtually depleted the habitat for these very peaceful and beautiful creatures. But the dolphins in Kratie and near the Lao border, the only locations where they continue to live in Cambodia, are hopefully having a bit of a comeback. That's because they are the only real tourist attraction in the area and the steady influx of travelers who want to see them has revived the local economy. What's more, since 2006, a Japanese NGO has been promoting peaceful co-existence between humans and dolphin in the area, and is trying to educate locals about the advantages the dolphins bring to the slowly recovering economy of the charming but dilapidated riverside town.

The dolphins live near the village of Kampi,

DAMMING THE MIGHTY RIVER

The Mekong, the world's 11th-longest river, runs for some 4,300 kilometers from its source on the Tibetan plateau through China, Burma, Thailand, Laos, Cambodia, and Vietnam before it flows into the South China Sea. Cambodia is the most dependent of all these countries on the water flow.

The flood waters that pour into the Tonlé Sap Lake assure the country's economic survival; any serious changes in the annual floods could lead to famine. But these changes are coming, mostly from China, where major dams are being built, which are already having a catastrophic impact on the fishery industry in Cambodia.

In order to develop the resource possibilities of the river, the Mekong Committee was founded in 1957, with backing from the United States, which feared that an impoverished Mekong basin would be a breeding ground for communism. The Mekong Committee advocated the constructions of large-scale dams, but by the time American influence had waned with the United States' defeat in Southeast Asia in 1975 and as Cambodia slipped into isolation, no large-scale projects had gotten off the ground. In 1978, the Interim Mekong Committee was founded, but with Cambodia isolated and Thailand, the most economically powerful member, preferring to spurn cooperation and go ahead with its own dam projects, dialogue collapsed and did not resume in a meaningful way until the Mekong River Commission was founded in 1995. This new outfit learned from past mistakes and is more concerned with the impact of changes in the river on the environment and the people living along its banks than it is with large-scale mega-projects.

China is not part of the Mekong River Commission and because of the huge imbalance of power between the lower Mekong nations and its gigantic neighbor to the north, the organization has been accused of turning a blind eye to Chinese priorities in recent years – while at the same time trying to engage the Chinese in dialogue and cooperation, with limited success. The future of the river looks uncertain, if recent Chinese developments are anything to go by. Since the completion of the Manwan Dam in 1996, the fish catch in Cambodia has dropped by half, boats get stuck on the already tricky river more frequently, and many endangered species, including the Irrawaddy dolphin, have been driven close to extinction. Despite this, China is building another dam, due to be finished in 2009, and is planning 12 more. Ever-increasing pollution, the price of China's economic rise, is having a massive impact, with run-offs from heavy industry and agricultural pesticides severely affecting nations downstream.

where boats are available for around US$3 per person (the price depends on how much water is in the river and how far the boatmen have to go). There's also a US$2 fee for going to watch the dolphins. The money apparently goes towards community development and the Kampi tourist police.

The dolphins are often visible right from the banks of the Mekong, but it's more atmospheric to hire a boat and enjoy these amazing animals, as well as the local birdlife, close up from the water. If you go on a dolphin-watching excursion, don't expect the dolphins to rush right up to the boat or do pirouettes in the middle of the river. Irrawaddy dolphins are rather reserved creatures and are likely to keep a safe distance from the boats. But sightings are virtually guaranteed.

The best time to catch sight of the dolphins is just after the rainy season, when there's plenty of water in the river, preferably in the early morning or late afternoon. Some environmentalists urge visitors not to take motorized boats out onto the river, as there's little doubt that the fees earned from tourism alone will not save this very rare animal.

A smaller population of Irrawaddy dolphins can be observed north of Stung Treng near the Laotian border.

The village of Kampi is the setting-off point for river trips to see the Irrawaddy dolphins. Kampi lies 17 kilometers north of Kratie along a paved road that passes through picturesque fishing communities; you could easily cycle there. Alternatively, *motodups* will take travelers there for US$3.50 round-trip or US$15 in a car.

Phnom Sombok

Phnom Sombok is a small and active hillside temple north of Kratie. As the hill is the only elevation around Kratie, it offers the best views across the Mekong in the area. Phnom Sombok is actually two small hills, one called Phnom Proh (Mountain of Man), the other Phnom Srei (Mountain of Woman). Phnom Srei is slightly higher. Besides the active temple, a number of *stupas* stand around the hillside. Some of the

paintings inside the temple hall offer a vivid depiction of hell.

Phnom Sombok, some 10 kilometers north of Kratie, is best visited as part a trip north to Kampi to see the Irrawaddy dolphins. Travelers taking a lift with one of Kratie's *motodups* might have to pay an extra dollar or two for the detour. If you are just heading for Phnom Sombok, US$3 round-trip should do it.

Sambor

Sambor was once the site of a pre-Angkor era settlement. Today, the main attraction is a large, modern pagoda, the biggest in Cambodia, with a mini zoo attached and no traces of the much older culture remaining. The animals live in deplorable conditions. Entrance is free.

The village of Sambor lies some 15 kilometers north of Kratie and is easily reached by motorcycle. A *motodup* should charge no more than US$7 for the round-trip journey. It's US$23 for a car. The temple is just outside the village.

Wat Roka Kandal

Built in the late 18th century and recently restored with assistance from a German trade association, the beautiful Wat Roka Kandal is one of the few temples in the area constructed from wood. It now houses a small arts and crafts center. Entrance is free.

Wat Roka Kandal lies a few kilometers south of Kratie and can be reached by motorbike in a few minutes. A round-trip ride with a *motodup* shouldn't cost more than US$2.

Chhlong

Few visitors make it to Chhlong, which is a shame. The area around this small port town on the Mekong was a center of rubber cultivation during the French occupation, and there are a few magnificent, if dilapidated, buildings in town to testify to this relatively glorious past. Equally attractive, traditional and very well kept Khmer houses on stilts make up the rest of Chhlong and give the small town a rather friendly feeling.

The former governor's residence, fully

restored, is now a boutique hotel called **Le Relais de Chhlong** (tel. 012/991801, www.nicimex.com, US$80–100), offering the only swimming pool in town. Owned by the same people as the beautifully restored Villa in Battambang, this attractive hotel has just six rooms, some with views of the Mekong; the cost is a little steep considering its very remote location. The only alternative in town seems to be the **99 Mekong Guest House** (tel. 012/203896, US$4), which may double as a place used by the hour. It offers cheap, bare rooms in a wooden house on stilts on the unsurfaced river road.

Chhlong lies some 30 kilometers south of Kratie on Route 73. From Chhlong, it's possible to carry on south to Kompong Cham, a couple of hours away on an excellent road that passes through several small picturesque villages. Some stretches of the road down from Kratie are in deplorable condition, especially when it rains, but most of the way is surfaced. Minibuses from Kompong Cham or Kratie may also pass through Chhlong, if conditions allow. Ask in either town for information.

Snuol

When I first came to Snuol in 2001, the small town was knee-deep in mud. I walked up to a shop by the market to buy some water and was greeted in perfect English by a man sitting in a reclining camping chair, as mired in mud as the rest of Snuol. He told me that he'd fought for the United States during the Vietnam War and that he'd been stuck in Snuol for more than a decade.

Snuol remains a small, dusty, and unattractive town at the crossing of Route 7, between Phnom Penh and Kratie and Route 76, which leads east from here to Sen Monorom, Mondulkiri's provincial capital. It's 135 kilometers to Kompong Cham in the southwest and 125 kilometers to Sen Monorom to the east. Snuol is only 20 kilometers from the Vietnamese border, which is now open to foreigners. The town offers a market, a few flea-bag hotels, basic restaurants around the market, and some mechanics, who can fix cars and motorbikes. It's definitely not a place worth staying in its own right, but getting stuck here is not the end of the world; it just feels like it. The mud's still around during the rains.

There are no banks in Snuol, but money-changers around the market will be able to help out in an emergency. Don't expect a great rate.

It's possible to catch pickups and passing buses from Snuol to either Kratie to the north, Phnom Penh and Kompong Cham to the west, or Sen Monorom to the east.

Stung Treng

Stung Treng is the provincial capital and the largest town in the province of the same name. Stung Treng was part of the Khmer Empire, and later part of the Lan Xang and Champassak kingdoms of Laos before reverting back to Cambodia during the French occupation. Quite a few local inhabitants speak Laotian. Most people in the province live along the Mekong, about a third of them around the town. Stung Treng fell to the Khmer Rouge in the early 1970s and was an unsafe area to travel into the late 1990s, when river pirates regularly robbed passing slow-boats. These activities have now stopped and the province is as safe and relaxed as any other in Cambodia. In remote areas of the province, a few Khmer Loeu villages can be found.

Stretched out along the high banks of the Mekong at the confluence with the Tonlé Se San River, the friendly town of Stung Treng is not particularly attractive, nor is there anything specific to see, though interesting river trips are possible. The Mekong tributary originates in Vietnam and flows through the northeastern province of Ratanakiri before reaching Stung Treng. The town serves as a jumping-off

© TOM VATER

a pier by the Mekong River in Stung Treng

point for Ratanakiri and is the last place of any size or importance before the Laotian border to the north, which is open for international travelers with a Laotian visa. The best thing to do in Stung Treng is to watch the sun go down over the Mekong.

SPORTS AND RECREATION
River Cruises

Stung Treng is a good place to organize a cruise on the Mekong. The stretch up the Laotian border is picturesque, with plenty of rocks breaking through the water's surface, forming small islands when the water is low. There are fishing villages on both banks of the river and waterfalls close to the border. It's possible to spot Irrawaddy dolphins just before the border, though the population is much smaller here than in Kratie.

Mr. T. at Riverside Guest House offers one- to three-day trips up the river towards the Laotian border. One-day trips on a speedboat, very fast but not too safe, cost US$100 for up to three passengers. On a normal long-tail boat, with a capacity of four passengers,

the same trip would also cost US$100. The big boat, which holds up to 10 passengers, costs US$150 for the day, and, due to its meandering speed, offers by far the best views and experience. A two-day trip on the long-tail is US$180, on the big boat US$200. Only the big boat does three-day trips, which cost US$250. All trips include gas, food, water, a guide; for the overnighters, trips also include a homestay in a Khmer village, or, during the dry season, camping on a sandbar in the river.

SHOPPING

In addition to the delightful market in Stung Treng, a visit to **Mekong Blue** (www.mekong-blue.com, Mon.–Fri. 7:30–11:30 A.M. and 2–5 P.M.), a weaving center, is definitely worth a visit. About 50 local women work here producing fine silks that have been awarded the UNESCO Seal of Excellence. The center is operated by an NGO that has been active in the Stung Treng area since 2003. It trains people in skills that will help pay a livable wage, and offers educational programs covering health and literacy. Mekong Blue is located outside of

Stung Treng on the banks of the Se Kong River, east of the Mekong. Ask a *motodup* to take you there. It is also possible to order silk items online. Check the website for a catalogue.

ACCOMMODATIONS
Under US$15

As the name suggests, the **Riverside Guest House** (tel. 074/439454, US$3–4) is right by the riverfront. This traveler-friendly guesthouse has cheap and cheerless rooms, but it has a good restaurant and small bar, which serves cocktails in the evenings and offers Internet access. The owner, Mr. T., can organize a variety of river trips, and provides first-rate travel information. The excellent Tree Top Eco-Lodge in Banlung is owned by the same family.

The very simple **Dara Guest House** (no phone, US$3), next door to the Riverside, has similar rooms as well as noisy bats in the roof. The owner, Mr. Taing, speaks French and there's also a restaurant.

A real step up in comfort, if not location, is the **Ly Ly Guest House** (tel. 012/937859, US$7) next to the market, a block removed from the river. Rooms are smart and clean, and have TV. Somewhat grander is the newly refurbished **Hotel Sekong** (tel. 016/611911, US$15), on the riverfront, which has an impressive entrance and clean, spacious rooms with air-conditioning, hot water, and TV. There's a small restaurant, offering Khmer snacks.

US$15-25

The **Sok Sambath Hotel** (tel. 074/973790), a block from the riverfront and opposite a market, was the best place in town for a long time. It offers clean and simple rooms with TV and hot water, most for around US$10, or US$15 with air-conditioning—with a few pricier and larger rooms as well. The hotel was closed and being refurbished at the time of research; rates after reopening are likely to be slightly higher. It now has serious competition from the **Gold River Hotel** (tel. 092/495556), also known as the Tonlé Mee Hotel. The property is located next to the riverfront pagoda in town.

Large, modern rooms with smart bathrooms, air-conditioning, and hot water cost US$20, while huge VIP rooms with the same facilities are US$30.

FOOD

Stung Treng is no culinary paradise. In the evenings, drink and snack stalls set up along the riverfront road. For a large variety of Khmer dishes (US$3–6), head to the **Sok Sambath Hotel** near the market. The **Riverside Restaurant,** part of Riverside Guest House, does decent travelers' fare, with main dishes around US$2–4, while **Riches Restaurant** (tel. 012/302017), near the riverfront pagoda, has much the same menu, but seems a better place to hang out in the evenings. The owner, Mr. Nak, also provides bus and minibus tickets. Both kitchens close at 10:30 P.M.

The **Mekong Blue Café** (Mon.–Sat. 7:30 A.M.–5 P.M.) is attached to the NGO operation of the same name, and offers breakfast and lunch. Most main dishes, such as fish *amok* and barbecued beef salad, cost around US$5.

INFORMATION AND SERVICES
Money

There's an ACLEDA Bank in Stung Treng that cashes travelers checks, changes dollars to riel, and has an ATM that accepts Visa cards only.

Health and Emergencies

No adequate health services exist in Stung Treng at this time. If you have an accident or fall ill, try to get to Phnom Penh as quickly as possible. The health posts in the area will not be able to provide even the most basic treatment. A few years ago, a lone motorcyclist crashed his bike, broke his leg, and passed out. Local people took him to a nearby health post and when the poor traveler regained consciousness, his leg had been amputated. That said, the Stung Treng Hospital sometimes has doctors from UNICEF present who might be able to help.

Internet Access

The Riverside Guest House has Internet access.

GETTING THERE
Air
There's an airfield six kilometers from town, but at the time of research, no flights landed in Stung Treng.

Boat
The most scenic and adventurous way to get from Stung Treng to the Laotian border is by boat. The regular ferry does not run anymore, but you can rent your own boat for up to four passengers; it takes about 3.5 hours and costs US$50. Boats pass rapids and giant boulders sticking out of the water, framed by dense forests, until reaching the Preah Muht waterfalls on the border, giving the journey a Conradian flair. There are border posts on this route, so you must possess a Laotian visa.

It's also possible to charter a speedboat from Stung Treng all the way down to Phnom Penh, though this can be pricey. Alternatively, go down to the river and ask any of the berthing cargo boats whether they might give you lift, but keep in mind that travel times are flexible and the journey can take several days. If they have room, most crews are happy to take on a few passengers. Make sure you take food, water, sunblock, and insect repellent.

To Kratie, a speedboat with two or three passengers costs US$180 and takes 3.5 hours. A slower boat to Kratie taking up to four people costs US$200 and takes five hours.

Regional Road Transport
The Sorya Bus Company (tel. 023/210359) has one bus a day leaving for Stung Treng from the southwest corner of Phsar Thmey (Central Market) in Phnom Penh at 7:15 A.M. Sorya Bus Company buses from Stung Treng to Phnom Penh also leave just once a day from near the ferry pier, at 7:15 A.M., go via Kratie and Kompong Cham and take about nine hours and cost US$10. The section from Stung Treng to Kratie takes about two hours. The road from Stung Treng to Banlung, Ratanakiri's capital, remains unsurfaced and, at least in the rainy season, treacherous, though buses now ply the road all the way from Phnom Penh in the dry

season, via Stung Treng. A share taxi from Stung Treng to Phnom Penh takes six hours (US$22). It's also possible to catch a share taxi from here to Banlung for around US$8. In the dry season, this journey should take about three hours. During the rains, it could take all day.

GETTING AROUND
Stung Treng is small enough to explore on foot, but if you need wheels, a *motodup* will be happy to take you around, from 1,000–2,000 riel a journey. If you want to hire a *motodup* for a day's excursions, expect to pay no more than US$8.

VICINITY OF STUNG TRENG
Thala Boravit
This site near Stung Treng may be historically significant. It was built during the Chenla Empire, sometime between the 6th and 8th century, and might have once been an impressive trading town, linking trade posts in today's southern Laos to temple sites farther south. Today, however, there are just a few stones lying about. There's another temple site amid rice fields nearby, but all that remains are some carved stones on the ground.

Thala Boravit lies on the western bank of the Mekong, opposite the town of Stung Treng and a little downstream. Catch a boat to the village of the same name, then follow the road straight on, away from the river. After a few hundred meters, there's a trail to the right leading to the site.

Phnom Preah Tihut
Another Chenla-era temple site that's been entirely destroyed, possibly by hungry looters during the civil war, this small hill-side area on the western edge of Strung Treng town was once a sprawling temple complex. The hillock here is covered with traces of structures long gone.

Siem Pang
This picturesque village lies on the banks of the Se Kong River, in the far north of Stung Treng Province. The population of this remote

settlement is half Khmer and half Laotian; both languages are spoken. Local boatmen offer trips to several Khmer Loeu villages in this area. Siem Pang has several very basic guesthouses and restaurants. Virachay National Park, which stretches across Stung Treng and Ratanakiri Provinces, has an office (www.bpamp.org) here, from where trips into the park can be organized, though the access points in Ratanakiri are more organized.

Travelers have two options to reach this remote location. Boats leave from Stung Treng in the mornings and take about eight hours (US$6). The return trip is a bit quicker. The trip is much faster by road. On a motorbike, the journey should not take more than three hours. Share taxis are sometimes available, but don't expect anything to move in the rainy season. Check for road conditions in Stung Treng first.

Banlung

Slap-bang in the center of Ratanakiri Province and connected to the outside world via a dirt road to Stung Treng, Banlung was built in 1979. It has replaced Lumphat, which was bombed flat during the Vietnam War, as provincial capital. The town of 20,000 is still very much in the early stages of its role as a capital. No more than several blocks of traditional Khmer houses on stilts, shacks, and a few rows of newer concrete buildings rise out of the red dusty soil that covers visitors in minutes—unless it rains, in which case they'll be splattered with mud from head to toe every time they venture out. Yes, Banlung is the dust and mud capital of the world.

The market building was constructed in 1997 and forms the center of town. In the early mornings, the area in front of the market hall is crowded with Khmer Loeu, the region's ethnic minorities, who make up 75 percent of the population of Ratanakiri. Vendors sell produce, which they have carried for many miles from their villages to town. Dust devils chase each other across the unsurfaced roads, and you feel a long way from the center of things—but, perhaps for this reason, the atmosphere is great and very relaxed. Bartering goes on everywhere and indigenous families come and go, carrying their supplies in rattan baskets strapped to their backs, supported with cord across their foreheads.

Nevertheless, you could be forgiven for asking why you've come to Banlung, which is the very definition of remoteness. At night, the brightest light in town is the moon. Several international NGOs have their offices here and you might bump into their staff in the town's few watering holes. The real attractions are outside of town, towards the Lao and Vietnam border and to the south towards Mondulkiri. Guided treks from Banlung into the nearby Virachay National Park and other remote destinations have really taken off in recent years and are the main reason to visit the province.

SIGHTS
The Market
The market, built in 1997, is the only point of interest in Banlung and offers an enormous variety of products. Cashews are ever-present and sold by the sack. Local vegetables and countless different fish pastes, the country's staple diet, are on display. A long row of meat stalls has set up shop behind the main building, touting chicken, buffalo, and pork, with the odd rare bird added to the display. Inside the market building, you can stock up on household goods and cheap clothes.

Heavy tobacco smoke wafts across the market area, strong and bitter. The Khmer Loeu, who make the market come alive, smoke from a very young age, and often both boys and girls have a small wooden pipe stuck between their teeth.

BANLUNG

Boeng Kansaign Lake

COCONUT SHAKE RESTAURANT

TERRES ROUGES LODGE

LAKESIDE CHENG LOK HOTEL

LAKESIDE LODGE

VIRACHAY NATIONAL PARK OFFICE

To KCHARAY CEMETERIES

RATANAK HOTEL

POST

GECKO HOUSE

REDLAND INTERNET

MR. CHANGE TORN

TRIBAL HOTEL

A'DAM RESTAURANT

TAXI STAND

ACLEDA BANK

Market

SAL'S RESTAURANT

TREE TOP ECO-LODGE

AIRPORT

0   0.25 mi
0   0.25 km

© AVALON TRAVEL

MAP AREA

To Yaklom Hill Lodge

NORDEN HOUSE

INFORMATION CENTER

KYEAK LOM LAKE

0   0.5 mi
0   0.5 km

ENTERTAINMENT
Bars
Gecko House (tel. 012/422228) is Banlung's first bar, with a cosmopolitan ambience, cold beer, cool music, and very friendly staff. The menu is extensive and features Khmer standards such as egg noodles, glass noodles, and rice noodles with vegetable and meat for around US$3. Excellent morning glory with garlic and oyster sauce is just US$1.50 per plate. For those in search of Western food, the menu features a variety of burgers (including tofu burgers) and pasta dishes from US$3.

SPORTS AND RECREATION
Trekking
With numerous NGOs and guesthouses now involved in ecotourism projects, the number of treks into the province increases every year. Due to the remoteness of Ratanakiri, trekkers are likely to have unique experiences in forest areas that have barely seen any human activity

THE KHMER LOEU: CAMBODIA'S INDIGENOUS PEOPLE

There are less than 100,000 Khmer Loeu (Upper Khmer), also called Chunchiet, living in Cambodia. The French called these populations *montagnards*, a term that survived into the Vietnam War, when many of the minorities fought for, as well as against, the United States. It's estimated that Cambodia's indigenous people comprise 1-2 percent of the country's total population. Most Khmer Loeu live in northeastern Cambodia.

In Ratanakiri, 75 percent of the population belongs to an indigenous group; in Mondulkiri, it's about 60 percent – though these numbers are likely to be quickly diluted as many Khmer move into these two provinces in search of opportunities. In Ratanakiri, the Tumpuon are the largest group, along with the Charay and the Kreung. In Mondulkiri, the Bunong form the bulk of the indigenous population, followed by Stieng, Kreung, Kraowl, and Tumpuon. In Kratie and Stung Treng provinces, small pockets of these groups can also be found.

Some ethnic minorities are also said to live in remote regions of the Cardamom Mountains in the west of Cambodia. These ethnic communities have little in common with their lowland compatriots, and have had limited contact with the rest of the country.

During the Khmer Rouge years, thousands of indigenous people were killed or repeatedly moved and forced into communes. In Ratanakiri, more than half the tribal population is said to have perished between 1975 and 1979. In those years, the Khmer Loeu were forbidden to practice their traditional way of life. While spiritual beliefs have survived in some ways, other aspects of their culture – their rich tradition of textiles, for example – have virtually vanished. The fact that the Khmer Loeu no longer dress the way minorities in Thailand and Vietnam do may save them from some of the more sordid aspects of exploitative tourism we know from Cambodia's neighbors, but they will have their hands full with the challenges ahead nonetheless.

Most Khmer Loeu are subsistence farmers and live in small village communities. Traditionally, everything they need to survive comes from the forest and the modest fields they plant near their villages. Forest is cleared and burned to establish agricultural land, which is cultivated with hill rice and intercropped with a wide variety of vegetables. However, recent human population growth and infrastructure development have put pressure on this system of subsistence agriculture. Today, the Khmer Loeu no longer clear new forest. Almost every household is aware that it is forbidden by Cambodian law to cut new forest. No wonder then, that the Khmer Loeu are concerned about outsiders cutting down the forests. When asked who exactly owns the forest, they answer that the forest is owned by everyone. This egalitarian attitude makes them vulnerable to land grabbing, a common problem.

The Khmer Loeu practice animism, the belief in natural spirits combined with ancestor worship. While the Khmer Loeu's past is fractured by recent conflict and relocation, virtually every aspect of life continues to be influenced by spiritual beliefs. But these beliefs are fading fast. Buddhism in Cambodia has strong roots in animist traditions and some Khmer Loeu, especially those married to Khmer, have started practicing Buddhism.

In recent years, a growing number of Khmer Loeu have converted to Christianity. One reason cited is poverty, as families don't have the money or livestock to carry out the ceremonies prescribed by their old traditions. Also, a perception has been fostered that they will have better lives if they convert. The process of conversion is driven by development agencies sponsored by Christian churches, who arrive in northeastern Cambodia in ever-increasing numbers with money and bibles in their pockets – a threat to Khmer Loeu culture as serious as land grabs.

in many years (other than logging and poaching, of course).

Treks to Virachay National Park must be booked at the park office in town. For treks elsewhere in the area, try Sopath at the Lakeside Lodge (tel. 092/785259). He organizes a trek into community forests for US$20, which includes food, water, transportation, and guide. He also provides an overnight elephant trek combined with a homestay in the Krueng Village of Labang for US$40, which includes food, water, accommodations, and guide. Another elephant trek leads to the Ka Tieng waterfall.

Experienced local tour guide Sitha (tel. 012/764714, http://jungletrek.blogspot.com), who is based at the A'Dam Restaurant in town, speaks English proficiently, knows the region well, and offers a good variety of treks to waterfalls and local villages.

SHOPPING

The market is more of a sight than a place to pick up souvenirs, though handwoven baskets are available. Some hotels retail gemstones

mined in the province. These are cut, but not set, in Banlung. Beware of fakes.

It's also possible to pick up some traditional Khmer Loeu textiles, wooden pipes, and carvings. Check around the hotels or the shops on the road to the market.

ACCOMMODATIONS

It's almost worth coming to Banlung for the accommodations alone, as there are now a handful of excellent places to stay in and around town.

Under US$15

The **(Tree Top Eco-Lodge** (tel. 011/600381, www.treetop-ecolodge.com, US$10) is a couple of minutes' walk south of town, just beyond the A'Dam Restaurant, and offers the best budget rooms in Banlung. Located at the end of a dirt track and overlooking a luscious, narrow valley, wooden bungalows in the traditional Khmer style, constructed on stilts, are connected by wooden walkways. All bungalows are spacious and have large verandas. The simple rooms are an absolute delight, equipped with huge

© TOM VATER

a traditional Khmer-style bungalow at the Tree Top Eco-Lodge in Banlung

platform beds and mosquito nets. The bathrooms—spacious, modern, and smart—are also worth a mention. For now, there's no hot water, but this, according to the friendly Khmer Chinese owners, is likely to change soon.

On the shore of Boeng Kansaign Lake in town, the **Lakeside Lodge** (tel. 012/727787 or 092/785259, US$7–10) is a backpacker favorite run by the very friendly trekking guide Sopath. It offers small, clean rooms (some with fans, some air-conditioned) in a former governor's mansion, which was one of the first larger houses built in Banlung in 1980. Treks in the area can be booked here.

US$15-25

The popular **Tribal Hotel** (tel. 075/974074) is not tribal at all, but offers clean, modern rooms in the heart of town for US$8–20, as well as older rooms for US$3–5. The onsite restaurant isn't bad.

Right by the shore of Boeng Kansaign, the **Lakeside Cheng Lok Hotel** (tel. 075/390063, US$20–25) is Banlung's best proper Cambodian-style hotel and the place where government big-wigs stay. Large, smart, and clean bungalows and rooms have air-conditioning, TV, and hot water, and some overlook the lake. A small roofed restaurant serving Khmer food is set in a fenced-in, tired-looking garden, but the Cheng Lok is a good value if your priority is comfort.

A recent addition to Banlung's growing hotel scene is **Norden House** (tel. 012/880327, www.nordenhouseyaklom.com, US$25), on the road to the Yeak Lom Lake. Spacious and smart concrete bungalows with hot water, TV, and a small balcony make for a comfortable stay amid a well-maintained garden. The restaurant serves Scandinavian specials, as well as Asian and European standards. There's a small fleet of dirt bikes (250cc) and a 4WD available for rent. Internet is free for guests.

US$25-50

The ◖ **Yaklom Hill Lodge** (tel. 012/799211, www.yaklom.com) is some five kilometers out of town, and hard to reach in the rainy season,

but it offers great bungalows with hot water in a peaceful jungle-like garden with rich birdlife. Electricity is available only in the daytime and the lake is a 40-minute walk away, but the place is friendly and some staff members belong to the local indigenous minorities. Bungalows range from singles and doubles (US$18) to a traditional hill tribe home that sleeps eight people (US$50), all with bathrooms. The Yaklom Hill Lodge is intent on preserving the environment around the resort and offers ecotours. The property has been approved by the International Ecotourism Club as well as several other ecotourism organizations and is involved in numerous community projects in the Banlung area.

US$50-100

For a bit of l'Indochine nostalgia, **Terres Rouges Lodge** (tel. 075/974051, www.ratanakiri-lodge.com, US$35–80) offers luxury rooms and bungalows with a strong period feel. It's furnished with antiques and even the wall decorations are in great taste. The bathrooms in the more expensive rooms are superb. The resort, in a well-kept garden on the shore road of Boeng Kansaign, is very professionally run, has a restaurant and a decent size swimming pool, and is the best place in the area to forget about the dusty roads for a couple of days.

FOOD

The **A'Dam Restaurant,** near the Tribal Hotel, is the evening hangout for the local NGO workers, of which Banlung has a small but noticeable population. Western comfort food and Khmer standards from US$2, and, best of all, a good pool table, are the main attractions. The restaurant has a great trekking guide named Sitha and is open until the last customer leaves.

Sal's Restaurant, near the airport, is another favorite with the NGO crowd and has a similar menu. A hundred meters beyond Terres Rouge, and overlooking Boeng Kansaign, the **Coconut Shake Restaurant** offers cheap and basic Western and Khmer dishes, including, you'd never guess, coconut shakes.

INFORMATION AND SERVICES
Virachay National Park Office
For permission to enter Virachay National Park as well as information on this remote and threatened region, visit the park office in Banlung (tel. 075/974176, www.bpamp.org). It's not possible to enter the park without a guide, though you can choose to embark on one of the park's official treks. The friendly office has a 3D map of the park and some information on the wildlife, and offers tailor-made treks.

Health and Emergencies
Banlung has a hospital, but it's to be avoided. No adequate health services exist in Ratanakiri province at this time. If you have an accident or fall ill, try to get to Phnom Penh as quickly as possible. The health posts in the area will not be able to provide even the most basic treatment.

Money
There's an ACLEDA Bank in Banlung that cashes travelers checks and changes dollars to riel. It also has an ATM, which is likely to have Visa facilities soon. Money-changers can be found around the market, easily recognizable by the glass counters full of money piles.

Internet Access
Internet in Banlung is slow, slow, slow, and around US$2 an hour. The best place is **Redland Internet,** near the A'Dam Restaurant.

Motorcycle Rental
Several guesthouses rent motorbikes. In town, right next to the main traffic circle, **Mr. Change Torn** rents out dirt bikes for US$15 a day and is the best place to head for spare parts and repairs.

GETTING THERE
Until a few years ago, regular flights connected Phnom Penh with Banlung, but the unsurfaced airstrip in Banlung has lain dormant since the disastrous 2007 air-crash of a machine owned by PMT Airlines in Bokor National Park on the south coast. It's a shame, because the flight in old Chinese propeller machines was one of Southeast Asia's most adventurous air journeys.

You might be able to jump a plane with the **Missionary Aviation Fellowship** (tel. 012/879426, www.mafcambodia.org), which operates irregular flights in a five-seat Cessna from Phnom Penh. It's hoped that regular air traffic will resume soon.

In the meantime, direct buses operated by the Sorya Bus Company (tel. 023/210359) leave from the southwest corner of Phsar Thmey (Central Market) in Phnom Penh at 6:15 A.M. every morning. The company runs two buses daily from Banlung back to the capital via Kratie and Kompong Cham, one at 6:15 A.M., the other at 7:30 A.M. The Hua Lin Transportation Company buses (tel. 023/223025) leave daily at the same time from its offices near the Olympic Stadium (opposite Wat Preah Puth Meanbon) in Phnom Penh. From Banlung, the Hua Lin buses also depart at 6:15 A.M. Both companies charge US$17 for a seat. Tickets can be purchased through most guesthouses and hotels in Banlung. Journey time is 8–12 hours, depending on weather and road conditions. Buses are unlikely to run in the rainy season until the roads have been surfaced.

A share taxi, which leaves early in the morning from the southwest corner of Phsar Thmey (Central Market) in Phnom Penh, costs almost as much and may be faster, though less comfortable. Some travelers break up the journey in Kratie or Stung Treng, where there are additional transportation options. From Kratie, a share taxi takes six hours (US$12.50); from Stung Treng, it is just three hours (US$8). These journey times become meaningless in the rainy season, when anything could happen.

Alternatively, you could rent a motorbike and drive yourself. Be sure to have a cell phone with you in case you break down on the more remote stretches between Stung Treng and Banlung.

GETTING AROUND
Banlung is definitely small enough to walk around. For destinations out of town, it's

© TOM VATER

motorbike on Route 19 in Ratanakiri

best to travel by motorbike. For the various attractions farther away, a guide is highly recommended. If your guesthouse or hotel cannot suggest anyone, ask for someone at the Ratanak Hotel: I met an excellent local teacher there who knew the province like the back of his hand. You could either hop on the back of the guide's bike, or rent one of your own and have the guide drive on his bike. Norden House and a number of other places rent motorbikes, from small 100ccs (US$5–7/day) to dirt bikes (US$10–15/day). Always wear a helmet, which should be provided with your rental bike.

If you travel by bike, make sure your cameras and any other high-tech gear are well wrapped. The roads of Ratanakiri are phenomenally dusty in the dry season and the dust is so fine, it will reach your camera sensor without you ever taking your camera out of your bag.

Some resorts also offer rides in four-wheel-drives, which is definitely the most comfortable, but also most expensive, way to get around the province (US$50–80/day).

VICINITY OF BANLUNG
C Yeak Lom Lake

Estimated at 700,000 years old, this almost perfectly circular crater lake is 50 meters deep, crystal clear, and surrounded by dense jungle and bamboo thickets. It offers romantic vistas and is a great place for a secluded dip in crystal-clear water. The water is placid and dead tree trunks rise from a deep unfathomable blue to the surface. Flocks of ducks break the smooth waters, and in the afternoons, egrets and other birds are easily observed. Myths and legends surround this lake, and the local Khmer Loeu tribes believe that there are spiritual beings living in its waters.

On the lake's shores, a small information center (entry US$1) exhibits instruments, tools, and household items of the Tumpuon, one of several ethnic minorities living in the area. Two small wooden piers reach over the water—making them ideal picnic spots, or diving boards, as the local kids like to demonstrate.

The lake is part of a conservation area and will hopefully remain protected, but there have been rumors that the jungle will soon be cut down to make room for an upscale resort.

Yeak Lom Lake lies five kilometers outside of Banlung. If you head out of town to the hill tribe monument traffic circle and turn right, it's just over a kilometer from there. If you don't have your own transportation, a *motodup* will gladly take you for US$2.

Voen Said

Voen Said is a small village on the southern bank of the Tonlé San. From here it's possible to visit Cambodian and Laotian minority villages, as well as a Chinese settlement in the area. The Tumpuon village of Kachon lies on the river an hour towards Vietnam. Some Cambodian minorities, including the Tumpuon and Charay, bury their dead in elaborate grave sites, one of which can be visited here (entrance US$1).

Voen Said lies 35 kilometers northwest of Banlung. In the rainy season, the road is likely to be impassable.

【 Charay Cemeteries

The Charay, one of Ratanakiri's ethnic minorities, live in villages along the Tonlé Se San River (as well as across the nearby border in Vietnam) and can be reached in a long day trip. The most frequently visited settlement is called Dal Village. The Charay houses are built on low stilts in forest clearings close to the river. The community lives virtually outside of the money economy; they have few possessions that don't come from the forest. Note that many women are extremely camera-shy or may demand money for as much as pointing a camera anywhere in the villages.

The graves, which can be found with the help of a guide from the village, are remarkable for their carvings. The graves lie spread out in the forest, in the undergrowth near the banks of the Tonlé San. They are not tended, and older graves are usually entirely subsumed by weeds. Most graves are bordered by rickety fences and wooden totem poles. Some have grass roofs. Household goods, forest products such as gourds and carvings, lie arranged within the grave area. Visitors should not move or take any of the objects in the gravesites nor offer the Charay money for such items.

The Charay villages are not easy to reach and it is best to have a *motodup* drive you. Head for the village of An Dong Meas, a small settlement on the banks of the Tonlé Se San River, 80 kilometers northeast of Banlung. Rent a boat here (US$15) to take you up towards Vietnam and the Charay villages. This trip is not advisable in the rainy season.

【 Virachay National Park

Virachay National Park covers an area of 3,325 square kilometers along the northern parts of Ratanakiri and Stung Treng Provinces along the border with Laos and is covered in tropical rainforest. Founded in 1993 and administrated by the Ministry for the Environment, the park was established to contain logging in the area, though large parts of the park have already been cleared of trees and wildlife.

Other parts of the park have never been explored, not even by the park rangers. Some of

---

THE GRAVES OF THE KHMER LOEU

Large carved wooden figures loom out of the jungle like totem poles, some wearing *kramas*, others carrying wooden machine guns. Weeds and bamboo have totally enveloped the icons, which serve as fence posts for the burial plots. Inside the plots, various offerings include carved wooden guns on the burial mounds. Traditionally, when a member of the community passes away, the Khmer Loeu (the Charay and Tumpuon) construct a grave, bury the dead, and leave it for a year, before they return and sacrifice a buffalo by cutting its hind-legs. Only then is the soul of the departed sent on its proper last journey.

Cambodia's rarest animals are said to survive in the park's core area, which is inaccessible to visitors.

Access to the park is only allowed in the company of park rangers. For all inquiries and bookings, contact the head office (tel. 075/974176, www.bpamp.org) in Banlung. The fee of US$13 per day includes a ranger guide and a contribution to a development fund to manage ecotourism projects. This fee is compulsory.

Through ecotourism initiatives started by park authorities, visitors can go on one-day or multi-day treks through parts of the park. The three-night **O'Lapeung River Valley Trek** involves a homestay in an ethnic minority village, a trip into a secluded valley, viewing remnants of the Ho Chi Minh Trail, and a kayaking excursion. The seven-night **Phnom Veal Thom Trek** involves village homestays, boat trips, and a long walk to a grassland area, which is home to deer, bears, hornbill, wild pig, and gibbons. On top of the park fee, trekkers have to pay for homestay (US$2.50), transportation (US$17) from Banlung to the starting point of the trek in Taveng Village, as well as boats (US$15) inside the park. It's unlikely that trekkers will encounter the larger mammals, such as tigers, that are

LUMPHAT, THE SREPOK RIVER, AND THE WORLD'S GREATEST WAR MOVIE

A ruined city in the Cambodian jungle, close to the Vietnamese border, on the banks of the Srepok River . . . Lumphat, the formerly well-developed capital of Ratanakiri with its own airport and secondary school, means nothing to Western readers – but the city is at the heart of one of the most enduring pop-cultural myths of our time.

In the 1979 Vietnam War movie *Apocalypse Now,* directed by Francis Ford Coppola, Martin Sheen's protagonist Willard followed the Srepok River (called Nung River in the movie) in a patrol boat deep into Cambodia. He was on a mission to locate and kill Colonel Kurtz, a renegade U.S. General, who had trained ethnic minorities, so-called *montagnards,* in the fight against the Viet Cong. The hill tribes had taken the colonel for a god, who in turn had supposedly gone insane.

Joseph Conrad's novel *Heart of Darkness* provided the template for the movie. Conrad's story, published in 1898, is a surreal journey into the heart of the Belgian Congo under the brutal control of King Leopold (a journey that the writer had undertaken himself in the 1880s), as well as a journey into the human condition. By the time Marlow, Conrad's template for Martin Sheen's Willard, finds Mr. Kurtz, the chief of the Inner Station, a ruthless ivory trader and the greatest anti-hero of Western literature, the old man is dying. It's up to Marlow to carry the truth of Kurtz's brutality back to the Europe. The text is an enduring modern icon and its title has become a media by-word for genocide and famine. The Heart of Darkness is a cultural symbol of 20th-century history. *Apocalypse Now* has nothing to do with any real Heart of Darkness, but the movie provides an imaginary link between Conrad, the Vietnam War, and Cambodia.

So much for the story. The reality is quite different. The Srepok River runs right through Lumphat and is best accessible here. The river is shallow and wide; in the dry season, it's hardly a meter deep. The water is green and barely moving. Unless the water levels were very much higher 40 years ago, no patrol boat ever navigated this river. Most importantly, the Srepok runs from east to west, in the opposite direction

to the movie river. Does it matter? Of course not. Lumphat is fascinating in its own right.

During the real war, rather than the imagined one, in the late 1960s, the United States tried to cut the Ho Chi Minh Trail (the vast network of jungle supply lines of the North Vietnamese that led from North Vietnam, though Laos and Cambodia into South Vietnam) with mass carpet bombings. No one knows how many people died in these bombings, but estimates are in the hundreds of thousands. The traffic on the trail never really slowed, despite almost a decade's worth of bombing, but obvious targets were obliterated completely. Lumphat happened to be located slap-bang in the middle of the Ho Chi Minh Trail and was bombed into the dust. One local man described the planes as gods from the sky that brought only fire.

By the early 1970s, the area was controlled by the Viet Cong and the Khmer Rouge. The Khmer Rouge killed many of the survivors of the bombing. Today, the remaining citizens explain how their friends and relatives were taken away for "training" and never seen again.

In the years since, there has been a little regeneration and numerous Khmer houses on stilts now dot the area where the town of Lumphat once stood. The old market square is still clearly discernible. Many of the 1960s-era buildings are lying in ruins over a wide area among wild-growing scrub. A bullet-marked water tower – surrounded by bomb craters, electricity works, and several formerly handsome homes – stand out amongst the ruins, as does the ghostly secondary school, a little outside of town, reached via several traffic circles with fallen statues that connect dirt roads leading into nowhere. The town has turned into both a wasteland and a village.

For those with an interest in the aforementioned cultural reference points (and there seem to be many, judging by the numerous travel blogs that boast of having reached this "Inner Station"), today's Lumphat is a monument to the gap between our actions and the sometimes devastating results these actions bring with them.

said to be living in the park. As entry to the park is only possible in the presence of a ranger, it is the park authorities who usually organize transport from Banlung to the park boundaries.

Gem Mines near Chum Rum Bei

Ratanakiri means "Gemstone Mountain" in English and there are a number of mines around the province. The area around Chum Rum Bei is the most accessible. Don't expect walk-in tunnels. Gemstones and zircon are dug up from square holes in the ground. Soil is winched to the surface, where it is sifted through. If you are tempted to buy stones, be sure you know what you are looking at. Some of the stones are fakes or just cheap, imperfect specimens and it takes a practiced eye to recognize the difference.

The village of Chum Rum Bei lies some 30 kilometers south of Banlung. A round-trip on a *motodup* is likely to cost US$15.

◖ Lumphat

In the 1960s, Lumphat was the provincial capital of Ratanakiri. Bombed by the United States and never reconstructed, Lumphat feels like an open-air museum demonstrating what war can do. Numerous ruins, including the waterworks, an airport, a secondary school, and a water tower, are spread over a wide area of brush, dotted with bomb craters and home to newly emerging village life. Basic food can be found at the stalls around the market. There's nowhere to stay in Lumphat; spending a few hours here on a day trip from Banlung is recommended. The town is the beginning of the Death Highway, the 299-kilometer jungle road that connects Ratanakiri and Mondulkiri Provinces.

Lumphat is 35 kilometers south of Banlung. Take the road towards Stung Treng, then turn left after about 10 kilometers. The 25-kilometer stretch south to Lumphat is good, hard dirt.

THE ROAD TO SEN MONOROM

In Lumphat, riders who want to move south into Mondulkiri will have to cross the Srepok River on a raft. Then riders will need to embark on approximately 100 kilometers of trails and ruts, mostly through logged wasteland or

© TOM VATER

a bridge across the Srepok River, which runs through the ruined city of Lumphat

recently replanted forest until the settlement of **Khon Nhek** (pronounced "cognac"), just inside the neighboring province. Occasionally, a Khmer Loeu village will loom out of the dust by the side of the tracks.

Several rivers need to be waded and bikes may have to be carried to avoid having water get in the engine. Trails and tracks disappear or break up all the time, so this road should not be attempted without a local who is both familiar with the route and an experienced rider. In the rainy season, it should not be attempted at all. Even in the best of circumstances, it is a bone-shattering experience, best broken up by staying in Khon Nhek, where there's at least food and karaoke.

South of Khon Nhek, the road improves considerably and leads through beautiful forest areas for another 80 kilometers. It then once more reaches something that can be called a real road, which covers the final 40 kilometers into Sen Monorom, Mondulkiri's capital.

The Death Highway is a great ride, but it's not a joke. If you break down, you will need to improvise. You can't rely on telephone reception. In fact, you can't rely on anything but yourself and the people you are with. Carry enough drinking water and leave with a full tank. If you plan to overnight in the jungle, be sure to have a mosquito net with you. There's gas, food, and very basic accommodations available in Khon Nhek. Without any real mishaps and if you don't linger too long in Khon Nhek, the entire Death Highway can be done in a nine-hour day.

Sen Monorom

Sen Monorom, the provincial capital of Mondulkiri, is located more than 1,000 meters above sea level among rolling hills overgrown by tall grasses. It's the only real town in the province. The jungle in this area has long been cut down, and the windswept highlands are cooler than the rest of the country—and are almost reminiscent of Scotland. If you want to escape the heat, this is the place to come.

Sen Monorom developed quite a bit in the last few years, from a mud-caked settlement with a single hotel in the middle of nowhere to a moderately thriving community, thanks largely to the presence of foreign NGOs and tourism—though it's still in the middle of nowhere.

The town now has a frontier vibe: you're likely to feel you've truly arrived in the Wild East when you reach Sen Monorom, with its abandoned airstrip (soon to be built over), a dozen hotels, a handful of restaurants, and two bars. The population of some 8,000 is predominantly Khmer, but the Phnong (or Bunong), the largest indigenous minority in northeastern Cambodia, definitely have a presence.

There is nothing much to do and there are no sights as such in Sen Monorom. But Sen Monorom is the only base for excursions around the province, and trips into the surrounding countryside tend keep to visitors here longer than they expected.

Beyond Sen Monorom, the province meanders east towards Vietnam. Large stretches of primary rainforest remain, but are being heavily logged. To see any jungle, you have to go on a long day trip. Approximately 60 percent of people in Mondulkiri province belong to an indigenous group. Most of them are Bunong (54 percent), followed by Stieng (3 percent), Kreung (1 percent), Kraowl (1 percent), and Tumpuon (1 percent). Ethnic Khmers make up 35 percent of the local population, while Vietnamese comprise 1 percent and Cham make up 3 percent. To experience Bunong culture, visitors have to venture out to the villages.

SIGHTS
The Market
The only obvious attraction in town is the market, not so much for its produce, but for the seriously rustic atmosphere between the rickety wooden stalls, which stand in a foot of mud in

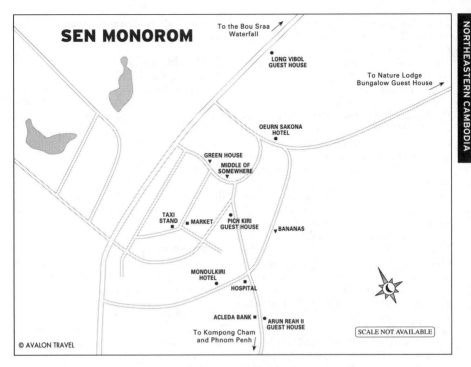

SEN MONOROM

To the Bou Sraa Waterfall

LONG VIBOL GUEST HOUSE

To Nature Lodge Bungalow Guest House

OEURN SAKONA HOTEL

GREEN HOUSE
MIDDLE OF SOMEWHERE

TAXI STAND

MARKET

PICH KIRI GUEST HOUSE

BANANAS

MONDULKIRI HOTEL

HOSPITAL

ACLEDA BANK

ARUN REAH II GUEST HOUSE

To Kompong Cham and Phnom Penh

SCALE NOT AVAILABLE

© AVALON TRAVEL

the rainy season. Impromptu gambling dens set up in the afternoons between the shacks and game meat can still occasionally be seen in market stalls.

ENTERTAINMENT
Bars

Nighthawks are almost spoiled for choice in Sen Monorom, considering the town's remoteness. **Bananas,** a little north of the hospital, is the favorite meeting place for the local expatriate NGO community, offering a menu of Western dishes as well as cold beer. It stays open till the last customer leaves. Alternatively, try the **Green House** in the center of town, which also provides Internet access. Next door, the **Middle of Somewhere** watering hole, run by an affable American, is the place to inquire about the Elephants Livelihood Initiative Environment, an NGO that cares for domesticated and injured elephants.

ACCOMMODATIONS
Under US$15

Right in town, the ◖ **Pich Kiri Guest House** (tel. 012/932102, US$5–10) is Sen Monorom's oldest hotel. It has 25 decent rooms with TV and cold shower arranged around a large parking area. Breakfast is patchy and there's no restaurant, but the guesthouse is close to the town center. The older rooms in the wooden part of the building are cheaper. The owner, Madame Deu, does not speak a word of English, but is a charming host nonetheless and can arrange motorbike rental and elephant treks.

Favored by NGO workers, the **Long Vibol Guest House** (tel. 012/944647, US$5–10) offers large, clean rooms with TV and hot shower in a beautiful garden, but Mr. Vibol, one of the town's most established tour guides, seems somewhat jaded. What's more, the guesthouse is a little out of town.

The **Arun Reah II Guest House** (tel.

012/856667, arunreah_mondulkiri@yahoo.
com.kh, US$6–10) offers simple but clean
bungalows with hot water, TV, and good views
across windswept Mondulkiri. The restaurant
serves cheap Khmer dishes from US$1 and
there's Internet access.

For something completely different, head to
the **Nature Lodge Bungalow Guest House**
(tel. 073/230272, www.naturelodgecambodia.
com, US$5–10), a couple of kilometers out of
town. It's run by a Khmer-Israeli couple and
offers guests tranquility and the opportunity
to stay in simple but smart huts or to camp in
an attractive garden. The resort does not use
generators and produces its own electricity (24
hours). Hot showers, a swimming pond, and
even a sauna facility are available for guests.
Nature Lodge organizes trips around Sen
Monorom as well as occasional parties. The
restaurant serves a wide variety of vegetarian
dishes (as well as options for carnivores) from
around Asia, the West, and the Middle East.

US$15-25

The **Mondulkiri Hotel** (tel. 012/390139, www.
mondulkiri-hotel.com, US$15–30), opposite
the hospital, is Sen Monorom's first modern
(and large) hotel. It has clean and comfortable,
if uninteresting, rooms with fridge, TV, and
air-conditioning. There are several smart bungalows within the hotel gardens and a restaurant serving Khmer and Chinese dishes.

The **Oeurn Sakona Hotel** (tel. 012/950680,
US$10–25), also in town, is similar if smaller.
Downstairs rooms have hot water and air-conditioning, while upstairs rooms have cold-wa-
ter showers and fans.

FOOD

For a selection of Western dishes, check out
Bananas (tel. 092/412680, US$3–5), a
German-run restaurant-cum-bar. It offers good
home-cooking at relatively high prices, until
you remember that this is Mondulkiri, an unlikely place to enjoy a good roast for US$7. A
number of simple Khmer restaurants can be
found around town. They manage to rustle up
an omelet with fresh baguette in the mornings

and standard Khmer dishes for lunch and dinner from US$2.

INFORMATION AND SERVICES

The small tourist office in town is one of the
very few in Cambodia that shows any kind of
activity. The staff speak English and can help
with motorbike rental, elephant treks, and
homestays in Bunong villages.

Money

There's an ACLEDA Bank in Sen Monorom
that cashes travelers checks and changes dollars
to riel. Money-changers can be found around
the market.

Internet Access

You can check Internet at the **Arun Reah II
Guest House** or the **Green House** (www.
thegreen-house.blogspot.com).

GETTING THERE

The airstrip in town remains closed (and it's
said it will soon give way to new developments),
but transportation options for Sen Monorom
have increased in recent years. During the dry
season, an air-conditioned bus operated by the
Hua Lian Bus Company (US$12) leaves Phnom
Penh at 7 A.M. and takes 8–12 hours. The journey is slightly faster though less comfortable in
a share taxi, i.e. pickup (US$10), which leaves
early in the morning from the southwest corner
of Phsar Thmey (Central Market).

For the most part the road isn't surfaced
yet, so all bets are off in the rainy season. The
buses cease to operate and some travelers have
reported being abandoned in the small and unattractive town of Snuol, or worse, breaking
down in their pickups somewhere farther east
and having to spend the night (which can be
cold) out in the open.

GETTING AROUND

Transportation options around Mondulkiri are
extremely limited. If you drive yourself, several
guesthouses and some stalls in the market rent
motorbikes. But you will still need a guide to

find your way around the myriad small trails that cross the region. Alternatively, you can hire a bike with a driver and let the trusty *motodup* (US$10–20/day) find the way to outlying villages and waterfalls. It's also possible to rent a four-wheel-drive for some excursions. Expect to pay US$50 a day, and don't believe stories about nighttime safaris. All I saw on one such excursion were a few rabbits.

VICINITY OF SEN MONOROM
◖ Elephant Treks

The villages of the Bunong minority are scattered all over Mondulkiri, and a few communities have become somewhat used to foreigners and have begun to organize elephant treks. The easiest, most straightforward way to do a trek is to book one with your guesthouse or hotel in Sen Monorom. Expect to pay about US$30 a day, or US$60 for two days with food and a homestay in a Bunong village. Your hotel will provide transport options to get to the village where the treks start, either Budang, some 10 kilometers south of Sen Monorom, or the settlement of Bulung, a little closer, but to the north of the provincial capital. As the guesthouses take a big cut, it might be better to go directly to Budang or Bulung and negotiate there with the Bunong. Any *motodup* will take you out there (it's about a half-hour ride from Sen Monorom).

An alternative is to visit **Elephants Livelihood Initiative Environment** (ELIE, tel. 012/1613833, http://elie-cambodia.org), a British-run NGO that aims to protect Mondulkiri's remaining domestic population. ELIE has rented farmland for several domestic elephants and their *mahoots* (handlers), and welcomes sick and injured elephants. Visitors can take day-long treks on elephant back for US$50, which includes food and accommodations—though this organization mainly looks for long-term, paying volunteers. Interested in being an assistant *mahoot* for a week or two?

Bou Sraa Waterfall

The Bou Sraa waterfall, located in attractive forest, carries water over two tiers year-round,

an elephant ride in Mondulkiri

© AROON THAEWCHATTURAT

but is most impressive just after the rainy season in November. The lower fall drops about 25 meters. The pools below the falls are too shallow for a real swim, but local kids like to shriek around in the shallow water. Be careful when descending by the side of the falls, as it's quite steep. Snacks and drinks are available by the falls. You can go on a 15-minute elephant ride here for 6,000 riel.

The falls lie some 35 kilometers east of Sen Monorom and are easy to get to on a graded toll road. Motorbike fees for the toll road are 3,000–5,000 riel.

Monorom Waterfall

The Monorom Waterfall is a smaller affair than Bou Sraa, but it does have a pool big enough for a swim and it's possible to jump from the top of the 10-meter cliff the water rushes across. At least the local kids do it.

The falls lie three kilometers northwest of Sen Monorom, which makes for a nice walk. Alternatively, a *motodup* can take you for US$3 round-trip (with waiting).

THE BUNONG AND THEIR ELEPHANTS

Cambodia is one of the last countries in Southeast Asia to retain a sizeable population of wild and domestic elephants. The elephant is central to Bunong culture. The Bunong have always shared their lives with elephants, which are treated like humans.

If an elephant gets sick or is injured, the Bunong will perform a ceremony to heal the animal; it is taboo to eat elephant meat. Prior to the Khmer Rouge years, almost every village had some elephants and the number of elephants owned by a family indicated its wealth and social status.

Moe Chan, an elder from Pautrom, a Bunong village in Mondulkiri, used to be an elephant catcher. He recounts, "When I was young, we used to ride all the way to Vietnam to buy musical instruments. We used to catch a wild elephant with three or four domestic elephants. But the tradition died out a long time ago. The last elephant trainer who knew how to teach domestic elephants how to hunt and capture a wild elephant died a long time ago. And I am one of the last catchers left."

When the Khmer Rouge came to power and forced the Bunong to move to Koh Nhek District in the north of Mondulkiri, the community's elephants were set free or sold by the Bunong, or killed by the communists. By the time the Bunong returned to their villages in the 1980s, the number of wild elephants had declined sharply. Furthermore, since conservation efforts were introduced in the mid-1990s, it's forbidden to capture them.

Today, it is thought that the Bunong own no more than 100 domestic elephants. Some Bunong believe that having a baby elephant makes the spirits angry, others perceive a baby elephant as good luck and a marriage ceremony for the elephants is arranged. Nevertheless, elephants rarely get opportunity to breed, and are likely to disappear from the villages of Mondulkiri within the next 20 years.

Moe Chan is realistic: "The Bunong have always used elephants for transport of forest product, rice, or to visit relatives and I guess the motorbike will do that in the future." He smiles sadly, "But of course the motorbike cannot go everywhere in the forest." The remaining pachyderms owned by the Bunong are most likely to find employment in Mondulkiri's burgeoning tourist industry.

Yet even today, when the Bunong sit in their homes and talk of the past, the legend of the elephant is retold again and again: Once upon a time, two young Bunong boys sat by a river fishing. After a successful catch, the older boy grilled and ate his fish. Soon he felt his body break out in a rash and began to scratch feverishly. His skin suddenly turned hard and grey and the boy grew and grew quickly in front of his brother's eyes. When he reached an enormous size and stopped growing, he said to his brother: "Please run to the village and tell our friends what has happened. I don't want to be the only one looking like this." The younger brother followed the elephant's instructions and soon the villagers all grilled their catches and ate with great joy. The villagers all began to itch and scratch. And after a short while, they all turned into elephants. The young boy had to prepare food for these giants who refused to consume anything but cooked rice. One day, the boy jumped up in protest. "I can't cook this much rice anymore," he said and flung the bowl of boiled rice to the ground. Everywhere the rice fell, lush vegetation sprung up from the dry soil and the elephant grass soon covered an area as far as the boy could see. The remaining people quickly trained the elephants to carry huge loads and it wasn't long until the elephants complained about their work. But the men countered, "Your bodies are so enormous, you should be able to carry anything." One day, a giant called Nut arrived and turned the elephants' tongues upside down, then pulled their lips away from their faces, stretching them longer and longer until the elephants could complain no more.

Mimong

Mimong, a small and somewhat impromptu settlement west of Sen Monorom, is the heart of Cambodia's gold rush. The nearby village of Preah Mias, some six kilometers away, is basically an open gold mine. It's possible to climb down into the open mines where the soil is extracted and filtered, but bear in mind that several miners die in accidents every year. The miners, most of them ethnic Khmer, along with some Chinese and Vietnamese, do not mind being photographed. There's a simple guesthouse in Mimong where rooms are US$5 a night.

Mimong is at the end of a bad road, some 45 kilometers west of Sen Monorom. On the back of a bike, it should take about four hours in the dry season and is pretty impossible in the rainy season.

BACKGROUND

The Land

GEOGRAPHY

Cambodia is a Southeast Asian country that borders on Thailand in the west and northwest, Laos in the north, Vietnam in the east and southeast. The country's southern coast faces the Gulf of Thailand. Cambodia stretches over 181,035 square kilometers.

Under French colonial rule, Cambodia was part of Indochina, along with Laos and Vietnam, and the country's current borders were largely drawn up by the French. The country is divided into 21 provinces, which are in turn divided into districts.

The Tonlé Sap Basin covers two-thirds of Cambodia and lies at an altitude of 5–30 meters above sea level. This gigantic low-lying area, with the Tonlé Sap Lake, Southeast Asia's largest body of freshwater in its center, and the Tonlé Sap and Mekong Rivers to the lake's east, is partially flooded during the rainy season, which generates the nutrient-rich soil that a large part of the population relies on for agriculture. The basin is hemmed in by the Dangrek Mountains to the north, the Cardamom Mountains to the west, the Elephant Mountains to the southeast, and the high plateaus of Mondulkiri and Ratanakiri to the east.

Cambodia's coast is lined with beaches and mangrove forests and numerous islands of varying sizes lie in the Gulf off the country's shores.

© AROON THAEWCHATTURAT

Phnom Aural, in the Cardamom Mountains, is the country's highest peak at 1,813 meters.

CLIMATE

Cambodia lies between the 10th and 15th degrees in the northern hemisphere and is a tropical country. The rainy season, from May to October, is brought on by monsoons coming from the southwest. This period is also characterized by high humidity, especially in September and October. From November till March, the dry season raises temperatures up to 40°C. April tends to be uncomfortably hot. The best time to visit Cambodia is from November to January when temperatures and humidity are lowest.

In recent years, these seasonal patterns have been disrupted by climate change, posing serious challenges to farmers. In 2008, heavy rains engulfed much of the country until early December.

FLORA
Forest

Cambodia has two types of forest. Evergreen forest grows above 700 meters, while tropical forests grow below this altitude. Kirirom National Park, a strange exception to this distribution of flora, has pine forests. Many tree species long threatened elsewhere in Asia still grow in profusion in Cambodia. Generally, the tree life is similar to Indonesia and quite different from China. Mangrove forests cover large stretches of the country's coast. Until fairly recently, Cambodia was home to some of the largest and most undisturbed forest areas in Asia.

Grasslands

Large tracts of Cambodia are covered by low-lying savannah-type grasslands. The soil in these areas is mostly poor and the vegetation is almost desert-like.

FAUNA

Cambodia has a varied fauna and is home to many unique animals, including some very rare large mammals that live in the country's forests. But as rapid development depletes the country's forest cover, and as poachers endanger animals, many species are likely to face extinction over the next few years.

Visitors almost never encounter the rarer

© AROON THAEWCHATTURAT

view of Mondulkiri's protected forests, in northeastern Cambodia

STRANGE CREATURES IN THE JUNGLE

For decades, Cambodia's jungles were virtually inaccessible to anyone but soldiers and hardened poachers. The U.S. bombing campaigns, the Khmer Rouge revolution, and the civil war blocked all development of the country's extensive biospheres, but also made scientific expeditions into remote regions impossible.

In recent years, the Cambodian government and private companies have been cutting down the country's forests, and habitats are shrinking at an alarming rate. This is especially tragic since Cambodia's forests are so remote that they are home not just to some of the last remaining tigers and elephants living in the wild in Southeast Asia, but also to animal species that have never been classified or captured on film.

In 2000, Fauna and Flora International undertook a trip into the Cardamom Mountains and came across a rare species of wolf snake and a large population of Siamese crocodiles, thought to have been extinct in the wild. The expedition also heard of sightings of the kting voar, a snake-eating cow reputedly living in Cambodia, though the scientific community isn't convinced that this particular animal actually exists (or if repeated findings of its strange horns are a hoax).

In 2007, a colony of endangered vultures was discovered in the northeastern part of the country, while an expedition along the Mekong River turned up a Cantor's giant soft-shell turtle, thought to have been extinct, which grows to more than two meters. In 2008, 42,000 black-shanked doucs and 2,500 yellow-cheeked crested gibbons were discovered in Cambodia. Both species were thought to exist only in Vietnam. Cambodia's national animal, the kouprey, a large forest-dwelling ox, stands up to two meters tall at the shoulder, weighs more than 1,000 kilograms, and is extremely endangered. This jungle cow is so rare, it wasn't even discovered until 1937. Today only 200 kouprey are thought to survive in Cambodia, southern Laos, and Vietnam.

Further scientific expeditions are likely to turn up more creatures thought to have become extinct or never seen before, but it's a race against time, as biospheres are shrinking rapidly. Besides logging, the international trade in exotic species, slash-and-burn agriculture, road construction, and the presence of unexploded ordnance pose a serious threat to animals in Cambodia.

---

species, and wildlife organizations do most of their surveys with infrared cameras that are left in the jungle for weeks. The chance of encountering a wild elephant or tiger in Cambodia is extremely remote. More common sights include monkeys, snakes, and birds.

Endangered species include tigers and elephants, as well as dolphins, gaur, clouded leopards, sun bears, numerous species of wild cats, pangolins, and the Siamese crocodile, which was thought to be extinct until some were spotted in the Cardamom Mountains a few years ago. For the rhino, once indigenous to Cambodia, it's already too late.

Mammals

Cambodia has a huge variety of mammals, most notable amongst them the Asian elephant and the tiger. Other wild cats, such as panthers and leopards, are also indigenous to Cambodia. Deep in Cambodia's forests, several bear species continue to survive. Wild deer such as the banteng and gaur have made headlines recently because they have been hunted close to extinction—as have some other large mammals. A number of deer, including the mouse deer, and wild boar survive in Cambodia's forests. Many smaller mammal species also live in Cambodia—among them numerous types of monkeys, such as rare lemurs and loris and the more common macaques and gibbons, along with a wide variety of rodents, from rice paddy rats and badgers to squirrels.

Marine mammals such as dugong and whales in the Gulf of Thailand are becoming increasingly rare, and the Irrawaddy dolphins

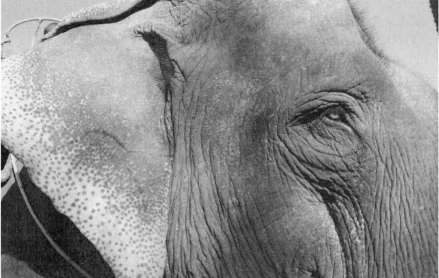

Cambodia's wilderness is home to some of the last remaining elephants in Southeast Asia.

are fighting for survival in the upper reaches of the Cambodian stretch of the Mekong River.

Birds

More than 500 bird species are said to be native to Cambodia, including cormorants, cranes, numerous types of hornbills, egrets, herons, parrots, and pheasants. The greater adjutant, a huge stork with a wingspan of more than 2.5 meters, nests only in Assam and Cambodia. Predatory birds include the crested serpent eagle as well as several types of owls.

Reptiles

Opinions vary on just how many types of reptiles live in Cambodia, not least because so little research has been done in recent decades. Some of the country's wilderness areas are home to extremely rare turtles, lizards, crocodiles, and snakes, with some species only recently discovered. Large saltwater crocodiles are now extremely rare in Cambodia.

Reptiles are especially vulnerable to trafficking. While wildlife NGOs and government agencies occasionally intercept the illegal transport of turtles and snakes, these successes catch only a fraction of the animals smuggled out of the country.

Freshwater Life

More than 850 species of fish are said to live in the Tonlé Sap Lake and the Mekong River, though only about 40 of those have any nutritional significance. Turtles and crocodiles, though no longer common, still survive in remote river areas, and the upper reaches of the Mekong in Cambodia are home to two shrinking populations of Irrawaddy dolphins.

Sealife

Cambodia's coastline is dotted with coral-fringed reefs. These are home to a huge variety of fish, including small sharks and rays, as well as dolphins and whales. Occasionally, whale shark sightings are reported.

ENVIRONMENTAL ISSUES

With Cambodia's economy booming in recent years, environmental considerations have taken a back seat for policy makers in Phnom

CAMBODIA'S NATURAL WEALTH: TROPICAL FORESTS AND LOGGING AND BEYOND

During 40 years of the civil war, wood was a major income source for the various factions fighting each other. Battles raged over forest territory, yet only a handful of people benefited from the logging. It is estimated that in 1970, more than 70 percent of the country was under primary forest cover; today it is said to be around 3 percent. As the war ground to a halt, the Cambodian government pledged reform to international donors, and consequently logging decreased slightly. But it did not stop. When the IMF threatened Cambodia in 1997 to withhold aid funds if the logging did not stop, the government threatened right back that it would reintroduce damaging past logging practices, if the money was not paid. The gambit paid off. In the late 1990s, foreign companies enjoyed a 100 percent export duty exemption for timber products.

It's only gotten worse. While the government allegedly abandoned commercial logging in 2003, the UK watchdog Global Witness monitored continued large-scale logging until the organization was thrown out of the country by Prime Minister Hun Sen in 2006. Since then, Global Witness has issued a report, the research for which was gathered in secret, which alleges that military units closely tied to the government have been plundering Cambodia's forest resources faster than ever. The report accuses the Cambodian government of "building a shadow state on patronage, coercion and corruption."

There are possible solutions to the loss of forest cover, but the authorities' greed and the willingness to use force at the drop of a hat, lack of education among the population, and the continued acquiescence of Western donor governments and organizations stand in the way of implementing efficient policies.

Some of the Khmer Loeu have their own forest management practices based on re-

---

Penh. The extraordinarily rapid depletion of natural resources does not benefit ordinary Cambodians and widens the gap between a tiny self-enriching elite and the vast majority of the population. While NGOs try and counter some of this expansion, as often as not, the effect of foreign donor money can be described as corrosive, enabling the allegedly cash-strapped government to pursue exploitative environmental policies with impunity.

Logging and Land Grabs

Cambodia is facing severe environmental degradation, not least because of continued widespread illegal logging. Land-grabbing has become a serious issue, and in the past two years, the Cambodian government has sold significant parts of the country, including islands, beaches, and forest areas, to foreign investors. Other large tracts of land have been grabbed from local people by Khmer businesspeople with political influence in order to cultivate monocultures such as rubber and cashew trees. The locals, who usually do not have titles to the land, are simply removed, by force if necessary. Land-grabbing has been the biggest factor in the displacement of people in Cambodia since the days of forced relocation under the Khmer Rouge. Some foreign observers estimate as much as a staggering 45 percent of the country has been leased or sold to foreigners since the year 2000.

Monocultures

Until the global economic downturn in 2008, Cambodian economic growth hovered at 10 percent per year, a result of international investment and the country's cash crop expansion program. To achieve high productivity, crops have been planted on giant monoculture plantations. Monocultures require external input to sustain themselves and to produce high yields.

spect for and co-existence with nature. According to Bunong belief (shared with other indigenous peoples throughout Southeast Asia), some actions in the forest are governed by religious rules that keep man and nature in balance, avoiding widespread habitat destruction. Each community assigns areas of forest as Spirit Forest, not to be exploited in any way. The Bunong belief system is an efficient form of responsible resource management refined by hundreds of years of firsthand experience. It's part of the community's identity and part of Cambodia's spiritual and natural heritage. No wonder then, that the Khmer Loeu are frightened of outsiders cutting down the forests. When asked about who exactly owns the forest, they answer that the forest is owned by everyone. This egalitarian attitude makes them and the country's last great wilderness areas vulnerable to land-grabbing.

The effects of logging are far-reaching. Once hillsides are denuded, erosion sets in when the rains come and silt is washed into the rivers. Not only does this destroy infrastructure and farmland, but it also threatens the Tonlé Sap Lake, which already has a silting problem, because the flooded forests along its shores have been cut down – the spawning grounds for the fish that provide much of the protein for the nation. Many voices in the NGO community allege that as long as Cambodia is run by soldiers, trees will continue to be felled and no amount of legislation or logging bans will fundamentally change this.

Between 1990 and 2005, Cambodia lost as much rain forest as it still has today; while the country remains under 59 percent forest cover, only 3.1 percent of that is rain forest. The loss of forest since 1990 is just under 20 percent, the loss of rain forest since then is 85 percent.

The resulting loss of nutritious soil through erosion is extremely high. Soil mulching—the introduction of other plant species into plantations to enrich the soil—is considered to be an obstacle to monoculture management, hence plantation floors are cleared of other species.

Dams

Numerous dams have been constructed in the Tonlé Sap watershed areas and in the upper reaches of the Mekong River. This causes the fragmentation of floodplain habitats. While mega-dam projects have been widely recognized to have a detrimental effect on biodiversity and people, China plans to dam the Mekong further.

Overfishing

Large-scale fishing, the expansion of the fishing industry, and fishing with destructive gear has severely affected the fish stock in the Tonlé Sap Lake. Attempts by the Cambodian government to reduce the catch of small fish have not been successfully enforced. Illegal fishing is widely practiced and the fish population in the Tonlé Sap continues to decline sharply. The Gulf of Thailand was overfished in the 1960s, but due to the long civil conflict, fish stocks there have somewhat recovered.

Dynamite Fishing

Many of the coral reefs around the Cambodian islands in the Gulf of Thailand have been damaged by dynamite fishing. Fishing with grenades, both in rivers and around the islands, was common throughout the 1990s. More recently, dynamite fishing has been significantly reduced due to partially successful drives to limit civilians from storing and using weapons, awareness campaigns, some coast guard action, as well as growing tourism around the islands.

History

There are no people in Southeast Asia who remain so connected to—if not burdened by—their history as the Cambodians. The descendents of the master builders of Angkor almost destroyed themselves in a vicious communist revolution. Both momentous periods—the regional supremacy of the Khmer Empire between 800 and 1400 and the almost four years of terror under the Khmer Rouge between 1975 and 1979—continue to hold a powerful sway over the nation's psyche, society, and politics and keep attracting scores of international observers, academics, and writers.

THE FIRST KHMER (4200-500 B.C.)

The origins of the Khmer are uncertain. Prehistoric finds from around Cambodia suggest that people lived in caves in the region as far back as 4200 B.C., if not much longer. Pottery dated back to this time is very similar to pottery produced in Cambodia today and historians make much of this fact—some things in Cambodia have not changed for more than 6,000 years. It is possible that even then Cambodians lived in simple wooden houses on stilts, planted rice, and caught fish. What is certain is that people lived in small village communities, and that big changes came along with an influx of people from what is today India around the time of Christ.

FUNAN (500 B.C.-A.D. 550)

The Indians brought a written language with them (Sanskrit), a religion (Hinduism), as well as new ways of looking at the world, ideas about social hierarchies, the concept of the god king, architecture, politics, and astronomy, as well as a name—Kambuja. There's been some debate about where this name comes from—research suggests that the Kambojas were an Indo-Iranian tribe that slowly migrated from today's Afghanistan into India and Sri Lanka, eventually set sail for Southeast Asia, and founded a Kambuja colony on the Mekong River, probably in today's South Vietnam, which at the time was populated by Khmer.

A myth of origin tells a different story, also with Indian connections. A Brahmin named Kaundinya sailed a ship to the Far East and encountered the princess of a local ruler who tried to attack him. Kaundinya used his magical bow to shoot an arrow into the boat of the princess who, perhaps in fear, agreed to marry him. To be able to give his daughter a dowry, the so-called dragon or *naga* king drank the water that covered his land, built the couple a new capital, and called it Kambuja. The name does not appear in Cambodian inscriptions until the 9th century A.D. Prior to that, though, the story was recorded by Chinese who were trading in the region.

Unfortunately, there are no contemporary descriptions of the era available to us today. But several archaeological sites in today's eastern Cambodia (including Angkor Borei near Takeo) and Vietnam's Mekong Delta point to the establishment of a first kingdom, or at least a group of allied city-states from the 1st century A.D. onwards, though the origins of this entity could lie much further back. The Chinese called it Funan, the Khmer Bnam. Since World War II, Roman, Chinese, and Indian goods have been found at digs, pointing to maritime trade. It is assumed that the kingdom's influence stretched all the way into what is today Laos, Thailand, Burma, and even the Malay peninsula. Kambuja seemed to be a halfway point of trade between India and China and was perhaps the first Southeast Asian empire.

CHENLA (A.D. 550-802)

The Chenla Empire started as a dependent of Funan in the middle of the 6th century A.D. and quickly absorbed the earlier empire, perhaps because of disruption of traditional trade routes between Europe and China, following the collapse of the Roman Empire. The Chenla Empire was less seafaring than its predecessor. Its capital, Isanapura, was located near Kompong Thom and included the temples of Sambor Prei

THE KINGS AND THEIR TEMPLES

The most successful rulers of Angkor built temples and cities to support themselves. The following chart illustrates who built what, giving an overview of the development of temple construction during the Khmer Empire.

King	Reign	Capital	Temples Constructed
Jayavarman II	A.D. 802–850	Hariharilaya, Mhanddrabarapeata	Phnom Kulen
Indravarman I	A.D. 877–889	Hariharilaya	Bakong, Preah Ko
Yasovarman I	A.D. 889–910	Hariharilaya, Yasodharapura	Phnom Bakheng, Lolei, Phnom Krom, Eastern Baray, Preah Vihear
Jayavarman IV	A.D. 928–944	Koh Ker	Koh Ker
Rajendravarman II	A.D. 944–968	Yasodharapura	Preah Rup, Eastern Mebon
Jayavarman V	A.D. 968–1001	Yasodharapura	Banteay Srei, Ta Keo
Suryavarman I	A.D. 1010–1050	Yasodharapura	Banteay Srei, Kbal Spean, West Baray, Preah Vihear
Udayadityavarman II	A.D. 1050–1066	Yasodharapura	West Mebon, Baphuon
Suryavarman II	A.D. 1113–1150	Angkor Wat	Angkor Wat, Beng Melea, Banteay Samre, Wat Athvea
Jayavarman VII	A.D. 1181–1220	Angkor Thom	Angkor Thom, Ta Prohm, Neak Pean, Banteay Chhmar, Preah Khan, Bayon

Kuk, which give an impression of how relatively powerful this early Khmer Empire might have been. Some scholars have pointed out that Chenla may well have been more of a shifting set of alliances of local chieftains than anything resembling a centralized state. By the late 7th century A.D., Chenla was divided into a northern and southern half, based in southern Laos and the Mekong Delta before breaking into smaller states in the early 8th century A.D. These weakened states were continually invaded by Javan kings during the 8th and early 9th centuries, which pushed the remaining local chieftains northwest of the Tonlé Sap Lake, into the region that later became Angkor.

ANGKOR (A.D. 802-1431)

Jayavarman II had grown up at the Javan courts (or had been kept a hostage there), returned to Kambuja and conquered as well as united several Chenla courts in A.D. 790; he thus established his authority as king and kick-started a period of 600 years during which Angkor was the world's biggest, most powerful empire. Eventually he founded a city, Hariharalaya, in the area near Roluos, some 15 kilometers from Siem Reap, and declared himself a god king in 802. Hariharalaya was a long way from the sea and right at the northwestern end of the Tonlé Sap Lake, a strategically advantageous location, given that the greatest dangers to the Khmer king came from enemy navies. This move enabled the Jayavarman II to declare independence from Java. But rather than rest on his laurels, the god king, or *devaraja,* decided to continue uniting parts of what is today Cambodia under his authority and fought numerous wars against his enemies until his death in A.D. 850. His son Jayavarman III consolidated his father's authority, and in A.D. 877, Indravarman I became the first god king to build significant structures in the Angkor region, such as the Preah Ko and Bakong temples. His son, Yasovarman I, built the adjacent Lolei temple and founded a new capital called Yasodharapura, which settled around the sacred mountain temple of Phnom Bakeng. Yasodharapura was the first Angkor capital. Yasovarman I also built the first massive reservoir, so important for the Khmer Empire's growing wealth and stability. Now called the Eastern Baray, this artificial lake was 7.5 kilometers long and 1.8 kilometers wide and its waters are estimated to have irrigated more than 8,000 hectares of farmland. The hilltop temple of Preah Vihear on the Cambodian–Thai border is also attributed Yasovarman I. For a while, though, Yasodharapura was abandoned and the capital was moved to Koh Ker, some 80 kilometers to the northeast.

Jayavarman IV, who seems to have come from a different part of the royal family, ruled there A.D. 928–944 and was the first Khmer king to introduce sandstone in his temple architecture. The most remarkable result is the massive pyramid-shaped temple of Prasat Thom at Koh Ker.

The capital returned to Angkor in 944 under Rajendravarman II, who promptly built the Eastern Mebon and began construction of Banteay Srei while extending the Angkor Empire into Thailand, Laos, and even southern China. Rajendravarman II was the first Khmer god king to sack the kingdom of Champa to the east. He was succeeded by his 10-year-old son Jayavarman V. Surprisingly, the young man managed to remain in charge for more than 30 years. He built a new city called Jayendranagari, and the temples of Banteay Srei and Takeo were constructed during his reign.

Poets, philosophers, and artists found a home at his court, but following his death in 1000, the empire subsided into turmoil for a decade.

Then Suryavarman I took over for 40 years and extended his realm's borders all the way to Lopburi in Thailand. He also began construction on the Western Baray, an even-larger reservoir that measured 8 kilometers by 2.2 kilometers and was designed to expand the king's economic power. Following the death of Suryavarman I in 1050, chaos ensued once more, until Suryavarman II took over in 1113. One of the greatest of Angkor's rulers, he reigned for 37 years and had Angkor Wat, a temple dedicated to Vishnu, constructed in that time. He extended his troops' reach to the borders of Bagan (Burma) and farther into the Malay Peninsula. He died around 1150.

Shortly after, the Cham and Khmer had a huge naval battle in which the Khmer Empire was defeated and declared a vassal state of Champa. Jayavarman VII, the last great king of the Khmer, a follower of Mahayana Buddhism and a military leader, retook Angkor from the Cham and ascended to the throne in 1181. He continued to fight the Cham for 22 years, until that eastern empire's defeat in 1203. More importantly, he built Angkor Thom, the Khmer Empire's most magnificent city—and the one we are left with today. In its center, the Bayon, a massive Buddhist temple, was not only dominated by the famous stone towers of the *bodhisattva,* but also featured detailed murals of ordinary Cambodian life during his rule. Jayavarman VII also laid out a grid of high roads that connected all the outlying provincial capitals of the Khmer Empire, and built more than a hundred hospitals. The overgrown forest temple of Ta Prohm was constructed under his reign. With its last true god king, the Khmer Empire had reached its peak.

Following Jayavarman VII's death, Angkor gradually lost power, as Champa to the east and the kingdom of Sukothai to the west began to assert themselves. In the middle of the 12th century, Jayavarman VIII came to power. A strong believer in Hinduism, this king had thousands of Buddha statues destroyed, and paid tribute to

Kublai Khan out of fear of China to the north. Jayavarman VIII was eventually removed by his son-in-law Srindravarman, who was an adherent of Theravada Buddhism. His reign is remarkable in so far as it was recorded by the Chinese diplomat Chou Ta-Kuan, who described not only the temples of Angkor, but also the daily life of its people—thus giving us the only eyewitness account of life in the Khmer Empire.

Knowledge of what happened in the following decades and centuries is sketchy. Perhaps Theravada Buddhism undermined the authority of the *devaraja,* the god king. Perhaps the empire's infrastructure was neglected, as the king could no longer muster thousands of slaves for his massive projects. Perhaps the neglect affected the rice harvests and caused floods and droughts. Another explanation points to the logging of trees in the Kulen hills to make space for fields to accommodate a quickly growing population. The subsequent erosion may have silted up the sophisticated network of canals and irrigation channels around Angkor and paralyzed its agriculture and trade. To the west, the Siamese kingdom of Ayutthaya conquered Sukothai to its north and then attacked Angkor several times, finally conquering and plundering the Khmer capital in 1431.

CAMBODIA IN LIMBO (1432-1863)

It's unlikely that Angkor was abandoned altogether at any time from the Siamese invasion of 1431 until the first French explorers came across the ruins in 1860—even then, Angkor Wat was active and more than a thousand monks lived around the temple. Unfortunately, hardly any inscriptions were carved into stone between the middle of the 14th century and the beginning of the 16th century and the only references to Cambodia during this period can be found in Chinese and Thai chronicles.

Research hints at the possibility that Angkor, apart from being sacked by its enemies and having overreached itself, was no longer economically viable, as it was too far from the sea where all the lucrative trade was happening. Several new capitals were built at the confluence of the Mekong and Tonlé Sap Rivers. From here, Khmer rulers could control the trade on the Tonlé Sap Lake as well as the flow of goods on the Mekong, down from Laos and up from the Mekong Delta. But moving the capital farther east did not end the strife with Siam, and while Cambodia enjoyed periods of stability and wealth because of increasing trade in the region, the country was also encroached upon by Vietnam to the east.

King Ang Chan, who ruled what was left of the Khmer Empire 1516–1566, established a capital at Loveck. For the first time, significant numbers of Westerners—adventurers, mercenaries, and traders—visited Cambodia. Towards the end of the 16th century, Chinese, Indonesian, Japanese, Malay, Portuguese, Spanish, Arab, and a few British and Dutch settlers made their home in the capital. When the Siamese threatened the Cambodians again, King Satha asked the Spanish for military help. By the time Spanish mercenaries arrived, it was too late. The Siamese attacked Loveck in 1593 and left a governor in the city. The Khmer were now ruled by foreigners.

In the meantime, the Vietnamese had defeated the Cham once and for all, many of whom fled into Cambodia. Soon the Vietnamese dominated and controlled the Mekong Delta and the Khmer kings no longer had effective access to the sea. The widespread distrust of the Vietnamese may have originated in this period. During the 17th and 18th centuries, Cambodia's neighbors were preoccupied with their own conflicts—while Vietnam fought a long civil war in the 17th century, Ayutthaya was destroyed by the Burmese in 1767. In the late 18th and early 19th centuries, Cambodia tried to play off its larger neighbors and lost parts of its territory as a consequence. Vietnam gobbled up the Mekong Delta and expanded its territory to its present borders by the late 18th century, while the Siamese annexed Battambang, Sisophon, and Siem Reap provinces in 1794. For a while, Cambodia was controlled by both neighboring states. But while the Thais shared a common culture and religion with the Cambodians and merely aspired to control them politically, Vietnam viewed the Khmer as barbarians who needed to be civilized—in step with the thinking of Western colonial powers at the time.

THE FRENCH IN CAMBODIA (1863-1953)

The French arrived in Southeast Asia in the late 1850s and soon decided that Cambodia would make an ideal buffer zone between their new colony of Cochinchina and Siam, which lay within the sphere of influence of Britain, France's main colonial competitor. King Norodom, who'd been on a very wobbly throne since 1860—the Siamese had seen to it that Norodom had not been officially crowned yet—saw a chance to free Cambodia from the dominance of both the Siamese and the Vietnamese and allowed Cambodia to become a French protectorate. Some historians say that this may have saved the country from disintegrating altogether.

In 1863, Cambodia became a French protectorate and a year later, Norodom was officially crowned in a bizarre ceremony supervised by Siamese and French officials. In 1884, the French forced the weak king to accept increased French authority. A year later, they had a major uprising on their hands that took thousands of soldiers more than a year to quell. But by 1887, French Indochina, including all of today's Vietnam and Cambodia, had been formed. King Norodom died in 1904 and was replaced by the more pliable Sisowath. In effect, Cambodia was run by the French Resident-General, who was appointed from Paris. The bureaucracy around the Resident-General, the men who now ruled Cambodia, was largely run by Vietnamese, whom the French thought more capable than the Khmer, a situation that soon bread resentment.

Economically, the French brought only modest advancements to Cambodia. The colonizers built some roads and a couple of railway lines. Rubber, corn, and rice were cultivated for export. Besides that, the French collected a lot of taxes, more than anywhere else in Indochina. In 1906, thousands of farmers demonstrated in Phnom Penh, to no avail. In 1907, Siam was pressured to return Battambang, Sisophon, and Siem Reap provinces to Cambodia and Angkor once again became part of Cambodian, if occupied, soil. The French did little to educate the Khmer, which gave Vietnamese and Chinese businessmen the opportunity to run the banking and trade system, and also made organized resistance more difficult. Cambodians, long used to cruel god kings, saw little reason to rebel, so long as a Cambodian monarch headed the country. Armed rebellions did occasionally take place, but only in the 1930s did small groups of Khmer intellectuals begin to criticize the colonial enterprise.

Resistance to the French became a moot point when the Japanese entered Cambodia in 1941 and ordered the French Vichy government to continue administrating Cambodia. The same year, King Monivong died and the throne was handed to the young Norodom Sihanouk, the great-grandson of King Norodom, thought to be too young to be of any danger. In March 1945, Cambodia, at the behest of the Japanese, declared independence, and remained just that—for seven months, until Allied troops regained control of the country. After the war, the French were determined to recover Indochina, but by then, effective rebel groups such as the Khmer Issarak and the Viet Minh had formed. Under increased pressure, the French allowed elections in 1946 and 1947 that weakened Sihanouk's hand, as he tried to negotiate his own independence deal with the French. But the king largely ignored the democratic movement in his country. Instead, he dissolved parliament, suspended the constitution and became prime minister in 1952.

INDEPENDENCE UNDER SIHANOUK (1953-1970)

In 1953, after some wrangling between Sihanouk and the French, Cambodia was granted full independence. Indochina, following humiliating defeats of the French army at the hands of the Vietnamese, ceased to exist. In some ways, Cambodia, under the sometimes watchful and autocratic eye of its former king,

KING NORODOM SIHANOUK: FATHER OF A SHATTERED NATION

One of Southeast Asia's most enigmatic leaders, King-Father Norodom Sihanouk, as his current official title goes, is a political survivor who has changed his alliances and titles so many times that he made the *Guinness Book of Records* as the politician who has held the greatest variety of political offices. Sihanouk is a wily politician, an alleged playboy – said to have fathered at least 14 children – as well as a man who understands himself as the father of his people. Young Sihanouk's extravagant private life filled gossip columns around the world in the 1950s and 1960s, but his long political career – amazing, bizarre, and catastrophic in turn – reflects the extreme shifts Cambodia has made in the second half of the 20th century.

The son of King Norodom Suramarit, Norodom Sihanouk was born in 1922. The future king attended primary school in Phnom Penh, before being sent to Vietnam for his secondary education until his coronation in 1941. At the time, the French still ruled Cambodia and expected the young king to be a pliant tool. They were wrong. Gradually, King Sihanouk distanced his country from France, achieving independence in 1953. Two years later he abdicated, became prime minister, and claimed neutrality for his country in the increasingly divisive cold war that was about to engulf the region. He also became an autocratic nationalist. In 1963, he made himself head of state for life. While some Cambodians today remember the late 1950s and 1960s as a time of stability, in which Sihanouk played in jazz bands, helped reinvent Cambodian architecture, and made a string of self-aggrandizing feature films, the period was also marked by the brutal repression of his adversaries, especially of the Left, and periodic neglect of state affairs.

In 1965, Sihanouk changed his neutralist stance when he broke off diplomatic relations with the United States, after South Vietnamese and American forces had made incursions into Cambodia. Sihanouk aligned himself with China and the North Vietnamese communists. Soon after, while on a trip abroad, he was toppled by the U.S.-backed right-wing general Lon Nol. Sihanouk went to China and began an unholy alliance with the communist Khmer Rouge – a term he had coined himself, and which was to haunt him and his country for decades to come. In the coming months, thousands of poor farmers joined the Khmer Rouge, partly because they wanted to fight for their king, partly as a reaction of extensive U.S. bombing campaigns. In 1975, the Khmer Rouge toppled the Lon Nol regime and made Sihanouk head of state, while driving the Cambodian people into the killing fields. A year later, Pol Pot put Sihanouk under house arrest. The king remained trapped in the Royal Palace in Phnom Penh until the Vietnamese invaded in 1979. The Khmer Rouge had killed five of his children by then. Nevertheless, Sihanouk formed an alliance with the genocidal communists once more. With support from the U.S. and China, Sihanouk's own troops, the Khmer Rouge, and other allies continued to fight the new Vietnamese-backed government until 1991, when he returned from exile to Cambodia and once more became head of state and later king.

Since his return, King Sihanouk's role has been symbolic. He has let his people know that the dirty politics of the 1990s were not to his taste and he finally abdicated in favor of his son King Sihamoni in 2004. In recent years, the king-father has been using his website (http://norodomsihanouk.info) to communicate with the public. While many observers think he shares much responsibility for the suffering of Cambodians, he remains above all what he always was – a great communicator who can play to many different audiences, seemingly without contradicting himself.

bloomed in its newfound independence. But discontent over repressive actions against political opponents and the increasing American presence in the region—despite the proclamations at the Geneva Conference in 1954, that Cambodia would be a neutralist country—made for a short Cambodian honeymoon.

In 1955, King Sihanouk abdicated in order to become more directly involved in politics, and founded a party that preached loyalty to the monarchy and to the Buddhist religion, which implied that social equalities in Cambodia were down to karma, rather than the struggle of people and ideologies. He then rigged and overwhelmingly won elections and humiliated his opponents in public, soon driving most of his opposition underground, whilst gallivanting around the country, shooting feature films, designing hotels, and indulging in earthly pleasures. And while Cambodia was one of the richest countries in the region during his long reign (1954–1970), the nation was slowly crumbling from without and within. Sihanouk distrusted the Americans and Thais and let the Viet Cong, who were fighting the South Vietnamese and American influence in Southern Vietnam, establish bases in northeastern Cambodia, which the United States soon bombed, allegedly with Sihanouk's tacit agreement.

A small Paris-educated Left, amongst them one Saloth Sar, slowly became more influential. Sihanouk called them the Khmer Rouge and invited some of them, including Khieu Samphan, later head of state during the communist years, to join his government. Nevertheless, throughout the 1960s, leftists were persecuted, detained, and killed by Sihanouk's security police. But while Sihanouk alienated the Left, he could not make peace with the Right either. He nationalized banking, insurance companies, and a trade organization in order to eliminate the influence of foreigners, especially Chinese and Vietnamese, which led to widespread corruption and cronyism. Now both sides of the political divide as well as large sections of the population were becoming fed up with the former king. The National Assembly elections in 1966 swung the country to the Right under the leadership of General Lon Nol. In 1967, following the nationalization of rice exports, farmers protested violently in Samlot, near Battambang, and Sihanouk had 10,000 of them killed. The god king's world was caving in. By 1968, he also had a small but growing communist armed resistance on his hands; by 1970, it controlled about a fifth of the country. Meanwhile, the United States, searching for Viet Cong bases in Cambodia, continued to carpet bomb the northeastern part of the country, killing thousands of civilians. Sihanouk chose to ignore many of these developments and busied himself with his feature film projects. Soon he had conservatives, perhaps with the help of the CIA, plotting a coup.

CAMBODIA UNDER GENERAL LON NOL (1970-1975)

In March 1970, after Prime Minister Lon Nol had signed a declaration supporting a vote against the prince, the National Assembly voted in a new, insignificant chief of state, while Lon Nol remained prime minister. The Khmer Republic was born. Sihanouk, in China at the time and suddenly deposed, made a spectacular political summersault and allied himself with the Vietnamese and Cambodian communists, whom his army had been fighting just a month before. Lon Nol promptly had thousands of Vietnamese civilians killed, and demanded that all North Vietnamese forces leave Cambodia immediately. As the United States and the South Vietnamese were running armed incursions into Cambodia, the communists did not leave, but pushed deeper into Cambodian territory. Lon Nol's troops fought two offensives against the North Vietnamese in 1970 and 1971. But with renewed U.S. military aid, corruption in the armed forces was so rampant that the Cambodian army was soon an ineffective fighting force, led by an equally ineffective Lon Nol, who had suffered a stroke and immersed himself in Buddhist mysticism.

By the end of 1972, the Khmer Republic was in control of little more than Phnom Penh and a few provincial capitals. But the Lon Nol government lasted another four years, thanks to a brutal bombing campaign by the United States, which, in the first half of 1973, dropped more than 100,000 tons of ordnance onto Cambodia—authorized by President Nixon and Henry Kissinger, his national security advisor.

But it was all to no avail. The Cambodian communists, the Khmer Rouge, simply hardened under the bombardment, killed all their erstwhile North Vietnamese sponsors, and began to turn those parts of the countryside under their control into collectives. By early 1975, the rebels controlled the river supply roots into Phnom Penh, which had swollen with two million refugees fleeing the bombing, which is said to have claimed half a million lives.

DEMOCRATIC KAMPUCHEA AND THE TERROR OF THE KHMER ROUGE (1975-1979)

On April 17, 1975, Khmer Rouge troops, many of them as young as 15, poured into Phnom Penh. The initial joy about the end of the war evaporated quickly. The victors had not come to celebrate, but to launch the radical revolution that became Democratic Kampuchea. In the weeks that followed, all borders were closed, and money, education, Buddhism, private property, and freedom of expression and movement were abolished. The inhabitants of Phnom Penh and all other cities were herded into the countryside to work. Thousands perished immediately. The communists had made it their priority to increase the country's rice output for export, which was to finance industrialization in turn.

But the changes did not stop there. Angkar, the revolutionary organization made up of members of the communist party, also banned family life and any individual expression, right down to clothes. In the new communist utopia, everyone would be the same. For some time, no one even knew who the leaders of the revolution were. Outside observers were told that Sihanouk, who had aligned himself with the communists following his ouster, was still in charge. Those who had been driven from the cities were labeled "new people" and were put to work growing rice. Initially, some "new

people" were elated—for the first time in years, the country was at peace and there was enough to eat in most areas. The "base people," rural Cambodians, on the other hand, had tasted authority for the first time, freed from the shackles of the monarchy and Buddhism. The young Khmer Rouge warriors, at the forefront of the communist movement, were all "base people." After victory over the hated Vietnamese and the Americans, they drove the revolution forward with increasingly vicious zeal.

Perhaps 100,000 people who were part of the establishment of the Khmer Republic—this included teachers, monks, policemen, engineers, and many others—were killed. But it was the radical policies of Angkar, above all over-working the population and not willing to or being able to distribute enough food, that killed more than a million Cambodians, perhaps one in seven people, between 1975 and 1979.

In 1976, Sihanouk was placed under house arrest and Comrade Pol Pot, a.k.a. Saloth Sar, was announced as prime minister. A constitution was published shortly after. In early 1976, a National Assembly was elected. "New people" were not allowed to vote and the assembly met only once, to pass the constitution. The new government announced a four-year plan to triple the rice yield per hectare, irrespective of soil conditions. Other crops were to be grown for export. The Cambodians were expected to work long days year-round to meet the revolutionary goals. Nevertheless, by 1976, rice, some of which had been exported, was in short supply and the population began to starve in many areas. More severe famines followed in 1977 and 1978.

In the meantime, Pol Pot had become paranoid about opposing forces within his own party—which, as far as the population was concerned, did not even exist—and began a cycle of internal purges that were to sweep away thousands of his erstwhile comrades in the coming years. Many of his former allies ended up at S-21 Tuol Sleng in Phnom Penh, a former school turned interrogation center, where some 17,000 people were tortured and subsequently taken away to be executed. All of them had confessed to having worked for the CIA, the KGB, or the Vietnamese security services. Other such centers operated around the country. While Cambodia was now almost totally isolated, the Chinese supplied the government with military equipment in order to foment the traditional antagonism of the Khmer towards the Vietnamese, who were backed by the Soviets and distrusted by the Chinese. Pol Pot, like Lon Nol and Sihanouk before him, would have liked to absorb a part of the Mekong Delta—Kampuchea Krom—into Democratic Kampuchea. Needled on by his Chinese sponsors, he soon ran brutal incursions into Vietnam, indiscriminately killing thousands of civilians, both Vietnamese and Khmer.

In response, Vietnamese troops invaded Cambodia on Christmas Day 1978 and on January 7, 1979, entered Phnom Penh, ending the Khmer Rouge reign of terror. At the time, the capital had fewer than 50,000 inhabitants. Pol Pot fled in a helicopter. But Cambodia's horrors were far from over.

THE VIETNAMESE LIBERATION AND OCCUPATION (1979-1991)

The country the Vietnamese encountered was on its knees, dotted with mass graves and starving masses of people. Yet thousands of Cambodians, while relieved that the Khmer Rouge had fallen, had no intention of living under the authority of their traditional enemies, the Vietnamese, and fled west into Thailand.

The Vietnamese installed a regime in Phnom Penh and renamed the country the People's Republic of Kampuchea. The agricultural collectives were dissolved. In the wake of the Khmer Rouge fall, widespread famine occurred. While some foreign aid poured in and the occupiers did their best to feed a helpless, traumatized, and antagonistic population, the United States and China made sure that only limited amounts of help reached the Cambodian people. In response to Vietnam's invasion and liberation of Cambodia, China, with the support of the United States, attacked Vietnam in February 1979. After two weeks of massacres and counter-

massacres along the countries' common border, the Chinese withdrew, unable to force a change in Vietnamese foreign policy.

The Vietnamese soon had even bigger problems on their hands. In the provinces, three different resistance forces had formed—the Khmer Rouge, FUNCINPEC, a royalist grouping under Sihanouk's son Prince Ranariddh, and the right-wing KPNLAF. These groups initially fought independently against the Vietnamese, but they formed a coalition in 1982, which was recognized as Cambodia's legitimate government by the United Nations. Thailand also sided with the United States and China, allowing the various anti-Vietnamese factions to arm in the numerous refugee camps along Cambodia's border. The Khmer Rouge troops, supplied with money and new weapons, quickly reformed into an effective guerilla force. Not only had the United States and China rewarded one of the 20th century's most heinous regimes, the superpowers also condemned the Cambodian people to 18 years more suffering. Many provinces fell under the control of one rebel faction or another, while the new government in Phnom Penh was made up of Khmer Rouge who had defected to Vietnam prior to the fall, amongst them Heng Samrin, Chea Sim, and Hun Sen.

The civil war continued unabated until 1989, when after lengthy negotiations, the Vietnamese left. In October 1991, the four warring factions signed a peace deal in Paris and formed a unity government under Prince Sihanouk, who returned to Cambodia in 1991 for the first time in 12 years. The United States and China withdrew their support of the rebel movements, marking the beginning of the downfall of the Khmer Rouge.

UNTAC AND THE 1993 ELECTION (1992-1993)

The Paris agreements made the formation of UNTAC possible. The United Nations Transitional Authority in Cambodia poured more than 20,000 personnel into the country with the aim of disarming the various factions and organizing free and fair elections. But the most expensive United Nations action ever—at

US$2 billion, much of which was wasted in inflated salaries—proved to be a flawed enterprise, a story of mismanagement and incompetence with tragic consequences for Cambodia.

The Khmer Rouge refused to disarm, barred the United Nations from entering the territories under its occupation, and massacred Vietnamese civilians, as well as U.N. soldiers and Cambodian civilians. Consequently, the other factions also refused to disarm. Yet, despite the Khmer Rouge's threats to execute voters, elections for a National Assembly took place on May 22, 1993. Approximately 90 percent of Cambodia's registered voters turned out, a clear signal for peace. FUNCINPEC won 45 percent of the vote, while the CPP, the Vietnamese-installed ruling government, garnered just 38 percent. The CPP refused to accept the election results and Sihanouk stepped in, made himself king once more, and announced the CPP's Hun Sen and his own son, FUNCINPEC's Prince Ranariddh, as joint prime ministers. The United Nations could do little to counter the fact that the will of the people had been betrayed in the country's first democratic election in more than 20 years.

Hun Sen soon outmaneuvered the prince and set about intimidating opponents while embarking on a nationwide program of building schools. Young, brash, and ruthless, the war hero who'd lost an eye in the battle for Phnom Penh (fighting with the Vietnamese liberators) was digging in. Despite the political wrangling, a fragile peace seemed to have almost arrived.

THE END OF THE CIVIL WAR (1993-1997)

Meanwhile, the Khmer Rouge, encamped near the Thai border in Pailin, was growing rich from gemstone and logging deals with the Thai military. They boycotted the elections and were in no mood to concede defeat. The guerillas continued in their attempts to destabilize the country while fishing for a slice of power. In 1994, Khmer Rouge fighters attacked a train in southeastern Cambodia and killed a number of tourists and Cambodians. Both FUNCINPEC and the CPP courted the Khmer Rouge leaders to shift camps,

and in 1996, Ieng Sary, head of one of the main Khmer Rouge factions, moved his troops over to the government side. With Ieng Sary and Pailin gone over, Pol Pot and his remaining troops clung to the small enclave of Anlong Veng in the far northwest of the country.

In the meantime, Sam Rainsy, a FUNCINPEC minister fired for his attacks on government corruption, started his own party, the Sam Rainsy Party (SRP). With all this political maneuvering and sporadic fighting, nothing much was done for the Cambodian people, and by the mid-1990s, the countryside still languished in abject poverty.

A FRAGILE PEACE (1997-2008)

In 1997, a grenade attack on a Sam Rainsy gathering in Phnom Penh killed numerous activists and rumors of a coup swirled around the capital. Soon after, Hun Sen seized control of the government during two days of bloody fighting. Prince Ranariddh and Sam Rainsy left the country. In 1998, new elections were contested by all parties (except the Khmer Rouge) and Hun Sen's CPP extended its stranglehold on power. The other parties refused to accept election results, but a power-sharing deal between the CPP and FUNCINPEC was eventually worked out, while Sam Rainsy went into the opposition.

The fortunes of the Khmer Rouge continued to decline during the late 1990s, but echoes of their reign of terror continued to reverberate around the world. In 1997, Pol Pot had one of his closest advisors, Son Sen, and his entire family massacred, and was put on trial by his erstwhile comrades, now led by the former general Ta Mok, nicknamed "The Butcher." The Khmer Rouge leader, Brother Number 1, was sentenced to house arrest and died in April 1998, possibly poisoned, escaping any kind of justice. Shortly after, the last Khmer Rouge leaders, amongst them Khieu Samphan and Nuon Chea, defected to the government. The Khmer Rouge had ceased to exist as a military force. Negotiations for a tribunal to investigate the Khmer Rouge war crimes began and were to drag on for years.

In 1999, Cambodia joined ASEAN. In 2002, local elections were largely peaceful, as were national polls in 2003. The CPP extended its powerbase in the countryside, while Sam Rainsy made gains amongst urbanites, especially the young, not least for his speeches against the Vietnamese. FUNCINPEC, involved in ever more infighting and corruption, lost its second-party status. It took almost a year of negotiations before a government, dominated by the CPP, with FUNCINPEC as a weak partner, was formed. Hun Sen, now virtually without effective opposition, had consolidated his power and Cambodia had become one of the most corrupt states in the world. Crucially, though, through a mixture of diplomacy and fear, Hun Sen had achieved the almost unthinkable: Cambodia, however battered and dysfunctional, was at peace.

In 2004, King Sihanouk abdicated, presumably for the last time, and his son Sihamoni ascended to the throne. Meanwhile, Prince Ranariddh was forced out of FUNCINPEC for trying to sell the party headquarters and then forced out of the country by Hun Sen. FUNCINPEC virtually collapsed, and the 2008 election, fought against a bitter and politically motivated conflict with Thailand over the temple of Preah Vihear, brought Hun Sen's CPP an overwhelming majority.

SELLING THE NATION (2008-PRESENT)

A decade after the cessation of serious armed conflict, Cambodia was doing well: Tourists were visiting the country in record numbers, the economy was booming, investment was strong. But there was a shadow side, which may yet come to dominate the life of ordinary people in the coming years. Government corruption has become so prevalent that large portions of Cambodia's land have been sold to foreign investors, resulting in the biggest displacement of Cambodians since the Khmer Rouge years. In 2009, some 150,000 Cambodians faced eviction from their homes. Despite logging and land laws, influential business tycoons and elements of the military continue to deplete the country's resources. Intimidation of the press is common, political opponents are still being assassinated, and foreign NGOs reporting on abuses have been shown the door.

Some observers have noted that the culture of impunity that has befallen the country is not unlike the lawlessness of the final days of the Lon Nol regime in the early 1970s, just prior to the Khmer Rouge revolution. Cambodia remains on a threshold, seemingly unable to decide whether to join the larger world or bask in a semi-isolated limbo.

Government and Economy

GOVERNMENT
Organization

Cambodia is a multi-party democracy under a constitutional monarch. Since 2004, the head of state has been King Norodom Sihamoni. The Cambodian people go to the ballot every five years and elect a National Assembly of 123 elected members. The government is formed by the winning parties.

In the elections of 2008, the CPP won 69 seats and 47.3 percent of the vote, the Sam Rainsy party won 28 seats and 21.9 percent of the vote, and FUNCINPEC won 26 seats and 20.8 percent of the vote. The CPP's Hun Sen is the current prime minister.

Cambodia has the largest government (in relation to its population) in the world. It currently has seven deputy prime ministers, 15 senior ministers, 28 ministers, 135 secretaries of state, and 146 undersecretaries of state. The 58-person-strong Cambodian Senate is dominated by CPP nominees, with nominees of the other two main parties, as well as a couple of the king's nominees and two parliamentarian nominees. Chea Sim is the current senate president.

Political Parties

Cambodia's political life is dominated by three parties. The CPP (Cambodia's People's Party) is currently Cambodia's strongest party and evolved out of the PRPK, the People's Revolutionary Party of Kampuchea, installed in 1979 by the Vietnamese. The FUNCINPEC Party (Front Uni National Pur Un Cambodge Independent, Neutre, Pacifique et Coopeativ) was founded by Sihanouk as a rebel movement against the Vietnamese. Due to corruption, the party had significant losses in the 2008 elections and seems doomed to obscurity. The SRP (Sam Rainsy Party) is Cambodia's third force. Led by a former FUNCINPEC finance minister Sam Rainsy, the party has made significant gains in recent elections on a platform of anti-corruption and anti-Vietnamese xenophobia.

The Military

Cambodia's current military force, the RCAF (Royal Cambodian Armed Forces), was founded in 1993, following the establishment of a democratically elected government. Throughout the 1990s, the RCAF absorbed soldiers from the other civil war factions. In 2000, it began to demobilize some of its soldiers to reflect Cambodia's peacetime conditions. The military is divided into army, navy, air force, and military police, and it operates under the jurisdiction of the Ministry of Defense. Cambodia's monarch is the supreme commander of the RCAF, while the prime minister is the commander-in-chief.

Judicial System

Cambodia has lower courts, an appeals court, and a Supreme Court, as well as a military court. The 1993 constitution guarantees an independent judiciary, though this remains largely an aspiration—with few judges properly trained and many of them allegedly in the pockets of influential politicians. The courts are further weakened by police corruption, substandard police procedures, and a brutal prison system. Justice remains elusive for Cambodians.

© TOM VATER

a staff member of an archaeological team of the Cambodian government at work in Sambor Prei Kuk

Slightly different circumstances apply to the Extraordinary Chambers in the Courts of Cambodia for the Prosecution of Crimes Committed during the Period of Democratic Kampuchea (Extraordinary Chambers or ECCC), an international court set up by the United Nations to deal with the remaining leaders of the Khmer Rouge.

Corruption

According to an international survey on corruption perception in 2008 by Transparency International (www.transparency.org), Cambodia was number 166 out of 180 surveyed nations, following Myanmar at 178 as the most corrupt Southeast Asian nation. This translates into land-grabbing, illegal logging, a compromised judiciary and police force, and a culture of impunity that reigns as much on the streets of the capital as it does in the provinces. Cambodians know from long and bitter experience that in order to get anything done, someone will have to be paid.

ECONOMY

Since the end of the political wrangling in Phnom Penh in the late 1990s, Cambodia's economy has grown rapidly. Yet even today, annual per capita income is just over US$500 and the country remains one of the poorest in the region. Due to massive wealth disparity, this means that people in the countryside remain extremely poor, with thousands in need of food aid, despite the fact that Cambodia grows sufficient rice to feed itself. Some of the urban population benefits from the massive recent economic gains, but 35 percent of Cambodians live below the poverty line. Today, foreign investment outstrips (official) foreign aid and prior to the global financial crisis, the Cambodian economy was growing at around 10 percent. But with continuing resource depletion on a massive scale, the vast majority of the population mired in abject poverty and global economic influence on the country, continued growth, for which a modicum of stability is required, is somewhat uncertain. Rice, fish, wood, and clothes are Cambodia's major exports. The kingdom is a member of the World Trade Organization.

Agriculture

According to 2004 figures, 75 percent of Cambodians are farmers. Most rural households are engaged in agriculture or fishing, sometimes both. Besides rice, the main crops are rubber, corn, vegetables, tapioca, and cashews. About 85 percent of agricultural land is used to grow rice.

The Garment Industry

Cambodia's garment industry almost went under in 2005, when a WTO agreement on clothing expired, which forced Cambodia to compete directly with countries that pay even lower wages to its workers, such as China and India. Amazingly, the industry has rebounded and accounts for some 70 percent of Cambodia's exports today. More than 350,000 people are employed in the garment industry.

Tourism

Tourism has grown rapidly since 1999. With two international airports open and another two planned, some two million tourists visited the country in 2008, most of them to see the ruins of Angkor. By far the largest numbers of foreign visitors come from Korea and Japan, followed by the United States (in 2007, 6.8 percent of tourists were Americans). As infrastructure improves and more sites of tourist interest become accessible, it is hoped that the industry will diversify away from the major Angkor ruins and promote other attractions around the country in order to distribute income from tourism more widely.

People and Culture

DEMOGRAPHICS

When the Khmer Rouge took power in 1975, Cambodia's population stood at around 7.2 million. An estimated 1–2 million people died between 1975 and 1978. In 1981, the population was around 6.3 million. In 2008, the population was around 14.3 million, with a median age of 21 years and a population growth rate of just 1.7 percent. Infant mortality is 98 per 1,000 and life expectancy is 62 years, four years higher on average for women than it is for men. The literacy rate is about 73 percent.

Cambodia is a multiethnic society with a majority of ethnic Khmer (about 90 percent). The remaining populations are Vietnamese (5 percent), Chinese (5 percent), Cham, and indigenous peoples. Given the large ethnic Khmer majority, Cambodia is one of Southeast Asia's most ethnically homogenous countries.

ETHNIC GROUPS
The Khmer

The Khmer, much like the Thais next door, typically appear ready to smile and be helpful, and are in constant search of harmonious relations. This tolerance finds its limits in the notion of "face," common to many Southeast Asian people. Nothing worries a Khmer more than loss of face—that is, to somehow look bad in front of other people, especially friends or foreigners. This has wide-ranging consequences in everyday contact with Cambodians. If you ask for directions and the person you are asking does not know where to send you, he/she will avoid giving the impression of being uninformed and is more likely to send you in any direction that springs to mind. Also extremely important is the Khmer's position in society, defined by status (wealth), gender, and age. Visitors will notice that farmers often appear to be subservient when in contact with educated or wealthy Khmer, or even foreigners. That's because the ancient hierarchical codes of Cambodian society define everyone's relation to everyone else. Every Khmer respects the authority vested by power or money in other Khmer he or she may encounter. Old people are rarely questioned or criticized and political power is rarely openly challenged.

The Vietnamese

The relationship between the Khmer and their neighbors to the east is difficult. In Cambodia's long-gone semi-mythical past, wars between the Angkor Empire and the Cham, who came from Vietnam, were frequent. In the 19th and early 20th centuries, the French brought lots of Vietnamese into Cambodia to help with skilled tasks like accounting and administration, responsibilities that the colonial power did not trust to the Khmer. In the 1970s, both the right-wing general Lon Nol and later the hard-line communist Khmer Rouge murdered large numbers of Vietnamese. Throughout Pol Pot's reign, Khmer Rouge troops invaded Vietnamese villages and killed countless civilians. When the Vietnamese invaded Cambodia in 1979 to stop these brutal incursions, and brought an end to the reign of terror the Khmer Rouge had unleashed, the historical resentment barely wavered. Opposition leader Sam Rainsy

has made a career out of verbally attacking the Vietnamese. Most Vietnamese in Cambodia today work as fishermen (the floating villages on the Tonlé Sap Lake are largely populated by Vietnamese who returned in the 1980s) or in construction.

The Chinese

The Chinese have been living in Cambodia for some 700 years and while retaining a distinct culture and way of life, many have intermarried with Khmer and speak Khmer. Prior to 1975, the Chinese dominated business and trade and usually belonged to the upper echelons of society, as they do in other Southeast Asian nations. During the Khmer Rouge era, the Chinese either left or were killed. Today, an estimated one million people in Cambodia are said to be Chinese-Khmer. In a country entirely drained of its intellectual resources, the Chinese community fulfills a vital function in helping to power the re-emerging economy. Go to a car showroom or a computer shop in Phnom Penh today, and chances are that the owner will be Chinese or Chinese-Khmer.

The Cham

The Cham once ruled most of southern Vietnam, but following the dominance of the Vietnamese in the region, many Cham fled to Cambodia from the 15th century on. In the 17th and 18th centuries, large parts of the community converted to Islam. During the Khmer Rouge years, Pol Pot's communists killed many Cham and burned down their mosques. Today, the Cham, thought to number less than half a million, generally live in small village communities along the Mekong and to the south of Phnom Penh, and have a fairly harmonious relationship with their Khmer neighbors.

The Khmer Loeu (Chunchiet)

In Cambodia, indigenous minorities are often called Khmer Loeu, which means "upland Khmer," and are therefore referred to as "hill tribes" or "highlanders." The hill tribes of the northeast are called *chunchiet* by the Khmer, a term the minorities reject. In French, they are called *montagnards*. Most of the indigenous peoples live in the four northeastern provinces—Kratie, Mondulkiri, Ratanakiri, and Stung Treng. Some indigenous peoples also inhabit most other provinces in the country.

Due to the lack of population studies, it is difficult to quantify the total number of ethnic groups in Cambodia. The National Population Census (1998) identified 17 indigenous groups based on their languages, but there could be more. Recent assessments showed that around 160,000 Cambodians are from indigenous groups, accounting for 1.5 percent of the total population. While speaking distinct languages and following their own religious practices, the indigenous peoples of Cambodia have much in common. Most importantly, they depend almost entirely on their natural environment for their livelihoods, having formed a close symbiosis with the land they inhabit. The Bunong especially have long functioned as caretakers of the forests of Mondulkiri. As such, their future is intimately linked to that of Cambodia's forests. During the Khmer Rouge years, most were forcibly resettled into communes, just like ethnic Khmer, and were forbidden to practice their animist rituals and their traditional lifestyles. The Bunong had their elephants taken away, many of which were killed by Pol Pot's communists.

Today, most ethnic Khmer regard the Khmer Loeu as backward, and land-grabs in the minorities' village areas are common. Western missionaries pose another serious threat to their unique cultures. Some ecotourism projects run by NGOs are beginning to work with the minorities, if only to stop them from using the slash and burn agriculture they have practiced for generations. The aim is to save Cambodia's dwindling forest reserves, but as one VSO staff in Ratanakiri put it, that policy may just pave the way for professional loggers to move in anyway and cut down the trees.

FESTIVALS AND CULTURAL EVENTS
Chinese New Year
Primarily celebrated by the Chinese and Vietnamese communities in Cambodia, Chinese New Year, or Tet, takes place over a week in January or early February. Many shops will be closed at this time. The holidays are traditionally spent attending lavish family reunions and dinners.

Choul Chnam (Khmer New Year)
Khmer New Year is one of the most important festivals for Cambodians. The three-day event, which falls in April, celebrates the beginning of the Buddhist faith. At this time, a new Buddhist deity or *Tevoda* is welcomed with offerings of incense, food, and glasses of water, which people leave outside the doors of their homes. On the first couple of days of the festival, people visit their local temple and bring food offerings to the monks. Young people dance and take the opportunity to get to know the opposite sex a little better. On the third day, Buddha statues are washed and the water is collected for a ritual wash. In practice, though, this usually ends as a massive water fight inside the pagodas. What's more, the battle-style water-throwing that takes place in neighboring Thailand is catching on in Cambodia too. In recent years, the government has had to ban high-powered water guns, a somewhat ironic move in a country that, until recently, was armed to the teeth. During Khmer New Year, be prepared to share Angkor with thousands of celebrating Cambodians, who travel from all over the country to picnic and celebrate among the ruins.

Viskha Puja (Buddha Day)
The Buddha's birth, enlightenment, and death are celebrated on a full moon day in May. Local people visit their pagodas, offer food to the monks, and, in the evening, meditate and pray in the temples.

Chrat Preah Angal (The Royal Plowing Ceremony)
The Royal Plowing Ceremony is a somewhat archaic event that takes place at the beginning of the planting season in May. The

BROKEN KNEES AND TEENAGE LOVE: THE GAME OF *ANGKUN*

During Khmer New Year, families and friends spend much of their time outside, often on street corners, playing a number of games to pass the day. One of the most popular and most passionately fought-over games is *angkun*, the knee bone game. Usually there are two teams, one made up of boys, the other of girls. Players of one team throw large inedible seeds to hit a master seed placed in the ground and owned by the competing team. Every time a contestant hits the master *angkun* with his own *angkun*, he must use the latter to knock the knee of one of his opponents, which can lead to minor adrenaline-driven street battles between the sexes.

It's great fun to watch, and if you linger, you may well be asked to participate. Watch your knees.

empty space in front of the National Museum is plowed, more or less symbolically, by several oxen. Then, eight royal oxen are each offered seven bowls of food, including rice, corn, green beans, grass, sesame, water, and wine to predict the future of the farming season. Those offerings preferred by the oxen are said to be especially suitable for planting in the coming year. If the oxen eat grass, then the coming season is likely to be terrible. If one of the oxen goes for the wine, the kingdom is said to be in trouble. The tradition, which is hundreds of years old, but had been discontinued between 1970 and 1994, is followed closely by all Khmer, the majority of whom are farmers.

Bonn Pchum Ben (The Ancestor Worship Festival)

The festival of the dead takes place in September or October and lasts for two weeks. During this time, it's believed that the souls of the dead are looking for their relatives and are likely to be disappointed if they don't find offerings in seven temples around the capital. In order to appease the dead, people will bring food to the temples, which is blessed and later eaten by the monks. It is said that the dead pick this time for the monks, who traditionally have problems finding enough food during the rainy season. The final day of Bonn Pchum Ben is the most important, when people gather at the temples and pray with the monks for the wellbeing of the souls of the dead.

Bonn Om Tuk (The Water Festival)

At the end of the rainy season, as the water levels in the Mekong subside, the Tonlé Sap River reverses its direction and drains the Tonlé Sap Lake back into the Mekong. Bonn Om Tuk, a three-day event, celebrates the changing direction of the river around the full moon with boat races in front of the Royal Palace. Tens of thousands of people attend. It's not certain what the origins of the festival are. More than 200 boats from all over the country race in front of the royal family, perhaps in reference to ancient naval battles between the Khmer and the Cham on the Tonlé Sap Lake.

The boats, around 25 meters long and decked out with garlands, are rowed by 20–30 men and women. The riverfront takes on a fantastic carnival atmosphere, and is crowded with hawkers and patrons. After dark, a boat procession circulates on the river, accompanied by fireworks. Bands set up on small stages and blast music at the passing crowds. Each of the 10 boats in the procession carries a board with a brightly lit up image: the first represents the colors of the king, the second those of parliament, and the third shows a map of Cambodia. The remaining boats represent various ministries. The same program repeats itself each day. On the third day of the festival, the king makes a brief appearance in front of the Royal Palace. The best views of this spectacle can be enjoyed from the first floor of the FCC. Alternatively, wander through the happy crowds along Sisowath Quay, bearing in mind that there are pickpockets afoot.

During the three-day holiday, Phnom Penh is extremely crowded and hotels are often fully booked. Buses from outside the capital may take longer than usual, and might even get stuck on the outskirts of town. The first few blocks off the riverfront are closed to traffic.

CLOTHES

According to Chou Ta-Kuan, a Chinese diplomat who visited the imperial city of Angkor Thom in August 1296, both Cambodian men and women wore only a strip of cloth around the waist. This included not just ordinary people, but also the wives of the king. This changed with the arrival of the French and the introduction of Christian ideas of modesty. The minorities in the northeast had their own textile traditions, but these were largely lost during the Khmer Rouge years, when everyone in the country wore the same clothes—black pajamas. The main traditional garment for farmers and workers, the *sampot*, a wraparound rectangular piece of cloth similar to the sarong, is now for the most part just worn in the privacy of the home to relax after work. High-society Khmer wear a more sophisticated version of the same garment, the *sampot chang kben*, which is twisted and pulled between the legs, then tucked into a cloth belt at the back. Cambodian men and women of all backgrounds wear this piece of clothing for special occasions, such as wedding parties. Besides these traditional cotton garments, finer silk versions are also produced, especially by the Cham.

Traditional dress in Cambodia is slowly going out of fashion, especially in urban areas and among the younger generation. Blouses, shirts, and jackets now complement the *sampot* as upper garments. The ever-present *krama*, the cotton head-scarf worn by almost everyone a decade ago, is becoming a rare sight in Phnom Penh, though not in the countryside. Young Cambodians wear jeans and T-shirts.

THE *KRAMA*: CAMBODIA'S ALL-PURPOSE SCARF

The cotton *krama* is one of the most common objects in Cambodia, worn by virtually every adult in the countryside. The checkered scarf comes in many colors and sizes and Cambodians find seemingly endless uses for it. They're used as shade and dust protection, hammocks or carry-bags for infants, containers, and towels – and farmers even tie them around their legs to help them climb trees. Some mothers sew *krama* together to make dolls for their children. During the Khmer Rouge years, the Khmer were forced to wear a red checkered *krama*. Nowadays, young urbanites have begun to shy away from wearing the scarves.

Many of the *krama* offered to tourists are woven from mixed synthetic threads. A small *krama* should cost around 4,000 riel (US$1). The bigger the size, the bigger the price. Don't be shy to bargain.

THE POSITION OF WOMEN IN CAMBODIA

Traditionally, in Cambodia the man is the head of the family and the woman expected to be a loyal wife. Decades of civil war and insecurity have further weakened the position of women in Cambodia, with high incidences of violence against women within the family recorded. The flourishing sex industry also demeans the position of women.

On the other hand, within the family circle, women partake in important decisions—such as education, or the choice of a husband or wife for their children—and they often manage to mediate in family conflicts that might otherwise be resolved with violence.

Women take part in public life and a small number of women have managed to establish themselves as entrepreneurs, actresses, and politicians, a development that will hopefully continue. But the disparate literacy rates for men and women tell the story: In 2004, 84.7 percent of men could read and write, while only 64.1 percent of women could claim the same privilege.

LANGUAGE

Khmer, or Cambodian, is spoken by the population of Cambodia and is the country's official language. The older languages Sanskrit and Pali have a significant influence on Khmer, due to the foreign influences of Hinduism and Buddhism on the country. Khmer has its own script and several dialects are spoken around the country and beyond its borders. Notable local dialect variations include Phnom Penh, Battambang, Khmer Surin, the Khmer spoken by some people in northeast Thailand, and Khmer Krom, the Khmer spoken by some people in the Mekong Delta. The dialects are close enough to be mutually intelligible.

RELIGION

Early Khmer Empires were generally Hindu, though a few early kings were Buddhists. Since the 13th century, Buddhism has been at the heart of Cambodian cultural life and identity. Non-Buddhists include Muslims, recently converted Christians, and a smattering of indigenous people adhering to animism.

Buddhism

Buddhism has been present in Cambodia for almost 2,000 years, probably as long as Hinduism. Initially, different Buddhist currents existed under the early Khmer Hindu empires. During the early Funan kingdom, Buddhism was already marginally present and tolerated. King Jayavarman II (802–869), an early king of the Angkor Empire, was a Hindu but was very tolerant of Mahayana Buddhism. Gradually, the Khmer Empire shifted away from Hinduism. Jayavarman VII (1181–1215), one most powerful kings of the Angkor era, was a devout Mahayana Buddhist who attempted to achieve enlightenment by working to save his people. This monarch moved away from the god-king concept consistent with Hindu thinking. Instead of supporting a vast Brahmanic clergy, he founded the *sangha,* an assembly of monks, and established libraries and public works.

Jayavarman VII sent his son to Sri Lanka to study Theravada Buddhism and in the 13th century, the Angkor Empire adopted Theravada Buddhism as a new state religion. It has been the dominant faith ever since, except during a brief resurgence of Hinduism following Jayavarman VII's death, and, more recently, during the Khmer Rouge years. The goal of Theravada Buddhism is enlightenment, the reaching of Nirvana, the end of all suffering. This goal is achieved by leading a life free of desire in the hope for a higher level of reincarnation next time around.

Religion has always been used in politics in Cambodia. During the 17th–19th century, Thai influence over the Cambodian monarchy extended into the Cambodian Sangha (the national Buddhist council), which in 1855 split into two factions: the Dhammayuttika Nikaya (Thammayut sect), which was connected to Thailand, followed a strict discipline, and was supported by the monarchy; and the Maha Nikaya, to which most of today's monks in Cambodia belong.

Following independence from France in 1953, King Sihanouk managed to impress the idea of institutionalized inequality on his people by aligning himself with Buddhism and Hinduism. One was born a king or a peasant, the reasons for which lay in a past life, the monarch argued, supported by the Buddhist clergy. The Khmer Rouge tried to destroy Buddhism and during their terror reign between 1975 and 1979, thousands of monks were killed and most of the country's temples were destroyed. The teaching of Buddhism was interrupted for several years and scholars fled or were executed.

Following the fall of the Khmer Rouge, the Vietnamese attempted to create one *sangha.* In 1981, a monk who had gone into exile to Vietnam during the Khmer Rouge years was officially ordained by the government as the new *sangharaja* of Cambodia. As soon as the

monks disembarking from a journey on the Sangker River in Battambang

Vietnamese had left, the ruling CPP aligned itself with the *sangha,* declaring Buddhism Cambodia's state religion, but in 1991 King Sihanouk appointed new *sangharajas* for both Buddhist factions. Within the *sangha,* further divisions exist, primarily between traditionalists and modernists. Members of the traditionalist wing value repetition of Khmer and Pali passages to accrue merit. This stems partly from the fact that the traditionalists reject study of Buddhist philosophy, because they don't understand the texts.

To this day, prominent members of the Maha Nikaya, especially the *boran* grouping, an ultraconservative movement of monks, promotes government policies and even calls for the arrest of monks who are not prepared to toe the government line. Modernists, on the other hand, are keen to use their influence in daily Cambodian life to effect social change. Finally, the so-called Young Monks Movement is in favor of openly facing down the government over corruption. Members of the Dhammayuttika Nikaya tend to stay out

of politics, follow a more literal interpretation of Buddhist scriptures and value discipline and study over political engagement.

More than 90 percent of today's Cambodians are Buddhist. New temples continue to be constructed all over the countryside, and, irrespective of its political links, Buddhism can provide much needed social cohesion in a country in which no one trusts anyone outside the family, a consequence of decades of war. On the other hand, the traditional Buddhist tendency to accept one's misfortune as something caused in a previous life continues to affect Cambodians.

THE *WAT*

A *wat,* a Buddhist monastery (this defines the entire compound, not just the prayer hall), is the religious and social center of every community in Cambodia. Local people flock here on holidays to make merit and donate foodstuff to the monks in the hope of shortening their cycle of rebirths and reaching nirvana. Normally 5–100 monks reside in a *wat,* which generally consists of a prayer hall, a sanctuary, accommodations for monks (and sometimes nuns), as well as a kitchen, a bell tower, and a pond. The sanctuary contains a shrine with Buddha statues and is used only by the monks. Large ceremonies involving the local community take place in the prayer hall. Stupas containing the ashes of monks and local residents, or Buddhist relics, are usually dotted around the *wat* or just outside its compound. Most *wats* have a gate, somewhat removed from the compound and often found at the turnoff of a temple road from a main road.

Many *wats* were destroyed during the Khmer Rouge years or used as stables and warehouses. Plenty of money has been raised since to rebuild monasteries, and nowadays even historical *wats,* some almost 100 years old and constructed from wood, are being knocked down to make way for new structures, invariably made from concrete.

THE LIFE OF A MONK

Monks are very much part of daily life in Cambodia and every young Cambodian male is expected to join the monastery for a year or less. In times of economic hardship, a family might receive its only food from the local *wat,* because one of their children serves as a novice there. Most novices do not become fully fledged monks *(bikkhu).* Novices can be as young as seven, but to become a *bikkhu,* one needs to be at least 20.

The lives of monks are governed by Buddhist law. All Buddhists are supposed to follow five basic precepts: not to lie, not to kill, not to steal, not to engage in sexual misconduct, and not to consume intoxicants. Everyone living in a *wat* must follow a further five precepts: not to eat after noon, not to consume entertainment (such as watching TV or going to a party), not to use personal adornments, not to sleep in a comfortable bed, and not to have contact with money. Furthermore, all monks are supposed to be celibate. *Bikkhu* have to follow 227 rules on top of the 10 precepts. Monks are also not

supposed to be involved in politics, or appear in court. Some of these rules have been updated or are simply ignored. Monks are allowed to vote in Cambodia, though this is opposed by senior conservative members of the *sangha.*

Women are not ordained at all, but older women, especially widows, often shave their heads, join the monastery, and become nuns.

Islam

Most of the Muslim minority (less than 1 percent of the population) living in Cambodia have ancestors that arrived sometime in the 15th century, after the defeat of the Cham by the Khmer and the end of the Cham Empire. Large Cham Muslim communities can be found along the Mekong around Kompong Cham, as well as south of Phnom Penh on the road to Kampot. The Cham maintain some of their pre-Muslim animist beliefs, and in contrast to other Muslims, only go to prayer once a week.

Hinduism

Hinduism was the dominant religion in Cambodia for more than a thousand years until the 13th century, when it was gradually replaced by Buddhism. Subsequent Hindu empires in Cambodia followed either Shiva or Vishnu, or a combination of both deities. While there's no Hindu community in Cambodia today, many elements of Hinduism survive in daily religious life—statues of the elephant god Ganesh are still common for example.

Christianity

Christianity didn't make significant inroads in early Cambodia, and the few churches that did exist prior to the Khmer Rouge were destroyed by the communists. In the 1980s, many Cambodians, coerced by Christian relief operations, converted to Christianity in the refugee camps along the Thai border. Many of these people returned back to Buddhism as soon as they had reestablished their lives in Cambodia.

More recently, Christian groups, especially missionary outfits, have come back to

Cambodia and are engaged in persuading or forcing, depending on the observer's point of view, the minority groups in the northeast away from their animist beliefs. This has contributed to the Khmer Loeu losing their roots and becoming more marginalized than they already were. Typically, missionaries approach the most destitute elements of the population and help them out of trouble—in return for converting. The Cambodian government sees the minorities as a problem rather than an asset and missionary organizations take heart from this.

Animism

Animism, the worship of nature and natural spirits, lies at the center of the belief systems of Cambodia's minorities. Animism is fast becoming rare in Cambodia, as missionaries make more and more inroads into traditional societies.

Superstition

Superstitions are an integral part of daily life in Cambodia. This has much to do with the fact that, until very recently, information exchange in Cambodian society has been based on oral beliefs—country life in Asia is cut off from the rest of the world by lack of mobility and education at the best of times, but Cambodia's catastrophic recent past has not only kept many folk beliefs and superstitions alive, but has also created an atmosphere where change is unwelcome. Hence, outmoded beliefs manage to accrue plenty of mileage.

When an apparently larger than average number of people was struck by lightning in 2008, many Cambodians turned to old beliefs to explain the increase in these deaths. According to the word on the street, breaking a promise to someone or having a mole on one's calves appear to be equally valid reasons to be struck.

The Arts

ARCHITECTURE
Temple Art and Architecture

The temples of the Angkor Empire and its predecessors are all we have left of a culture that dominated Southeast Asia for centuries. Cambodian temple ruins date from around A.D. 500–1220. At the time they were built, the temples were surrounded by infrastructure that supported thousands of people, be they temple staff, soldiers, farmers, slaves, or other subjects. Most Cambodians lived in wooden buildings then (much like today), and naturally, there is nothing left of those. Hence it is the religious structures that tell us about the cultural and political development of the Khmer Empires.

PRE-ANGKORIAN (500-800)

Early Cambodian temple architecture was heavily influenced by architectural ideas and techniques from India. As the early Khmer kings were Hindus and the state religion of the Angkor Empires prior to the 11th century was Hinduism

(though Buddhism was tolerated), every aspect of temple building was defined by the Hindu worldview. Central to this view was the cult of the god king who saw his creations as a miniature map of the universe over which he reigned. Architectural elements that can traced back to India include the symmetry of temple layouts, the temple ponds or moats (symbolizing the cosmic ocean), and the central tower (prasat). But the Angkor architects soon began to interpret these influences from the west and architectural ideas from Java and China changed the temples over time.

Some of Angkor's major monuments, including Angkor Wat, are temple mountains: earthly representations of Mount Meru, home of the Hindu pantheon. Temple mountains are shrines built on a multilevel base. Initially, at Bakong for example, just one tower would stand on the base. But by the 10th century, five towers, one in the center of the temple mountain's platform, the others at the four corners, had become the established norm.

But not all major Khmer temples follow this design. Ta Prohm was a flat temple compound. Concentric walls surrounded the sanctuary, symbolizing the mountain chains surrounding Mount Meru. In between these walls, enclosures were lined by roofed galleries. In order to step from one enclosure into another, you had to pass through a *gopura,* an entrance hall, often mounted by towers. *Gopuras* were often flanked by stone guards and decorated with impressively carved lintels (cross beams above doorway). Above the lintels, triangular pediments also featured carvings. On some door frames to the *gopuras,* Sanskrit writing was carved into the sandstone. Blind windows and doors were also common elements. As most temples opened to the East, blind doors were introduced at the remaining sides to maintain symmetry. Blind windows were used to decorate blank walls. At the heart of every temple lay the sanctuary, a small hall buried underneath the central tower *(prasat).* The temple foundations were often built from laterite, clay that hardened when exposed to the sun, but this material was usually hidden from view, as laterite is not suitable for carving. Other temple structures included libraries (though these may have served as shrines rather than as repositories for scriptures or manuscripts) and the barays, massive reservoirs built for irrigation purposes and possibly also religious reasons.

The earliest substantial temple ruins in Cambodia date back to the early 7th-century Chenla Empire, a pre-cursor to Angkor. Its capital, Isanapura, can still be visited today, at Sambor Prei Kuk in Kompong Thom Province. These temples were built from brick with carvings usually added onto stucco on top of the brick, though some brick carvings can also be found. Early Khmer temples often feature a lingam, a phallic representation of Shiva, in their sanctuaries. Some of the largest linga can be found at Koh Ker.

ANGKORIAN (800-1220)

At the beginning of the 9th century, Jayavarman II was the first Khmer king to build a capital to the northwest of the Tonlé Sap Lake at Hariharalaya (the Roluos group of temples). Subsequent kings added temple structures, such as the Bakong temple mountain, dedicated to Shiva; Preah Ko, with its red brick towers and finely carved lintels; as well as Lolei (also at Roluos), a temple with four brick towers and fine carvings of Indra, the Sun God.

From the 10th century on, the Khmer increasingly used sandstone. At first, because the stone had to be laboriously extracted from the Kulen mountains, only small parts of the temples were made of sandstone. But as the empire grew in wealth, sandstone became increasingly popular. Ta Keo, built in the 10th century, was the first temple built almost entirely from sandstone.

During Jayavarman VII's reign in the 13th century, new building elements were added. *Dharamshalas,* rest houses for pilgrims, spread along the Angkorian highways across the kingdom. Next to some later temples, such as Ta Prohm, a hall of dancers, decorated with dancing *apsaras,* was erected. The exact function for these buildings is not known, though they may indeed have served as dance halls.

Many temples are decorated with bas-reliefs: figures or scenes that stick out from the background, carved into stone walls or lintels. Fine examples of bas-reliefs can be seen at the 10th-century temple of Banteay Srei, but the greatest masterpiece is the outer gallery of Angkor Wat, which features some 12,000 square meters of continuous narrative depicting mythological scenes as well as historical battles. The outer walls of the Bayon, on the other hand, are covered in bas-reliefs depicting life of ordinary Khmer going about their daily chores, giving visitors a unique insight into how humans fit into all this architectural grandeur.

Impressive, too, are the stairs leading up to the temple towers, which often have an ascent of up to 70 degrees. This rather impractical design may have served a visual purpose, with the small base of the tower making the entire structure look more heaven-bound.

Incredible carvings lend Angkor its unique, otherworldly character—just as much as monumental proportions do—and some motifs return again and again to engage the visitor. *Apsaras,* heavenly nymphs cast in stone, originate in the *Mahabharata* and lend the temple ruins a very sensuous ambience. Stories in the Hindu myth tell of how the gods used these celestial dancers to seduce demons, heroes, and holy men. *Devatas* are similar female deities to *apsaras,* though they never dance. *Dvarapalas* are temple guards, sometimes carrying a stick, carved near the entrance doors to the shrines. *Nagas,* mythical multi-headed snakes, are prominent parts of Khmer mythology. They can often be found as part of lintels or as freestanding sculptures, sometimes shielding Buddha in meditation. Some larger temples have causeways flanked by balustrades shaped as *nagas.* Often these *nagas* are held by gods and demons, symbolizing the churning of the ocean and the fight between the two parties for *amrita,* the nectar of immortality, a central story in Hindu mythology. *Garudas* are half-man, half-bird creatures who serve as transport for Vishnu. *Garudas* can be found as part of lintels, or as part of *naga* heads. Sometimes they appear to be the enemies of the mythical snakes, at other times the two are part of the same harmonious sculpture.

French Urban Architecture (1870-1952)

The French left a wealth of interesting, if mostly crumbling, architecture behind. The absolute highlight is the Bokor Palace on the southeast coast, which is unfortunately being developed into a casino complex. Phnom Penh still has a fair legacy of French buildings. The beautiful art deco Central Market (Phsar Thmey), built in the 1920s and 1930s, was being restored in 2009. Sadly, many French buildings have been knocked down to be replaced by chrome and glass monstrosities. In the provinces, almost every small town has a few blocks of French townhouses still standing and restoration is underway for some of these buildings. Especially attractive are the colonial remnants of Kampot, Battambang, Kratie, and Chhlong, as well as the now fully restored area around the Old Market in Siem Reap.

Urban Architecture Under King Sihanouk (1953-1970)

After the departure of the French, King Sihanouk personally got involved in how his newly independent kingdom was to look. The king actively promoted a new building style, the so-called New Khmer Architecture, largely the brainchild of architect Vann Molyvann. Traces of this movement, which sought to combine traditional Khmer and modern aesthetics, can still be seen around the Cambodian capital and in some provincial towns. The large apartment blocks in Phnom Penh dating from the 1950s and 1960s were mostly built by resident Chinese merchants.

Rural Architecture

Most Cambodians live as they have always lived. The typical family home is constructed on high stilts, which keeps animals out of the living space, protects from flooding, and offers shade and storage space underneath the home. The higher the stilts, the wealthier the owner is likely to be. A narrow stairway leads to the first floor, which is usually fronted by a veranda. The first floor might be divided into a couple of living spaces, one for the parents to sleep in, another one for the children and possible guests. Everyone sleeps on thin mats. A kitchen is usually separated from this large room. Bathroom and toilet, if they exist, can be found in a concrete or wood outhouse, somewhere behind the main building. Most houses in the country are surrounded by a small garden. Sometimes there's also a small pond. Despite the fact that the buildings are simple, they are clean and comfortable and offer a higher standard of living than the overcrowded tenement blocks in Phnom Penh.

MUSIC

The typical Khmer orchestra is called *phleng pinpeat* and usually performs in temples on public holidays or during special religious ceremonies. The main instruments used are gongs, flutes, a type of xylophone, violins, and horns, often made from animal horn. For the Western

DENGUE FEVER: THE NEW BEAT OF CAMBODIA

Travelers are rightly worried about contracting dengue fever in the remoter parts of tropical countries, especially in the rainy season, but there's one variety it's worth catching up with: the musical kind.

In 2001, two brothers from Los Angeles, Ethan and Zac Holtzman, formed a band called Dengue Fever – after Ethan had visited Cambodia. In LA, they looked for and found a Cambodian singer, Chhom Nimol, a karaoke star who'd moved to the United States to make money for her family back home and was performing regularly in Little Phnom Penh in Long Beach. The band put out their first album in 2003, an eclectic mix of Cambodian pop tunes from the 1960s as well as some original songs. The brothers wrote the lyrics and had them translated into Khmer before Chhom could sing them.

In 2005, the band visited Cambodia and was incredibly well received. A documentary feature of the trip, *Sleepwalking Through the Mekong,* was released shortly after. Since then, the band has made several more albums, most recently on Peter Gabriel's Real World label.

Dengue Fever is highly entertaining, but it has also performed a great service to music, specifically Cambodian music. In the 1960s, Cambodian bands had a pretty original take on rock and roll. The bands sang in Khmer, and the sounds they produced had a raw, real quality, usually unheard of so far away from the United States or Britian. Most of the musicians of that era were killed by Pol Pot's Khmer Rouge. A few escaped into exile. Dengue Fever rediscovered the song material that had fallen into obscurity and re-introduced Cambodians, as well as the rest of the world, to a sound that was almost killed by genocide. Even King Sihanouk liked Dengue Fever. Check them out on www.denguefevermusic.com.

listener, this music may sound a bit arbitrary and off-key. Songs appear to meander without a particular structure.

Played outside the temple, traditional Khmer music often features sentimental lyrics about love and farewells, about the simple life of the farmer. The Khmer Rouge picked up on these folk traditions and subverted them for propaganda purposes. Since the 1990s, some of these music traditions have been revived, especially at temple fairs. In the 1950s, the French introduced jazz to Phnom Penh's nightclubs and classic dances such as the waltz and the tango also became popular among the Cambodian elite. In the 1960s, rock music, first imported, then homegrown, also made some inroads; several tapes that have surfaced in recent years attest to a pretty wild music scene.

Today's pop music is divided into sentimental ballads, harking back to the 1960s, or rock music and techno introduced from Thailand and loosely translated into Khmer. Most popular is karaoke. Even small country towns and villages will have several karaoke bars in which local men, with or without the help of the resident taxi girls, will engage in drunken musical performance late into the night. A basic karaoke bar has a TV, a stereo system, a DVD player, and a microphone: quite an investment, though this is recouped quickly, as men, young and old, compulsively perform heartbreaking melodies for their friends, for the hostesses, and for themselves.

DANCE

Cambodia has quite a dance culture, with three distinct types of dances. Best known is the royal ballet *(apsara),* considered the classic dance of Cambodia. Once upon a time, this dance was performed purely for the enjoyment of the royal family, but in recent years, it has become very much a tourist attraction. Also popular, though increasingly fading, is the lively folk dance, far less restrained and artificial than the *apsara* dance, and popular in the countryside. Dances revolve around themes that farmers can relate to, such as the

THE GREATEST MOVIE SET IN THE WORLD

Cambodia has long been used as a movie location. Foreign documentaries were shot around the country as early as the 1920s. In the 1950s, Khmer filmmakers began to shoot their own features, and by the 1960s, a small but vibrant film industry had established itself, turning out some 300 popular movies until the Khmer Rouge takeover.

The first big-budget foreign film made in Cambodia is an excellent adaptation of Joseph Conrad's *Lord Jim* (1965), which was partly shot around Angkor and stars Peter O'Toole.

King Norodom Sihanouk, then prince, was also an ardent filmmaker and, in the 1960s, produced, directed, and wrote numerous romantic melodramas in which he often took the lead role. Some of his films can be found in the video shops around Phnom Penh and are still shown regularly on Cambodian TV.

Following its takeover in 1975, the Khmer Rouge destroyed Cambodia's film industry. The communists did produce some propaganda films, however.

The best-known foreign movie about life under the Khmer Rouge is *The Killing Fields* by Roland Joffe, shot in Thailand in 1984. This brilliant movie follows the true story of journalist Dith Pran on his journey through the Cambodian genocide.

Since the end of the civil war, Cambodian and foreign filmmakers have slowly begun to rediscover the country for the cinema. Cambodian director Rithy Panh's interesting 1994 movie *The Rice People* deals with the aftermath of the Khmer Rouge reign and was the first Cambodian film ever submitted for an Oscar. Panh is the director of Bophana, the audiovisual center in Phnom Penh that aims to preserve Cambodia's film, photographic, and audio history. Less serious, but seriously successful, are locally made horror-cheapies.

Angelina Jolie, a.k.a. Lara Croft, rediscovered the country for the international cinema with *Tomb Raider,* an action flick based on a computer game, which was shot around Angkor. Jolie loved the country so much, she adopted a Cambodian child, a boy called Maddox, and is involved in various NGO projects.

Wong Kar-Wai's 2001 *In the Mood For Love* was partly shot in Angkor and the 2003 French production *Two Brothers* by Jean-Jacques Annaud, a film about two tigers set during the French colonial period, followed shortly after.

The most interesting recent foreign film about Cambodia is perhaps Matt Dillon's *City of Ghosts,* shot independently in 2002. The plot, which follows a young American man (Dillon) looking for his crooked boss and possible father (James Caan) in Southeast Asia, is forgettable, but the performances of the ensemble cast (featuring Gérard Depardieu, Stellan Skarsgård, and excellent Cambodian newcomer Kem Sereyvuth), against the mesmerizing backdrop of a beaten, raw country trying to get back on its feet, are remarkable. Dillon goes all the way for local color and comes up with a dark and brooding tale that perfectly portrays a moment in Cambodia's painful rebirth. The Khmer rock and roll soundtrack is great too.

beginning of the rains, the harvest, or even a fruit. These dances go back to the region's pre-Buddhist times and have their roots in animism. Finally, there's *ram vong,* a dance that is purely designed for enjoyment. Any Khmer festival, celebration or even an evening in a nightclub will feature this dance. Dancers move in single line in a circle against the clock and turn their hands back and forth, inspired by simple *apsara* dance movements, in time to the music.

THEATER

The royal theater is based on the *Reamker,* the Khmer version of the Ramayana, a 2,000-year-old Hindu epic. The story of how Rama frees his wife Sita with the help of Hanuman, god of the monkeys, from the evil clutches of Ravana, is performed by masked dancers. Theater in the Western sense has barely made any inroads in Cambodia, though a rock opera, called *Where Elephants Weep,* was launched in late 2008, to be televised, though it immediately ran foul with the Supreme Council of Buddhist Monks and had to be modified.

LITERATURE

Cambodian folk literature is a rich seam of stories with both entertainment as well as educational value that is traditionally handed down from generation to generation. Fairy tales, fables, ghost stories, and stories illustrating aspects of Cambodian history, usually with a great bloodthirsty hero who kills thousands of enemies in great battles, are common genres. Most of this literature is designed to teach the common man that he must accept the prevailing power structures. During the Sihanouk and Lon Nol years, a handful of Cambodian writers produced novels, short stories, and political nonfiction. Those writers who survived the Khmer Rouge (by fleeing the country), can be divided into left- and right-wingers. While the left-wingers were resurrected under the Vietnamese occupation, no literary scene has managed to reestablish itself in Cambodia.

CINEMA

The first films made by Cambodians for Cambodians were silent movies, shot in the 1950s. In the 1960s, more than 300 movies were made in Cambodia and cinemas opened in the capital and some smaller towns. Today, the 1960s are considered the golden age of Cambodian cinema. King Sihanouk, a cinema enthusiast, made a string of feature films in the late 1960s, often using the Angkor temples as backdrops. Many of the actors and directors involved in the golden age of Cambodian cinema were killed by the Khmer Rouge and many of the films were lost.

In the 1980s, after the Vietnamese had expelled the Khmer Rouge from government, foreign films with socialist messages became the vogue, but no Cambodian film industry was re-established. Only at the end of the 1980s did some production companies start business again, but most of these local efforts were hampered by the emergence of VCRs and the consequent closure of the few cinemas open at the time.

In the 1990s, the film industry made a comeback, first with a deluge of cheap karaoke videos, then slowly with cheap horror flicks. Rithy Panh, who had escaped the Khmer Rouge, trained to be a filmmaker in France and has since made several internationally acclaimed features and documentaries dealing with Cambodia's recent tragic past. Widespread DVD piracy is seen as a major reason why the local film industry has not developed faster in recent years.

ESSENTIALS

Getting There

AIR

Cambodia currently has two international airports, one in Phnom Penh and one in Siem Reap. It is expected that Sihanoukville Airport will also eventually receive international flights. While Cambodia is no international hub, connections have improved dramatically in recent years and should continue to do so, especially after Bangkok Airways lost its monopoly on flights from Bangkok into Siem Reap in 2009.

For now the majority of foreign travelers arrive in Siem Reap, which, has frequent flights to Bangkok. It also has international connections to Kuala Lumpur in Malaysia; Kunming,

Cheng Du, and Hong Kong in China; and Seoul in South Korea. A smaller number of international flights connect to Phnom Penh from Beijing, Cheng Du, Guangzhou, Shanghai, and Hong Kong in China; Seoul in South Korea; Kuala Lumpur in Malaysia; Singapore; Ho Chi Minh City and Hanoi in Vietnam; Vientiane in Laos; and Taipei in Taiwan. Both airports are quite small but modern, and arrival and departure procedures are smooth and professional. Snacks and drinks are available. Unlike at land borders, tourists are not hit for bribes at the airports. Monument Books has branches in the departure lounges in Phnom Penh and Siem Reap. In Phnom

Penh, the departure lounge also has a bar and a comfortable smoking area, which dispenses free cigarettes.

Arriving by Air

Getting your visa and clearing customs is little more than a formality in Cambodia (unless you are on a black list). An official taxi from Siem Reap Airport to your hotel will cost you US$5. The journey takes around 20 minutes. A *motodup* will do the run for US$2. A taxi from Phnom Penh International into town costs US$9 and takes about 30 minutes; a *motodup* does the run for US$2. As a rule, hotels are happy to pick up guests from either airport free of charge or for a nominal fee, but you will need to arrange this with your hotel in advance.

Departing by Air

A departure tax of US$25 is payable on international flights. For domestic flights, the departure tax is US$6.

OVERLAND

Cambodia shares land borders with Thailand, Laos, and Vietnam. A number of international border crossings, where Cambodian visas are issued on the spot, connect the kingdom to its neighbors. Some of these land crossings are frequently used by foreigners, while others are so remote that they hardly see any international traffic. Cambodia's international borders are generally open daily 6 A.M.–8 P.M.

You will need a visa for Laos or Vietnam in order to cross any land borders into these countries. If you enter Thailand from Cambodia overland, without having previously applied for a tourist visa, you will only get a 15-day entry stamp. If you arrive by plane from Cambodia, you will get 30 days.

In order to enter Cambodia and get a visa, you will need a passport photograph, hard to come by at the remote crossings. Cambodian immigration officers are engaged in a number of scams to force foreign visitors to pay more for their visas than they should. Entering from Thailand, especially via Poipet or Koh Kong,

you may be forced to pay 1,000 or 1,100 baht (US$30 or US$33) instead of the official rate of US$20. Arriving from Laos, extra fees are also often demanded. Some guidebooks encourage their readers to confront officers. Remember that at the border crossings, the officials you are dealing with are the local—and only—authority. Threatening them or getting noisy is likely to be counterproductive. Get your Cambodian visa in advance if you want to avoid the problem altogether. Never try to cross into Cambodia without a visa or at an unauthorized crossing. Besides the fact that this is against the laws of the country you are leaving and the one you are entering, sections of Cambodia's border are heavily mined.

Border Crossings with Thailand

Cambodia and Thailand currently have six international border crossings. Cambodian visas are issued at all these crossings. There's one exception: Crossing from Thailand at Preah Vihear, when this is possible, does not entitle visitors to carry on further into Cambodia, as the hilltop temple is not an international border crossing.

POIPET/ARANYAPHRATET

The most popular overland route into Cambodia is the border crossing at Poipet (Aranyaphratet on the Thai side). It's possible to make the 465-kilometer run between Bangkok and Siem Reap in a day.

But be forewarned: While through-tickets from Khao San Road in Bangkok cost just 400–800 baht, they are often a scam. Tourists are cheated in a number of ways. Usually, onward transportation on the Cambodian side is so slow that travelers arrive in Siem Reap very late and are forced into a hotel that pays commission to the transport company that brought them. Those who try and change hotels might get into an ugly argument. Sometimes tourists have been taken through other, far more remote border crossings, where they were hit by additional scams.

The safest and quickest way is to do the journey independently. On the Thai side of the border, which can be reached from Bangkok by train, bus, or minibus, things are pretty straightforward. There are ATMs and shops at the border and Aranyaphratet has reasonable accommodations and a half-decent hospital. From town, it's six kilometers to the border, best traveled in a tuk-tuk. Across the border in Cambodia, it's best to leave Poipet as quickly as possible. Note that buses leave Poipet in the mornings (until 8 A.M.). The best way to avoid any hassles is to stay in Aranyaphratet overnight and then connect to a morning bus out of Poipet. If you arrive in Poipet during the day, get in a share taxi or hire a taxi to get out of town. Otherwise you might find yourself at the mercy of hordes of touts eager for your money. Do not stay there overnight unless you absolutely have to; if you do, the casinos located in the no-man's-land between the immigration posts are your best bet. To get out by bus, head for the bus station, 1.5 kilometers away from the border along Route 5 and then turn right. Don't get roped into the free shuttle service to the bus station, as it will take you to a "Tourist Lounge" where tickets to onward destinations are sold at inflated prices. Instead, try and book your own bus ticket with one of the bus company offices at the station. Buses go around the southern shore of the Tonlé Sap Lake. It's a bumpy ride, no matter what mode of transportation you choose. Route 5 from the border as far as Sisophon, about 50 kilometers away, is mostly okay. After that, Route 6 towards Siem Reap still has stretches in appalling condition, especially in the rainy season, though the entire stretch is in the process of being surfaced.

KOH KONG/HAT LEK
After Poipet, the Hat Lek border crossing near Koh Kong is the most popular overland route from Thailand into Cambodia. Frequent minibuses from Trat, the last Thai town of note before the Hat Lek border crossing, take 90 minutes and cost 120 baht. There's nothing much to see in Hat Lek, except for a small market along the road. Coming from Thailand, a

motorcycle taxi from the border to Koh Kong will set you back 50–70 baht.

PHSAR PROM/BAN PAKARD
The closest border to Pailin is not a particularly convenient spot to cross into Cambodia as the roads around Pailin are in terrible condition. A *motodup* from Pailin to the border post, some 20 kilometers out of town costs US$5. A taxi from Battambang will cost you US$50 in the dry season. Once the rains have started, check in Battambang about local road conditions. On the Thai side, minibuses take two hours to Chanthaburi and cost 100 baht. From Chanthaburi, frequent buses leave for Bangkok, four hours away.

To get to this border from Bangkok, head for the Eastern Bus Terminal at Ekkamai and jump on one of the frequent buses for Chanthaburi. Journey time is about four hours. In Chanthaburi, regular minibuses (100 baht per head) make the run to the border in under two hours.

DAUN LEM/BAN LAEM
Located north of the Pailin border crossing, this is a remote international border where Cambodian tourist visas should be available for US$20, though this is at the discretion of the immigration officers on duty. Crossing into Thailand, getting a 15-day entry stamp should not be a problem for most nationalities. There are some casinos on the Cambodian side, hence the crossing's international status. The village on the Cambodian side is called Daun Lem; on the Thai side, it's Ban Laem. The border is open daily 7 A.M.–8 P.M. There is onward travel available on the Thai side. Don't count on that on the Cambodian side.

ANLONG VENG/CHONG SA-NGAM
The closest border crossing to Anlong Veng is at Chong Sa-Ngam, some eight kilometers from Pol Pot's grave and just three kilometers from Ta Mok's jungle hideaway. The border is open to foreigners coming from either side. On the Thai side, the nearest village is Khu San in Si Saket Province, from where there are direct buses to Bangkok and elsewhere

in Thailand. The village has a bank with ATM as well as simple guesthouses. The border is open daily 7 A.M.–8 P.M. To get to the Chong Sa-Ngam border, try and hitch a ride with Cambodian traders from Anlong Veng who cross the border in the morning, otherwise you might be in for a long walk on the Thai side.

From Bangkok, the quickest way to this remote and rather inconvenient border (unless you plan to see Khmer temples of Issan on the way) is a flight to the regional hub of Ubon Ratchasima. From this small city, you can get a regular bus to Khu San in Si Saket province, the closest village to the border. Alternatively, there's a regular bus from Bangkok's Eastern Bus Terminal to Si Saket town (eight hours), from where you can catch several local buses a day to the border. Also, in the mornings plenty of *songthaews* (local converted pickup trucks with benches in the back) on their way from Si Saket to the border markets can give you a lift. Note that since the border spat over the Preah Vihear temple, the Thai military has set up a number of roadblocks in this area, though foreigners are never stopped.

O'SMACH/CHONG JOM
You could also cross the border at O'Smach (Chong Jom on the Thai side), farther west, though this border is farther from Anlong Veng, there's no public transport on the Cambodian side, and the road is not as good. To get to O'Smach, grab a regular bus from the Thai town of Surin (80 baht), which takes around 90 minutes to the border. From the O'Smach border to Siem Reap is a 125-kilometer ride via Samrong, most likely only possible in an expensive taxi.

Border Crossing with Laos
In order to enter Laos, travelers will have to have a valid Lao visa in their passports. Coming into Cambodia from Laos, tourist visas are issued on the spot for US$20, business visas for US$25, though immigration officials often demand extra fees at this crossing.

DOM KRALOR/VOENG KAM
Onward travel from Stung Treng to the Laotian border and beyond is a little bit confusing, but easily done. From Stung Treng, you have two possibilities to get to the border. The easiest way is to travel by road (Route 7), which has recently been upgraded. The border at Dom Kralor is about 55 kilometers from Stung Treng and minibuses now ply this route irregularly for US$5. The Sorya Bus Company bus from Phnom Penh (departs at 7 A.M.) to Stung Treng also carries on all the way to the border. Once at the border, you might have to walk between the two border posts, a distance of two kilometers. Also note that there is no regular transport onwards on the Laotian side, though through tickets can be booked in Stung Treng. Alternatively, you can take a boat to the riverine border crossing of Koh Chheuteal Thom. If there's a boat going, you should be able to get a seat for US$5. It's also possible to hire a boat to go to the border for around US$30. A minibus to Dom Det in Laos leaves Stung Treng at 8 A.M. and costs US$10 and then carries on to Dom Khone (US$12), Don Khong (US$15), and Pakse (US$15). Numerous tour agencies in Laos (in Pakse) offer through-tickets to Stung Treng, at much the same prices. This way, travelers avoid getting stuck somewhere in the deep south of Laos where transportation options are limited. Immigration officials may demand extra fees (about US$2) for stamping you in. On the Lao side, the village of Voeng Kam has a small market, which can be visited from the Cambodian side, even without a Lao visa. There's a small and adequate guesthouse (US$7) and some small restaurants here.

Coming from Laos into Cambodia is straightforward; tourist and business visas are now issued at both border crossings.

Border Crossings with Vietnam
Coming from Vietnam, Cambodian visas are available on arrival at all of the border crossings detailed here. Make sure you have a passport photo for the Cambodian authorities. Going into Vietnam, you will have to have a visa issued by a Vietnamese consulate.

TOUR COMPANIES AND TRAVEL AGENTS

While just a few years ago, large parts of Cambodia were inaccessible to all but the most hardy travelers, in-country travel agents and international operators now offer tours that go well beyond the ruins of Angkor. Cambodia is a country where visitors will hugely benefit from personal encounters they might have with the Khmer people, and independent travel is generally straightforward to most points of interest. Nevertheless, there are exceptions, and going with a group and a guide does have distinct benefits.

Whether you want a tailor-made historical tour of the Angkor temples or a trek into the wilds of Ratanakiri, it's all possible and it need not hurt your wallet if you don't expect five-star service, which in any case is hard to come by outside of Phnom Penh and Siem Reap. On the other hand, if you'd like to see the temples in style, then there's barely a limit to how much you can spend. Some local operators work closely with local communities and involve them in the tour programs, making the trip a more personal experience. Finally, for adventure seekers, several motorbike touring companies offer visitors the opportunity to experience some really off-the-beaten-track trips to jungle temples and remote villages on challenging roads.

CAMBODIA TRAVEL SPECIALISTS IN THE UNITED STATES

- **Abercrombie and Kent** (U.S. tel. 800/323-7308, www.abercrombiekent.com) offers luxury tours around Cambodia, usually in conjunction with a visit to either Thailand and/or Vietnam.

- **Asiatranspacific** (U.S. tel. 800/642-2742, www.asiatranspacific.com) organizes a range of interesting high-end tours around Indochina. The company's Angkor program includes a sumptuous dinner inside a temple ruin and a meeting with a representative of the World Monument Fund.

- **Wilderness Travel** (U.S. tel. 800/368-2794, www.wildernesstravel.com) also arranges tours in style, at slightly lower prices. It offers a 13-day temple package, which takes in some remote locations around the country, and other Southeast Asian itineraries that include Angkor.

O'YADAW/LE TANH

Opened in 2008, this small border crossing 75 kilometers east of Banlung in Ratanakiri is hard to reach. There's no regular direct transportation on either side of this border and a taxi ride there from Banlung costs around US$50. The border on the Vietnamese side is called Le Tanh. In Pleiku, the nearest city on the Vietnamese side, some 80 kilometers from the border, head for the central market where you might be able to find a yellow local bus going to Duc Co for about 15,000 dong. In Duc Co, you will have to find a *moto* to take you to the border at Le Tanh.

TRAPAENG THLONG/XA MUT

The border at Trapaeng Thlong (Xa Mut on the Vietnamese side) off Route 7, a few kilometers before the town of Memot, is hardly used by foreigners and there's no regular transportation on either side. The turnoff off Route 7 to the right (coming from Kompong Cham) is clearly signposted. Once there's a decent road on the Vietnamese side, this crossing might become part of the fast overland route between Siem Reap and Ho Chi Minh City.

TRAPAENG SRE/LOC NINH

In 2008, the border at Trapaeng Sre (Loc Ninh on the Vietnamese side) opened off Route 7, some 40 kilometers south of Snuol. There is, for now, no regular transport on either side of the border, but eventually, a quick connection between Ho Chi Minh City and this border post is likely to be established.

BAVET/MOC BAI

Daily buses from Sorya Transport, Neak

TOUR OPERATORS IN ASIA

- **AboutAsia** (U.S. tel. 914/595-6949, tel. 092/121059, www.asiatravel-cambodia. com) has an office in the United States, but is based in Cambodia. It organizes tour packages around the temples and the country that involve the local community.

- **Asian Trails** (tel. 023/216555, www.asian-trails.info), a tour operator from Thailand, offers a wide range of two- to ten-day trips around Cambodia at competitive midrange prices.

- **Exotissimo** (tel. 063/964323, www.cambodia.exotissimo.com), a Vietnam-based operator, offers interesting, high-standard camping tours around some of the more remote temples.

- **Green Elephant Travel** (tel. 063/965776, www.greenelephanttravel.com) is based in Siem Reap and operates a variety of tours with an emphasis on minimizing your carbon footprint (some of them are almost entirely walking and cycling). Prices are midrange to high-end, depending on the level of comfort.

ADVENTURE AND MOTORBIKE TRAVEL IN CAMBODIA

- **Dancing Roads** (tel. 012/753008, www. dancingroads.com) offers a wide variety of dirt-bike tours around the temples, the northeast, the coast, and the Cardamom Mountains, as well as two-week bicycle tours to remote parts of the country.

- **Hidden Cambodia** (tel. 012/655201, www. hiddencambodia.com) also offers dirt-bike tours, as well as Angkor packages, sustainable ecotourism trips, and humanitarian tours into the countryside to aid village development.

- **Red Raid** (bmerklen@camnet.com.kh, www.motorcycletourscambodia.com) has a varied program of dirt-bike tours around the remoter parts of Cambodia, as well as cross-border tours into Laos and Southern China.

Krohhorm Bus Company, GST, and Mekong Express (US$7–12) and minibuses from Capitol Guesthouse (154A, Street 182, tel. 023/217627) in Phnom Penh travel along Route 1 east of Phnom Penh across the border, and all the way to Ho Chi Minh City. This is the fastest overland connection between Phnom Penh and Saigon—the trip should not take more than six hours, including formalities at the border. Guesthouses and travel agents in Ho Chi Minh City offer frequent buses and similar ticket prices to Phnom Penh.

KAAM SAMNOR/VING XUONG

To reach this popular border crossing from Phnom Penh, you have two options. Capitol Guesthouse (154A, Street 182, tel. 023/217627) in Phnom Penh and Neak Krohhorm Bus Company offer combined boat and bus tickets for US$10. If you want to travel independently, grab a share taxi at Central Market to Neak Loeung on the banks of the Mekong and then board a ferry down to the village of Kaam Samnor. It's a short ride with a *motodup* to the Vietnamese immigration post and from there another few kilometers in a minibus to Chau Doc, from where there are regular buses to Ho Chi Minh City. From Ho Chi Minh City, grab a bus to Chau Doc (six hours), from where minibuses (US$3, one hour) head to Vinh Xuong.

PHNOM DEN/TINH BIEN

This border crossing in Takeo Province can be reached in a share taxi from Phnom Penh (ask around Central Market). Seats are around US$10. Alternatively, a private taxi from Kampot or Kep will set you back around US$30 and takes about three hours. On the

Vietnamese side, there's transport to Chau Doc, 10 kilometers away, from where onward travel to Ho Chi Minh City is available. From Ho Chi Minh City, catch a bus to Chau Doc, which takes around six hours. From there, it's a 40-minute *motodup* ride to the border. The *motodups* operating this route are cutthroats and may demand horrendous prices either way. As there's little alternative, you might not have a choice but to pay US$7–10 a *moto*. The *motodups* on the Vietnamese side also engage in a couple of other scams, such as taking passengers to a private bus stop rather than the public terminal in Chau Doc. Don't pay anything until you get to your destination, though in general, there's little to be done about the transport scams at this border. The border is usually open daily 8 A.M.–5 P.M.

PREK CHAK/XA XIA

The ride to the border takes about an hour from Kep and leads through picturesque countryside. Two roads lead to the closest border crossing of Prek Chak (Xa Xia on the Vietnamese side). One follows the coastline from Kep, while another, better road goes via Kompong Trach. A *motodup* from Kampot will cost you about US$10, a little less from Kep. A taxi should be around US$25. On the Vietnamese side, the nearest town to the border is Ha Tien, from where a *motodup* will charge around US$3 to get to Xa Xia, a trip of about 10 kilometers. Ha Tien lies in the Mekong Delta and one day soon, direct transport from here to the tourist island of Phu Qoc in Vietnam should become a reality.

Getting Around

AIR

Generally speaking, travel in Cambodia is adventurous. Planes are the easiest way to get around, but domestic flights are far more limited now than just a few years ago. At the time of research, the only regular flights (several times daily with Siem Reap Airways) were from Phnom Penh to Siem Reap and back, though this is likely to change in 2010. The coastal resort of Sihanoukville has a fully equipped airport and there are unsurfaced airstrips in a number of smaller towns, including Banlung in Ratanakiri and Sen Monorom in Mondulkiri, as well as in Koh Kong on the coast. But none of these see any regular traffic.

If you're interested in traveling to the provinces by air, you might be able to catch a plane of the Missionary Aviation Fellowship (tel. 012/879426, www.mafcambodia.org), which operates irregular flights in a five-seat Cessna from Phnom Penh. This outfit carts missionaries and NGO staff around the country and occasionally has empty seats on its flights. Check on the website and contact the airline via email or phone.

TRAIN

Cambodia's railway system is in bad shape, but picked up investment from Japan in 2008. Plans were drawn up to have the railway system back to pre–Khmer Rouge standards by 2010, but, with many delays in the restoration process, this is no longer a realistic target.

In the 1990s, train travel was extremely dangerous. Passengers in the front wagon, in front of the engine, traveled free because there was a real risk that the train could hit a mine placed on the tracks. Nowadays it's safe but slow. Rolling stock and tracks are in appalling condition.

As of 2009, there was just one passenger train a week between Phnom Penh and Battambang, requiring a torturous 14 hours of travel (compared to three hours by taxi or five hours by bus) for just 300 kilometers. Many carriages no longer have seats and are packed with locals, so it's a rewarding if arduous experience to travel this route. The tracks will be extended all the way to the Thai border at Poipet, where it will be possible to connect to the Thai rail network.

A Bamboo Train waits for departure at Ou Dambang, a small station near Battambang.

The other main train line leads south from Phnom Penh to the coast and Sihanoukville, via Kampot, but only cargo trains operate on this route. If you're feeling adventurous, you might be able to catch a ride on either of these routes, hobo-style.

The only other trains operating in Cambodia are the illegal but delightful Bamboo Trains, homemade handcars that ferry passengers along short lengths of track in areas where roads are still in bad condition. Something of a tourist attraction near Battambang, the Bamboo Trains also exist around Pursat.

BOAT

A few years ago, river traffic on the Mekong was frequent and it was possible to catch a ferry all the way from Phnom Penh to Stung Treng, at least during and after the rainy season when water levels were adequate. With improving road conditions, many of the regular routes have closed down—Cambodians prefer to go by bus.

Notable exceptions are the daily ferries from Phnom Penh to Siem Reap and from Siem Reap to Battambang. Neither ride should be considered safe by Western standards. It's not unheard of for a boat to run out of gas halfway through the journey or for luggage to be dumped overboard and lost. The trip from Siem Reap to Battambang is the more spectacular of the two. In Siem Reap, a number of boat excursions across the Tonlé Sap Lake can be arranged.

The ferry between Koh Kong and Sihanoukville is less reliable than it once was and no longer operates in the rainy season. When buses started plying the same route, the boat operator raised his prices—perhaps not the best business strategy. Speedboats operate between Koh Kong and several Thai islands. For more information call Neptune Resort (tel. 011/984512) in Koh Kong. In Sihanoukville, motorboats, sailboats, and kayaks can be rented to explore the Cambodian coastline. The temple of Angkor Borei, near Takeo, can be reached by boat in the rainy season, a beautiful trip. Multi-day boat trips on the Mekong can be arranged locally in Kratie and Stung Treng.

passengers sharing transport on a pickup truck in Kampot

© AROON THAEWCHATTURAT

BUS AND TAXI

The regional bus system in Cambodia is steadily growing, with more and more companies competing for passengers. Every provincial capital and some smaller towns are now reachable on regular buses, though some routes, especially in the northeastern provinces of Ratanakiri and Mondulkiri, may not operate during the rainy season.

Most buses have air-conditioning, as well as a TV set, which blasts karaoke or action thrillers at passengers, often at top volume and with maximum distortion. Some buses have toilets, and all stop every few hours at roadside restaurants with basic facilities. Thankfully, none of the journey times are epic, except for the trips to the northeastern part of the country. A bus trip from Phnom Penh to Siem Reap takes five hours. Bus travel can be slow, but it is also cheap and safe and you'll share your journey with local people.

A faster and somewhat more risky and uncomfortable alternative is the increasing traffic of regular share taxis or minibuses. Share taxis tend to be either Toyota Camrys or pickup trucks. In more remote areas, or during the rainy season, pickups may be the only way to get around. That can be a real adventure and you might find yourself sitting on top of a crate of fermented fish or scores of tied up, distressed chickens for several hours. Minibuses and share taxis leave when they are full and to have even a little comfort, you'll need to book two seats for yourself. (The front seat next to the driver counts as two seats and is probably the most comfortable option.)

You can also book an entire taxi for yourself, which can be especially worthwhile if you can get a group of four or five people together. A major advantage is that you can tell the driver to stop off anywhere en route. A private taxi from Phnom Penh to Siem Reap costs US$50–70. In remote areas where roads are bad, renting a private taxi is more expensive.

RENTAL CAR OR MOTORBIKE

It's quite straightforward to rent a car, with or without a private driver. Most people opt for

MOTORCYCLE SAFETY TIPS

Cambodia is a great country for back-roads motorbike tours. While such undertakings are not always entirely safe, riders with off-road experience will find even a day trip through the countryside a real adventure. Longer tours can take visitors to remote and rarely seen locations almost untouched by tourism.

It's really quite important that visitors who rent motorbikes in Cambodia can actually drive. As it's not necessary to have a valid drivers license in order to rent a vehicle, some people who have never driven anywhere are tempted to rent heavy motorbikes, often with tragic consequences. Cambodia is definitely not a place to learn to drive. If you can't drive, don't rent a bike and start here.

The main rule to remember while driving in Cambodia, is that "might is right." The larger vehicle generally has right of way and it is not uncommon for fast cars to overtake slow-moving vehicles in blind corners without any consideration for oncoming traffic. Drivers joining main roads from side streets usually don't pay attention to passing cars as they pull into traffic. Motorcycles often drive against the traffic while trying to cross to their side of the road, which can make driving, especially in the capital, seem like a videogame. Remember, you have only one life.

At night, slow rural traffic tends to lack lights; driving after sundown is not recommended.

Hardly anyone wears a helmet in Cambodia, which tempts many visitors to forgo helmets themselves. Yes, it's more romantic to drive down an empty country road at 80 kilometers an hour with the hot wind blowing through your hair, but it's not worth the risk.

Once off the main roads, drivers will have hard soil, dust, sand, or mud to contend with. In the rainy season, roads become so muddy that many of the remoter parts of Cambodia are virtually cut off from the outside world. A few of Cambodia's larger temples, such as Preah Khan and Preah Vihear, both near Tbeng Meanchey, are, for now at least, best reached by motorbike.

If you are driving your motorbike mostly off-road, make sure you keep the chain well-oiled, avoid buying gas from roadside stalls, and check your tire pressure regularly. Consider taking some spare parts (the clutch handle often breaks) and wear protective clothing.

It's best not to drive alone through remote areas, as there'll be limited assistance in case of a breakdown or accident. Mobile phone reception can be patchy in remote areas.

the driver, thus reducing their own responsibility and increasing their safety, as a Cambodian driver is more familiar with the local driving culture and should, at least in theory, be better equipped to keep the vehicle safe. This might not always be obvious when you are being thrown around the backseat doing 80 kilometers an hour across a sea of potholes with smoke-belching trucks bearing down on you. The difference in price between driving and being driven is marginal.

A car around Phnom Penh, Angkor, or Battambang is likely to cost US$25–40, including gas. Gas is not cheap in Cambodia, about US$1 per liter, and fluctuations in gas prices will influence rates. For longer drives between major cities, prices vary. Even small towns have gas stations, though plenty of private operators sell gas from small stalls by the roadside, often storing the fuel in soft drink bottles. Note that this gas is often low quality and should be used only in an emergency.

One of the best ways to explore the more remote parts of Cambodia is by motorbike, preferably on a 250cc dirt bike. Motorbikes can be rented in most towns where there's tourism. Small 100cc Chinese or Thai mopeds cost US$5–8 per day, or less if you rent for longer than week. Most 250cc dirt bikes can be rented for US$10–20, depending on where you rent them, how long you rent them, and what condition they're in. Dirt bikes can only be rented in Phnom Penh, Sihanoukville, Battambang, and Banlung. Check the bikes as best as you can, some are in appalling condition. Tourists are not allowed to drive around the Angkor temples and consequently, motorbikes can't be rented in Siem Reap. There is an occasional ban on foreign drivers in Sihanoukville; check the latest details when you get there.

There are real advantages to exploring the provinces at length with a guide and bikes from an experienced dirt bike tour company. Red Raid (www.motorcycletourscambodia.com) is highly recommended, and Dancing Roads (www.dancingroads.com) and Hidden Cambodia (www.hiddencambodia.com) are equally competent. These excellent outfits have offices in Siem Reap and Phnom Penh and offer guides, route suggestions, and some degree of safety back-up, coupled with local knowledge, which reduces driving risks dramatically. Red Raid, which has been operating on Cambodia's trails since 2001, has guides who speak English, German, or French, and offers helicopter rescue in case of a serious accident. Prices aren't cheap (and the larger the group, the lower the price), so count on at least US$150 a day for bike, fuel, guide, and back-up. You'll be glad for it when your bike's frame collapses on a muddy jungle trail 200 kilometers from the nearest road.

For detailed route descriptions all across the country, *Ultimate Cambodia Travel Guide* by motorcycle writer Matt Jacobson is recommended.

Drivers License
When renting a motorbike or car, a drivers license is rarely demanded. Rental agents prefer to retain the driver's passport (but make sure you carry a photocopy with you at all times if your passport stays with the rental agency). In case of an accident, having an International Driving License could be of help, but the foreign driver is usually pronounced to be at fault—whatever the circumstances of the incident.

Insurance
Renting a vehicle in Cambodia does not mean you are insured driving it. If you damage the vehicle, the shop will demand cash compensation as per the rental agreement. The same applies if the vehicle is stolen. In case of an accident involving another vehicle or people, foreign drivers are liable to pay whatever damages are demanded. The local police are likely to side with the Cambodian party. In case of personal injury, personal travel insurance should cover possibly horrendous medical costs. If you rent a vehicle with a driver, that vehicle is usually insured and the driver or rental agent bears all responsibilities.

Visas and Officialdom

VISA REQUIREMENTS
Foreign visitors, including Americans, require a visa to enter Cambodia. At international airports and all land border crossings mentioned in this guide, tourist visas (US$20) as well as business visas (US$25) are issued on the spot. Those who are considering working, investing, or setting up a business in Cambodia should apply for a business visa. Tourist visas are valid for a month and are single entry. It's possible to get an online e-visa (http://evisa.mfaic.gov.kh, US$25), which is also valid for one month but non-extendable. Regular tourist visas, whether issued by a Cambodian embassy abroad or at a border, can only be extended once, for one more month, for US$35. Business visas can be extended several times. A year extension is US$200.

Immigration and government officials from Cambodia, Thailand, Laos, and Vietnam are involved in discussions on whether to issue joint tourist visas for visitors wishing to travel between these countries. As of 2009, no decision had been reached.

CAMBODIAN EMBASSIES AND CONSULATES ABROAD

- **Australia:** 5 Canterbury Crescent, Deakin, tel. 02/6273 1259, Cambodianembassy@ozemail.com.au

- **Canada:** Consulate of Cambodia, 903-168 Chadwick Court, North Vancouver, BC, tel. 604/980-1718, dglo@shaw.ca

- **Japan:** 8-6-9, Akasaka, Minato-Ku, Tokyo, tel. 03/5412 8521 or 03/5412 8522, aap33850@hkg.odn.ne.jp

- **Laos:** Thadeua Road, KM2, Vientiane, tel. 021/314950, recamlao@laotel.com

- **Singapore:** 400 Orchard Road, #10-03/04 Orchard Towers, tel. 6732 4764, cambodiaembasy@pacific.net.sg

- **Thailand:** 185, Rajdamri Road, Lumpini, Pathumwan, tel. 02/254 6630, recbkk@cscoms.com

  Royal Consulate General of Cambodia, No. 666, Sowanasone Road Tambun Thakasem, Ampheu Meung Sa Kaew, tel. 01/723 6017, consulsk@cscoms.com

- **United Kingdom:** 64 Brondesbury Park, Willesden Green, London, tel. 020/8451 7850, cambodianembassy@btconnect.com

- **United States:** 4530 16th Street, N.W., Washington DC, tel. 202/726-7742, rec.dc@hotmail.com

  Royal Honorary Consulate of Cambodia, 422 Ord Street, Suite G, Los Angeles, tel. 213/625-7777, cambodiaconsulate@usa.net

  Royal Honorary Consulate of Cambodia, 1818 Westlake Avenue N., Suite #315, Seattle, tel. 206/217-0830, consul-huoth@diplomats.com

- **Vietnam:** 71A, Tran Hung Dao St., Hanoi, tel. 04/942 4789, arch@fpt.vn

  Royal Consulate General of Cambodia, No. 41, Phung Khac Khoan, Ho Chi Minh City, tel. 08/829 2751, cambocg@hcm.vnn.vn

FOREIGN EMBASSIES IN CAMBODIA

Numerous countries have embassies in Phnom Penh. Those who don't probably have an embassy in Bangkok. The **United States Embassy** (1 Street 96, tel. 023/728000, http://cambodia.usembassy.gov) is located in a new, fortified building near Wat Phnom and contains Phnom Penh's only McDonald's. The embassy is open for U.S. citizen services Monday–Thursday 1–4 P.M. The Consular Section is closed for both American and Cambodian holidays and is closed to the public on Fridays. However, the American Citizen Services unit will assist U.S. citizens with emergencies 24 hours a day, seven days a week. There's no special emergency number.

The **British Embassy** is at 27–29 Street 75 (tel. 023/427124, http://ukincambodia.fco.gov. uk/en). Office hours are Monday–Thursday 8:15 A.M.–noon and 3–4:45 P.M., and Friday 8:15 A.M.–1:15 P.M. The **Australian Embassy** is on Street 254 (Villa11, R V Senei Vannavaut Oum, tel. 023/213470, www.dfat.gov.au/missions/countries/kh.html).

After almost being damaged by a government-sponsored mob in 2003, the **Thai Embassy** (tel. 023/726306–10, www.mfa.go.th/web/1830.php?depcode=20800100) relocated to 196 Preah Norodom Boulevard. The **Vietnamese Embassy** (tel. 023/726284) is at 436, Monivong Boulevard. Note that there are Vietnamese consulates in Sihanoukville and Battambang.

Other embassies in Cambodia include **China** (256 Mao Tse Tung Boulevard, tel. 023/720920), **France** (1 Monivong Boulevard, tel. 023/430020), **Germany**

(76–78 Street 214, tel. 023/216381), **India** (777 Monivong Boulevard, tel. 023/210912), **Japan** (194 Norodom Boulevard, tel. 023/217161), **Laos** (15–17 Mao Tse Tung Boulevard, tel. 023/982632), **Malaysia** (5 Street 242, tel. 023/216177), **Myanmar** (181 Norodom Boulevard, tel. 023/223761), **The Philippines** (33 Street 294, tel. 023/222303), and **Singapore** (92 Norodom Boulevard, tel. 023/221875).

Accommodations and Food

ACCOMMODATIONS

A wide range of good-value accommodation awaits visitors in Cambodia's main towns and tourist spots. Siem Reap offers more than 8,000 beds, from US$5 for a cell in a backpacker flophouse to US$1,000 for a chance to wallow in five-star luxuries for a night. In the midrange bracket, the town near the Angkor temples also offers great places to stay, from modern boutique guesthouses to smart hotels with a whiff of colonial nostalgia.

Phnom Penh too offers a wealth of different sleeping options, and a number of stylish upscale hotels have recently opened in the capital. Sihanoukville welcomes visitors with quality beach accommodations. In neighboring Kampot and Kep, old villas and townhouses have been refurbished and turned into midrange and upscale hotels. In the remote towns of the northeastern part of the country, Banlung in Ratanakiri and Sen Monorom in Mondulkiri, a number of attractive ecolodges have opened.

Elsewhere around the country, in the smaller provincial capitals, good-value Khmer hotels, usually with clean and quite simple air-conditioned rooms, can be had for under US$15.

FOOD AND DRINK

For many first-time visitors, the essence of Cambodian food might not be obvious, or if it is, the thought of partaking in typical Cambodian cuisine might not appear such an altogether attractive option. After all, Cambodia's staple diet consists *prahoc,* a strong-smelling fermented fish paste, and rice.

Rice *(bai)* is the most important food in the country and more than 2,000 species once grew in Cambodia. There's hardly a dish that does not contain rice, including noodles made from rice, desserts, cakes, and alcoholic beverages, and no Khmer meal is complete without boiled rice. Also central to Khmer cooking is fish, both from lakes and rivers and the Gulf of Thailand. Fish is smoked, fried, boiled, grilled, fermented, or served in soup. Perhaps even more important, especially for the country's poor, who can't afford fish or meat, is *prahoc,* which serves as a condiment to every Cambodian meal. But there's plenty of variety to be discovered beyond *prahoc,* which the uninitiated should perhaps first try in a restaurant before indulging in the market variety. Soups and fried dishes with fish, meat, and vegetables are an integral part of Cambodia's staple food, and fruit is amazingly abundant and varied. Chou Ta-Kuan, a Chinese diplomat who spent almost a year in Angkor during the late 13th century, reported the consumption of vegetables like mustard greens, cucumbers, squash, leeks, eggplants, onion, and fruit such as watermelons, oranges, lychees, pomegranates, lotus roots, and bananas. All are still common in Cambodia today.

Cambodia's cuisine is not unlike that of its two larger neighbors, Thailand and Vietnam, and many dishes available in those countries are also Cambodian standards, though local flavors vary. The Cambodians are not nearly as obsessed with chili as the Thais and aim for milder, more rounded flavors, infused with herbs, pepper, and sugar. Tamarind is used in soups and sauces, and turmeric, ginger, lemongrass, kaffir lime, and galangal are integral building blocks of many Khmer dishes. *Kroeng,* a typical Khmer sauce, contains cardamom,

PRAHOC: CAMBODIA'S NATIONAL DISH

Every chef worth his fish will tell you that there can't be a Cambodian cuisine without *prahoc*. *Prahoc*, fermented fish paste, is a Cambodian standard. The pungent dish (enter any market in the country and you will encounter its fine odor soon enough) is part of the national psyche and even Prime Minister Hun Sen prides himself on being able to make an excellent *prahoc*. In a reference to a political opponent, Hun Sen once said that a Khmer who does not know how to make *prahoc* will never lead the country.

More importantly, for millions of Cambodians, it is the only source of protein. *Prahoc* is the Khmer name of the freshwater fish that is used for the paste, which is eaten with rice and vegetables, but is served with pretty much all other food as well.

Apart from being Cambodia's most popu-lar dish, *prahoc* remains a crucial measure for the wellbeing of the country's poorest. In 2008, prices for *prahoc* shot up, in line with high inflation and rising food costs. Almost three million people, the country's poorest, were severely affected, not least because they could no longer afford *prahoc:* the prices for the fish had rapidly risen from US$0.12 to US$0.50. While most poor families tried to produce extra *prahoc* for sale in previous years, they could now no longer generate enough of the paste to feed themselves.

If you're scared of trying the common market variety, you can taste *prahoc* in one of Phnom Penh's upscale restaurants, like Malis. The five-star *prahoc* at these eateries is made from fresh fish and lacks the ferocious smell.

© AROON THAEWCHATTURAT

prahoc for sale in the Old Market, Phsar Chas, in Siem Reap

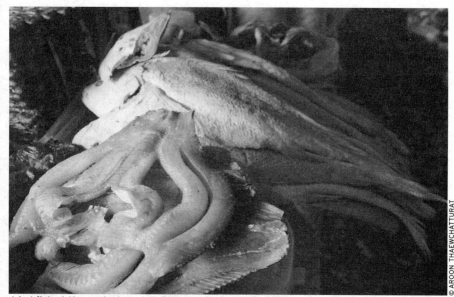

dried fish at the central market, Phsar Nath, in Battambang

© AROON THAEWCHATTURAT

cinnamon, nutmeg, cloves, and star anise, as well as aforementioned ingredients. As recently as a decade ago, Cambodians cooked a great deal with marijuana, until Western pressure removed the evil weed from market stalls.

The closer you get to the border with Thailand, the more Thai dishes will appear on local menus, and the same goes for the country's the border with Vietnam. In a larger international context, Cambodia lies, geographically and culturally, between India and China and this is reflected in its kitchen—think curry (with coconut milk) and spring rolls, both integral dishes to any local menu, done in Cambodian style, of course. The French presence in the country has also left its culinary legacy: No other Southeast Asian nation consumes as much bread, mostly traditional French baguette, sold fresh in the mornings on busy street corners. Sandwiches filled with pickled vegetables and paté are served from roadside stalls.

At home, families usually sit in a circle on a mat on the floor to eat. Cambodians eat mostly with chopsticks. For breakfast, noodle soup with vegetables and meat is a favorite. In the countryside, there's little else to eat in the mornings. For lunch and dinner, most Cambodians try to eat at home. A usual meal consists of boiled rice, along with soup *(samlor), prahoc,* and fried fish or meat, as well as unripe papaya or mango. Street stalls usually set up in Cambodian towns in the afternoons, often around the market or by a bridge, serving a variety of fried dishes, sandwiches, sugar cane juice, and some very sweet fruit desserts. Small-town restaurants usually have no menu and display the available pre-cooked meals in large pots. Just point at the desired dish and it will be served with rice.

Typical, widely available standards include:

- **Amok trey:** Fish cooked in coconut milk, wrapped in banana leaves and steamed. This is one of the most popular dishes in Cambodia.

- **Loc lac:** Cubes of stir-fried beef, served with onions and rice on salad (cucumbers and

CAMBODIAN FRUIT

Cambodia is a great place to sample a huge selection of tropical fruits, some familiar to Western visitors, others inviting discovery. What follows is a list of the most commonly available varieties.

- **Avocado** – *avocaa* (Season: May-Aug.)
  The avocado can be round, oblong, pear- or bottle-shaped, and has a yellowish green to dark green skin. The skin is shiny or thick and leathery. The fruit has a large seed, which constitutes half of its weight.

- **Banana** – *jeik* (Season: All year)
  Many varieties of banana grow in Cambodia. Bananas are usually seedless and can be short and fat or long and slim.

- **Cashew** – *svai jantee* (Season: March-June)
  The cashew apple is eaten fresh, candied or stewed, and has a sweet and astringent taste. The cashew nut is the actual fruit.

- **Coconut** – *dawng* (Season: All year)
  While the young green coconut fruit is cut open for its clear and nutritious juice, the milk of the ripe coconut is used as a cooking ingredient.

- **Custard apple** – *dtiep bpai* (Season: June-Sept.)
  The custard apple is about the size of a baseball, greenish with powdery surface and is sweet in taste. The flesh is white and comes apart in segments – each segment contains black seeds.

- **Dragon fruit** – *srawgahneeak* (Season: All year)
  The dragon fruit has shiny reddish to pink skin with greenish scales. The flesh is often white, sometimes reddish, and has small black seeds mixed in. Its taste is not unlike that of a pear.

- **Durian** – *toorayn* (Season: April-June)
  The durian is a huge fruit with a hard green to yellow spiky rind and a very distinctive and strong smell many foreigners find hard to take. If you can get past the odor, the durian is deliciously sweet and extremely high in fat.

- **Guava** – *dtraw bai* (Season: All year)
  The guava can be round or pear-shaped. Size is variable, from that of a lime to a grapefruit. Its flesh is soft and white or pink, with a lot of small seeds. It is usually consumed fresh and has a sweet taste.

- **Jackfruit** – *knao* (Season: All year)
  The jackfruit, huge and green, with yellow flesh, looks a bit similar to the durian, but lacks the pungent smell.

- **Lime** – *plai kro ch'mah* (Season: All year)
  The lime is a small fruit with smooth green or yellow skin. The juice is used for drinks and as food flavoring.

- **Longan** – *mien* (Season: Aug.-Sept.)
  The longan is a small round fruit, about the size of a grape, with a thin brown leathery shell and blackish stone seeds. The flesh is juicy white and sweet in taste.

- **Lotus seeds** – *chook* (Season: All year)
  Lotus seeds grow in green pods that look like shower heads. Each pod contains many oval seeds that have a green smooth skin. To eat, peel the skin away. The youngest seeds have the sweetest taste.

- **Lychee** – *guhlean* (Season: April-June)
  The lychee is about the size of a plum, heart-shaped with bright red to purplish leathery skin. The flesh is milky white with a sweet taste, and has reddish to brown stone seeds.

- **Mango** – *suh-ai* (Season: All year)
  There are many types of mango. In Cambodia, it is eaten both raw and ripe. The raw mango is green to dark green according to variety and can be sour. A ripe mango is usually yellow and has a sweet taste.

- **Mangosteen** – *mawkuht* (Season: Aug.-Nov.)
  The mangosteen is a smooth berry, dark purple when ripe. The flesh is white and is divided into several segments. It has a pleasantly sweet taste.

(continued on next page)

CAMBODIAN FRUIT (continued)

- **Orange** – *plai kroidt poosat* (Season: Nov.-Feb.) Oranges in Cambodia generally have green skin and taste a bit sour.

- **Papaya** – *la-hong* (Season: All year) The papaya is a fleshy fruit with thin and smooth skin. The skin turns from green to yellow or orange while ripening. It has a sweet taste and its aroma can be overwhelming when very ripe. The papaya is an excellent laxative.

- **Pineapple** – *manawa* (Season: All year) The Cambodian pineapple is deliciously juicy, a perfect combination of sweet and sour.

- **Pomegranate** – *dtoteum* (Season: All year) The pomegranate is about the size of tennis ball, with smooth yellow or reddish skin. The fruit contains several segments and each has many gemstone-like seeds. It's sweet in taste.

- **Pomelo** – *kroitlaung* (Season: All year) The pomelo is a larger version of the grapefruit, though less juicy and less bitter.

- **Rambutan** – *sao mao* (Season: May–Sept.) The rambutan is about the size of a plum, ellipsoid, purplish-red covered in dense hair. The flesh is white and juicy and contains white seeds. It has a sweet taste.

- **Santol** – *kom peeng riech* (Season: June-Aug.) The santol is about the size of a tennis ball with yellow-brownish color and thick rind. It has several large seeds covered by white pulp, which is sweet to sub-acid. Usually it is eaten fresh by peeling the rind off, cutting the fruit into small pieces, and dipping it into a mixture of salt, sugar, and chili powder. Santol pickles are also popular. It has laxative effect.

- **Sapodilla** – *leumuht* (Season: Aug.-Sept.) The sapodilla, or chiku, has a brown thin rind and black seeds. The soft brown flesh has a sweet taste.

- **Soursop** – *dtiep barang* (Season: All year) The soursop has green leathery skin and soft, curved spines. Its flesh is whitish and juicy with hard black seeds. It has a sweet and sour taste and makes good material for a milkshake.

- **Starfruit** – *speu* (Season: All year) The starfruit is shiny yellow-green when ripe, with five pronounced ribs. It has a sweet citrus flavor. It is eaten fresh, in salads, or pulped into a drink.

- **Sugar cane** – *aumpo* (Season: All year) Sugar cane is a perennial crop. The cane is eaten fresh by peeling off its hard skin. Cut yourself a piece and chew it, but spit out the fiber. More convenient is the freshly squeezed juice, available from mobile stalls.

- **Tamarind** – *ompeul khoua* (Season: All year) The tamarind has brown skin, and grows in straight or curved pods. The mature pods have brown flesh and black seeds. The fruit is used as a cooking ingredient and as a snack. The flesh is used for flavoring soups.

- **Watermelon** – *aolak* (Season: All year) The watermelon has smooth greenish to dark skin and is round or oval in shape. The juicy flesh is usually red, and sometimes yellow, peppered with small flat brown seeds. It has a sweet, refreshing taste.

---

tomatoes seasoned with a lime sauce or black pepper). Sometimes includes a fried egg on top.

- ***Bai cha:*** Rice fried in soy sauce, generally with garlic, pork, and herbs, though ingredients vary wildly.

- ***Bok l'hong:*** A papaya salad with a lime sauce base and baby tomatoes, string beans, peanuts, dried fish, fermented crabs, and chili, similar but not as fierce as Thailand's *somtam.*

- ***Kuytheaw:*** Beef noodle soup.

- **Somlar kari:** Red coconut chicken soup with sweet potatoes and bamboo shoots.

- **Somlar machu yuon:** Tamarind-based soup with fish or meat and pineapple, tomatoes, and onions.

In recent years, thanks to tourism, a wide variety of international cuisine, sometimes awful, sometimes splendid, has become available in Phnom Penh and Siem Reap. Sometimes it's even found in some provincial capitals, but on the whole, once you are in the provinces, you are likely to have to stick to Cambodian staples. Also note that international food is significantly more expensive than the local food.

Nonalcoholic Drinks

In small-town restaurants, very weak cold or hot tea is usually served with the food. If a village has a shop, it's likely to sell American soft drinks and small bottles of drinking water. Roadside stalls often sell juices, especially sugar cane juice. If you have a sensitive stomach, avoid the ice. In tourist restaurants, fruit shakes and juices are usually on the menu, though it's worth asking if the juices are canned or fresh. Cambodian coffee is strong and bitter and is often drunk with sweet condensed canned milk. Coffee is also served with ice.

Alcoholic Drinks

The two most popular beers are Angkor and Anchor, available in cans and bottles and usually drunk with ice. Again, be careful with the ice in the beer, especially in the provinces. Popular foreign beers include Beer Lao, Tiger, and Heineken. Traditional Khmer restaurants are populated by armies of beer girls in skimpy uniforms who encourage customers to drink the brand they represent. Local liqueurs are usually made from rice and tend to be great facilitators of terrific hangovers, if consumed in any volume. Shops in Phnom Penh and Siem Reap sell a wide variety of foreign-made spirits and wines.

Tips for Travelers

TRAVELERS WITH DISABILITIES

Cambodia is not easy on travelers with disabilities, despite the fact that a significant section of the population has to cope with disabilities caused by land mines and unexploded ordnance. No matter where you go in Cambodia, tarmac tends to be potholed; sidewalks are cracked, uneven, and crumbling; and special facilities, such as ramps for wheelchair users, are virtually nonexistent. Notable exceptions are the two international airports and a few luxury hotels.

Unfortunately, the temples of Angkor prove to be a real challenge for travelers with disabilities. Virtually every temple visit requires some climbing—though the central tower of Angkor Wat has been closed off to all tourists because the crumbling steps leading to the top are so steep and worn away that even able-bodied tourists risk breaking their limbs.

On the plus side, ground-level rooms are available in many Cambodian hotels and if you need help, it's cheap to hire someone to help you get around. In some temples, such as Ta Prohm and Beng Melea, ramps have been built that make access somewhat easier. Check travel blogs and forums for other visitors' experiences before you set off.

TRAVELING WITH CHILDREN

Traveling through Cambodia with kids can be an extremely rewarding experience. Cambodians love children and foreign kids are likely to be quickly integrated into any social gathering. If you travel with infants, Siem Reap and Phnom Penh provide enough infrastructure and services not to have to worry, though this is not the case away from these main centers. Keep in mind that medical services remain limited, and make sure your child drinks enough, does not sunburn, and does not eat objects off the sidewalk.

LIVING IN CAMBODIA

Staying in Cambodia appears to be so easy that some people who had planned to pass through the country on their travels simply forget to leave. Long-term visa formalities are not complicated and the investment climate welcomes foreigners. Jobs for people with skills and even for those who merely pretend to have skills appear plentiful. In Phnom Penh and Siem Reap, pretty much everything an expatriate might need is available. Moving from a developed country to Cambodia is not without its challenges, though. Interfacing with a very different society, whose values may not make sense or don't even become apparent during a first visit, takes time. If you do decide to stay on, be patient and remember you are a guest.

For nuts and bolts information on moving to Cambodia, check out these websites:

- www.talesofasia.com/cambodia.htm

- www.expatinterviews.com/cambodia

- www.ispp.edu.kh
  (click on New in Cambodia)

- http://seniors.lovetoknow.com/
  Retire_in_Cambodia

Beyond the health issues, the chaotic traffic, especially in Phnom Penh, is an issue for children old enough to walk around by themselves. The same goes for the countryside, as children, even teenagers, are unlikely to understand the dangers of land mines.

WOMEN TRAVELING ALONE

Women travelers must always be careful in Cambodia and should not travel to remote areas alone or walk around in quiet city areas after dark, even in areas frequented by tourists. Violence against Cambodian women is high and several foreign women have been attacked and raped in recent years. Drive-by snatchings of handbags have also increased significantly in Phnom Penh in recent years.

GAY AND LESBIAN TRAVELERS

Cambodia is a gay-friendly country. That's not to say that homosexuality is celebrated in this conservative Buddhist nation, but what with former King Sihanouk commenting positively about gay rights, gay and lesbian visitors are generally welcome. Phnom Penh and Siem Reap have several gay hangouts.

Whether you're gay or straight, you shouldn't be demonstrative in public, as this might lead to offense.

VOLUNTEER OPPORTUNITIES

Following decades of conflict, Cambodia is still an extremely poor country. There are a plethora of aid projects in the country, some definitely more beneficial and philanthropic than others. Make no mistake, development and aid are businesses. That said, there are some worthwhile projects. Orphanages, schools, and environmental protection top the lists.

The **Cooperation Committee for Cambodia** (tel. 023/214152, www.ccc-cambodia.org) is an umbrella organization for local and international NGOs (nongovernmental organizations) operating in Cambodia. The committee's website features a handy map of the country indicating what projects (with project descriptions and website links) currently run in which areas of the country.

Also check the following programs, organizations, and charities for aid projects in Cambodia:

The **Peace Corps** (www.peacecorps.gov) has been sending volunteers to countries around the globe since 1961, when this U.S. government program was founded by President John F. Kennedy. The Peace Corps has been active in Cambodia since 2006 and is involved in teacher training. Tours usually last two years and are preceded by language and project-specific training.

PHOTOGRAPHY IN CAMBODIA

Cambodia is a very photogenic country with spectacular temples that change personality with the shifting light of day, colonial architecture, river and lake vistas, jungle and white-sand beaches, and most importantly the country's enigmatic and friendly people. Here are a few basic tips on how to get the best shots on your travels.

Light: As in all countries close to the equator, early morning (between sunrise and 9 A.M.) and in the afternoon (between 4 P.M. and sunset), the so-called golden hours, are the best times to take pictures outside. Note that the light varies considerably from season to season. The Cambodian landscape generally looks best during and after the rainy season, from June to December, before the plants wilt and dust covers everything. Some really dramatic light can be caught during the rains. The Angkor ruins look very otherworldly on storm-laden days in the summer.

People: For the most part, Cambodian people are happy to be photographed, though it is always polite to ask. Photography in temples is usually also not a problem, but it is advisable to ask before photographing monks. There are notable exceptions to this liberal attitude: Photography of police and military, as well as of military installations, should be avoided. The Kompong Loeu, the indigenous people of Ratanakiri and Mondulkiri, generally don't like to be photographed at all and may run away as soon as you pull out your camera. In some minority villages, the influx of tourists has led to demands for money. Photographers have to decide for themselves whether this is a good way to get a snapshot.

Dust: The main enemy of camera gear in Cambodia, apart from heat and rain, is the dust. Especially in the northeast during the dry season, the fine red dust that swirls around anywhere there's a road has a way of entering cameras and dirtying sensors, even if the lens is never separated from the body. Even fixed lens cameras are not immune from this hazard. Always make sure photography gear is well wrapped in plastic before setting off on a motorbike trip.

Gear: Cameras and camera accessories are not particularly cheap in Cambodia and visitors who intend to buy a camera during their trip around Asia would be better off doing so in Singapore, Malaysia or Thailand. That said, there's a Canon shop (The Royal Cambodia Company, 437 Monivong Boulevard, tel. 023/428955, www.royalgroup.com.kh) in Phnom Penh that can undertake basic repairs of Canon models. Memory cards and film are available in Phnom Penh, Siem Reap, and, to a lesser degree in Sihanoukville. Some smaller towns may have photo-shops that sell cheap compact cameras, film and occasionally some memory cards.

Film Developing: Having your pictures developed is not a problem in Phnom Penh, whether you use a digital or film camera. Be aware though that it's unlikely that a shop in Cambodia will handle your negatives with particular care. If you want to be certain no scratches appear on your films, have them developed when you get home.

Safety: Finally, always make sure your camera is securely stored when you take a walk in the busy streets of the capital. Fly-by robberies, typically two kids on a motorcycle zipping past and grabbing whatever you have over your shoulder, are not common, but they are occurring more and more often. The risk increases if you take your camera out at night.

GoAbroad (U.S. tel. 720/570-1702, www.goabroad.com) is a U.S.-based organization that connects young people with jobs and volunteer opportunities abroad. They publish a long list of teaching and care opportunities in Cambodia.

HealthCareVolunteer (www.health-carevolunteer.com) is the world's largest listing of health-related volunteer opportunities around the world. This U.S.-based group offers volunteer placements for skilled health professionals in a dental clinic and a private medical clinic in Cambodia.

VSO (Voluntary Services Overseas, www. vso.org.uk), a U.K.-based charity, sends skilled volunteers to partake in aid projects around the world, including many placements Cambodia. Candidates are expected to stay at least a year or two with their projects.

Globalteer (www.globalteer.org) is another U.K.-based nonprofit that places volunteers in aid programs around the world, including interesting and rewarding short-term projects in Cambodia.

ECOTOURISM

Cambodia is trying to diversify its tourism industry in order to lure visitors away from the overcrowded temples. Ecotourism is the new, much-talked-about future of travel in Cambodia; or is it? Ecotourism projects (both privately operated and NGO-based initiatives) are all the rage in Southeast Asia. While many projects actively contribute to more sustainable tourism practices and the protection of the environment, some merely aspire to such lofty goals—and a few simply use the catchword to draw in patrons. Ecotourism is dependent on Cambodia's rapidly shrinking natural wealth and beauty and there's a danger that areas pioneered by ecotour operators will soon be gobbled up by loggers, plantation owners, or other investors. Most importantly, if ecotourism is to work, projects must be run within local communities. Without direct participation by and benefit for ordinary Cambodians, ecotourism merely exploits natural resources without giving anything back, a typical precursor of mass tourism. Visitors interested in ecotourism should be careful to check who benefits from their money. Numerous homestay options and ecofriendly tourism projects are mentioned in this guide.

CONDUCT AND CUSTOMS

A reasonably smart appearance and a smile go a long way in Cambodia. Remember that the kingdom is very conservative, and given its recent tragic history, not enamored by cultural challenges or rapid social change. Hence, the way you look is very important. Beachwear should only be worn on a beach designated for tourism. When entering (active) temples, make sure that your clothing is respectful and that upper arms and legs are always covered. Also, if you enter a temple's prayer hall or a private home, be sure to remove your shoes and don't point the soles of your feet towards a Buddha statue or a person. Females visiting pagodas should be sure never to touch a monk. If you want to pass something to a monk, do it through a (male) third person. Couples showing affection in public will be looked at with disdain. When dealing with officials, patience and politeness will eventually get results. Getting impatient, noisy, or patronizing towards anyone, but especially policemen and immigration officials, has the opposite effect. Finally, if you eat with chopsticks, lay them vertically across your bowl when you have finished eating. Leaving them stuck in the bowl is associated with incense burning for the dead.

WHAT TO TAKE

It's hot and sticky in Cambodia, so it's tempting to walk around in shorts or a bikini. Keep in mind, though, that Cambodia is conservative and locals are genuinely offended and embarrassed by foreigners letting it all hang out. Light cotton clothes are best, and a jacket will come in handy in northeastern Cambodia. You'll also want to bring an adapter plug and current converter. If you plan to spend prolonged periods in remote areas, you won't regret investing in a mosquito net.

Health and Safety

BEFORE YOU GO
Resources

Numerous specialty travel health guides have been published in recent years. Whether it's worth lugging one of these around in your luggage depends on your priorities and where you intend to go. *Staying Healthy in Asia, Africa and Latin America,* by Dirk G. Schroeder (Avalon Travel Publishing, 2000) is an excellent guide to problems and diseases you might encounter in the tropics and is small enough to fit in your backpack. For up-to-date information, take a look at the Cambodia page of the Center of Disease Control and Prevention (CDC) at wwwn.cdc.gov/travel/destination-Cambodia.aspx.

Vaccinations

All adults should have up-to-date inoculations for measles, mumps, rubella, diphtheria, tetanus, and polio whether they plan to travel or not. Visitors to Cambodia should also be vaccinated against Hepatitis A. Those intending to work in the health sector or likely to have sexual contact with the local population should also get a Hepatitis B vaccine. A typhoid shot is recommended for those who spend a lot of time in rural areas, as is vaccination against Japanese encephalitis if you plan to spend extended periods in remote rural areas.

STAYING HEALTHY

Cambodia poses more health challenges than other Southeast Asian countries. Food hygiene is so-so and medical facilities are limited. Travel can be arduous and exhausting and the heat can have more severe consequences than travelers might realize at first. Always stay hydrated, especially when climbing the temples of Angkor for hours on end. It's best to carry a supply of oral rehydration powders, available (in different flavors) in the United States, to counteract dehydration, diarrhea, sunstroke, infections, and hangovers. Wash your hands every time before you eat and avoid eating raw, unpeeled food in cheap local restaurants. Western food, including salads, is mostly safe to eat because it's served only in tourist areas. Also be careful with shellfish. If you are a long way from the coast, or if it's not quite fresh, don't eat it. Keep the flies out of your food and drink, as they can be persistent. Never drink the tap water and brush your teeth with bottled water, which is available virtually everywhere. Ice cubes seem okay in the bigger cities, but anyone who's spent a little time traveling around the country will have seen the extremely unhygienic ice trucks delivering large blocks of frozen water covered in saw dust to provincial restaurants.

Cambodia is a tropical country and visitors will notice that the Khmer go to extreme lengths to avoid the sun. People who work outdoors are generally covered up from head to toe. Visitors are unlikely to follow local routine, nor will they stay indoors between 10 A.M.–3 P.M. and should therefore wear long sleeves and pants (which in any case, the conservative Khmer will appreciate), a hat, and strong sunscreen. The effects of the sun are especially powerful when on long trips through the temples. Traveling on the roofs of river ferries and train carriages can also lead to serious burns without the passenger even noticing. Treat sunburn with aloe vera cream and avoid repeated burns.

DISEASES AND COMMON AILMENTS
Fungal Infections

By far the most common infections visitors to Cambodia suffer from are fungal infections, brought on by high temperatures and humidity. Common types include athlete's foot, which occurs between the toes, fingers, and in the groin area, as well as ringworm, which occurs all over the body. To avoid fungal infections, wear loose cotton clothes and wash yourself frequently. Dry thoroughly after taking a shower, and do as the locals do and use talcum powder. If you do develop an infection, apply antifungal cream regularly.

Diarrhea and Dysentery

The second most common ailment travelers suffer from when in Cambodia is diarrhea, though incidents are nowhere near as common as when traveling on the Indian subcontinent. If you do get diarrhea, drink plenty of water, eat very plain food (such as boiled rice), and use oral rehydration salts. Avoid stomach blockers (such as Imodium), which will merely clog your insides, rather than ridding you of the bug that's causing your discomfort. If you develop a fever or find blood in your stool, go to a doctor for a stool test. This can be an impossible undertaking in the remoter parts of Cambodia, so if you do not get better, then travel to Phnom Penh or Siem Reap as quickly as possible and seek treatment there. Diarrhea symptoms could also point to a case of amoebic or bacillic dysentery, which require professional diagnosis and treatment with either drugs that clean your intestines or with antibiotics. Most travelers to Cambodia never experience diarrhea, never mind dysentery, and pass their time in Cambodia with a perfectly normal stomach.

Malaria

Malaria is a serious problem in Cambodia and several thousand Khmer succumb to the parasitical disease every year, with thousands more infected. In the border regions of Cambodia and Thailand, malaria is almost entirely resistant to most prophylaxis, because thousands of refugees, living in camps in the area, were dosed with preventive medications in the 1980s and 1990s. Malaria is also present in the northeastern provinces of Mondulkiri and Ratanakiri, as well as in Kompong Cham and around Pursat, though it is not as resistant to drugs there. Around the Tonlé Sap Lake, in Siem Reap, and in Sihanoukville, malaria is rare, and it is virtually unheard of in Phnom Penh. Doctors prescribe different prophylaxis, so make sure you get the right one for Cambodia if you choose to take preventative

steps. Note that immunity is not 100 percent certain if you do take medication, and malaria contracted despite the use of prophylaxis is very hard to treat. Prevention and common sense are still the best ways to avoid contracting the disease. Most importantly, do not get bitten at dusk or at night, when malaria-carrying mosquitoes are most active. If you do think you have contracted malaria, then consult a doctor immediately. Symptoms include fever, diarrhea, stomach cramps, and aching joints. Remember that untreated malaria can be fatal.

Dengue Fever

Dengue fever, once also called "bone-breaking fever" by the British in India, is transmitted around the clock by mosquitoes. There's no medication to counteract the illness' crippling effects, so those who are infected need to drink as much oral rehydration salts and water as possible and get plenty of rest. Even though there's no treatment for most strains, get a blood test if you suspect having dengue fever as there's a fatal variety that does need to be treated. In Cambodia, dengue fever is especially prevalent in Phnom Penh, as well as in Battambang and Kratie, more rarely around remote temples such as Preah Vihear and Koh Ker, as well as parts of Ratanakiri and Mondulkiri. Symptoms are usually severe and include high fever, nausea, vomiting, muscle pains, and skin rashes. Avoid taking Aspirin to counteract the disease's effects. Full recovery may take several weeks.

HIV/AIDS

Contact with blood and bodily fluids can lead to contracting the human immunodeficiency virus (HIV), which can lead to acquired immune deficiency syndrome (AIDS), which is fatal. Besides sexual contact, dirty needles can also lead to transmission of the virus, so be careful with acupuncture and tattoo needles and avoid intravenous drug use. If you need an injection in a Cambodian hospital, ask for a fresh, wrapped syringe. Complete abstinence is the safest way to avoid contracting AIDS or STDs (sexually transmitted diseases), but this is not an option for everyone. Always use a condom, whether you have sexual contact with Cambodians or other travelers. Condoms are widely available in Cambodia and locals usually know them as Number 1, the most popular brand in the country. Condoms produced in the United States are likely to be of higher quality than Cambodian ones.

BITES AND STINGS
Mosquitoes
A whole world of insects and reptiles seems to be out there to make locals and visitors alike miserable. Mosquitoes are top of the list of annoying creatures and are responsible for spreading malaria, dengue fever, and Japanese encephalitis. They are most prevalent during or after the rainy season, when much of the country is flooded. Mosquitoes breed in ponds and rice fields. It's best not to get bitten at all, so stay indoors during the hour before dusk, when they are most active; wear long sleeves, trousers, and socks after dark; and use an effective repellent. If your room is not mosquito-free, as is often the case in wooden houses, sleep under a net. Some guesthouses provide nets in their rooms. If you sleep in the jungle, always use a net. Mosquito coil, widely available in Cambodia, does not kill the insects, but keeps them at bay. Try not to sleep inhaling the smoke from the coil. If you have no other option, turn the fan in your room on full speed to keep them off your skin.

Sandflies
Some beaches around Koh Kong are plagued by sandflies. They bite, you scratch, the bites become infected. There's nothing much you can do against sandflies and beaches infested by these bugs tend to be a drag.

Other Insect Bites
When walking in the jungle, be aware that ticks may fall onto your skin from branches. Use a pair of tweezers to remove these nasty creatures, by carefully pulling them out by the head. Scorpions and spiders, including tarantulas, are common in Cambodia. The scorpions tend to be of the large black variety and their sting is

not fatal, hardly more serious than a wasp sting. Spiders bite humans only very rarely.

Leeches
Leeches are very common on moist forest floors and are often not detected by trekkers until their shoes have filled up with their own blood. To prevent leeches from climbing into your shoes, soak your socks in tobacco prior to setting off. If you find leeches on your body, use a cigarette lighter or salt to get them off your skin. If you pull them off, the wound may become infected.

Snake Bites
Cambodia is home to a number of poisonous snakes. Always wear shoes and long trousers when walking through grassland and forest. If you get bitten, do not attempt to suck out the poison or cut the wound. Keep still, and if possible, have yourself transported to a hospital (that means Phnom Penh or Siem Reap), though there are few (if any) antivenins available in Cambodia. If the snake that bit you is dead, take it with you for identification.

Rabies
Some doctors suggest taking a rabies vaccine if you are planning to spend a long time in rural areas or caves, but for most travelers that's not necessary. If you get bitten by an animal, wash the wound with soap and water, and iodine if available, and go to a hospital as quickly as possible. The danger of contracting rabies is substantially reduced by cleaning the wound immediately. If the animal is dead, take it with you.

Marine Dangers
It's perfectly safe to swim and dive through Cambodia's coral gardens, but a few tips minimize potential risks. Touching or walking on coral not only destroys these tiny organisms, it can also cause serious cuts. Sea urchins are the most obvious annoyance when you enter tropical waters. The spines of these creatures are long and nasty, go through rubber shoes like butter, and can cause infections. Make sure you do not

leave any bits of spines in your wounds and clean them thoroughly. Reef sharks and barracuda, both common in Cambodian waters and often encountered by divers, are more glamorous, but largely imagined, hazards. Unprovoked attacks by these beautiful fish are virtually unheard of, though there's no need to touch or crowd them. In the extremely unlikely event that you encounter anything larger than a reef shark in the Gulf of Thailand, such as an oceanic shark, you are a very lucky diver indeed. There are occasional sightings of whale sharks. The whale shark is the world's biggest fish and is completely harmless. Do not stick your hand into rock crevices as this may bring out a snapping moray eel. Beware of some jellyfish species that trail miles of stinging thread.

Fake Medicines

There are reports of Cambodian clinics and pharmacies prescribing and selling phony pharmaceuticals. The consequences of taking pirated medicines can be serious, so don't purchase anything from hole-in-the-wall outlets and doctors. In Phnom Penh and Siem Reap, the branches of the U-Care pharmacy (daily 8 A.M.–9 P.M.) are reliable.

MEDICAL FACILITIES

Medical facilities of international standard were virtually unheard of in Cambodia as recently as 2007. Since then, the 24-hour Royal Angkor International Hospital (tel. 063/761888, 012/235888, or 063/399111, www.royalangkorhospital.com) in Siem Reap has been treating those with wads of cash or travel insurance. Accident victims in Phnom Penh are often taken to Calmette Hospital, which lacks basic hygiene and equipment, while its staff appears to suffer from a serious lack of work ethics. Avoid this hospital if you can. In the capital, the best place to head is International SOS (161, Street 51, tel. 023/216911 or 012/816911, www.internationalsos.com), which can treat smaller injuries and ailments and help with evacuation procedures in serious cases. Provincial hospitals and other hospitals in the capital, as well as private clinics and dentists, are best avoided. In an emergency in the provinces, contact a nearby NGO and ask for advice.

EVACUATION SERVICES

In Phnom Penh, International SOS (tel. 023/216911 or 012/816911, www.internationalsos.com) can arrange for a plane to pick you up and take you to Singapore or Bangkok for emergency medical treatment. In Siem Reap, the Royal Angkor International Hospital (tel. 063/761888, 012/235888, or 063/399111, www.royalangkorhospital.com) can help with similar arrangements. Make sure you have travel insurance that covers medevac, which can cost up to US$20,000.

SAFETY

Generally, Cambodia is a pretty safe country for travelers. The riskiest aspect of Cambodian life affecting visitors is no doubt the traffic. Ordinary Cambodians want no harm to come to foreign visitors. While some civilians still own guns, armed robbery is relatively rare, though it's wise not to walk around late at night, especially in the capital. Take a taxi instead and always keep your belongings close. Bag snatchers on motorbikes are becoming more common. If possible, check your passports and valuables into the hotel safe, but don't be too paranoid about hotel theft. While theft does take place in midrange establishments, especially in Phnom Penh, it is rare. If you do have everything stolen in a hotel and it looks like an inside job, get in touch with your embassy if the police prove to be unhelpful; embassy staff might, in some cases, be able to mediate.

No doubt, Cambodia as a whole and Phnom Penh in particular offer many opportunities to engage in nefarious behavior. Before you embark on an activity you would not consider at home, remind yourself that looking for the company of thieves in an impoverished, at times desperate, country carries incalculable risks. Tourists who indulge in drugs or prostitution or any other illegal activity in Cambodia are on their own and will need to rely on their own wits to get out of potentially tight spots.

THE CURSE OF THE LANDMINES

The war in Cambodia ended a decade ago, but its deadly legacy continues to harm Cambodian people – in fact, the war lives on underground. Thousands of landmines and UXO (unexploded ordnance) lie buried in Cambodia's fertile soil. The United States attacks against North Vietnam on Cambodian soil in the 1960s, the Khmer Rouge government in the 1970s, and the Vietnamese army and the Cambodian army in the 1980s and 1990s have all contributed to Cambodia's accumulation of landmines and buried bombs, and have made the kingdom the most heavily mined country on the planet.

The result is a human tragedy of epic proportions: Cambodia has one of the world's highest rates for landmine victims – one in every 275 people has been maimed by a mine or by UXO.

NGOs and government agencies have been working on mine clearance for many years. The Cambodian Mine Action Center (CMAC) is the biggest organization, with more than 2,300 staff. The Hazardous Areas Life (Support) Organization (HALO Trust) has 1,200 staff. The Mines Advisory Group (MAG) trains Cambodians in mine clearance and also carries out de-mining. The Royal Cambodian Armed Forces conduct de-mining in support of government priorities, such as the development of infrastructure. All these groups are gathered under the Cambodian Mine Action and Victim Assistance Authority (CMAA), which was set up to regulate and coordinate mine action throughout the country.

Cambodia ratified the International Mine Ban Treaty in 1999 and aims to be mine-impact-free by 2012, though this does not seem to be a realistic target. De-mining work in Cambodia relies almost entirely on international funding. On January 19, 2007, seven de-miners from CMAC died, and the NGO's work drew concerns among donors when CMAC and higher authorities blocked an investigation into the incident. This raised questions about the competence of the de-miners and the transparency of the Cambodian government.

Despite these problems, the situation is improving, with a steady decline in casualties figure from 875 in 2005 to 450 in 2006. No matter whether an area has been de-mined or not, the risks never disappear completely. It is quite common for long-buried UXO to rise to the ground surface during the rainy season, thus making areas that had already been de-mined unsafe once more. *Never, ever leave well-trodden paths, always listen to the advice of local people, and don't go trekking into the wilderness by yourself.*

Traffic

Cambodia offers some of the most dangerous driving conditions in Southeast Asia. With the construction of new roads and rising incomes, the number of vehicles has increased dramatically in the past decade. The local driving style is haphazard, and accidents, often fatal, are shockingly frequent. Cambodia has no effective drivers license system in place. Many cars driving around the country have no plates and are not insured. People die on Cambodia's roads every day and the average Cambodian who has crashed his bike or car on a highway will not be picked up by an ambulance. At best he will end up in a provincial hospital where there are virtually no facilities. If the injuries are severe, the accident victim almost always dies. And the same goes for foreigners who don't have travel insurance. Those who do have insurance will want to be airlifted to Singapore or Bangkok in case of a serious accident. Several tourists die in traffic accidents every year.

Until a few years ago, Phnom Penh was one of the most traffic-free cities in Asia. Now, traffic jams in the early mornings and early evenings block the main arteries, but it's still not nearly as bad as in Bangkok or Ho Chi Minh City. During the water festival, traffic in the capital is brought to a virtual standstill.

In Cambodia, people drive on the right-hand side of the road. Driving at night is not recommended. Plenty of nighttime traffic in the countryside doesn't use any kind of lighting, while most drivers on the roads of Phnom Penh in the small hours appear to be drunk.

Major towns are linked by surfaced highways. Notable exceptions are the northeastern provinces of Ratanakiri and Mondulkiri, where there are no surfaced roads at all.

All this is not to say that one should not drive in Cambodia. I've logged thousands of kilometers around the country, on both motorbikes and in cars. Drive responsibly, wear a helmet, and give way.

Police

The Cambodian police is underpaid—regular street cops earn as little as US$25 a month—and has a reputation for corruption. Make sure you follow traffic rules, otherwise you might be asked to pay anything from a few dollars to outrageous demands of US$50 for a minor infraction at one of the numerous informal roadblocks the authorities have set up, primarily in Phnom Penh. In case of a robbery, the police are likely to be of little help, and do not, as a rule, investigate or fill out the necessary insurance forms unless they are induced to do so. You can reach the tourist police in Phnom Penh at 012/942484.

Drugs

Recreational drugs are illegal in Cambodia. That includes marijuana, despite the fact that the plant is traditionally used in Cambodian cooking and is available more or less openly in Phnom Penh. Marijuana's availability may have more to do with the general culture of impunity than with a policy of tolerance, and tourists occasionally are arrested for flaunting that impunity or for becoming involved in big deals. While it may be possible to pay to get out of a tight spot, there is no guarantee for this—and Cambodian prisons have a reputation as fearsome places best avoided. If you do indulge, be very discreet. Several pizza outlets in the capital offer so-called "happy" pizzas, topped with ganja. Strictly speaking, they are illegal, but they are sold openly.

Most other drugs seem to have reached Phnom Penh. Opium from Laos (none grows

in Cambodia) and cheap amphetamines from Thailand are sometimes offered to tourists on Phnom Penh's riverfront. Given that you don't know what you're getting and that a thousand eyes will watch your every move, succumbing to temptation could be a really bad idea. The Siem Reap that visitors experience is virtually drug-free, though marijuana is occasionally offered to young tourists.

Prostitution

Most visitors will notice that Cambodia's nightlife has a dark edge. Prostitution, though illegal, is nothing new to Cambodia and very much part of ordinary life in towns across the country. Countless local brothels cater to Cambodian men. But with the arrival of highly paid U.N. personnel in the early 1990s, the sex business got a serious shot in the arm and expanded rapidly. Today, it's everywhere. Check into a midrange guesthouse or hotel, and you might be offered a massage of dubious intent at the reception desk as you check in. Go to any number of bars in the capital, and you will be accosted by armies of cash-strapped hostesses, usually called taxi girls, eager to be taken home.

Several bars also employ male sex workers. The economic and social circumstances are no different for these male escorts as they are for the taxi girls.

Many of Cambodia's sex workers are migrants, legal or otherwise, from Vietnam. Tens of thousands of girls and young women are pressed into the sex business, and pedophilia has become an increasing problem in recent years, not just amongst Cambodians. Foreigners too search for underage sex in Cambodia. British rock star Gary Glitter, who had been convicted in the United Kingdom in 1999 for storing images of sex with minors on his computer, spent quite some time in Cambodia, until he was deported in 2002. In 2005, Glitter was convicted of sex with minors in Vietnam, where he served prison time until 2008. But Glitter is just one high-profile case amongst many. As long as sex with minors is practiced by Cambodians, as long as the police turn a blind eye to people with cash or clout, and as long as young girls and

UNTAC, AIDS, AND TAXI GIRLS: CAMBODIA'S SEX INDUSTRY

As Cambodia emerged from decades of war in the early 1990s, the country was facing a multitude of serious problems, including a massive gender imbalance: It's estimated that for every 100 men, there were 135 women under the age of 20. The survivors were poorer than they had ever been since French rule in the 1920s and a severe lack of education, coupled with virtually no infrastructure and the exploitation of the poor by corrupt officials and business leaders, only exacerbated the situation for young women. Polygamy became widespread. While women headed 30 percent of all households, almost half the population was under 15 years of age. Half of all women could not read.

When 22,000 United Nations Transitional Authority in Cambodia (UNTAC) troops, along with foreign businessmen and NGO staff, arrived in 1992, the number of sex workers, so-called "taxi girls," in the capital increased from an estimated 1,000 to more than 20,000 in two years. Initially most of these women were Vietnamese, but they were soon joined by Thais, Filipinas, and, of course, Cambodian women. At the height of the UNTAC presence in 1993, more than 100,000 women worked in the sex industry. An HIV/AIDS epidemic, which continues to this day, was the immediate result.

The foreigners had little notion of Khmer cultural attitudes towards sex, and the sex workers had no knowledge of the risks of sexually transmitted diseases. At the same time, casinos and red light districts were established for Thais along the border within Cambodia, in order to circumvent Thailand's strict gambling laws. Thousands of Thais flocked into Koh Kong and Poipet in search of sex workers. Sex tourists from Western countries discovered Cambodia and many of the bars in Phnom Penh, Siem Reap, Sihanoukville, and Battambang began catering specifically to Western men looking for female company.

According to the United Nations Development Program (UNDP), HIV was first detected in Cambodia in 1991. The first confirmed AIDS case followed in 1993. By 1997, more than 200,000 adults were living with HIV/AIDS. The overall infection rate was 3.3 percent among all adults, and more than 30 percent among sex workers. Due to the easy availability of condoms and several governmental and NGO awareness campaigns, the infection rate declined to 1.9 percent by 2003. But the epidemic is shifting – to women. Husband-to-wife and mother-to-child transmissions are now the most common ways to get infected.

Today, more than 90 percent of Cambodians are aware of the disease and the Ministry of Education includes HIV education in its national curriculum. What's more, Cambodia is one of the few developing nations that has made antiretroviral medication available to some citizens with HIV/AIDS. But with drug users and freelance sex workers barely targeted, education will remain crucial to further reductions.

sometimes boys can barely survive on the money their parents make planting rice, the problem is unlikely to go away.

Thanks to NGO and government initiatives, the openness with which sex criminals broke the law just a few years ago has gone. Many of the cruelest manifestations of the business have shifted into a murky underground scene, invisible to casual visitors. If you have any information regarding the sexual exploitation of children, call the national help hotline (tel. 023/997919).

Demonstrations and Elections

Cambodia's political life is often tumultuous and sometimes violent. Demonstrators may clash with security forces, and political acts of violence, such as assassinations of vocal social critics and political candidates, are unfortunately far too common, especially around election time. For foreign visitors, there's no reason to become involved in the twists and turns of Cambodian politics and it's best to stay away from large political gatherings.

Information and Services

TOURIST INFORMATION

Cambodia's tourist offices are not well equipped to deal with requests for information and staff rarely speak English. In many guesthouses, smaller hotels, and eco-lodges around the country, staff can be quite informed about the local area. There are no Cambodian tourist offices abroad.

For up-to-date listings, the so-called Canby Guides, which cover Siem Reap, Phnom Penh, and Sihanoukville, are of some use. In Siem Reap and Phnom Penh, Pocket Cambodia Guides offer tips on dining, sleeping, and partying.

The best independent Internet source on travel in Cambodia is www.talesofasia.com. For hotels, currency rates, weather, and some cultural information, visit www.tourismcambodia.com.

MAPS

Reliable provincial maps can be bought in bookshops and at the Central Market in Phnom Penh. The German Embassy in Phnom Penh has published a good Cambodian road atlas in Khmer and English, which is free and can be found in some hotels. The petroleum company Total has published a similar atlas, in French and English, with some travel information included. Try and find it at Monument Books (111, Norodom Blvd., tel. 023/217617) in Phnom Penh.

MONEY

Cambodia's official currency is the riel, but U.S. dollars and, in the western part of the country, Thai baht are also widely used. Tourists who use only dollars tend to pay a bit more than those who try to conduct at least simple transactions, such as bills in guesthouses and restaurants, in riel. In the countryside, dollars will be accepted, but local people generally stick to the riel. There are no coins in Cambodia and the riel comes in 100, 200, 500, 1,000, 2,000, 5,000, 10,000, 20,000, 50,000, and 100,000

bills. In tourist areas, prices on menus and expensive souvenirs tend to be in U.S. dollars. This guide quotes prices as they are quoted in the country.

Your change in any transaction could be in riel or U.S. dollars or even Thai baht. Change smaller than US$1 will invariably be in riel.

ATMs always dispense U.S. dollars, generally can be accessed with Visa and MasterCard, and are found in the major cities. In provincial capitals, bank machines are only likely to accept Visa cards. ANZ Bank has the largest number of ATMs, but in the provinces, only ACLEDA Bank offers international banking services and ATMs.

Changing money in tourist centers and provincial banks is generally not a problem, especially if you change Euros. Banks will give you U.S. dollars in exchange. If you want to stock up on riel, head for a money-changer. Their stalls are usually located around market areas. Don't expect better rates than the official exchange rate, though. Travelers checks can be changed in banks in major cities and provincial capitals as long as they are in U.S. dollars or Euros. Expect to pay 2 percent commission.

Major credit cards are becoming more accepted at hotels and restaurants, as well as some upmarket shops and all airlines operating in Cambodia. Be careful, though, as there's often a 5 percent charge to the customer. It's also possible to get cash advances on major credit cards in Phnom Penh, Siem Reap, and the provincial capitals, though sometimes only Visa cards are accepted. Major hotels in Siem Reap and Phnom Penh also offer cash advances, but besides the 5 percent or so surcharge, the exchange rate is also not as competitive as the banks'.

Tipping may not be common in Cambodia, but in restaurants and hotels, it is welcome as the staff earn very little. Bargaining is part of virtually every money transaction in the street or at the local market. Bargain for taxi, tuk-tuk, and *motodup* fares, but keep it all in proportion:

Saving 1,000 riel, which you will hardly notice spending, means depriving a Cambodian of a significant part of his daily income.

COMMUNICATIONS AND MEDIA
Internet Access

Internet cafés are widespread in Cambodia and even smaller towns usually have one or two. In Phnom Penh and Siem Reap, Internet access is often provided in bars and restaurants, and some hotels now offer in-room Wi-Fi. Compared to the United States, Internet speed is slow in Cambodia. Since power outages are relatively common, you should frequently save important documents while you're working. The more sophisticated Internet cafés will have USB ports on their computers, as well as printing and CD-burning facilities and Internet phone software. Calling abroad is cheapest via the Internet. Rates range 300–1,300 riel, depending on the country you call. It's cheapest to call the United States and European countries, while calls to neighboring countries such as Thailand can be more expensive.

Telephones
CELL PHONES

Because of Cambodia's abominable infrastructure, cell phones have been the preferred choice of communication for years. Tall glass boxes, covered with stickers of phone prefixes, are the equivalent of a phone box in the West. Behind the glass box a local with a bag full of phones (one for each prefix) will hand you the one that corresponds to the number you want to ring. Rates are very reasonable, around 300–500 riel per minute. This is cheaper than using a landline if you want to make a regional call.

Since 2009, foreigners have been able to buy SIM cards, which can be topped up with prepaid cards everywhere in Cambodia. If you are refused a SIM card, ask a Cambodian to help. A *motodup* will most likely be glad to help out. SIM cards cost around US$10, depending on the prefix you purchase. Roaming charges for international mobiles are hefty in Cambodia. Mobile numbers start with 01, 08, and 09.

PUBLIC TELEPHONES

The years of civil war destroyed Cambodia's

the stall of a money-changer at the Central Market in Phnom Penh

© AROON THAEWCHATTURAT

telephone system, but it is slowly being rebuilt. Local calls are cheap, while regional calls are better made on a local mobile. Big cities and towns are all on a national grid now and have their own local codes. Nevertheless, many hotel numbers in this guide are for mobile phones. There are few public phone booths in Cambodia, but those that do exist can be used for international calls, providing you have a MPTC or Camintel phone card (available at hotels, post offices, and some shops for US$5–50). Using an Internet phone in an Internet café is usually cheaper, quicker, and more convenient.

TV, Radio, and Film

A couple of decades ago, the country's media barely existed. Cambodian television and radio have come into their own in recent years and besides the rather staid and controlled government channels, several private channels bombard the population with a mixture of game shows, soap operas upholding traditional stereotypes, karaoke clips, and news that is shaped by whoever owns the station. Press freedom in Cambodia is limited, assassinations of local journalists are not unheard of, and the flow of real information from the mass media to the people is poor. Contemporary Cambodian movies tend to be cheap romances or gruesome no-budget horror flicks. There are notable exceptions by a new generation of Cambodian filmmakers, such as Rithy Pan with his movie *The Rice People.*

Radio Love FM 97.5 MHz is the country's only English-language radio station and plays Western pop music. Radio Australia 101.5 FM, BBC World Service Radio FM 100, and the Voice of America broadcast in and around Phnom Penh and Siem Reap. Several television channels feature news in English. All other broadcasting is in Khmer, though satellite TV (including UBC) is widely available.

The English-Language Press

The *Cambodia Daily* (www.cambodiadaily. com) and the *Phnom Penh Post* (www.phnompenhpost.com) are the two most important English-language newspapers published in Cambodia. The *Daily* carries international news culled from mainstream American and European papers and does some fine local reporting. The *Phnom Penh Post* used to be a critical, courageous, and well-informed biweekly publication, but went daily in 2008, losing some of its bite in the process. *Asia Life* (www.asialifehcmc.com) is a free monthly listings publication with tourist-friendly articles. The monthly *South Eastern Globe* (www.se-globe.com), published since 2006, is Cambodia's only professionally produced and critical news magazine. With substantial features, great photography, and its finger on Cambodia's pulse, this publication is a good introduction to what's going on in the country and the region.

WEIGHTS AND MEASURES

Cambodia uses the metric system. Electricity is 220 volts, and power cuts are common in the provinces and not unheard of in the capital. Siem Reap seems to have the most reliable power supply. Electrical sockets are of the two-prong variety, either with round pins, as in the United States, or with flat pins, as in neighboring Thailand.

RESOURCES

Glossary

anastylosis archaeological technique to reconstruct monuments by dismantling and subsequent rebuilding a structure

apsara heavenly nymph, often depicted on Khmer temple walls

asura demon

baht Thai currency

barang Western foreigner

baray ancient water reservoir

bodhisattva a person or being who uses his wisdom to help others towards enlightenment

boeung lake

Brahma important Hindu deity, creator of the world

Cham this term refers to two groups of people, the people who lived in Champa, an empire which spread across today's Central and South Vietnam between the 2nd and 15th century. Today's Cham are a Muslim minority in Cambodia.

chedi a cone-shaped edifice under which Buddhist relics or the ashes of a Buddhist teacher are buried.

chunchiet Khmer term for Cambodia's indigenous minorities

cyclo bicycle-powered rickshaw

deva god

devaraja god king

devata female guardian spirit

Ganesh popular Hindu deity with an elephant head, son of Shiva, remover of obstacles

garuda mythical half-man, half-bird figure

gopura pavilion, entrance hall in Hindu temples

Kampuchea the name Cambodians call their country

Khmer an ethnic Cambodian, the Cambodian language

Khmer Issarak Cambodian nationalist rebel movement of the 1940s

Khmer Krom ethnic Khmer living in Vietnam's Mekong Delta

Khmer Loeu Cambodia's indigenous minorities

Khmer Rouge term coined by King Sihanouk for Cambodia's communist movement, which seized power in 1975 and engaged in a cruel four-year socialist experiment, costing the lives of millions of Cambodians

kimji fermented cabbage, a standard Korean dish

kouprey possibly extinct Cambodian jungle ox

krama Cambodia's traditional, all-purpose scarf

Krishna one of the most popular gods in the Hindu pantheon, seen by some Hindus as an avatar of Vishnu, by others as a Supreme Being; he is depicted as god child, lover or Supreme Being

Lakshmi Hindu goddess of wealth and prosperity; she is the consort of Vishnu and married Rama (under the name of Sita)

linga, lingam phallic symbol

lintel a carved sandstone block above doorways into temples

Mahayana also called Great Vehicle, a branch of Buddhism

mahoot elephant handler

montagnard French term for Indochina's indigenous minorities

motodup motorcycle taxi driver

Mount Meru home of Shiva, in Hindu mythology

naga mythical snake, often featured in Khmer architecture

nagara Sanskrit for capital; Angkor is supposedly a mutation of this word

Norry unofficial hand car used by local people on some of Cambodia's railway tracks

Pali Indian language and part origin of the Khmer language

payapee the Irrawaddy dolphin

phnom hill or mountain

pho Vietnamese noodle soup

phsar market

prahoc fermented fish paste, the staple protein source for most Cambodians

prasat temple or palace hall, or general word for temple

preah sacred

Rama incarnation of Vishnu and hero of the Ramayana and Reamker

Ravana demon of the Ramayana and Reamker

Reamker Khmer version of the Ramayana, an epic Hindu poem

riel Cambodia's currency

sampot traditional piece of cloth that is wrapped around the waist (like a sarong)

sangha assembly of monks

sangharaja head of assembly of monks

Sanskrit Indian language and part origin of the Khmer language

Shiva Hinduism's most important deity, creator and destroyer of the universe

stung river

stupa a cone-shaped edifice under which Buddhist relics or the ashes of a Buddhist teacher are buried

temple mountain architectural design that represents the mythological mountain, Mount Meru, home to the Hindu pantheon

thali Indian meal of rice, several types of vegetables, fish or meat, yogurt, chapati, and rice

-varman suffix attached to the names of Khmer rulers, means as much as "protected by"

vihear main building of a Buddhist pagoda

Vishnu important Hindu deity, protector of the world

wat Thai word designating a contemporary Cambodian Buddhist temple complex

yoni female fertility symbol and the counterpart to the lingam

yuon derogatory word the Khmer use for the Vietnamese

ABBREVIATIONS

ASEAN Association of Southeast Asian Nations

CIA Central Intelligence Agency, the United States' secret service

CPP Cambodian People Party

DK Democratic Kampuchea, the Khmer Rouge incarnation of the country

EFEO Ecole Francaise d'Extreme Orient

FUNCINPEC Front Uni National pur un Cambodge Independent, Neutre, Pacifique et Coopeativ, Cambodia's royalist political party

KGB Soviet-era Russian secret service

KPNLAF right-wing rebel force aligned with the Khmer Rouge and FUNCINPEC to fight the liberation of Cambodia by the Vietnamese

KR Khmer Rouge

NGO nongovernmental organization

NVA/NLF The North Vietnamese Army/National Front for the Liberation of South Vietnam

PRPK People's Revolutionary Party of Kampuchea

RCAF Royal Cambodian Armed Forces

SRP Sam Rainsy Party

UNESCO United Nations Educational, Scientific and Cultural Organization

UNTAC United Nations Transitional Authority in Cambodia

Khmer Phrasebook

PRONUNCIATION GUIDE

Khmer, unlike Lao, Thai, and Vietnamese, is not a tonal language, which means that one word has one meaning that does not change with slight changes in pronunciation. Khmer grammar is simple, sentences follow a subject, verb, object structure, and nouns do not change with singular and plural. Nevertheless, speaking Khmer is not easy as there are some sounds that cannot be easily replicated by English speakers. What follows are approximations.

Vowels

No one knows how many vowels there are in Khmer, as the language has not been properly set out by local scholars. The precise number of vowels therefore varies from dialect to dialect. For the purposes of this phrasebook, commonly used vowel sounds are described here.

a	as in "cat"
ah	as in "father"
ai	as in "sky"
ao	as in "cow"
au	as in "bond"
aw	as in "draw"
ay	as in "play"
e	as in "bet"
ea	as in "yeah"
ee	as in "tea"
eh	as in "telephone"
eu	as in the French "peuple"
ew	as in "few"
i	as in "bit"
o	as in "toe"
oa	as in "toe" but the vowel is cut short
oo	as in "zoo"
oy	as in "toy"
u	as in "fun"
uh	as in "album"

Consonants

Khmer consonants often occur in clusters that are hard for nonnative-speakers to pronounce. Some of the very common, but, for the Western ear, not exactly definable consonants, are listed here.

bp	no such sound in English; in between "b" and "p"
ch	as in "child"
dt	no such sound in English; in between "d" and "t"
g	as in "go"
j	as in "June"
k	as in "king"
ng	as in "ring"
ny	as in "union"
ph	as in "plain"
r	as in "red" but with a hard rolling sound
th	as in "tell"
wr	as in "red"

Stress

Most Khmer words have one or two syllables and the stress usually falls on the second syllable. Longer words tend to be modern and often refer to science or arts. Such words borrow from Sanskrit, Pali, and French.

BASIC AND COURTEOUS EXPRESSIONS

Hello (formal). *juhm reeab sooa.*
Hello. *soo'as dai.*
Good morning (used rarely). *a'roon soo'as dai.*
Good evening (used rarely). *prolop soo'as dai.*
Good night (used rarely). *reea trai soo'as dai.*
Good night (I go to bed). *k'ngnyom dto dtaic.*
How are you? *soksabai?*
Very well, thank you. *k'ngnyom soksabai jeea-dteh.*
Okay; good. *k'ngnyom meun aidteh.*
Not okay; bad. *k'ngnyom meun soksabai dteh.*
So-so. *k'ngnyom tawm madah dteh.*
And you? *joa ngea win?*
Please. *somehdtah.*
Thank you. *awkuhn.*
Thank you very much. *awkuhn chahran.*
You're very kind. *ngea geu chet bahn na.*

You're welcome. *man aidteh.*
Goodbye. *lee-a haoee.*
See you later. *dchooab kneer pail graoee.*
yes *dcha* (f.), *baht* (m.)
no *ahdtay*
I don't know. *k'ngnyom adt dang.*
Just a moment, please. *Som mehdah jahm mooee playt.*
Excuse me/Sorry. *somdtuh.*
My name is . . . *k'ngnyom chmooa . . .*
What is your name? *dtaeu ngea chmooa ai?*
Pleased to meet you. *wridt reeay.*
Do you speak English? *tah ngea niyai anglais?*
Is there anyone here who speaks English? *meean ngea nah niyai anglais no dteeni?*
I don't speak Khmer. *k'ngnyom meun niyai peeyai-sah khmer.*
Please speak slowly. *som niyai yuhdt yuhdt.*
I understand. *k'ngnyom yuhl.*
I don't understand. *k'ngnyom adt yuhl.*
No problem. *aut bannye hah.*
How do you say . . . in English? *dtah . . . hao dtah meud jeea peeyai-sah anglais?*
Would you like . . . *dtah ngeea jawng . . .*
Let's go to . . . *dtaw ngoam kngeea dto . . .*

TERMS OF ADDRESS

I *k'ngnyom*
you (formal) *ngea*
you (informal) *ain/hain*
you (plural) *ngea dtaeng aw kngeea*
he/him *kuhadt*
she/her *kuhadt* (older), *ngeeang* (younger)
we/us *yeung/puhyeung*
they/them *puhkai*
Mr., sir *looc*
Mrs., madam *looc srey*
Miss, young lady *ganyah*
husband *p'dtai*
wife *prawpuhn*
friend *meutpe*
sweetheart *ouhnsamlann* (f.), *bawngsamlann* (m.)
boyfriend *meut praw*
girlfriend *meut srei*
son *gawn praws*

daughter *gawn srei*
brother *bawng praw* (older), *ba-own praw* (younger)
sister *bawng srei* (older), *ba-own* (younger)
father *aeu puhk*
mother *madai*
grandfather *dtah*
grandmother *yai*

TRANSPORTATION

Where is . . . ? *gawn lain nah . . . ?*
How far is it to . . . ? *jangnai baun nah dto . . . ?*
from . . . to . . . *bpee . . . dto . . .*
Where (Which) is the way to . . . ? *ploeu nah dto . . . ?*
the bus station *jomm nawd ruhtyunnkrong*
the bus stop *gnai lahnkrong chuk*
Where is this bus going? *dtah lahn krong nee dto nah?*
the taxi stand *jomm nawd lahn taxi*
the train station *sattanee ruhtpleum*
the boat *dtoo*
the dock *dto salang*
the airport *prawleean yuhnhoa*
I'd like to buy a ticket to . . . *k'ngnyom jomm dteng samboat . . .*
first/second class *muh/kraoee*
round-trip *dto mao*
reservation *kao*
baggage *aiwann*
Stop here, please. *som chuhb naeu dteeni.*
the entrance *plao jol*
the exit *plao chen*
the ticket office *gonlain dtinn sambot*
near *jet/kbai* (depends on context)
far *chnai*
to/toward *toeu gann*
by/through *chlong gadt*
from *bpee*
the right *s'damm*
the left *chueng*
straight ahead *dteu dtrong*
in front *bee muk*
beside *jet/kbai*
behind *kahng groaee*
the corner *gachrung*
the stoplight *pleung stop*
a turn *baud*

right here *dtrong dknai nee*
somewhere around here *meudtaum kbai nee*
road *plao*
street *plao*
highway *plao jiat*
kilometer *kilomedt*
bridge *speeann*
toll *loi kongtrau*
address *assaiyatahn*
north *kahngjeung*
south *kahngt'bong*
east *kahnggaot*
west *kahnglait*

ACCOMMODATIONS
hotel *santahgeea*
Is there a room available? *mien bantuhk tuhmnay?*
May I see it? *k'ngnyom saum meul banh dteh?*
What is the rate? *daumlai bannmahn?*
Is there something cheaper? *Mien ahseing taochieng ni?*
single room *bauntuhk samrahp maunuh menea*
double room *bauntuhk samrahp maunuh bpee nea*
double bed *krea kaying bpee nea*
twin beds *krea pbee*
with private bathroom *mien bahntuhkteuk*
hot water *teuk k'dao*
shower *teuk p'gah chuhk*
towels *gaun saing*
soap *saboo*
toilet paper *kreua dah juhd moat* (lit., tissue)
blanket *pooee*
sheets *gomrah bpook*
air-conditioned *mahsinn drawjea*
fan *gong hah*
key *sao*
manager *neakruhbkrong*

FOOD
I'm hungry. *k'ngnyom klienn bai.*
I'm thirsty. *k'ngnyom srai teuk.*
breakfast *ahhah beilbpreuk*
lunch *ahhah tngnai dtrong*

dinner *ahhah beileungnee-ek*
snack *jamngai ngahmleing*
menu *maunui*
order *g'mong*
the check *kat loi*
glass *kao*
fork *saum*
knife *gahmbut*
spoon *slahpreea*
napkin *kreua dah juhd moat* (lit., tissue)
soft drink *peasechia*
coffee *kahfai*
tea *dtai*
drinking water *teuk pak*
bottled carbonated water *teuk soda*
bottled uncarbonated water *teuk saut*
beer *s'rahbeer*
wine *s'rah*
milk *teukdawgo*
juice *teukplaicheu*
sugar *skaw*
salt *ahmball*
eggs *bpong dteea*
bread *nuhmbpang*
chili *mateh*
rice *bai*
soup *suhp*
fruit *plai cheu*
vegetables *baunlai*
fish *dtray*
shellfish *keptaepkluonaeng*
shrimp *baunggeea*
meat (without) *(komm dea) sait*
chicken *sait mauan*
pork *sait chruh*
beef *sait go*
fried *chah*
grilled *ang*
roasted *ang*
barbecue *ang*
spicy *hall*
not spicy *adt hall*

SHOPPING
money *loi*
bank *tauneeageea*
money-exchange bureau *gariyahlai dopra*
What is the exchange rate? (How many

riel for one dollar?) *muhi dollah p'do bahn baunnmahn loi riel?*

How much is the commission? *Bahn kaumissong baunmahn?*

Do you accept credit cards? *dta k'ngnyom ahg prao credit card?*

How much does it cost? *daumlai bannmahn?*

What is your final price? *dtai baunn neung?*

expensive *t'lai*

cheap *tao*

more *teym dtiedt*

less *teakchieng ngeh* (specific for food, money)

a little *baun teak*

too much *chrahn bpeik*

HEALTH

Help me please. *sommehdtah juhee k'ngnyom paung.*

I am ill. *k'ngnyom cheu.*

Call a doctor. *dooresap hao doctor.*

Take me to . . . *yau k'ngnyom dto . . .*

hospital *muhndtee pead*

drugstore *fahrmacee*

pain *cheu*

fever *krung k'dao*

headache *cheu k'bahl*

stomachache *cheu bpuh*

burn *rawleek*

cramp *lemool krawpeu*

nausea *mien ahram tahcheu*

vomiting *k'aood*

diarrhea *ree aht*

medicine *t'namm peadt*

antibiotic *t'namm p'sa*

pill; tablet *gruhap t'namm*

aspirin *aspirin*

bandage *baung ruhm raubuh*

sanitary napkins *samlay a-namai*

birth control pills *t'namm buhnyeea kaumnaodt*

condoms *sraom a-namai/condom*

toothbrush *chra*

toothpaste *t'namm-dogh-t'meung*

dental floss *ksai samahdt anchahn-t'meung*

dentist *pead t'meung*

toothache *cheu t'meung*

POST OFFICE AND COMMUNICATIONS

long-distance telephone *dtoolasap graheu prawteh* (lit., overseas call)

I would like to call . . . *k'ngnyom chaung dtoolasap . . .*

credit card *credit card*

post office *praysannee*

letter *saumbaut*

stamp *teamp*

postcard *bahn praysannee*

air mail *air mail*

package *geanjawb*

box *lang*

string *k'sai*

tape *scot*

AT THE BORDER

border *bruhmdain*

customs *goi*

immigration *police antao prawes*

inspection *chaik*

passport *passpaw-likatchlongdain*

profession *muhkrawbaw*

single *naolee-uh*

married *reapgah*

divorced *leanglea*

widowed *mehmai* (f.), *bpuhmai* (m.)

insurance *teeaneer-rapraung*

title *neeam k'puhng bpuh*

drivers license *banbahlbaw*

AT THE GAS STATION

gas station *sattani chiadtsang*

gasoline *sang*

full *peunn*

tire *saumbawgang*

air *bom k'chahl*

water *teuk*

oil (change) *p'dau prayn mahssin*

My . . . doesn't work. *. . . rawbau k'ngnyom kodt.*

battery *ahkuhi*

radiator *tuhng dteuk*

alternator *deenamo*

generator *mahssin pleun*

tow truck *lahn samdao*

repair shop *gaunlain chuha-chaul*

auto parts store *gaunlain luh gruhang lahn*

NUMBERS

0 *son*
1 *muhi*
2 *bpee*
3 *bai*
4 *buhan*
5 *pram*
6 *prammuhi*
7 *pram bpee*
8 *pram bai*
9 *pram buhan*
10 *daup*
11 *daup muhi*
12 *daup bpee*
13 *daup bai*
14 *daup buhan*
15 *daup pram*
16 *daup pram muhi*
17 *daup pram bpee*
18 *daup pram bai*
19 *daup pram buhan*
20 *maupay*
21 *maupay muhi*
30 *sahmsap*
40 *saisap*
50 *hasap*
60 *hoksap*
70 *jetsap*
80 *peadsap*
90 *gaosap*
100 *muhroi*
101 *muhroi muhi*
200 *bpee roi*
500 *pram roi*
1,000 *muhi-puh-aun*
10,000 *muhi meun*
100,000 *muhi sayn*
1,000,000 *muhi leean*
one-half *gaunnla*
one-third *muhi peeabai*
one-fourth *muhi peeabuhan*

TIME

What time is it? *maong baunmahn haoee?*
It's one o'clock. *maong muhi guht*
It's three in the afternoon. *maong bai rawseel.*
It's four in the morning. *maong buhan preuk.*
six-thirty *maong pram muhi gaunla*
a quarter till eleven *kwa dta pram maong dta muhi*
a quarter past five *maong pram leu dta pram ngeeadtee*
noon *tangngai dtrong*
midnight *ahtriadt*
one minute *muhi neeadtee*
one hour *muhi maong*

DAYS, MONTHS, AND SEASONS

Monday *tangngai jan*
Tuesday *tangngai aungkeea*
Wednesday *tangngai puht*
Thursday *tangngai prawhaw*
Friday *tangngai sauk*
Saturday *tangngai sao*
Sunday *tangngai ahteut*
January *kai meagreah*
February *kai guhmpeak*
March *kai mineea*
April *kai mehsah*
May *kai uhsapeea*
June *kai mi-tauknah*
July *kai gakadah*
August *kai saihah*
September *kai ganya*
October *kai tauklah*
November *kai wichikah*
December *kai t'noo*
dry season *kai reang*
hot season *kai k'daol*
rainy season *kai pleeang*
today *t'ngai ni*
tomorrow *t'ngai s'aik*
yesterday *masseu muhan*
now *ailaoni*
day *t'ngnai*
week *sabpadah*
month *kai*
year *chnam*
after *bauntoabp*
before *muhn*

Khmer Names

The Khmer language, *aksar Khmer,* has one of the longest alphabets in the world (35 consonants, 15 independent vowels, and 16 dependent vowels – the latter appear only in combination with a consonant) and is thought to have developed from Indian scripts. The first Khmer inscription dates from the 6th century.

SIEM REAP AND ANGKOR
Siem Reap

Siem Reap	សៀមរាប
Wat Bo	វត្តបូព
Wat Damnak	វត្តដំណាក
Wat Athvea	វត្តអធ្វា
Wat Thmei	វត្តថ្មី

Angkor

Angkor	អង្គរ
Angkor Wat	អង្គរវត្ត
Angkor Thom	អង្គរធំ
The Bayon	បាយ័ន
The Baphuon	បាពួន
The Phimeanakas	ភិមានអាកាស
Phnom Wat Bakheng	វត្តភ្នំបាខែង
Baksei Chamkrong	បក្សីចាំក្រុង
Thomanon	ធម្មនុន
Chaosay Tevoda	ចៅសាយទេវតា
Ta Keo	តាកែវ
Ta Prohm	តាព្រហ្ម
Banteay Kdei	បន្ទាយក្តី
Prasat Kravan	ប្រាសាទក្រវ៉ាន់
Pre Rup	ប្រែរូប
Eastern Mebon	មេបុណ្យខាងកើត

Neak Pean	នាកព័ន្ធ
Ta Som	តាសោម
Preah Khan	ព្រះខ័ន
The Western Baray and Western Mebon	បារាយខាងលិច និង មេបុណ្យខាងលិច
The Roluos Group of Temples	ប្រាសាទរលួស
The Bakong	បាគង
Banteay Samre	បន្ទាយសំរែ
Banteay Srei and Kbal Spean	បន្ទាយស្រី និង ក្បាលស្ពាន
Beng Melea	បឹងមាលា
Phnom Krom	ភ្នំក្រោម
Chong Khneas	ជុងឃ្នាស
Prek Toal	ព្រែកទួល
Kompong Phluk	កំពង់ភ្លុក
Kompong Kleang	កំពង់ឃ្លាំង
Phnom Kulen	ភ្នំគូលែន

PHNOM PENH

Phnom Penh	ភ្នំពេញ
Boeng Kak	បឹងកក់
Wat Phnom	វត្តភ្នំ
The Royal Palace and Silver Pagoda Complex	ព្រះបរមរាជវាំង វាំង និង វត្តព្រះកែវមរកត
The National Museum	សារមន្ទីរជាតិ
Wat Botum	វត្តរាជវរារាម
Wat Ounalom	វត្តឧណ្ណាលោម
The Cambodia Vietnam Monument	ស្នូកមិត្តភាពកម្ពុជាវៀតណាម
The Olympic Stadium	ពហុកីឡដ្ឋានជាតិ
The Independence Monument	វិមានឯករាជ្យ
Wat Moha Montrei	វត្តមហាមន្ត្រី
S-21 Tuol Sleng Museum	ស-២១ សារមន្ទីរឧក្រិដ្ឋទួលស្លែង

Wat Lanka	វត្តលង្កា
Bophana	បុប្ផាណា
Phsar Thmey (Central Market)	ផ្សារធំថ្មី
Phsar Toul Tom Poung (Russian Market)	ផ្សារទូលទំពូង
Phsar Chas (Old Market)	ផ្សារចាស់
Phsar Orussey (Orussey Market)	ផ្សារអូរុស្សី
Choeung Ek Killing Fields	វាលពិឃាតបឹងជើងឯក
Oudong	ឧដុង្គ
Tonlé Bati	ទន្លេបាទី
Phnom Chisor	ភ្នំជីសូ
Phnom Tamau Zoological Gardens and Wildlife Rescue Center	រមណីយដ្ឋាន និង សួនសត្វភ្នំតាម៉ៅ

THE COAST

Sihanoukville

Kompong Som (Sihanoukville)	កំពង់សោម
Kirirom National Park	ឧស្យានជាតិគីរីរម្យ
Ream National Park	ឧស្យានជាតិរាម
Koh Rong	កោះរ៉ុង
Koh Rong Samloen	កោះរ៉ុងសន្លើម
Koh Dek Koul	កោះដែកគោល
Koh Pos	កោះពស់
Koh Russei	កោះឫស្សី

Koh Kong

Koh Kong	កោះកុង
Koh Kong Island	កោះកោះកុង
Sre Ambel	ស្រែអំបិល

Kampot

Kampot	កំពត
Phnom Chhnork	ភ្នំឈ្នោក
Phnom Sorsia	ភ្នំសសៀរ
Tekchhou Zoo	សួនសត្វទឹកឈូរ
Bokor National Park	ឧស្យានជាតិបូកគោ
Bokor Hill Station	ស្ថានីយបូកគោ

Kep

Kep	កែប
Koh Tonsay	កោះទន្សាយ
Kompong Trach	កំពង់ត្រាច

Takeo

Takeo	តាខ្មៅ
Angkor Borei	អង្គរបុរី
Phnom Da	ភ្នំដា

THE TONLÉ SAP BASIN
Kompong Chhnang

Kompong Chhnang	កំពង់ឆ្នាំង
Prasat Srei	ប្រាសាទស្រី

Pursat

Pursat	ពោធិសាត់
Kompong Luong	កំពង់លួង
Phnom Aural National Park	រមណីយដ្ឋានជាតិភ្នំឱរ៉ាល់
Phnom Samkok National Park	រមណីយដ្ឋានភ្នំសំកុក

Battambang

Battambang	បាត់ដំបង
Battambang Museum	សារមន្ទីរបាត់ដំបង

The Bamboo Train	ឡូរី
Wat Ek Phnom	វត្តឯកភ្នំ
Wat Samrong	វត្តសំរោង
Wat Banan	វត្តបាណន់
Wat Phnom Sampeau	វត្តភ្នំសំពៅ
Kamping Poy Reservoir	កំពីងពួយ
Pailin	ប៉ៃលិន

Sisophon

Sisophon	ស៊ីសុផុន
Banteay Chhmar	បន្ទាយឆ្មារ
Banteay Top	បន្ទាយទ័ព

Poipet

Poipet	ប៉ោយប៉ែត

Anlong Veng

Anlong Veng	អន្លង់វែង
Kbal Tonsoung	ក្បាលទន្សោង

Tbeng Meanchey

Tbeng Meanchey	ត្បែងមានជ័យ
Preah Khan	ព្រះខ័ន
Koh Ker	កោះកែ
Preah Vihear	ព្រះវិហារ

Kompong Thom

Kompong Thom	កំពង់ធំ
Wat Kompong	វត្តកំពង់
Sambor Prei Kuk	សម្បូរប្រៃគុហ៍
Phnom Santuk	ភ្នំសន្ទុក

NORTHEASTERN CAMBODIA
Kompong Cham

Kompong Cham	កំពង់ចាម
Koh Paen Island	កោះប៉ែន
Wat Nokor	វត្តនគរ
Phnom Srei and Phnom Proh	ភ្នំស្រី និង ភ្នំប្រុស
Skuon	ស្គុន

Kratie

Kratie	ក្រចេះ
Koh Trong	កោះត្រង់
Phnom Sombok	ភ្នំសំបុក
Sambor	សម្បូរណ៍
Wat Roka Kandal	វត្តរកាកណ្ដាល
Chhlong	ឆ្លូង
Snuol	ស្នួល

Stung Treng

Stung Treng	ស្ទឹងត្រែង
Thala Boravit	ថ្លាបូរវិត
Phnom Preah Tihut	ភ្នំព្រះទីហុត
Siem Pang	សៀមប៉ាង

Banlung

Banlung	បានលុង
Ratanakiri	រតនគីរី
Yeak Lom Lake	បឹងយក្សឡោម
Voen Said	វ៉ឺនសៃ
Virachay National Park	រមណីយដ្ឋានវិរៈជ័យ
Chum Rum Bei	ជុំរុំបី
Lumphat	លំផាត់

Sen Monorom

Sen Monorom	សែនមនោរម្យ
Mondulkiri	មណ្ឌលគីរី
Bou Sraa Waterfall	ទឹកជ្រោះប៊ូស្រា
Monorom Waterfall	ទឹកជ្រោះ មនោរម្យ
Mimong	មីមុង

BORDER CROSSINGS
Thailand

Poipet	ប៉ោយប៉ែត
Koh Kong	កោះកុង
Phsar Prom	ផ្សារ ប្រហ្ម
Daun Lem	ដូនលែម
Anlong Veng	អន្លង់វែង
Chong Sa-Ngam	ចុងសាងាម
O'Smach	អូរស្មាច់

Laos

Dom Kralor	ដំក្រាឡ្យ

Vietnam

O'Yadaw	អូរយ៉ាដាវ
Trapaeng Thlong	ត្រពាំងថ្លុង
Trapaeng Sre	ត្រពាំងស្រែ
Bavet	បាវិត
Kaam Samnor	ក្អមសំណ
Phnom Den	ភ្នំដិន
Prek Chak	ព្រែកចាក

Suggested Reading

Cambodia, along with Vietnam, is the most extensively written about country in Southeast Asia and new titles on the country's history, most of them by foreign authors, are published every year. Many of the titles mentioned here, whether fiction or nonfiction, can be bought as pirate copies in Phnom Penh.

FICTION

Ryman, Geoff. *The King's Last Song*. Easthampton, MA: Small Beer Press, 2008. Uneven but entertaining historical novel juxtaposing scenes from the Angkor court with a crime story from the UNTAC years.

The Reamker. Phnom Penh: Reyum Publishing, 1999. The Khmer version of the *Ramayana*, a famous Hindu epic.

HISTORY AND POLITICS

Becker, Elisabeth. *When the War is Over*. New York: Simon & Schuster, 1986. Exhaustive telling of the Khmer Rouge revolution from the French colonial era to the death of Pol Pot in 1998 by a *Washington Post* journalist who managed to enter Cambodia during the Khmer Rouge years.

Cain, Kenneth, Heidi Postlewait and Andrew Thomson. *Emergency Sex*. London: Ebury Press, 2004. Both hilarious and dispiriting account of three United Nations workers trying to come to grips with post-war societies in Cambodia, Rwanda, Somalia, and Haiti.

Chandler, David. *A History of Cambodia*. Boulder, CO: Westview Press, 2007. Excellent history of Cambodia from its pre-Angkorian origins to its modern period.

Chandler, David. *Voices from S-21: Terror and History in Pol Pot's Secret Prison*. CA: University of California Press, 2000. A study of the archives of Tuol Sleng S-21, the Khmer

Rouge's interrogation camp in Phnom Penh, where some 17,000 people were tortured.

Coates, Karen. *Cambodia Now*. Jefferson, NC: MacFarland & Company, 2005. Captivating analysis of the legacy of the Khmer Rouge terror and how Cambodia deals with its dark past today.

Dunlop, Nick. *The Lost Executioner*. London: Bloomsbury Publishing, 2005. An incredible and personal account by an Irish photojournalist of his search and eventual finding of Comrade Duch, the commandant of the S-21 torture camp in Phnom Penh. Duch was allegedly responsible for more than 20,000 deaths during the Khmer Rouge years. *The Lost Executioner* asks serious questions about why it is taking so long for Khmer Rouge leaders to be brought to justice and contemplates the role of the media in conflict situations.

Kamm, Henry. *Cambodia: Report from a Stricken Land*. New York: Arcade Publishing, 1998. Somewhat revisionist but thorough history of Cambodia between 1970 and 1998, by a Pulitzer-winning *New York Times* correspondent.

Neveu, Roland. *The Fall of Phnom Penh*. Bangkok: Asia Horizons Books, 2007. Stunning photographic account of the fall of Phnom Penh to the Khmer Rouge in 1975 by a French photojournalist.

Osbourne, Milton. *Sihanouk—Prince of Light, Prince of Darkness*. Chiang Mai, Thailand: Silkworm Books, 1994. Critical biography of Cambodia's enigmatic former king.

Shawcross, William. *Sideshow: Kissinger, Nixon and the Destruction of Cambodia*. Pocket Books, 1979. Account of how Cambodia was manipulated and destroyed by the superpower policymakers and the Khmer Rouge.

Short, Philip. *Pol Pot: The History of a Nightmare*. London: John Murray Publishers, 2005. Solidly researched and engagingly written biography of Brother Number 1.

Ta-Kuan, Chou. *The Customs of Cambodia*. Chiang Mai, Thailand: Silkworm Books, 2007. Chou Ta-Kuan wrote the only surviving account of the Angkor Empire after visiting Cambodia in 1296. The text usually available in Cambodia was translated from Chinese into French in 1902, some time later from French into English. A new direct translation from Chinese into English by linguist Peter Harris, correcting mistakes from earlier editions, was published in 2007.

Vickery, Michael. *Cambodia 1975–1982*. Bangkok: White Lotus, 2001. Authoritative, landmark report by one of the leading scholars of Cambodian history, much maligned by revisionist writers. Somewhat dated, but still provides an interesting and unique perspective on the Khmer Rouge period and its causes.

PERSONAL ACCOUNTS OF THE KHMER ROUGE YEARS

Accounts from survivors have almost become a genre in themselves, as more and more refugees who fled to France or the United States put pen to paper, to recall the horrors Cambodia went through in the 1970s. The strength of these books is their subjectivity: The Cambodian tragedy is retold in very personal terms, offering an alternative perspective to academic analysis of the period.

Bizot, Francois. *The Gate*. New York: Vintage, 2004. Gripping telling of the French author's experience of being incarcerated by the Khmer Rouge.

Nath, Vann. *A Cambodian Prison Portrait*. Bangkok: White Lotus, 1998. A firsthand account of the infamous S-21 torture facility by the painter Vann Nath, one of the prison's seven survivors. Nath's harrowing images of Khmer Rouge torture practices are displayed at S-21, the Tuol Sleng Genocide Museum in Phnom Penh.

Seng, Thierry. *Daughter of the Killing Fields*. London: Fusion Press, 2005. Seng, now a high-profile human rights lawyer in Cambodia, was three years old when the Khmer Rouge took over. Besides retelling Seng's incredible story—from her father's death at the hands of the communists, to prison, refugee camps, and flight into a Christian family in the United States—this book is an interesting but at times lopsided retelling of recent Cambodian history.

Ung, Luong. *First They Killed My Father*. Harper Collins, 2001. Ung's account of life as a five-year-old under the Khmer Rouge is based on the author's journey through Cambodia's horrors, from work camp to work camp and finally, escape to Vietnam.

TRAVELOGUES

Livingston, Carol. *Gecko Tails, A Journey Through Cambodia*. London: Trafalgar Square, 1997. The first travelogue about Cambodia to be published in 30 years, this informative book chronicles the journeys and stories of a foreign correspondent in Cambodia in the early 1990s.

Pym, Christopher. *Mitsapim in Cambodia*. London: Hodder & Stoughton, 1960. Quaint travelogue that offers insights into Cambodia prior to the country's 30 years of conflict.

ARCHAEOLOGY

Dagens, Bruno. *Angkor, Heart of an Asian Empire*. London: Thames & Hudson, 1995. Small companion guide to the temples of Angkor with excellent illustrations and information on the Angkor Empire, its subsequent rediscoveries, and the ruins' fate in the 20th century.

Mouhot, Henri. *Travels in Siam, Cambodia, Laos and Annam*. Bangkok: White Lotus,

2000 reprint, orig. 1864. Mouhot, a natural history researcher, rediscovered the ruins of Angkor in the Cambodian jungle.

Rooney, Dawn F. *Angkor*. Hong Kong: Odyssey Publications, 2001. Brilliant illustrated introduction to the temples of Angkor.

NATURE AND FIELD GUIDES

Francis, Charles. *A Guide to the Mammals of Southeast Asia*. Princeton, NJ: Princeton Press, 2008. A complete, illustrated, and up-to-date guide to the mammals of mainland Southeast Asia.

Robson, Craig. *A Guide to the Birds of South East Asia*. London: New Holland Publishers, 2005. With 1250 native bird species covered on 142 color plates, this paperback edition is a handy title to have with you while exploring Cambodia's wilderness regions.

HEALTH AND PRACTICAL INFORMATION

Jacobson, Matt. *Ultimate Cambodia*. Phnom Penh: Coastal Books, 2008. A great guide for motorcycle enthusiasts.

Schroeder, Dirk. *Staying Healthy in Asia, Africa, and Latin America*. Emeryville, CA: Avalon Travel Publishing, 2000. An excellent resource that fits into your pocket for easy reference.

Internet Resources

Cambodia travel tips
www.talesofasia.com

Cambodia's best travel information website with particular attention to overland border crossings. Long-running institution by American expat writer and guesthouse owner Gordon Sharpless.

Cambodia blog and travel resource
www.andybrouwer.co.uk

Ten years of Cambodia travelogues, interviews, and photos by Andrew Brouwer, a long-term visitor to Cambodia.

Cambodia listings
www.canbypublications.com

Companion website to Cambodia's best free listings guide.

Cambodia restaurant and hotel listings
www.cambodiapocketguide.com

Companion website to listings pocket guides published in Phnom Penh and Siem Reap.

Hotels and tours
www.visit-mekong.com/cambodia

Hotel booking website, useful for Phnom Penh, Siem Reap, and Sihanoukville.

The official site for tourism in Cambodia
www.tourismcambodia.com

Government website with facts about the country, destination highlights, travel contacts, maps, and events calendars.

Recent Cambodian history in articles and photos
www.mekong.net/cambodia

Oral histories, photographs, and articles about Cambodia and Cambodians abroad.

Documentation Center of Cambodia
www.dccam.org

Since its inception in 1994, the Documentation Center of Cambodia (DC-Cam) has been at the forefront of documenting the myriad crimes and atrocities of the Khmer Rouge era. The website contains survivors' stories, extensive archives, and material on the Khmer Rouge Tribunal.

Khmer arts and culture
www.khmerculture.net
Website of Friends of Khmer Culture, an organization involved in Cambodian heritage.

Natural resource exploitation in Cambodia
www.globalwitness.org
Global Witness exposes the corrupt exploitation of natural resources and international trade systems, to drive campaigns that end impunity, resource-linked conflict, and human rights and environmental abuses. The organization was thrown out of Cambodia for reporting about illegal logging.

The Mekong River
www.mrcmekong.org
Website of the Mekong River Commission provides information on one of Asia's largest rivers.

Cambodia discussion groups
www.cambodia.org
Website featuring information on Cambodia and its people as well as news, discussion groups, and Khmer fonts.

Transitions Abroad
www.transitionsabroad.com
Information on working, studying, and volunteering abroad.

Index

List of Maps

Acknowledgments

Many people helped me deepen my understanding of Cambodia over the past decade. Without them, this book would never have come about. To those not mentioned here, my sincere apologies . . .

In Phnom Penh: Tassilo Brinzer, Arne Deepen, and Paul Brisby at The South Eastern Globe; Saket, Lo, and Poch at the Last Home Guest House; Joe Heffernan and Hort Sothea (FFI); Reinhard Trippmacher at Red Raid; Chea Sopheap at Bohr's Books; Hurley at La Cantina; Snow at Maxine's; Marc Eberle; Philippe Janowski; Ron Gluckman; Sopharoath Yi; and Youk Chang at DCCAM.

Around the country: Marcel Crompvoets at the Riel Bar in Kep; Hem John in Kompong Thom; Joe at Red Sun Falling in Kratie; Imke of Cloud 9 in Sihanoukville; Robert Remrev of Impian Divers in Koh Kong; Sambath Soung in Battambang; Tania and George (VSO) and Mr. Robert in Banlung; Barbara Lettner in Kampot; and Gordon Sharpless (www.tale-sofasia.com) in Siem Reap.

Thanks to these Cambodia experts and enthusiasts elsewhere for their insights: Fred Branfman, David Chandler, Cameron Cooper, Daniel Cooper, Janey Drummond, Luke Duggleby, Nic Dunlop, Daniel Ferguson, Andy Jones (Imaginative Traveler, Bangkok), Gerhard Joren, Greg Muller, and Roland Neveu.

Special thanks to Sopharoath Yi for help with the phrasebook.

At Avalon Travel, I'd like to thank my editor, Kathryn Ettinger, for her patience and the always concise answers to my questions, Brice Ticen for sound advice on the maps, and Domini Dragoone for sorting through the images.

Most of all, thanks to my wife, photographer Aroon Thaewchatturat (www.aroonthaew.com), for the excellent images and sound advice provided.

www.moon.com

DESTINATIONS | ACTIVITIES | BLOGS | MAPS | BOOKS

MOON.COM is all new, and ready to help plan your next trip! Filled with fresh trip ideas and strategies, author interviews, informative blogs, a detailed map library, and descriptions of all the Moon guidebooks, Moon.com is all you need to get out and explore the world—or even places in your own backyard. As always, when you travel with Moon, expect an experience that is uncommon and truly unique.

MAP SYMBOLS

▦ Expressway	◖ Highlight	✗ Airfield	⚲ Golf Course
⬚ Primary Road	○ City/Town	✈ Airport	₽ Parking Area
▦ Secondary Road	◉ State Capital	▲ Mountain	⬟ Archaeological Site
▦ Unpaved Road	⊛ National Capital	✛ Unique Natural Feature	⛪ Church
▬ Trail	★ Point of Interest		⛽ Gas Station
⋯ Ferry	• Accommodation	꩜ Waterfall	⬭ Glacier
▬ Railroad	▼ Restaurant/Bar	⚑ Park	▧ Mangrove
▨ Pedestrian Walkway	▪ Other Location	❶ Trailhead	▨ Reef
⬚ Stairs	⋀ Campground	⛷ Skiing Area	▨ Swamp

CONVERSION TABLES

°C = (°F – 32) / 1.8
°F = (°C x 1.8) + 32
1 inch = 2.54 centimeters (cm)
1 foot = 0.304 meters (m)
1 yard = 0.914 meters
1 mile = 1.6093 kilometers (km)
1 km = 0.6214 miles
1 fathom = 1.8288 m
1 chain = 20.1168 m
1 furlong = 201.168 m
1 acre = 0.4047 hectares
1 sq km = 100 hectares
1 sq mile = 2.59 square km
1 ounce = 28.35 grams
1 pound = 0.4536 kilograms
1 short ton = 0.90718 metric ton
1 short ton = 2,000 pounds
1 long ton = 1.016 metric tons
1 long ton = 2,240 pounds
1 metric ton = 1,000 kilograms
1 quart = 0.94635 liters
1 US gallon = 3.7854 liters
1 Imperial gallon = 4.5459 liters
1 nautical mile = 1.852 km

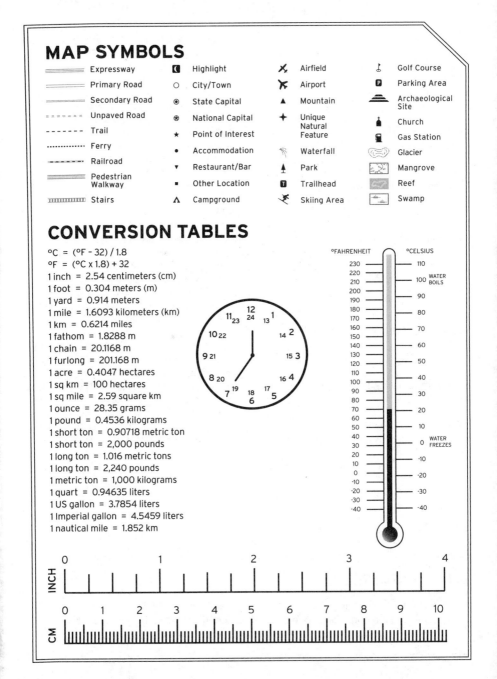

°FAHRENHEIT / °CELSIUS

°FAHRENHEIT	°CELSIUS	
230	110	
220	100	WATER BOILS
210		
200	90	
190		
180	80	
170		
160	70	
150		
140	60	
130		
120	50	
110		
100	40	
90	30	
80		
70	20	
60		
50	10	
40		
30	0	WATER FREEZES
20	-10	
10		
0	-20	
-10		
-20	-30	
-30		
-40	-40	

INCH: 0 1 2 3 4

CM: 0 1 2 3 4 5 6 7 8 9 10

MOON CAMBODIA

Avalon Travel
a member of the Perseus Books Group
1700 Fourth Street
Berkeley, CA 94710, USA
www.moon.com

Editor and Series Manager: Kathryn Ettinger
Copy Editor: Ellie Behrstock
Graphics Coordinators: Domini Dragoone, Amber
  Pirker
Production Coordinator: Domini Dragoone
Cover Designer: Domini Dragoone
Map Editor: Brice Ticen
Cartographer: Kat Bennett
Proofreader: Margo Winton
Indexer: Deana Shields

ISBN: 978-1-59880-214-6
ISSN: 1949-8306

Printing History
1st Edition – January 2010
5 4 3 2 1

Text © 2010 by Tom Vater.
Maps © 2010 by Avalon Travel.
All rights reserved.

Front cover photo: Monk's hand touching carving on
  Angkor Wat wall © Getty Images/The Image Bank/
  Keren Su.
Title page: © Tom Vater.
Front color images: pgs. 4, 5 (left, right), 6, 7
  (top right, bottom), 8, 9, 16, and 22 © Aroon
  Thaewchatturat; pgs. 5 (center), 7 (top left), 13, 14,
  20, 21, and 23 © Tom Vater; pg. 10 © 123rf.com/
  Komar; pg. 11 © 123rf.com/Galyna Andrushko; pg.
  12 © 123rf.com/Keith Levit; pg. 15 © 123rf.com/
  Dndavis; pg. 17 © 123rf.com/Artur Bogacki; pg. 19
  © 123rf.com/Suei Kae Wong.

Printed in Canada by Friesens

KEEPING CURRENT

If you have a favorite gem you'd like to see included in the next edition, or see anything
that needs updating, clarification, or correction, please drop us a line. Send your
comments via email to feedback@moon.com, or use the address above.